CASE STUDIES
IN US TRADE
NEGOTIATION

VOL. 2: RESOLVING DISPUTES

INSTITUTE FOR INTERNATIONAL ECONOMICS

CASE STUDIES
IN **US TRADE**
NEGOTIATION

VOL. 2: RESOLVING DISPUTES

CHARAN DEVEREAUX   ROBERT Z. LAWRENCE   MICHAEL D. WATKINS

Washington, DC
September 2006

Charan Devereaux is a senior researcher at the John F. Kennedy School of Government's Trade and Negotiations Program and the Harvard Law School Program on Negotiation, where she writes on international trade issues.

Robert Z. Lawrence, senior fellow at the Institute for International Economics since 2001, is the Albert L. Williams Professor of Trade and Investment at the John F. Kennedy School of Government at Harvard University. He was appointed by President Clinton to serve as a member of his Council of Economic Advisers in 1999. He held the New Century Chair as a nonresident senior fellow at the Brookings Institution and founded and edited the *Brookings Trade Forum*. He has been a senior fellow in the Economic Studies Program at Brookings, a professorial lecturer at the Johns Hopkins School of Advanced International Studies, and an instructor at Yale University. He is the author or coauthor of several books, including *Has Globalization Gone Far Enough? The Costs of Fragmented Markets* (2004) and *Crimes and Punishments? Retaliation under the WTO* (2003).

Michael D. Watkins is a professor of practice in organizational behavior at INSEAD, Fontainebleau, and was a professor at Harvard's Kennedy School of Government and the Business School. He also taught negotiation in the Senior Executive Program at the Program on Negotiation at Harvard Law School. He is founding partner of Genesis Advisers, a leadership strategy consultancy. He is the author of *The First 90 Days: Critical Success Strategies for New Leaders at all Levels* (Harvard Business School Press, 2003) and *Breakthrough Business Negotiation: A Toolbox for Managers* (Jossey-Bass, winner of the CPR Institute prize for best negotiation book in 2002).

INSTITUTE FOR INTERNATIONAL ECONOMICS
1750 Massachusetts Avenue, NW
Washington, DC 20036-1903
(202) 328-9000   FAX: (202) 659-3225
www.iie.com

C. Fred Bergsten, *Director*
Valerie Norville, *Director of Publications and Web Development*
Edward Tureen, *Director of Marketing*

Typesetting by BMWW
Printing by Automated Graphic Systems, Inc.

Printed in the United States of America
08 07 06   5 4 3 2 1

Library of Congress Cataloging-in-Publication Data

Devereaux, Charan.
   Case studies in US trade negotiation / Charan Devereaux, Robert Z. Lawrence, Michael D. Watkins.
      p. cm.
   Includes bibliographical references and index.
      ISBN-10: 0-88132-362-4 (v. 1 : alk. paper)
      ISBN-10: 0-88132-363-2 (v. 2 : alk. paper)
      ISBN-13: 978-0-88132-362-7 (v. 1 : alk. paper)
      ISBN-13: 978-0-88132-363-4 (v. 2 : alk. paper)
      1. United States—Commercial policy—History. 2. International trade.
   3. Foreign trade regulation—Cases.
   4. Agreement on Trade-Related Aspects of Intellectual Property Rights (1994)
   I. Lawrence, Robert Z., 1949–
   II. Watkins, Michael, 1956–   III. Title.

HF1455.D49 2006
382'.973—dc22   2006022687

The views expressed in this publication are those of the authors. This publication is part of the overall program of the Institute, as endorsed by its Board of Directors, but does not necessarily reflect the views of individual members of the Board or the Advisory Committee.

Contents

Figures

Preface

Trade policy is central to the Institute's research program. A number of our studies have analyzed the functioning of the World Trade Organization (WTO), and the General Agreement on Tariffs and Trade (GATT) before it, and proposed reform of the international trading rules; others have assessed bilateral and regional trade agreements; still others have measured the costs of protection and delved into the American trade policy-making process.

This new volume presents case studies on six major trade disputes and the efforts to resolve them through the dispute settlement mechanism in the WTO. Authors Charan Devereaux, Robert Z. Lawrence, and Michael Watkins pay particular attention to the United States and how these disputes play out in the American political context.

The six disputes presented here are the US-EU disputes over trade in hormone-treated beef, bananas, and genetically modified foods; US photography giant Eastman Kodak Co.'s efforts to penetrate the home market of its Japan-based rival Fuji Photo Film; the George W. Bush administration's decision to impose tariffs on some imported steel and the European Union's response to these tariffs; and the WTO challenge brought by Brazil against US cotton subsidies. A companion volume, *Making the Rules*, offers cases on important trade negotiations, all focused on the process of establishing how the trade system operates. The two volumes thus provide an important complement to the Institute's earlier studies on the substance of these topics.

The Institute for International Economics is a private, nonprofit institution for the study and discussion of international economic policy. Its purpose is to analyze important issues in that area and to develop and communicate practical new approaches for dealing with them. The Institute is completely nonpartisan.

The Institute is funded by a highly diversified group of philanthropic foundations, private corporations, and interested individuals. Major institutional grants are now being received from the William M. Keck, Jr. Foundation and the Starr Foundation. About 33 percent of the Institute's resources in our latest fiscal year were provided by contributors outside the United States, including about 16 percent from Japan.

The Institute's Board of Directors bears overall responsibilities for the Institute and gives general guidance and approval to its research program, including the identification of topics that are likely to become important over the medium run (one to three years) and that should be addressed by the Institute. The director, working closely with the staff and outside Advisory Committee, is responsible for the development of particular projects and makes the final decision to publish an individual study.

The Institute hopes that its studies and other activities will contribute to building a stronger foundation for international economic policy around the world. We invite readers of these publications to let us know how they think we can best accomplish this objective.

C. FRED BERGSTEN
Director
August 2006

Acknowledgments

In compiling this volume, we received help from a number of generous people who agreed to be interviewed for the case studies. Some of these individuals are quoted in the text, while others preferred to remain anonymous. We thank them for their time and assistance. We would also like to thank all those who read drafts and made suggestions, including Timothy Josling, David Orden, Robert Paarlberg, Kimberly Ann Elliott, and Alan Wolff.

We are grateful to the participants of the John F. Kennedy School of Government (KSG) Executive Program, "The Practice of Trade Policy: Economics, Negotiations, and Rules," and to the participants of the Institute for International Economics work sessions on "Case Studies on International Trade Rules Negotiation and Enforcement," who commented and offered their ideas on some of this work. Most of the case studies in this volume were developed as KSG cases, and we thank the staff of Harvard's KSG Case Program for their help.

Finally, we would like to thank Madona Devasahayam, Marla Banov, Helen Hillebrand, and Valerie Norville at the Institute for International Economics for their assistance with the editing and publishing process. Though there are many to thank, the views expressed here are the authors' and should not be attributed to anyone else.

Introduction

International trade negotiations once focused primarily on reducing border barriers such as tariffs and quotas that protected markets for manufactured goods. Such discussions took place in a rules-based, multilateral global system centered on the General Agreement on Tariffs and Trade—the GATT. The GATT was spectacularly successful in reducing border barriers. On average, tariffs on industrial goods fell from around 40 percent in 1947 to below 5 percent in the late 1980s. But as tariffs fell and markets opened, the challenges presented by the different laws and practices of trading nations became apparent. In response, the focus of trade policymaking shifted. Trade negotiations now often center on policies and rules once thought of as purely domestic in nature. Trading nations commonly seek not only to negotiate over tariffs but also to change practices by constraining, reconciling, or even harmonizing rules.

Our first volume, *Making the Rules,* presented case studies on negotiations to establish trade rules in this new context. However, the expanding depth and scope of trade rules has been accompanied by another important development. With the birth of the World Trade Organization (WTO) in 1995 came a new system for resolving trade disputes. By comparison, the early GATT system had limited provisions for dispute settlement: Adjudication was provided, but the emphasis was on diplomatic consultation and developing consensus. While the GATT evolved in the direction of a more juridical system, the WTO approach entails an even stronger, more routinized and juridical way of managing conflicts over trade. The result is a more powerful system with a greater ability to enforce trade rules—but also one that is more controversial.

The cases presented in this volume describe efforts to resolve trade disputes in the context of this new system. Our aim is to raise questions and stimulate discussion. To that end, the cases explore the substance of the conflicts and their political context, and also delve into the dispute resolution process. By examining important recent trade conflicts, the reader can come to understand not only the larger issues surrounding trade policy today but also how participants seek to exert influence in the dispute resolution system and how the system evolves as a result of these pressures.

We have sought, both in our introduction and in the cases themselves, to avoid policy advocacy. The idea is neither to undertake an analysis of trade disputes from the perspective of a particular discipline nor to provide prescriptions as to how the situation should be resolved or the dispute settlement mechanism changed. As in our first volume, we pay particular attention to the United States and how the disputes play out in the American political context. The cases involve conflicts with Europe, Japan, and Brazil over a wide array of products—notably, cotton, steel, beef, bananas, and camera film. They also span a broad range of trade rules on food safety, technical barriers, competition policies, subsidies, safeguards, and quotas. Some of the trade conflicts are long-term, initiated during the GATT and continuing to the present day. Others arose after the creation of the WTO. Some focus on how domestic government officials deal with the dispute at hand, while others highlight the roles of business and consumer groups. But all of the cases explore the interaction between the rules, the politics, and the process of resolving trade disputes.

The Cases

The six major disputes treated here are the US-EU fight over trade in hormone-treated beef, the US-EU dispute over trade in bananas, the efforts by the US photography giant Eastman Kodak Co. to penetrate the home market of its Japan-based rival Fuji Photo Film, the decision by the George W. Bush administration to impose tariffs on some imported steel and the European Union's response to these tariffs, the WTO challenge brought by Brazil against US cotton subsidies, and the US-EU dispute over trade in genetically modified (GM) foods. The cases are summarized below.

Food Fight: The United States, Europe, and Trade in Hormone-Treated Beef

The long-standing US-EU dispute over trade in beef began with the widespread adoption of growth-promoting hormones for raising beef cattle in the United States. In 1989, Europe banned the use of these hormones. The ban covered all beef, including meat imported from the United States. At the core of the dispute lay fundamental disagreements about trade in food.

The United States argued that the European regulatory process had been captured by politics. US officials were frustrated by what they saw as a political move to protect the EU beef market by invoking scientifically unsupported claims about the detrimental health effects of hormones. Europe defended its ban, asserting that health issues should be decided democratically—by politicians who answer to voters. The real issue, Europe argued, was that the US trade system was overly influenced by industry—the United States had soured the entire transatlantic trade relationship by responding to the demands of the beef lobby. Ultimately, the United States brought a case against Europe at the WTO.

Banana Wars: Challenges to the European Union's Banana Regime

Despite the growth and liberalization of world trade in the post–World War II era, international trade in bananas remained highly regulated, especially in Europe. The import of inexpensive bananas distributed by large US-based brands was limited by trade quotas in EU nations—a policy justified by the European Union as a way to assist former European colonies, long reliant on banana trade. This case describes efforts by the Office of the US Trade Representative (USTR), urged on by such major distributors of Central and Latin American bananas as the Chiquita and Dole corporations, to end European banana import restrictions. The United States brought a successful case against Europe at the WTO, and later imposed retaliatory tariffs following EU resistance to the WTO panel's findings.

Snapshot: Kodak v. Fuji

This case describes the issues that arose when the US photography giant Eastman Kodak Co. sought to penetrate the home market of its worldwide rival based in Japan, Fuji Photo Film. It examines the relationship between the USTR and its Japanese counterpart, the Japanese Fair Trade Commission. The case focuses on the question of whether domestic regulations may, because of their practical application, amount to trade barriers—as Kodak alleged in the instance of Japan.

Standing Up for Steel: The US Government Response to Steel Industry and Union Efforts to Win Protection from Imports, 1998–2003

The March 2002 decision by President George W. Bush to impose tariffs on some imported steel capped a long-running campaign by the US steel industry and its unions for assistance in dealing with surges of low-priced imported steel in the aftermath of the 1998 Asian financial crisis. The Bush decision came as a surprise to many who assumed that a free trade–oriented administration would not adopt measures likely to be viewed as protectionist. The case traces the history of the steel dispute through the Clinton and Bush administrations. It examines the behavior of lobby groups and Congress, particularly the role of subgroups (such as the so-called Congressional Steel Caucus, a group of members from steel-producing states) and committees within Congress. It describes the sorts of pressures that converge on the executive branch as it confronts the prospect of bringing action under section 201 of the US rules—a policy response that is allowed when imports injure a domestic industry. The case also describes the successful European challenge to these tariffs at the WTO and the US decision to remove them in the face of threatened retaliation.

Brazil's WTO Cotton Case: Negotiation Through Litigation

The United States is by far the world's largest exporter of cotton, accounting for between one-quarter and one-third of world exports. Like many other countries, the United States also provides subsidies to its cotton producers—$2.3 billion in 2001–02 alone. Between December 2000 and May 2002, the world price of cotton declined by 40 percent, shrinking the value of the global cotton market from $35 billion to $20 billion in just 18 months. It bottomed out at 39 cents a pound, a record-low level in real terms. The reasons for this dramatic price decline are complex, but nearly everyone pointed a finger at US subsidies. In September 2002, Brazil initiated a WTO case against the United States—the first-ever challenge of a developed country's agricultural subsidies by a developing country. West African countries also lobbied the WTO to include a separate initiative on cotton in the Cancún text. Many in the media have framed the cotton case as a litmus test of whether the WTO can work for the poor.

The US-EU Dispute over Trade in Genetically Modified Crops

In 1996, American farmers began planting GM corn and soybean crops. Use of these herbicide- and insect-resistant varieties skyrocketed in the United States. After some public debate, GM crops were generally treated the same as non-GM crops by the US regulatory system using existing laws. But not all countries were as quick to embrace agricultural biotechnology. The European Union developed a separate regulatory approach for GM products, including a different approach toward risk. Resistance to the technology grew in Europe, and many consumer groups, environmentalists, NGOs, and politicians rejected genetically modified organisms (GMOs). Ultimately, the European Union placed a de facto moratorium on the approval of new GM products in 1998, frustrating US exporters. The US position on GM crops has been that there is no scientific evidence that can justify Europe's de facto ban of such plant varieties. But some noted that though European GM policies restricted trade, the moratorium was not a simple case of protectionism. The Bush administration decided to challenge the European Union at the WTO, arguing that the moratorium against GMOs violated the SPS agreement.

The Evolution of the WTO Dispute Settlement System

The multilateral trading system's dispute resolution mechanism has evolved over the past 50 years in response to economic, institutional, and political forces. The success of the trading system, beginning with the GATT and continuing in the WTO, has dramatically increased the scope and depth of trade rules and the range of parties involved. This success has paradoxically resulted in more, and more difficult, disputes between trading nations. At the same time, structural, institutional, and psychological barriers make it difficult for the contending parties to resolve their own disputes through negotiation. Although the current WTO dispute resolution system represents a good mechanism, it nonetheless has strengths and weaknesses. Also, it has not prevented (and cannot prevent) countries from seeking to game the system by making strategic choices to advance their national interests.

The Increasing Scope and Depth of Trade Rules

From its inception with the GATT to the current WTO, the history of the international trading system is characterized by increasing complexity. On one hand, the system has achieved enormous increases in global welfare.[1] On the other hand, it has increased both the number and the difficulty of disputes that need to be resolved.

The GATT System

For the four decades before the establishment of the WTO, a surprisingly weak institutional framework governed global trade. In the original design for the postwar economy, participants in the 1944 Bretton Woods Conference sought to create not only the International Monetary Fund (IMF) and the World Bank but also a third institution—the International Trade Organization (ITO). Before the charter of the ITO was negotiated,

---

1. For a quantitative estimate, see, for example, Bradford, Grieco, and Hufbauer (2005).

however, an interim agreement known as the GATT came into effect and was used as the basis for negotiating tariff reductions. In March 1948, the ITO Charter was signed in Havana, Cuba. The commercial policy provisions of the charter were those of the GATT, but the agreement covered a wide range of additional issues, including fair labor standards, restrictive business practices, economic development and reconstruction, and special treatment of primary commodities. But because of opposition in the US Congress, the charter was never ratified.

Instead, until 1994, the trading system operated on the basis of the GATT. Given its original role as a provisional agreement, it is quite understandable that the GATT had a narrow mission focused on border barriers and a weak system for settling disputes and ensuring compliance.

According to its preamble, the purpose of the GATT was "to enter into reciprocal and mutually advantageous arrangements directed to the substantial reduction of tariffs and other barriers to trade and to the elimination of discriminatory treatment in international commerce." The GATT sought to eliminate discriminatory treatment by requiring most favored nation (MFN) treatment of all members (Article I) and national treatment for imported goods (Article III). The agreement did not compel harmonized standards or policies; it simply required that domestic and imported goods be treated in the same way. Provided they respected this principle, GATT signatories (known as "contracting parties") remained free to implement any domestic policies or rules they desired. Policies relating to measures such as standards and intellectual property were not covered by the GATT's disciplines.

The GATT was remarkably successful. Its membership grew from the 23 countries that drew up the original agreement to the 123 countries that became charter members of the WTO. During the GATT years, the volume of world trade increased more than thirteenfold.[2] In addition, tariffs came down steadily. The first seven rounds of GATT negotiations lowered average tariffs on industrial products from about 40 percent in 1947 to 4.7 percent in 1994.[3]

But increased trade and decreasing tariffs led to new pressures on the system. As the world economy became more integrated, there were growing calls for more governance. Complex cross-border economic activities required more secure frameworks in which to operate. When trade occurred mainly in simple, standardized commodities, the most important issues for trade policies were the border barriers that segregated markets

---

2. From 1950 to 1993, the volume of world trade increased 13.2 times (WTO, table II.1, "World Merchandise Exports, Production and Gross Domestic Product, 1950–2003," *International Trade Statistics 2004*, www.wto.org.

3. For more information, see WTO, "Statement of Ambassador Dr. Mounir Zahran, Chairman of the GATT 1947 contracting parties to the closing session, Geneva, December 12, 1995," press release 36, December 12, 1995; and WTO (2005).

internationally. Export success for those able to produce simple products—say, lumber—at relatively lower cost depends mainly on market access. If foreign lumber can be brought into a market at prices below those charged for domestic substitutes, it will not be difficult to find willing marketers and buyers.

Many other factors beyond market access duties affected the sale of more sophisticated products, however. For example, in order to sell automobiles in a foreign market, firms could be required to comply with complex domestic regulatory standards; they might also need to establish or find extensive networks for marketing, sales, and service. Firms therefore wanted hospitable rules governing standards and regulations—so-called technical barriers to trade. Moreover, they had to be concerned about rules relating to operating distribution networks in foreign countries. As sales grew and reached a sufficiently high level, many firms also considered establishing production facilities in foreign markets. Aided particularly by improvements in communications and transportation, firms were increasingly able to manufacture products by sourcing from multiple locations. Raw materials might best be sourced in one country, labor-intensive processes performed in another, and technologically sophisticated processes carried out in a third. Production abroad focused attention on many other aspects of domestic regulation and taxation. Firms planning to source in one country and sell in another preferred secure intellectual property rights and compatible technical standards and regulations. They sought to avoid government measures that constrained their operations through local content and domestic performance requirements. All these forces created firms' growing demand to include rules for these policies in trade agreements.

In addition, with deepening trading, financial, and investment relationships came increasing demands from developing countries. As they shifted away from import substitution to export promotion strategies, developing countries became more interested in and affected by trade rules. Many of these nations sought special preferences and differential treatment in the trading system, as well as more comprehensive rules and more effective enforcement.

These pressures became particularly evident during the Tokyo Round of GATT negotiations, which concluded in 1977. Though the GATT's focus remained on rules and barriers that were clearly related to trade in goods, the Tokyo Round agreement included an "enabling clause" that created more scope for special and differential treatment of developing countries. The agreement also contained seven plurilateral codes dealing with import licensing, technical barriers to trade, customs valuation, subsidies and countervailing duties, antidumping measures, civil aircraft, and government procurement.

The codes represented an expansion of the GATT's mission to cover nontariff barriers and rules governing fair trade, but contracting parties that did not sign the codes were not bound by them. The codes also had disparate and separate dispute settlement systems.

The Tokyo Round left many problems unresolved. As the many subsequent disputes between the United States and the European Union made clear, the combination of a weak dispute settlement system and opaque rules made it particularly difficult to impose disciplines on agricultural subsidies. In addition, many parties resorted to extralegal measures such as voluntary export restraints and, in the United States, unilateral retaliation that violated basic GATT principles (see Bhagwati and Patrick 1991).

The Uruguay Round: Expanding the Rules, Increasing Complexity

The next round of trade talks changed the game considerably. Concluded in 1994, the Uruguay Round Agreement dramatically increased the scope of trade rules beyond border barriers. It included agreements on services (the General Agreement on Trade in Services, GATS), Sanitary and Phytosanitary (SPS) Measures, Technical Barriers to Trade (TBT), Trade-Related Investment Measures (TRIMs), Trade-Related Aspects of Intellectual Property Rights (TRIPS), and a new agreement on Subsidies and Countervailing Measures (SCM). The TRIPS was particularly noteworthy, since it required countries to implement policy regimes that achieve a minimum level of intellectual property protection. Unlike the codes of the Tokyo Round, the Uruguay Round was a single undertaking to which all members agreed. It also included strengthened versions of the previous codes and created a much stronger and unified dispute settlement system. In short, the Uruguay Round dramatically increased the binding obligations of the members.

One result of expanding the scope of trade rules was a powerful change in the politics surrounding trade policymaking. When trade policies covered only border barriers, they brought a fairly narrow group of domestic producers and consumers into the political fray. But as the trading system expanded to constrain national regulatory policies, many more players entered the game. Some of these players saw trade agreements as an opportunity to further their agendas; others saw trade agreements as a threat.

Increasingly, the most important political agents—business interests, labor unions, and environmentalists—not only compete with their counterparts in other countries but also compete to have their concerns subject to international rules. Business complains that foreign firms are dumping underpriced products in the domestic market. Labor complains of "social dumping," or competition from producers in countries with particularly lenient labor and social standards. Environmentalists complain of "eco-dumping" when competition comes from companies operating in countries with lax environmental standards. Fearing that such foreign competition will force the erosion of domestic protections, these groups seek to prevent a race to the bottom by including labor and environmental standards in trade agreements.

Trade agreements have fundamentally altered the distribution of power over domestic (and international) decision making. Executives, legislators, bureaucrats, interest groups, and constituents that once were focused purely on domestic considerations are thus drawn into the trade arena. As new actors and interests are engaged, debates over trade become the battleground for political conflicts that reflect a wide range of concerns—much broader than the economic impact of trade. Attention is focused not only on how policies affect relative prices but also on shifts in the distribution of power.

For example, as the scope of trade agreements widened, the number of legislators and committees drawn into the policymaking process expanded accordingly. Until the Tokyo Round, responsibility for US trade policy was heavily concentrated in the Senate Finance Committee and the House Ways and Means Committee, because the major trade issue was tariffs—that is, essentially taxes. But the broadening of the purview of trade implied the need for others to be involved. In the Uruguay Round, a large number of committees felt obliged to participate in decision making and oversight.[4] On the one hand, the salience of trade as an issue made the trade committees more powerful; on the other hand, it also forced them to share their power to a greater degree.

Trade agreements have also changed the way that legislators put forward their policy agendas. Bundling particular issues into a trade agreement may help to overcome domestic opposition. Conservative legislators, for example, may not want to include labor standards in trade agreements, but some might go along if the agreement benefits their constituents who are exporters. Liberal legislators may resist freer trade, but might find agreements more appealing if they help strengthen labor standards abroad. Thus both the Right and the Left have tried to use trade agreements as a mechanism to advance their domestic policy agendas and constrain their opponents. On the right, trade agreements have been used to promote domestic reform and deregulation, as seen in the conditions associated with China's accession to the WTO. On the left, the promotion of a social clause in the European Union serves a parallel function. But those who are weakened by these maneuvers will inevitably question the process.

---

4. No longer could the chairs of the two tax-writing committees control the contents of trade bills: Participation spread to include the House Energy and Commerce Committee (domestic content, certification standards), the House Foreign Affairs and Senate Foreign Relations Committees (foreign loans, export controls), the Judiciary Committee (antitrust reciprocity), the House Financial Services and Senate Finance Committees (banking, foreign investment, the export-import bank), the Agriculture Committee (farm trade), the Armed Services Committee (procurement), and so forth.

Once the rules are set, new constraints are imposed on legislators, and their ability to grease the political wheels using regulations that have a protective effect is reduced (see O'Halloran 1997). One appeal (domestically) of the Clean Air Act's standards was that they discriminated against foreign petroleum refiners, but Venezuela forced these provisions to be changed by bringing a case to the GATT. Regulators face similar constraints. As long as trade policy was focused on border barriers, regulators could operate independently. Thus, an agency such as the Food and Drug Administration (FDA) was unconcerned about international policy. It faced little interference either in setting standards and/or in assessing conformity to them. But deeper integration and the efforts at achieving mutual recognition of conformity assessment between the United States and the European Union dramatically changed the demands on the FDA— and transformed the future environment in which it will operate.

The Result: More, and More Difficult, Disputes

As the rules have become more extensive, more players have entered the political game, and as the WTO membership has become more diverse, the number of trade disputes has increased dramatically. As figure 0.1 shows, in its first decade (1995–2004), the WTO caseload averaged 35 disputes a year, more than three times the average under the GATT in the 1980s, and seven times as many as the annual average number brought under the GATT between 1948 and 1989.

There has also been a marked increase in the diversity of countries involved in dispute settlement cases. Under the GATT, developing countries constituted only 21 percent of complainants and just 13 percent of respondents. But under the WTO, 38 percent of both complainants and respondents have been developing countries. Thus, developing countries are now both more likely to bring cases and to have cases brought against them.

The issues covered by the cases have undergone a considerable evolution as well. In the 1950s, for example, 38 percent of the disputes (20 cases) dealt with tariffs, 43 percent (23 cases) with nontariff barriers (such as quotas and discriminatory treatment) and 19 percent with unfair trade (dumping and subsidies). In those three categories, 23 percent of the cases dealt with agriculture.[5] In the 1980s, however, tariffs were just 14 percent of the cases, nontariff barriers 57 percent, and unfair trade 29 percent; 47 percent of these cases involved agriculture. Clearly, the focus has evolved away from tariffs and toward nontariff barriers and unfair trade, particularly in agriculture. In the 1990s, the mix of cases was even more diverse. Almost 30 percent of the 340 cases pertained to issues that were not even covered

---

5. These numbers rely on Hudec (1993) prior to 1990 and the WorldTradeLaw.net database thereafter.

Figure 0.1   Complaints under the GATT and WTO

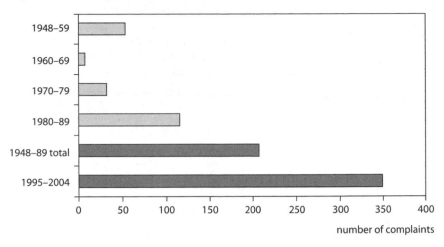

number of complaints

by the GATT agreement. As of 2004, there had been 60 cases devoted to dumping practices, 60 to subsidies and countervailing measures, 31 to safeguards (i.e., temporary restrictions of a product), 25 to TRIPS, 19 to TRIMs, 33 to technical barriers to trade, 14 to services, and 55 to agriculture.

Finally, while retaliation is still unusual, it has become more common. Under the GATT, no complaining party actually suspended its concessions to retaliate against a member that failed to come into compliance with a ruling. Indeed, only one party, the Netherlands, was even authorized to retaliate (against the United States, several times in the 1950s); it chose not to. By contrast, under the WTO, the United States has retaliated against the European Union (twice, over beef and bananas), as has the European Union against the United States (over foreign sales corporation, or FSC, export subsidies), and several other countries have been authorized to retaliate.

Barriers to Negotiated Agreement

Once we have established that the trading system is generating greater numbers of more difficult disputes, the next question is why the parties can't negotiate their own settlement. Why does the system need a separate institution—in the form of the WTO Dispute Settlement Body—to act as referee? Given that the parties have successfully negotiated the rules of the game, what is it that prevents them from resolving their own conflicts?

The answer is that while trade agreements are negotiated by many parties on a broad set of issues, disputes tend to arise between a few parties on a narrow set of issues. Negotiations to resolve such disputes are bound to be difficult, because (1) they tend to be zero-sum propositions, with clear winners and clear losers; (2) special interests that might have been overridden or placated when the full agreement was negotiated become fully mobilized to win—or avoid losing—a dispute (indeed, they may have initiated the dispute); and (3) once a conflict has begun to escalate, predictable transformations in the parties' attitudes create additional impediments to negotiated resolution. These barriers to negotiated agreement—structural, institutional, and psychological, respectively—are discussed in greater detail below (and see Arrow et al. 1995; Watkins 2000).

Structural Barriers

Structural barriers arise when a negotiation structure results in a narrow or nonexistent zone of possible agreement. Negotiation structure consists of the following five elements (developed in Watkins 2002):

- the parties, their interests, and alternatives to agreement;
- the agenda of issues to be negotiated;
- communication channels through which negotiations are conducted;
- linkages among sets of negotiations; and
- time constraints and action-forcing events.

Each of these elements can give rise to structural barriers. Perhaps the wrong parties are negotiating, or the negotiations involve too many or too few parties to proceed productively. The issue agenda may be too narrow, generating a zero-sum, win-lose situation—or it may be too complex to tackle successfully. The parties' communication channels may be inadequate for conveying their interests and positions. The negotiations may be linked to past or future negotiations in ways that raise issues of precedent. Finally, the negotiations may lack sufficient time in which to be conducted or, equally problematic, an action-forcing event to push the parties to reach closure.

In trade disputes, the most common structural barrier is the narrowness of the agenda to be negotiated. Trade agreements are crafted as package deals, as multiple parties bundle together many issues in order to fashion mutually beneficial trades. In this way, each party to the agreement is made better off than it would be under any no-agreement alternative.

But disputes tend to arise between two (or a few) parties over a much narrower set of concerns, often a single issue. As a result, the negotiations are very likely to be a zero-sum game. It should therefore be no surprise when the parties come to loggerheads in their efforts to negotiate settlements. For example, Europe and the United States were unable to negotiate a settlement after Europe banned hormone-treated beef. Because the dispute was over a single issue—trade in beef—its resolution would create a winner and a loser.

Political Barriers

Negotiations to resolve trade disputes are further complicated by two-level game dynamics. Negotiations *between* nations interact with negotiations *within* them, constraining the ability of leaders to settle disputes.[6] As discussed in the previous section, these interactions have become more complex and problematic as the concerns of trade negotiations have shifted to issues of deeper integration.

Negotiated agreements to resolve trade disputes are fiercely resisted by the interests within each country that stand to lose. In the steel case, for example, domestic interests initiated the dispute by persuading the Bush administration to impose tariffs and then fought to sustain them. Opponents of a settlement typically allege that those in favor of negotiating are selling out. They may foment internal political turmoil that impedes compromise, as leaders who appear too accommodating become the target of attacks from their internal opposition.

Leaders thus have to work hard internally to build support for agreement while they are negotiating externally. Efforts to synchronize external negotiations and internal coalition building involve a delicate balancing act, because the interactions of the two levels reduce tactical flexibility. By engaging in hard bargaining externally, for example, leaders may bolster their internal political support. But they also may commit themselves to untenable positions in the external negotiations. Later, they may be unable to retreat from these positions because doing so would result in an unacceptable loss of face.

Psychological Barriers

Finally, psychological transformations can further impede negotiations to resolve disputes. Psychological barriers are biases of perception and interpretation that reduce the potential for negotiated agreement.[7] The

---

6. For an extensive discussion on bureaucratic politics and its impact on decision making, see Allison (1971); see also Iklé (1964).

7. Such barriers include equity and justice seeking, biases in assimilation and construal, reactive devaluation of compromises and concessions, loss aversion, judgmental overconfidence, and dissonance reduction and avoidance (Arrow et al. 1965, 10–19; more generally, see chapter 1). More in-depth explorations of psychological barriers are presented in Robinson (1996a, 1996b) and Ross and Ward (1995). See also Cialdini (1993), and Zimbardo and Leippe (1991).

experience of conflict changes the parties' perceptions in ways that can make conflicts self-sustaining (Robinson 1996b). Specifically, the adversaries develop *partisan perceptions*—emotional associations and expectations that are irreversible.[8] Their views of the situation, and of the actions of the other side, become distorted in predictable patterns.

For example, contending parties often experience *goal transformation*—they go from simply wanting to protect themselves to wanting to hurt the other.[9] Feelings of victimization and a desire for retribution and revenge sustain conflicts long after the initial causes have ceased to be important. Siblings continue to fight for parents' attention long after they are adults, and nations argue over scraps of land that no longer have strategic importance. Some suggest that Europe brought the foreign sales corporation case against the United States in part out of frustration with the US-initiated WTO cases on beef and bananas and a desire to strike back.

When conflicts become bitter, the contending parties also begin to gather and interpret information about each other in ways that are profoundly biased—a phenomenon known as *naive realism*.[10] Research has shown that perceptions become distorted in three main ways. First, partisans assume that they themselves see things objectively while their opponents' views are extreme and distorted. Second, they tend to misjudge the other side's motivations, overestimating the importance of ideology and underestimating the situational pressures their counterparts face. Third, parties consistently overestimate the extent of the differences between themselves and the other side.

The result is the exaggeration of the actual differences between the sides, which are further exacerbated by the breakdown in communications that inevitably occurs when conflicts become more polarized. As a consequence, the parties experience *selective perception*—they interpret each other's actions in ways that confirm their preexisting beliefs and attitudes. They unconsciously overlook evidence that challenges their stereotypes, and they may also come to view the negotiation in purely win-lose terms. This behavior often contributes to making a failure to reach agreement a self-fulfilling prophecy.

---

8. See Rubin, Pruitt, and Kim (1994); they define residues as "persistent structural change—in an individual, group, or community—which is due to past escalation and encourages further escalation" (1994, 99).

9. Rubin, Pruitt, and Kim (1994, chapters 6, 7) provide an overview of these concepts and others related to conflict escalation.

10. See Robinson et al. (1995); by "naive realism," the authors mean lack of awareness of one's own subjectivity in making predictions about oneself and others. As Arrow et al. (1995, 13) note, "Disputants are bound to have differing recollections and interpretations of the past—of causes and effects, promises and betrayals, conciliatory initiatives and rebuffs. They are also bound to have differing interpretations or construals . . . of the content of any proposals designed to end that dispute."

An especially unfortunate consequence of partisan perceptions is that gestures meant to be conciliatory are often dismissed or ignored—a phenomenon known as *reactive devaluation*.[11] If one side believes that the other is intent on achieving total victory, any conciliatory gesture tends to be treated as either a trap or a sign of weakness. To conclude otherwise would require a fundamental reassessment of the other side. If the conciliatory overture is interpreted as a deception, the response is often counterdeception or rejection. If it is interpreted as a sign of weakness, the response may be to press forward aggressively.

The Need for Alternative Dispute Resolution Mechanisms

Together, structural, political, and psychological barriers narrow or eliminate the zone of possible agreement in direct party-to-party negotiations to resolve disputes. Fortunately, however, there are alterative dispute resolution (ADR) mechanisms—involving third-party intervention—that can help overcome these barriers. These mechanisms fall on a spectrum ranging from voluntary mediation to binding arbitration.

Given the potent barriers to negotiating settlements to trade disputes, it is not surprising that the members of the WTO decided that they needed an ADR mechanism. Seen in this light, the WTO Dispute Settlement Understanding (DSU) is a way for the parties to precommit, during broader rule-making negotiations, to use an alternative mechanism in the (likely) event that they are unable to resolve their disputes. This was, effectively, a way to tie the hands of the parties and to guide difficult-to-resolve disputes into a more productive channel.

In addition, the DSU process, once activated and under way, helps the parties to deal with internal political issues and, to some degree, surmount psychological barriers to agreement. Developments in the formal dispute resolution process may even serve to spur the parties to try to negotiate a deal—a phenomenon known as "bargaining in the shadow of the law" (Cooter, Marks, and Mnookin 1982). For example, the loss by the United States in the cotton case might have induced it to be more forthcoming in the Doha Round and Free Trade Area of the Americas (FTAA) negotiations with Brazil.

Designing Dispute Resolution Systems

Given that the trading system needs a distinct mechanism to resolve disputes, the next question is what type of mechanism is needed. What

---

11. Ross and Ward (1995, 270) define reactive devaluation as "the fact that the very act of offering a particular proposal or concession may diminish its apparent value or attractiveness in the eyes of the recipient."

Figure 0.2   Dispute resolution spectrum

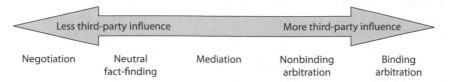

are the strengths and weaknesses of different approaches to dispute resolution systems design?

As figure 0.2 illustrates, ADR mechanisms can be arrayed on a spectrum that runs from pure negotiation to pure mediation to pure arbitration, and that includes a wide range of hybrids in between.[12] In pure negotiation the parties seek, unassisted, to negotiate resolutions to their disputes. As discussed in the previous section, the existence of powerful structural, institutional, and psychological barriers to negotiated agreement provides the impetus for seeking alternative approaches involving third parties. At the same time, negotiations among the contending parties may proceed in—indeed, may be stimulated by—parallel third-party processes ranging from mediation to arbitration.

In pure mediation, the contending parties invite an impartial, mutually acceptable third party to assist them in resolving their dispute. Participation in the process is voluntary, and the parties are free to exit the process and pursue other alternatives. Mediators help contending parties to overcome barriers to agreement by

- enhancing and shaping communications among the disputants;
- evaluating and critiquing the parties' positions;
- developing creative options;
- persuading the parties to make concessions;
- enabling the parties to save face by coordinating mutual concessions;
- absorbing anger or blame; and
- serving as a witness to agreement.

Mediation can in principle be quite helpful in overcoming psychological barriers to agreement. But because it is voluntary, it is seldom effective when there are significant structural or political impediments to resolving a dispute. In practice, mediative solutions to trade disputes are therefore quite rare.

---

12. For a good overview of the mediation process, see Moore (1996). For distinct types of intervention roles, see Watkins and Winters (1997).

At the other end of the ADR spectrum is binding arbitration. In a pure arbitration process, the parties are required to submit their dispute to a third party for investigation and adjudication. The arbitrator takes evidence and renders judgment according to some set of rules (in a code-based system), precedents (in a common law system), or a combination of both. In a pure arbitration system, the decision of the arbitrator is binding on the parties and fully enforceable. Put another way, the arbitrator has the coercive power necessary to (a) impel the parties to participate in the process and (b) impose and enforce terms of settlement on them, while the mediator must be acceptable to the disputants and seek only to influence them.

In contrast to mediation, arbitration can be quite effective in overcoming structural and political barriers to agreement. Arbitration rulings define a winner and a loser, and therefore address the zero-sum nature of most disputes. In addition, rulings give leaders a potent tool in overcoming internal resistance in the two-level game. Leaders can assert that they are committed to abide by the arbitrator's findings, and that a failure to do so would have much broader negative consequences for their constituencies.

Between the poles of pure mediation and pure arbitration are ADR processes in which the third party has some ability to press the parties to accept a specific settlement. At the mediation end of the spectrum, we find mediators whose reputations or positions give them clout. At the arbitration end of the spectrum, we find adjudication processes in which the findings of the arbitrator are not fully binding or enforceable.

Dispute Resolution in the Trading System

Having established a vocabulary for analyzing dispute settlement systems, we are ready to explore the evolution of dispute resolution in the multilateral trading system. In terms of the framework developed in the previous section, dispute resolution in the GATT began de facto as a mediation system and progressively evolved in the direction of becoming more like arbitration. The establishment of the WTO represents the logical conclusion of this process, enshrining a weak arbitration system in international law.

Dispute Resolution in the GATT

The ill-fated ITO Charter, which would have integrated the ITO into the United Nations system, contained elaborate provisions for adjudicating disputes among its members and even for appeals to the International

Court of Justice at The Hague.[13] The GATT, by contrast, had an uncertain link to the UN system and fairly limited provisions for dealing with member complaints, with no means of formal juridical dispute settlement. The major focus was on providing contracting parties with a mechanism for dealing with nullification or impairment of benefits under the agreement. Diplomatic methods of consultation were emphasized. Thus Article XXII required contracting parties to "accord sympathetic consideration to and adequate opportunity for consultation to" other GATT parties. Article XXIII allowed parties first to attempt bilateral negotiations and subsequently to refer the problem to the entire body.

Signatories to the GATT could file a complaint if another party violated an agreement or discipline under Article XXIII. Even if no specific agreement had been violated, a complaint could be launched if another party adopted measures that had the effect of undermining previously granted concessions (Article XXIII:1([b])). Article XXIII then called for the contracting parties as a whole to "promptly investigate any matter so referred to them" and "make appropriate recommendations" or "give a ruling on the matter as appropriate." It allowed them to "authorize the suspension of the application to any other contracting party of such concessions or other obligations as they determine to be appropriate in the circumstances."[14]

It is important to note that the GATT Secretariat did not police compliance. Instead, it offered assistance to contracting parties in settling disputes when parties felt that an agreement had been violated. In addition, the settlement system was weak, since the consensus rule by which GATT took decisions had the effect of making participation by defendants voluntary. Defendants could prevent the GATT from dealing with disputes and they could also block any rulings from being adopted.

Moreover, the GATT Agreement did not detail the precise manner in which the body as whole was to carry out its investigations and apply its rulings. Indeed, these practices changed over time, evolving in the direction of a more juridical approach. In its early years, complaints were dealt

---

13. See Article 96 of the Havana Charter on the International Court of Justice:

> 1. The Organization may, in accordance with arrangements made pursuant to paragraph 2 of Article 96 of the Charter of the United Nations, request from the International Court of Justice advisory opinions on legal questions arising within the scope of the activities of the Organization. . . .

> 5. The Organization shall consider itself bound by the opinion of the Court on any question referred by it to the Court. In so far as it does not accord with the opinion of the Court, the decision in question shall be modified.

14. There has been considerable debate over the reason for permitting these suspensions of concessions. Was the purpose to enforce compliance, provide compensation, or offer a safety valve? For an extensive discussion, see Lawrence (2004). The literature suggests some role for each of these explanations, but the maintenance of reciprocity appears paramount. In most instances, the suspension of concessions was supposed to be equal to the level of nullification or impairment.

with at semiannual plenary meetings; later they were delegated to working group, and finally to panels of neutral adjudicators. These panel proceedings, developed in 1955, were informal; both the judges and the advocates were diplomats rather than lawyers.[15] In contrast to working parties in which participants represented their countries, panel members were supposed to be neutral and not receive instructions from their governments. Nonetheless, as Robert Hudec observes in his history of GATT dispute settlement (1993, 12), "Legal rulings were drafted with an elusive diplomatic vagueness."

To use the terms defined above, this was a mediation system. Reliance on this approach accounts for some of the difficulties encountered by the "diplomatic" dispute resolution process practiced in the GATT during the late 1940s and 1950s. The parties voluntarily took their dispute to a group of "wise men" (i.e., mediators), who would help them work out an acceptable solution. The parties were free to accept or reject the recommendations. Solutions often had a compromise or split-the-difference character to them, consistent with the outcomes of most mediative processes. While this approach helped to resolve many trade disputes early in the history of the GATT, it may have actually encouraged parties to breach the rules, because they knew they were likely to retain some of their gains. Ultimately it was rejected by parties that wanted clear rulings in their favor when they felt the rules had been violated.

GATT participants therefore came to differ over how the dispute settlement system should operate. On the one hand, the European Community (EC) found itself in a defensive posture as a result of its Common Agricultural Policy (CAP)—which many other countries viewed as a highly protectionist instrument—and its preferential arrangements with former colonies. As a result the European Commission had a strong preference for approaches to dispute settlement that were diplomatic (mediation) rather than legal (arbitration). On the other hand, particularly in the 1960s, the developing-country members called not only for special and differential treatment for themselves but also for stricter enforcement of developed-country obligations, backed up by a system with multilateral retaliation against violators.[16]

The United States never wholly agreed with the EC's "diplomatic" approach, but for a period it took a rather strong stand with the EC on the side of "anti-legalism." The two trade superpowers preached that trade restrictions must be approached gradually, and with careful attention to social realities. They branded formal legal claims by other GATT members "legalistic," creating a climate in which such legal actions were

---

15. At the Ninth Session of the GATT Contracting Parties, the first Panel on Complaints was established in response to a dispute between Italy and Sweden (see Jackson 1969, 173).

16. In 1961 Uruguay launched a case challenging many practices in developed countries, particularly in agriculture.

viewed as unfriendly actions; indeed, there were no cases brought between 1963 and 1969 (see Hudec 1993). In the 1970s, however, the GATT began to move more toward a legalistic system of dispute settlement. Hudec (1993, 13) notes, "The primary pressure for rebuilding came from the United States, which abandoned its anti-legalist position when political developments at home created a need for stronger enforcement of US trade agreement rights." The United States sought to expand the ambit of the GATT by supporting the codes in the Tokyo Round and seeking tougher rules and time lines for dispute settlement. While the United States was able to have the GATT's dispute settlement system described in detail in a memorandum of understanding,[17] opposition forestalled any significant change in procedures (Jackson 1997a, 116).[18]

Dissatisfaction with the GATT dispute settlement system grew during the 1980s. One particular obstacle to success was the ability of disputing nations to block the adoption of panel reports. A second was related to enforcement. Although retaliation was authorized under the GATT, it was never actually implemented in any case. The weakness of the international dispute settlement system and the limited coverage of the rules became increasingly frustrating for the United States. Delay and uncertainty in the process, absence of legal rigor in rulings, uncertainty about adoption, and delay in compliance were all seen as problems (Howse and Trebilcock 1999, 55–56).

The United States responded by seeking to leverage its market power to reduce barriers to its exports, using unilateral measures without GATT authorization. Section 301 in the 1974 Trade Act provided a procedure for dealing with foreign measures that constrained US exports. In the mid-1980s, the United States dramatically stepped up its use of section 301 legislation to target foreign practices not covered under the GATT that it nonetheless deemed unreasonable. These included the failure to respect intellectual property, refusal to provide access to telecommunications, and other foreign regulatory practices deemed to discriminate against US products and firms. In the Omnibus Trade Act of 1988, the United States adopted Super 301, which contemplated bilateral negotiations and the unilateral adoption of sanctions by the United States in the event that they failed.

---

17. "Understanding Regarding Notification, Consultation, Dispute Settlement and Surveillance," GATT BISD [Basic Instruments and Selected Documents], 26th Supplement (1979): 210.

18. Since the 1950s, the GATT system had clearly evolved in the direction of a greater emphasis on rule-making and not simply the adjudication of disputes. In addition to replacing national representatives with neutral panelists in dispute settlement, the GATT case brought by Uruguay in 1962 produced a ruling that if a complaining party established "violation," this would be deemed a "prima facie nullification or impairment." As a result, the burden of proving that there was no nullification or impairment shifted to the responding parties. This concept was embraced in the 1979 understanding at the end of the Tokyo Round.

The WTO Dispute Settlement System

Out of a desire in part to restrain this US unilateralism, as well as to create a more effective system, the WTO DSU was negotiated in the Uruguay Round. The Uruguay Round Agreement also enhanced the power of the Dispute Settlement Body (DSB) to enforce trade rules. Because it required unanimity to prevent proceedings, no one country could block the panel from hearing a dispute. The single undertaking meant that all WTO rules and most agreements were subject to the DSU. WTO members therefore had the ability to implement cross-sectoral retaliation. For example, if a country violates the TRIPS agreement's intellectual property rules, it can be subject to the loss of other trade benefits, such as low tariffs on manufactured goods.[19] While members could no longer veto the adoption of panel rulings, they were given the right to appeal such rulings to the Appellate Body (AB) established in the DSU.

According to the DSU, parties may seek to resolve conflicts by using the good offices of the director-general or by agreeing to arbitration.[20] But they may also invoke the formal dispute settlement mechanism. The parties to the dispute are first required to engage in consultation. If these consultations are unsatisfactory, a complainant can request the establishment of a panel to hear the case within 60 days. To establish such a panel, the WTO DSB (the WTO members) draws on a roster of potential panelists nominated by WTO members. The panel then examines the case; after issuing an interim report, it delivers a final report with conclusions and, at its discretion, it provides suggestions as to how to the parties might come into compliance. If the panel finds that a member has failed to comply, absent an appeal by that member, it can make a recommendation as to how the member could come into compliance.[21] If complying immediately is impractical, the member is given "a reasonable period of time to do so" (DSU, Article 21.3).

The finding can then be appealed. If the member loses the appeal and fails to act within this period, the rules call for the parties to negotiate compensation, "pending full implementation." Compensation is "volun-

---

19. Article 22.3 of the WTO DSU tries to match the sector in which the violation occurs and the sector in which concessions are suspended. However, if such matching is deemed not "practicable or effective" by the complaining party, it may seek to suspend concessions in other sectors or in another covered agreement.

20. See Article 25 of the DSU: "Expeditious arbitration with the WTO as an alternative means of dispute settlement can facilitate the solution of certain disputes that concern issues that are clearly defined by both parties."

21. Panel reports must be adopted within 60 days, unless a consensus exists not to adopt or a party appeals the findings. Appeals, which are limited to issues of law and legal interpretation, are heard by an appellate body composed of seven members. Appeals proceedings must be completed within 90 days.

tary," however (Article 22.2, 22.1). Moreover, it is generally understood that any compensation provided should be on an MFN basis.[22] If, after 20 days, compensation cannot be agreed on, the complainant may request authorization from the DSB to suspend equivalent concessions.[23] In particular, "the level of the suspension of concessions . . . shall be equivalent to the level of nullification and impairment" (Article 22.4). The magnitude of the retaliation is determined by the DSB, generally on the recommendation of the original panel. Arbitration, to be completed within 60 days, may be sought to address the suspension, the procedures, and the principles of retaliation (Article 22.6).

Strengths and Weaknesses

To use the terms defined previously, the WTO dispute settlement mechanism is an example of a weak arbitration process. The parties are required to submit to the process if one party launches a complaint. The arbitrator (in this case, a panel) investigates and reaches conclusions based on specified rules (in this case, negotiated by the parties). The resulting rulings are binding on the parties. However, de jure the WTO system remains weaker than the pure arbitration processes common in domestic legal systems for four major reasons: precedents are not binding, enforcement is not automatic, standing is not assured, and remedies are limited. But in some instances the WTO practice actually comes closer to a domestic legal system than these principles might imply.

First, the WTO DSU is not a common-law system with binding precedents. Technically, there is no stare decisis. Each panel ruling is thus unique—only the members themselves can adopt rules that add to or subtract from the agreement. In principle, the adjudication is a process of dispute settlement, not a court case. In practice, however, panelists usually find the arguments made by other panelists to be persuasive and give considerable weight to precedent. Indeed, the Appellate Body, and hence the panels, actually follow precedent very closely. So in practice, if not by rule, the system in some ways mirrors domestic legal procedures. In addition, as Article 3.2 of the DSU notes, members recognize that the dispute settlement system clarifies the "existing provisions of these agreements in accordance with customary rules of interpretation of public international law."

---

22. The statement that "compensation is voluntary and, if granted, shall be consistent with the covered agreements" (DSU, Article 22.1) is generally understood to require that it be based on MFN principles.

23. According to Article 22.3 of the DSU, the complaining party should first seek to suspend concessions in the same sector as that in which the panel body has found a violation. If that party considers such action not practicable or effective it may seek to suspend concessions in other sectors under the same agreement; if this, in turn, is not practicable or effective, then obligations under another covered agreement may be suspended.

Second, WTO members do not automatically implement WTO rulings. Members have discretion as to whether or not they will comply. Although the WTO does review its members' trade policies, there is no central policing mechanism. The WTO itself does not investigate and prosecute its members for violations. Instead, only members believing their rights have been nullified or impaired can bring cases.[24] Nonetheless, in practice, compliance with both GATT and WTO rulings has been widespread.

Third, until 2005—when the two disputants, the United States and the European Union, agreed to open to the public the proceedings of the case in which the European Union challenged continued US retaliation over the banning of hormone-treated beef [25]—all panel proceedings occurred in closed sessions attended only by the participants in the dispute. Panelists may at their discretion choose to consult outside experts or read outside briefs, but they are not required to do so. Although private counsel can be employed to make their arguments, only governments have standing to bring cases. There is no private right of action.[26]

Fourth and finally, there are significant limits to the remedies available to the "winners." The panel's findings demand that the rule breakers bring their systems into compliance. But unlike rulings on contract cases in common-law legal systems, no attempt is made to compensate the winner for damages incurred during the period of noncompliance. This failure to require compensation has the advantage of avoiding further disputes over the size and payment of such damages. But it also has a downside: Parties expecting to lose have an incentive to draw out the process as long as possible. Parties also may engage in rule-breaking behavior with the knowledge that at most, they will be tasked with coming into compliance at a later date. Thus, the Bush administration imposed tariffs on steel in the full knowledge that they would be challenged and possibly overruled but correctly judged that the action would placate domestic interests for a significant period of time.

Moreover, if the losers do not bring their systems into compliance, at most they will be subject to retaliation. De jure, such retaliation is meant

24. One exception is disputes over prohibited subsidies. Violations of export subsidies for example may be challenged by any member regardless of whether that country believes it has been adversely affected.

25. As noted on the WTO Web site, "At the request of the parties in the disputes 'Continued suspension of obligations in the EC-hormones dispute' (US—Continued suspension of obligations in the EC-hormones dispute, DS320; Canada—Continued suspension of obligations in the EC-hormones dispute, DS321) the panels have agreed to open their proceedings with the parties on 12, 13 and 15 September 2005 for observation by WTO Members and the general public via closed-circuit broadcast to a separate viewing room at WTO Headquarters in Geneva" (www.wto.org).

26. The long-running dispute over bananas eventually allowed member states to employ private lawyers in their litigation; actions over turtles and shrimp as well as asbestos opened up the process to amicus curiae briefs.

to be temporary: countries still have an international legal obligation to comply. But in practice, because there are no additional trade consequences aside from retaliation, it can become the "permanent" solution to a dispute. In the beef hormone case, for example, retaliation has served as a de facto substitute for compliance. While in practice the dispute resolution procedure therefore can operate like a safety valve, overreliance on retaliation may undermine the system as a whole.

More generally, there remains a strong tension between the two roles of the dispute settlement system: It is both an institution that enforces rules and a framework for negotiation and compromise. In the first function, the emphasis is on adjudication—the consistent application of relevant rules and ensuring that the rules are followed. In the latter, the purpose is to find a solution the participants can live with.

Nonetheless, the formalization of the system and the inability of members to veto the proceedings have strengthened the WTO's ability to enforce rules and have broadened its jurisdiction. In emphasizing the significance of the change, Joseph Weiler (2001) describes the former dispute settlement under the GATT as "diplomacy by other means."[27] By contrast, he argues, the WTO system has now imported the norms, practices, and habits of legal culture: "Disputes are not settled, they are won or lost, parties go for the jugular, 'we can win in court' becomes for most lawyers an automatic trigger to 'we should bring the case.'" He adds, " The new ethos is no longer a 5–4 mentality, it is 'getting it [legally] right' or 'making it appeal proof'"(Weiler 2001, 340). Weiler probably overstates somewhat the contrast between the GATT and WTO since the GATT system had clearly evolved in a more juridical direction. Nonetheless, the questions he raises are important. Is the shift toward this more legalistic approach desirable? Opinions are mixed. On one side are those who point to the merits of a trading system based on enforceable rules and contrast it with a system based on power politics. The legal scholar John Jackson (1997b), for example, is firmly in this camp (see also Jackson 2004). He stresses the importance of such rules not just in making the system more fair but also in establishing a predictable framework for private decisions. He also points to the role of dispute settlement findings in filling in gaps and clarifying ambiguities that are inevitable in all rule-making systems.

On the other side are those who voice strong reservations, such as political scientist Claude Barfield (2001). In particular, Barfield believes that there is a serious imbalance between the legislative and judicial capacities of the WTO, made worse by the WTO DSU with its firm deadlines and certain rulings. To negotiate rules in the WTO is cumbersome and time-consuming. Inevitably, therefore, as the rules become more complex,

---

27. Under the GATT, "Crafting outcomes that would command the consent of both parties and thus be adopted was the principal task of the panelists" (Weiler 2001, 338).

Barfield is concerned that the DSB will be drawn into providing opinions and filling in gaps where the agreements themselves provide no guidance. Such a development is natural: If the US Congress met only once each decade, the US courts would become more active in making laws. Barfield worries that the DSB's growing role will shift power away from national governments toward panelists and thereby undermine national sovereignty. He therefore would like the Appellate Body to refuse to decide cases in which the rules are not clear.

When the WTO system for dispute settlement became more effective, it drew attention to the question of how the WTO deals with issues that may relate to trade—such as international environmental treaties, international labor standards, and human rights—when signatories do not have access to mandatory dispute settlement. Indeed, many have sought to have these issues included in trade agreements precisely to gain access to the dispute system. On the one hand, some observers fear that if more issues are included, the WTO risks losing its trade focus and experiencing excessive mission creep (Bhagwati 2002). Developing countries are also concerned that covering these issues in the WTO could make them subject to protectionism. In the 1980s it was already apparent that advocates of including services and intellectual property in the trading system were driven largely by their desire to use the dispute settlement system (see Devereaux 2005). On the other hand, those concerned about these other areas have become increasingly fearful that a narrow trade perspective will trump their interests.

Another controversy relates to the use of retaliation in the enforcement mechanism. Some object that the use of retaliation is ineffective in inducing compliance, others are concerned that it is protectionist, a third group complains about overriding national sovereignty, and a fourth believes that the system is inequitable (for discussion, see Lawrence 2004). Nevertheless, compliance with the WTO seems to be strong and, again, the system can operate as a safety valve—though this function, as noted above, is controversial.[28]

Gaming the System

At the same time, the WTO dispute resolution mechanism does not, and probably cannot, prevent nations from seeking to game the system. They may do so by intentionally breaching their commitments, in the full knowledge that they are likely to trigger WTO actions. In addition, once cases are under way, nations may employ a broad range of strategies in their efforts to either win or avoid losing.

---

28. For a discussion of possible reforms of the dispute settlement system, see Sutherland et al. (2004, chapter 6).

Rational Breach

The cases in this volume illustrate several reasons why nations may engage in a strategy of "rational breach." One overarching justification is the short-term political interests of leaders, which sometimes override the long-term economic interests of their nations. In the steel case, for example, the Bush administration certainly knew that its actions could be challenged in the WTO, but proceeded nonetheless so that it might satisfy powerful domestic constituencies—the steel companies and their unions.

In some cases, the breach of WTO commitments by one party paradoxically enables both the offender and the offended to achieve domestic political gains, albeit once again at the cost of overall economic welfare. Thus the European refusal to accept hormone-treated beef enabled the leaders in the European Union to assist their domestic farming constituencies and gain support from consumer groups. At the same time, the willingness of successive US administrations to pursue cases against the European Union in the WTO placated their farming constituencies. The result was a political win-win and an economic loss-loss.

Another important factor is the value of delay associated with breaching commitments and triggering WTO cases. Such a breach can be perfectly rational if the resulting (significant) time it takes for the case to be heard, appeals to be completed, and retaliation to be approved permits domestic industries to adjust and critical political events—for example, elections—to pass. In such situations (as the steel case makes clear), breach functions as a sort of political safety valve whose effectiveness rests in large part on the lack of provisions for recovering damages through WTO cases. The benefits achieved during the period between breach and retaliation are essentially costless for the offending party, unless, of course, the original violation triggers a tit-for-tat spiral of counterbreach.

Finally, breach can be used to intentionally push the envelope when rules are ambiguous. While WTO rulings do not officially create precedents, that outcome is almost unavoidable in practice. In addition, success in launching cases in areas where there is ambiguity is an effective mechanism for increasing the pressure on other parties to seek to extend or clarify the rules in subsequent rounds of trade negotiations. In the bananas case, for example, the European Union basically pretended to comply in the hope the United States might drop its challenge or at least delay its retaliation.

Strategies for Influencing Outcomes

Once launched, WTO cases go forward according to established principles and time frames. But such procedural norms by no means prevent the parties from crafting strategies designed to influence the ultimate outcome. It is possible for them to do so because negotiations among the players can be carried on in parallel with the more formal arbitration processes. These negotiations can powerfully influence how far the formal process proceeds or can lead to understandings between the contending parties once rulings have been made. In domestic legal systems, as already mentioned, this is known as "bargaining in the shadow of the law."

The goal in fashioning these strategies is to favorably influence counterparties' perceptions of their interests and alternatives—for example, in order to make a negotiated settlement appear preferable to risking a full-blown defeat. The tools most commonly relied on are coalition building and issue linkage.

The parties that file WTO cases often seek to build international alliances in order to bolster the importance of their case or to generate favorable public opinion in support of their positions. Complainants will lobby other members to join them in bringing cases as either complaining or third parties. In addition, though public opinion has no direct impact on WTO proceedings, parties may also seek to use it to impose a real, albeit non-trade-related, cost on the party that has breached its obligations. The public relations efforts by the West African countries in the cotton case served this purpose. At the same time, defendants will attempt to prevent these coalitions from forming. In the cotton case, for example, fear that the United States might retaliate through measures such as reducing foreign aid dissuaded the West African cotton producers from formally joining Brazil in launching WTO proceedings. But Brazil was able to counter this US threat by getting the vulnerable parties to play a critical role in influencing public opinion.

Issue linkage is the second major strategy employed by those seeking to influence perceptions of interests and alternatives during dispute settlement proceedings. The breaching parties typically seek to keep the terms of the dispute narrow, both to make the costs of accepting the breach palatable to the other side and to avoid sparking domestic political battles. The parties that file cases attempt to broaden the dispute for the converse reasons: Doing so enlarges the pie that is at risk, perhaps undermining domestic political support for leaders in the breaching party, and makes it easier to mobilize and sustain supportive domestic political coalitions. For example, the European Union challenged US exports in its case against foreign sales corporations in response to US victories on beef and bananas.

Questions to Consider

Many of the issues discussed in our introduction arise in the cases we have selected for this volume. First, all of the disputes deal with the behind-the-border or deeper integration concerns in trade policy. Second, none of the disputes could be amicably settled by the parties. Some were resolved, in the sense that the losing defendant withdrew its measure (steel) or the losing complainant dropped the matter (film), but in others compliance was difficult (bananas) or as yet impossible (beef, GMOs) to obtain. In several, while the cases themselves had varying degree of success, they were actually brought in order to make larger points and hence had significance beyond the measures concerned: for example, the Kodak-Fuji case to show that the informal barriers in Japan violated WTO rules, the cotton case to pressure on the United States to reduce farm subsidies in the Doha Round, and the beef hormone and GMO cases to challenge EU regulatory practices. As you read through each of the cases, consider five major questions.

What WTO Rules Were Challenged?

The case studies in this volume cover a wide range of policy issues that extend far beyond border barriers. They therefore allow for reflection on the precise nature of the agreements that constrain domestic policies and for consideration of whether these rules are appropriate. These WTO rules include the agreements on sanitary and phytosanitary standards (hormones and GMOs); technical barriers to trade (GMOs); agriculture, export, and domestic content subsidies (cotton); safeguards (steel); domestic measures that are not covered by GATT rules but that may nullify or impair a member's legitimate expectations of benefits (film); quotas (bananas); services (bananas); and dispute settlement rules (bananas). They involve the United States as a complainant (hormones, GMOs, film, and bananas) and respondent (cotton), in cases against both developed countries (Japan and the European Union) and developing countries (Brazil). As you read the cases, think about the nature of the rules in question, asking,

- Are the rules really necessary to ensure free trade?
- Are the rules too vague or unclear?
- Do the rules threaten national sovereignty?
- Are they fair?

Why Were the Rules (Allegedly) Breached?

The cases illustrate that countries may sometimes violate rules quite deliberately, knowing they might eventually pay a price at the WTO; at other times they may do so inadvertently because the rules themselves are complex or ambiguous, or because domestic policies were adopted with inadequate attention to their WTO implications. Once they were found in violation and lost their appeals, some respondents came into compliance when threatened with retaliation, while in other cases they did not and retaliation was authorized and applied (hormones, bananas). As you read the cases, consider why the rules were breached, asking,

- What implementation problems did the rules pose for members?
- Were these anticipated during the rule-making negotiations or did they emerge later on, during implementation?
- Did changing domestic economic and political conditions trigger the breach?
- Did the parties try to take advantage of loopholes? Were they successful?

Why Was the Breach Challenged?

Various courses of action are open to countries that believe their trading partners have violated an agreement. They can choose to ignore the violations, seek to negotiate with the trading partner, or choose to bring a case. If compliance is still not forthcoming after a WTO ruling, complainants can again choose to do nothing, seek authorization for retaliation, or retaliate in order to induce compliance. In making these choices, countries may be driven by a number of considerations and needs. These include promoting national economic interests, responding to domestic interest groups, preserving international relations, and setting a precedent for other rules and relationships with other trading partners. The cases provide examples of countries that choose not to file cases and those that do. In some cases, particular interests and concerns dominate; in others, the dispute has been brought to the WTO in order to make a point. In reading the cases, therefore, you should think about why the breach was challenged, asking whether this dispute was brought to the WTO

- simply to resolve the problems of particular producers;
- to clarify certain rules;
- to obtain through litigation what could not be obtained through agreement; or
- to create conditions for negotiation.

What "Influence Games" Are the Parties Playing?

The WTO DSU is a system through which players seek to advance their interests by litigation. They breach rules and file cases in order to achieve strategic objectives. To achieve advantage, they also craft and enact strategies—such as negotiation and coalition building—in parallel with the litigation process. As you read the cases, think about the game that is being played and the strategies the players are employing by asking,

- Who are the key players? What are their interests?
- What are their alternatives to complying with the rules? To permitting others to do so?
- What is the larger context in which the cases are filed? How is the subject of the dispute linked to other issues?
- Beyond filing and defending the cases, what do the parties do to try to influence their outcomes? To what extent do they engage in negotiation with the other side?
- What coalitions do they seek to build and why?
- To what other issues do they try to link their dispute and why?

How Well Did the Dispute Settlement System Work?

Finally, think about what the case tells us about the WTO dispute settlement system and its strengths and weaknesses. Some view the WTO system as a great achievement, while others have concerns. As you read the cases, consider the implications for the system by asking,

- Did the WTO operate in an equitable manner?
- Did the dispute settlement system provide effective relief for the complainant?
- Was it effective in achieving compliance?
- Did the result undermine national sovereignty? What are the merits in and the problems of relying on litigation to deal with conflicts over deeper integration?
- Was an important precedent set with implications for other policies?
- Did the case contribute to or detract from the long-run legitimacy of the WTO?
- How does the dispute system affect the balance of power of individual countries?
- How does the system affect the domestic balance of power within countries?

Food Fight: The United States, Europe, and Trade in Hormone-Treated Beef

In the summer of 1999, several McDonald's restaurants in southern France opened their doors to be greeted by steaming piles of fresh manure. French farmers had targeted McDonald's to protest recent actions by the United States in an ongoing trade dispute over beef treated with growth-promoting hormones. French displeasure echoed through the town of Auch, where 150 farmers occupied a McDonald's holding signs that declared "No hormones in foie gras country."[1] In nearby Millau, an attack on a McDonald's site under construction resulted in $65,000 worth of damage. Charged with willful destruction, five farmers were imprisoned. "You are right to be angry," French agricultural minister Jean Glavany told a crowd at a farming fair. "This attempt to impose hormone-treated beef on us is unbearable."[2]

French hostility toward the American hamburger had its roots in a long-standing US-EU dispute over trade in beef. Ten years earlier, in a much-

---

Food Fight: The United States, Europe, and Trade in Hormone-Treated Beef is an edited and revised version of the case with the same name originally written by Charan Devereaux for the Case Program at the John F. Kennedy School of Government. For copies or permission to reproduce the unabridged case please refer to www.ksgcase.harvard.edu or send a written request to Case Program, John F. Kennedy School of Government, Harvard University, 79 John F. Kennedy Street, Cambridge, MA 02138.

1. Craig R. Whitney, "Food Fight: French Impose Own Tariffs; Some Restaurants Retaliate Against US Goods over Beef Dispute," *The International Herald Tribune*, July 31, 1999, 9.

2. Glavany, quoted in Samer Iskandar, "Farm Protester Refuses to Leave French Jail Cell," *The Financial Times*, September 3, 1999, 3.

publicized effort to satisfy a health-conscious public, Europe had banned the use of growth-promoting hormones in raising beef cattle. The 1989 ban covered all beef—including meat imported from the United States, where growth-enhancing hormones were widely used. In retaliation, the United States imposed punitive tariffs on approximately $100 million worth of European food imports, including pork products, canned tomatoes, and some fermented beverages. With rhetoric running high on both sides, a standoff began. Europe and the United States were at an impasse.

In the years that followed, the rules changed. New multilateral institutions and agreements were put in place to govern disputes like the beef quarrel. The World Trade Organization (WTO), with its new dispute settlement mechanism, was born in 1995. Rules for managing the health and safety issues surrounding trade in food were promulgated by the 1994 Sanitary and Phytosanitary (SPS) agreement. And the role of an existing international scientific organization that evaluated food safety, the Codex Alimentarius Commission, was strengthened.

Despite these changes, the story was very much the same a decade later. Though the new WTO ruled against the European ban, the European Union continued to reject beef raised with growth-promoting hormones. Nor had the new SPS agreement resolved the dispute. In 1999, once again, the United States imposed punitive tariffs of approximately $117 million on foods imported from Europe, again focusing on pork but also national specialties such as Roquefort cheese, mustard, truffles, and foie gras. The rules had changed, but the endgame remained much the same: Europe and the United States were at an impasse (see timeline in appendix 1A).

At the core of the dispute lay fundamental disagreements about trade in food. The United States claimed that the European regulatory process had been captured by politics. US officials were frustrated by what they saw as a political move to protect the EU beef market by invoking scientifically unsupported claims about the harm caused by eating hormone-treated meat. Food regulation should be based on science, the United States argued, not on politics or protectionism. Europe defended its ban, asserting that health issues should be decided democratically—by politicians who answer to voters. European consumers had different standards than American consumers when it came to food. To justify their position, European officials invoked the "precautionary principle," which they claimed entitled the European Union to prohibit or restrict products that were suspected, but not proven, to be hazardous.

The real issue, Europe insisted, was that the US trade system was overly influenced by industry. The United States had soured the transatlantic trade relationship by responding to the demands of the beef lobby, European officials said. The "client relationship" between Congress, the US Department of Agriculture (USDA), the Office of the United States Trade Representative (USTR), and the beef industry made it difficult to settle the dispute in any politically palatable way, Europeans argued. US officials noted that little pressure was needed to motivate the government to initiate and pursue the case—the central issue was that Europe would not lift the ban. The standoff persisted: No hamburger would cross the Atlantic.

Background

The Context: Trade and Agriculture

Before the ban, Europe imported a modest amount of US beef—about $100 million annually (out of more than $1 billion worth that US beef producers shipped abroad each year)—a drop in the $166 billion bucket of two-way transatlantic trade. Most of the US shipments were pet foods and other low-grade meat products. But the beef dispute captured the attention of US congressional leaders, federal agency heads, powerful industry lobbies, top European officials, diplomats, consumer groups, and international organizations. By early 2000, the European Union had spent some 600 million euros on the hormone spat.[3] What was the big deal with beef?

Trade in food and agricultural products had often been a sticking point between the United States and Europe. As a result, agriculture remained essentially off the table in the first seven rounds of trade talks under the General Agreement on Tariffs and Trade (GATT) and was largely exempted from the disciplines that applied to manufactured goods (USDA 1998, 5). Though the subject of agriculture incited heated debates, little action was taken.

The differences between the United States and Europe grew out of their respective agricultural policies. From the early 1950s through the 1970s, agricultural trade was an exception to the trend of strong worldwide economic growth, falling from 34 percent of total world trade in 1950 to only 14 percent in 1976. Over the same period, higher productivity in agriculture led to lower crop prices and a need for fewer agricultural workers.

The response of US and European governments was to support agricultural prices and incomes. In Europe, the mechanism for doing so was the Common Agricultural Policy (CAP), initiated in 1962. Though the CAP controlled prices, it did not control production; as a result, there were large surpluses of some commodities. To reduce these surpluses, the European Community provided subsidies to farmers so they could sell their products on international markets without a loss. The United States

---

3. Geoff Winestock, "Column One: EU Beef Battle with US Began in a Rare Event—Italian Boys Grew Breasts; Ministers Banned Hormones—But Scientific Evidence Was Always Lacking," *The Wall Street Journal Europe*, March 2, 2000, 1.

also utilized price supports and subsidies in the agricultural sector, but it was moving to dismantle some of those price controls by the early 1970s. Its notable competitive advantage in many agricultural products, often attributable to industrial farming methods, put the United States in a strong export position. As a result, the United States gained enthusiasm for a liberal trade regime for farm products, focusing on its export commodities.

The beef dispute erupted at a time when the United States was pushing to lower agricultural subsidies and supports abroad—a move that would benefit the US agricultural industry. The year 1986 marked the beginning of the Uruguay Round of GATT trade talks, negotiations that the United States hoped would later be known as "the agriculture round" in recognition of progress in reducing agricultural trade barriers. For the first time, agriculture was prominent on the trade agenda.

It is important to note that both the United States and Europe actively protected their beef markets. Before the ban, most of the 50,000 metric tons of US beef shipped annually to Europe consisted of offal (tongue, liver, etc.), but significantly, the EC quota allowed in 10,000 tons of premium high-quality beef. In 1987, the United States exported about $145 million worth of beef to Europe and the EC exported about $449 million of beef (mostly canned) to the United States. Eighty percent of US meat exports to Europe consisted of sales to France and Britain.

The History: Beef and Hormones in the United States

In 1989, when the EC banned beef produced from cattle treated with growth-promoting hormones, more than half of the 35 million US cattle sent to market each year received such hormones. They included the natural substances oestradiol-17β, testosterone, and progesterone, as well as the synthetic hormones trenbolone and zeranol. By reducing the time required for a steer (a castrated young bull) to reach target weight (about 1,100 lbs.), hormone treatments saved cattle ranchers about 15 percent in feed costs. Producers maintained that hormones not only kept beef prices down but also turned out leaner meat. "Hormones increase lean production and reduce fat production, which is what consumers have told us that they want," says Chuck Lambert, chief economist at the National Cattlemen's Beef Association. "We are also able to do that at about a 15 percent increase in efficiency."[4]

The hormones in question had been approved for controlled usage by the US Food and Drug Administration (FDA) in the 1950s, 1960s, and

---

4. Unless otherwise noted, all quotes from Chuck Lambert are from a December 1999 interview with the author. According to Lambert, the feedlot process lasted 120 to 180 days on average for untreated cattle. The use of hormones enabled the time to drop to between 102 and 153 days.

1980s.[5] Administered subcutaneously, the hormones trickled into cattle from an implant under the skin of the ear. "Hormones are not implanted into edible tissue," Lambert notes. "In function, they are similar to Norplant or a slow-release cold capsule. One implant lasts about 100 days, as the hormones are slowly released into the system of the animal." A number of studies had concluded that these compounds were safe when administered properly. "Use of these hormones provides the best of all worlds," says Dr. Robert Livingston, formerly of the FDA's Center for Veterinary Medicine (FDA-CVM). "You get a better product quicker and cheaper. There are additional benefits, as well. For example, because less feed is being used more efficiently, you have less waste."[6] By 1999, 90 to 95 percent of grain-fed US beef cattle were being treated with growth-promoting hormones.[7]

Regulating Hormones: The DES Debate

Hormone use in the United States was not free of controversy. The first artificial animal-growth stimulant was a hormone called diethylstilbestrol, or DES. Discovered by an Iowa State College nutritionist and approved by the FDA in 1954, DES increased weight gain in cattle by 10 to 15 percent. As a result, DES-treated cattle consumed about 500 pounds less feed and went to market about five weeks sooner than untreated animals. Cattlemen flocked to DES feeds; by the early 1960s, as many as 95 percent of US cattle feeders used the hormone (Marcus 1994, 1).[8]

But use of DES was complicated by its status as a potent carcinogen.[9] In 1958, Congress passed the Food Additives Amendment, known as the Delaney Clause, which barred any substance known to cause cancer in humans or animals from being used in the food supply, either directly or in-

---

5. The pharmaceutical firms manufacturing the hormones included Eli Lilly, American Cyanmid, Roussel-Uclaf, Vineland Laboratories, Schering-Plough, Upjohn, and International Minerals and Chemicals.

6. Unless otherwise noted, all quotes from Robert Livingston are from a 2000 interview with the author.

7. The figure comes from Chuck Lambert, who notes that 15 percent of total US beef production comes from cows and bulls at the end of their productivity in the breeding herd or the dairy herd. These cattle typically do not receive growth hormones and are generally used in ground beef or processed products.

8. The four main manufacturers of agricultural DES were American Home Products Corporation, Dawes Laboratories, the Hess and Clark Division of Rhodia Inc., and Vineland Laboratories (Victor Cohn, "FDA Bans Most Uses of Controversial Drug," *The Washington Post*, June 28, 1979, A3).

9. From 1947 to 1971, between 500,000 and 3,000,000 women took DES to prevent miscarriage. In the 1970s, evidence first appeared linking DES to a rare form of vaginal cancer in the daughters of women who had taken the drug (Kuchler, McClelland, and Offutt 1989, 25).

directly.[10] "What that meant," explains former FDA-CVM director Lester Crawford, "was that use of DES had to stop."[11]

In 1961, however, Congress modified the Delaney Clause by passing what became known as the DES Proviso. It stipulated that if no DES residues remained in food-producing animals after the hormone was metabolized, DES did not have to be taken off the market. But the proviso was not a clear solution because available technology could not always detect hormone residues. Therefore, debate continued, as did the use of DES.

By the 1970s, the controversy became more publicly charged. The Senate, in an effort led by Edward M. Kennedy (D-MA) and William Proxmire (D-WI), twice passed bills prohibiting DES, both of which failed in the House (Marcus 1994, 2).[12] The USDA and the beef industry opposed a ban. The FDA issued bans in 1972 and 1973, but both were overturned on procedural grounds by the US Court of Appeals for the District of Columbia.[13]

Finally, in 1979, on FDA Commissioner Donald Kennedy's last day on the job, the FDA banned DES once and for all. Despite opposition from DES manufacturers, the beef industry, the USDA, and many in Congress, the hormone was removed from the market in an effort supervised by the FDA-CVM's Lester Crawford. "Every other country in the world had banned DES," says Crawford. "We were the only country still using it."

The next year, Allied Mills, a unit of Continental Grain, asked the FDA what to do about the illegal DES-implanted cattle brought to its feedlots. The FDA investigated and initially found 20,000 head of cattle that had been injected. A week later, it raised the number to nearly a half million. The FDA investigation concluded that hundreds of beef cattle businesses had ignored its DES ban.[14] The FDA went public, warning consumers not

---

10. Section 409 of the Food Additives Amendment of 1958 (21 U.S.C. 348(c)(3)(a): "No additive shall be deemed to be safe if it is found to induce cancer when ingested by man or animal."

11. Lester Crawford was interviewed by the author in 1999 and in 2000. After serving as director of the Center for Veterinary Medicine at the FDA (1978–80, 1982–85), he became the head of the USDA Meat Inspection Program. During that same year, in 1985, he also became the chairman of the UN Committee of Veterinary Medicine through the Codex Alimentarius; he became vice chairman of the Codex (1991–93) after four years as the US delegate (1987–91). In 1997 he became the director of the Center for Food and Nutrition Policy at Georgetown University. He returned to the FDA as acting commissioner in March 2004.

12. S. 963, which barred the administration of DES to any animal intended for use as food, was passed by voice vote in the Senate (61–29) in September 1975. The Senate also passed a measure banning DES in cattle feed in September 1972.

13. Victor Cohn, "FDA Bans Most Uses of Controversial Drug," *The Washington Post*, June 28, 1979, A3. See also Marcus (1994, 132).

14. "FDA Says About 10% of Cattlemen Used Growth Drug After Its Ban," *The Wall Street Journal*, July 15, 1980.

to eat beef. Former FDA-CVM Director Crawford explains, "We got DES off the market in 1979, but then what happened was the cattlemen were in revolt. They decided they would stockpile DES and use it anyway, even though it was banned. DES was the most effective treatment of its kind—it was terribly effective. The cattlemen also didn't want the government telling them what to do. Finally, in the 1970s and early 1980s, the US consumer movement was not very well developed." Observers suggest that violations of the ban were linked to the 25-year habit of using DES, as well as continuing doubt that it was dangerous.

In the end, one historian notes, the FDA probably spent more money regulating DES use in beef cattle than it did on any other drug (Marcus 1994, 2). The DES story is significant for a number of reasons. For one thing, DES shaped how beef was produced in the United States. Traditionally, cattle had been raised mainly by using open-field grazing. However, DES tipped the balance toward confined feeding, encouraging the creation of large commercial feedlots in the midwestern, western, and southern states (Marcus 1994, 1). Opinions differ about the pertinence of the DES story to the European hormone ban. According to some observers, it demonstrates that European fears about hormones are justified—after all, the United States had its own hormone scare. Others argue that the DES story proves that the FDA would ban growth-promoting hormones if necessary—even in a politically charged environment or in the face of industry opposition.

Though DES was ultimately banned in the United States, other growth-promoting hormones remained available to the US beef industry. FDA officials continued to stand behind their safety, and eventually the industry adopted these hormones in place of DES.

The Ban

The Birth of the Ban: Consumers, Politics, and Hormones

Prior to 1981, the EC had no universal policy on the use of growth-promoting hormones in meat animals. The use of hormones had been banned in Italy since 1961, in Denmark since 1963, and in Germany since 1977. Belgium and Greece had never permitted the use of hormones for fattening purposes. However, Spain, the United Kingdom, France, and the Netherlands permitted the use of most hormones for speeding growth in beef cattle.[15]

The move to impose a Europe-wide ban was spurred by the disturbing discovery in 1977 that 83 boys (ages 3 to 13) at the Sisters of the Sacred

---

15. Ireland banned the use of growth-promoting hormones in July 1985.

Heart of Jesus School in Milan, Italy, had sprouted breasts. Seventy-five girls (ages 3 to 8) also showed breast enlargement (Scaglioni et al. 1978). In addition, some of the nuns who taught at the school were admitted to the hospital with acute menstrual pain.[16] The medical researchers who investigated the incident found symptoms consistent with high doses of estrogen, but no evidence of exposure. The school cafeteria seemed the most likely source; in an August 1979 article in the respected medical journal *The Lancet*, researchers hypothesized that "although estrogen contamination was not detected when samples of school meats were tested, an uncontrolled supply of poultry or beef was suspected as being the cause of this outbreak" (Fara et al. 1979, 295). Observers suggested that students might have consumed unmetabolized estrogen as a result of an improperly inserted hormone implant. For example, if a farmer had inserted an implant into the neck of a steer, instead of the ear, and had done so too late, the neck meat would have carried high levels of the hormone. (Neck meat, an inexpensive cut, was often used in schools.)[17]

In 1980, soon after the *Lancet* article appeared, an Italian consumer group reported the discovery of 30,000 jars of baby food containing DES-contaminated French veal. One British tabloid ran the headline "Eat Steak, Change Your Sex."[18] Widespread publicity ensued about illegal use of DES injections in European veal production, especially in France. The cover of the German magazine *Der Spiegel* featured the face of a little girl superimposed on the body of a fully developed woman.[19]

After French television broadcast film of calves receiving hormone injections, the Union of French Consumers called for a boycott of veal. Pierre Mehaignerie, the French agriculture minister, denounced the demands of the consumer organizations as excessive, but veal sales in France subsequently dropped by 50 percent and in Italy by 60 percent.[20] The boycott later spread to Britain and Belgium. The Bureau of European Consumer's Unions (BEUC), a consumer's group financed by the European Commission and affiliated consumer groups, urged a broader veal

---

16. Geoff Winestock, "Column One: EU Beef Battle with US Began in a Rare Event—Italian Boys Grew Breasts; Ministers Banned Hormones—But Scientific Evidence Was Always Lacking," *The Wall Street Journal Europe*, March 2, 2000, 1.

17. Winestock, "Column One: EU Beef Battle with US," 1.

18. Winestock, "Column One: EU Beef Battle with US," 1.

19. As described in Kevin O'Sullivan, "Fundamental US-EU Divide on Hormone-Treated Beef," *The Irish Times*, May 8, 1999, 10.

20. Mehaignerie, cited in Ronald Koven, "Common Market Bans Hormones in Cattle Feed," *The Washington Post*, October 3, 1980, A25; for veal sales in France, see Roger Cohen, "Boycott Shows EEC's Consumer Power," *Reuter News*, October 16, 1980, and "Hormones; Campaign for Real Veal," *The Economist*, October 18, 1980, 51; in Italy, see Andrew Gowers and Ivo Dawnay, "Another Shot of Politics for the Beef Farmer; EEC Hormones Ban," *The Financial Times*, January 24, 1986, 15.

boycott throughout the European Community and lobbied European farm ministers to ban all hormones.[21]

On September 20, 1980, just weeks after the BEUC's call for a complete ban, the EC Council of Agriculture Ministers adopted a declaration that one of the hormones used for raising livestock should be banned and that there should be greater harmonization of legislation on veterinary medicines. The press cast the declaration as the result of a successful consumer rebellion throughout Western Europe. The BEUC was proud of the victory, especially in light of the fact that only 20 of the European Commission's 8,000 employees worked on consumer affairs (as opposed to the more than 600 who worked on Community agriculture). "It's an unprecedented victory—the greatest success we've ever had," exulted BEUC spokesman Yves Domzalski. "The veal issue is the only affair on which we have ever had a prompt response from the ministers."[22]

On October 31, 1980, the European Commission proposed even more stringent legislation that would ban the use of all hormone products in meat production, and later expanded the proposal.[23] Discussions in the European Parliament revealed that while a majority supported a ban, Belgium, Ireland, and the United Kingdom favored the use of some hormones to promote growth in meat animals. The United States, Argentina, Australia, Canada, New Zealand, and South Africa raised concerns about the potential impact of a ban on their exports to Europe.[24]

After much debate, the European Council adopted its first directive on the hormones issue in July 1981 (Directive 81/602/EEC). The Council banned only stilbenes—the type of hormone found in the baby food incident—and allowed the use of testosterone, progesterone, oestradiol-17β , trenbolone acetate (TBA), and zeranol to promote growth, pending further study of their effects on consumer health. The Council directed the Commission to provide this study on hormone safety by July 1, 1984. In

---

21. Founded in 1962, the Brussels-based BEUC represented 13 European Economic Community (EEC) consumer groups, including the Union of French Consumers. At the time of the veal boycott, the BEUC was also attacking the community's CAP for consistently forcing unjustifiably high food prices and consuming 70 percent of the EEC's $30 billion budget, with half that money spent on the storage or subsidized export of food. In 1980, the BEUC had a staff of 10 (Roger Cohen, "Boycott Shows EEC's Consumer Power," *Reuter News Agency*, October 16, 1980). It later became European Commission Directorate General 24 for Health and Consumer Protection.

22. Employment figures and Domzalski quoted in Cohen, "Boycott Shows EEC's Consumer Power."

23. The proposal banned all use of hormones except for zootechnical and therapeutic purposes, such as managing pregnancy in animals.

24. For more information on these events, see "EC Measures Concerning Meat and Meat Products (Hormones), Complaint by the United States," Report of the WTO Panel, WT/DS26/R/USA, August 18, 1997, 2:26–28.

the meantime, the regulations of individual member states would continue to govern the use of the five hormones.

The Lamming Group: A Scientific Review

As directed, the European Commission appointed a Scientific Group on Anabolic Agents in Animal Production, made up of 22 scientists and chaired by Professor G. E. Lamming of Britain's Nottingham University. The committee, which became known as the Lamming Group, began to explore the following question: Does the use for fattening purposes in animals of the substances oestradiol-17β, testosterone, progesterone, trenbolone, and zeranol present any harmful effect to health?

The Lamming Group's interim report, issued in September 1982, found that the three natural hormones (oestradiol-17β, testosterone, and progesterone) "would not present any harmful effects to the health of the consumer when used under the appropriate conditions as growth promoters in farm animals."[25] As Professor Lamming explained, "We found that the residues were not genotoxic—not cancerous—at high levels in susceptible test animals. The residue levels were low and insignificant and presented no danger to the consuming public."[26] As for the synthetic hormones trenbolone and zeranol, the group determined that additional information was needed before a final conclusion could be reached.[27]

The US Response

In response to the European debate, the FDA's Center on Veterinary Medicine set up a team in 1982 to meet with EC officials about hormones. "I was the head of that team," Lester Crawford recalls, "so I spent a lot of time with the EC people to try to work through their concerns about the US hormones." According to Crawford, the team did not have much experience dealing with their foreign peers, primarily because no world body oversaw the issue. FDA-CVM officials met regularly with their Canadian and British counterparts to share information, but, Crawford admits, "We were deathly naïve in the international arena. People concerned with hormones had not really been involved in international affairs. It was a huge tragedy because FDA wasn't really ready, but until the Reagan administration, FDA-CVM had to carry the whole burden."

---

25. Lamming et al. (1989, 389).

26. Lamming, quoted in Robin Herman, "Steroids in Your Hamburger; Growth-Promoting Chemicals, Banned in Europe, Are Considered Safe by Experts," *The Washington Post,* January 10, 1989, Z11.

27. See Lamming et al. (1989, 389); see also "EC Measures Concerning Meat and Meat Products (Hormones), Complaint by the United States," Report of the WTO Panel, WT/DS26/R/USA, August 18, 1997, 2:28.

Europe Bans Hormones

Several years later, hormone use in livestock was still a compelling public issue in Europe. Men were quoted as fearing for their masculinity and fertility, and even worried that eating hormone-treated beef could alter their sex.[28] European consumer groups, led by the BEUC and "green" groups, worked energetically in support of an outright ban. Observers remember the hormone debate getting tremendous coverage in the press. As one points out, "Americans don't really have much appreciation for food safety and they consider it almost kind of humorous. But in Europe it continues to be a leading political issue, and it was in 1984 and 1985." (Some argue less attention has been paid to food safety in the United States because the American regulatory system is more reliable.)

Despite the public outcry, the European Commission moved to deescalate the hormone issue. In June 1984 it proposed a new council directive amending the 1981 Hormone Directive. The Commission envisaged controlled use of the three natural hormones and a reexamination of the two synthetic hormones after scientific evaluation had been completed. But the European Parliament and the Council of Ministers rejected the proposal.[29] Instead, several member states—notably West Germany—pushed vigorously for a total ban of all the hormones in question. Ultimately, in an overwhelming vote, the European Parliament passed a resolution supporting a ban on all growth-promoting hormones, asserting that "scientific information about these substances is far from complete and that considerable doubt therefore exists about the desirability of their use and of their effect on human health."[30] The Parliament also noted, "There is overproduction of meat and meat products in the European Community, which adds considerably to the cost of the CAP."[31] One official at the European Directorate General for External Economic Relations reflects on the importance of the hormones ban to the Parliament: "This is the first time when the European Parliament flexed its muscles and opposed the Commission saying that this was a consumer concern and making the Commission tow the line they wanted. It is a warhorse for them" (quoted in Davis 2003, 336).

---

28. John Cherrington, "Hormone Fears Will Not Go Away," *The Financial Times*, November 26, 1985, 34.

29. "EC Measures Concerning Meat and Meat Products (Hormones), Complaint by the United States," Report of the WTO Panel, WT/DS26/R/USA, August 18, 1997, 2:29, 30.

30. Point E of Parliament's Resolution, *EC Official Journal*, no. 288, November 11, 1985, 158; quoted in "EC Measures Concerning Meat and Meat Products (Hormones), Complaint by Canada," Report of the WTO Panel, WT/DS48/R/CAN, August 18, 1997, 4:14.

31. *EC Official Journal*, no. 288, November 11, 1985, 158; quoted in "EC Measures Concerning Meat and Meat Products (Hormones), Complaint by Canada," 4:63.

In October 1985, following the Parliament vote, the Lamming Group was disbanded by Frans Andriessen, the EEC agriculture commissioner. Professor Lamming's subsequent warning—"If you legislate in haste, you repent at leisure"—was widely quoted in the press. At a November press conference, Andriessen countered, "Do you really believe that public opinion is concerned by scientific judgment or by a political decision? In public opinion, this is a very delicate issue that has to be dealt with in political terms. Scientific advice is important, but it is not decisive."[32] The overwhelming factor, Andriessen held, was the democratic nature of the European Parliament's vote. The Lamming Group took its own action by rebelling against its dissolution. Though the Commission told Lamming he could not legally release any of the committee's findings, 16 of the 22 scientists would later publish their final report in 1987. It concluded that the two synthetic hormones, trenbolone and zeranol, were safe with "accepted husbandry practices."[33]

Despite Lamming's warnings, the Commission amended its proposal to reflect the European Parliament's support of the ban and submitted it to the Council of Ministers. On December 31, 1985, the Council of Agriculture Ministers voted to adopt a ban on the use of hormones for growth promotion (Directive 85/649/EEC). (Britain and Denmark voted against it.) The directive's preamble began by emphasizing that differing rules on hormone use in different member countries had distorted trade in the European market and that "these distortions of competition and barriers to trade must therefore be removed."[34]

In addition to the desire to create a common regulatory standard across the European market, there were also concerns about the beef supply in Europe. BEUC director Tony Venables held that legislators were persuaded to support a complete ban by the existing beef surplus. "If we have a beef mountain of 700,000-odd tons, it only makes matters worse to use out-of-

---

32. Lamming and Andriessen, quoted in Andrew Gowers and Ivo Dawnay, "Another Shot of Politics for the Beef Farmer; EEC Hormones Ban," *The Financial Times*, January 24, 1986, 15.

33. "The levels of trenbolone and zeranol and their major metabolites found in edible tissue, following accepted husbandry practices, are substantially below the hormonally effective does in animal test systems and therefore do not present a harmful effect to health" (Lamming et al. 1987, 391).

34. "Whereas the administration to farm animals of certain substances having a hormonal action is at present regulated in different ways in the Member States; . . .whereas this divergence distorts the conditions of competition in products that are the subject of common market organizations and is a serious barrier to intra-Community trade; Whereas these distortions of competition and barriers to trade must therefore be removed by ensuring that all consumer are able to buy the products in question under largely identical conditions of supply and that these products correspond to their anxieties and expectations in the best possible manner. . ." Council Directive of 31 December 1985 prohibiting the use in livestock faring of certain substances having hormonal action (85/649/EEC), *Official Journal of the European Communities*, no. L 382/228.

date hormone growth methods," he said.[35] Some saw the ban as a way to curb the surplus by reducing production and increasing consumption. "The decision was done on non-scientific grounds against a background of considerable consumer pressure and emotion and a background of food surpluses at the time," recalled Professor Lamming. "It's a dangerous precedent if scientific evidence is ignored. It queries the whole theory of a scientific approach to drug evaluation."[36]

In short, scheduled to go into effect in January 1988 (and one year later in Britain), the ban was extremely popular. According to Lester Crawford, "People who were voting for the directive were in effect saying, 'We're against hormones in meat, we're against US beef coming in, and we're for vegetarians and we're for the BEUC.' There was absolutely nothing politically savory they could be for by voting against the hormone ban. It was positioned very skillfully by the BEUC. Very few voted against it because it was so politically popular. It was unbelievable."

The directive inspired a group of hormone manufacturers to form their own lobby, the European Federation of Animal Health (FEDESA, or Fédération Européenne de la Santé Animale), and launch a campaign against the ban. Sale of the five hormones in western Europe amounted to around $20 million before the ban—a relatively small fraction of the $1.4 billion animal-health market—but manufacturers worried that their other products would be perceived as unsafe.[37] The ban, FEDESA officials warned, threatened investment in other biotechnology products. "Sure we can survive without hormones," said one pharmaceutical executive. "But we are a science-based company, and if things are going to be banned in Europe on non-factual grounds, there's no future for us here."[38] FEDESA challenged the ban at the European Court of Justice, arguing that it had no scientific foundation. But the court said the ban was necessary to ensure that the different rules in different member states did not create barriers to trade or distort competition.[39]

Meanwhile, the USTR was surprised that the ban actually went through. Former USTR staffer Len Condon (later vice president of the American Meat Institute) recalls: "There was a lot of informal communication back and forth between Brussels and Washington and we were being told that

35. Venables, quoted in Andrew Gowers and Ivo Dawnay, "Another Shot of Politics for the Beef Farmer; EEC Hormones Ban," *The Financial Times,* January 24, 1986, 15.

36. Lamming, quoted in Robin Herman, "Steroids in Your Hamburger; Growth-Promoting Chemicals, Banned in Europe, Are Considered Safe by Experts," *The Washington Post,* January 10, 1989, Z11.

37. Sales figures from Tim Dickson, "Ban on Hormone Meat Proves Recipe for Strife," *The Financial Times,* December 29, 1988, 3.

38. Executive quoted in Gowers and Dawnay, "Another Shot of Politics for the Beef Farmer," 15.

39. The court ruled on the case on November 13, 1990. Lucy Kellaway, "Court Upholds Hormone Ban," *The Financial Times,* November 14, 1990, 32.

this directive wasn't really going anywhere. But suddenly it got adopted on the very last day of 1985. I remember we were informed by the USDA's meat inspection agency. They came over to visit us and told us it had been adopted and we had a problem."[40]

Hormones and International Institutions

US officials knew that a ban on hormones in meat production would have an impact on trade. One strategy was to seek out an international body to evaluate the safety of the hormones in question. If an international body found that the hormones were safe, US officials reasoned, Europe would be pressured to remove the ban. The FDA first approached the Paris-based OIE, the Office Internationale des Epizooties, or World Organization for Animal Health, which was responsible for international regulatory communications about live animals.[41] The OIE rejected the call to look at hormones. "Therefore," one US participant remembers, "We had no choice but to go to Codex."

Codex Considers Hormones

The Codex Alimentarius Commission (Latin for "food code") was established in 1962 by the UN Food and Agriculture Organization (FAO) and the World Health Organization (WHO) to consult on implementing the Joint Food Standards Program. The main goals of the program were to protect the health of consumers, ensure fair practices in food trade, and coordinate food standards.

The FDA proposed that a Codex committee on residues of veterinary drugs in foods be appointed. "Because of the hormone dispute, the US was looking for an international group to examine the issue," recalls former FDA-CVM Codex liaison Robert Livingston. "Since there was not an international expert committee within the Codex, they asked the Codex Alimentarius to evaluate the need for a Codex committee on veterinary drugs."

In 1985 an FAO/WHO committee recommended that Codex set up such a committee, concluding that "the question of the occurrence and safety of residues of veterinary drugs in foods of animal origin was of significance

---

40. Unless otherwise noted, all quotes from Len Condon are from a December 1999 interview with the author. Condon served at the USTR from 1981 to 1997. In 1997 he became a vice president of the American Meat Institute.

41. The OIE was established in 1924. As the world organization for animal health, the main objectives of the OIE are to (1) inform governments of the occurrence and course of animal diseases throughout the world, and of ways to control these diseases; (2) coordinate, at the international level, studies devoted to the surveillance and control of animal diseases; and (3) harmonize regulations for trade in animals and animal products among member countries (see www.oie.int, accessed June 1, 2000).

to public health and consumer concern, and posed potential problems to international trade." The Codex Commission expressed "strong support" for the recommendations and established the Codex Committee on Residues of Veterinary Drugs in Food (CCRVDF) (Codex Alimentarius Commission 1985, paras. 88–89).

At the 1985 Codex Commission meeting in Geneva, various countries vied to make their nationals chair of the new committee. Competition for the leadership position was fierce "because the future of veterinary-drug regulation and perhaps the emerging hormone ban was to be determined by the outcome of who hosted it," explains Lester Crawford. The contest came down to two nations—West Germany and the United States—and the matter was put to a secret ballot (Codex Alimentarius Commission 1985, para. 91). "It was a very close vote," Crawford remembers: "Most nations abstained—they did not want to get involved. The majority of nations in Codex were very small, and smaller nations did not like to get involved in a battle of the titans. If they had to decide between Europe and the United States, they'd take a bathroom break."

The United States emerged the victor, and the USDA's Crawford, a self-proclaimed "hormone man," was named chairman of the new CCRVDF.[42] The chairmanship was especially important for procedural reasons. The CCRVDF would not actually evaluate the residues of veterinary drugs in foods. For a drug to be evaluated, CCRVDF had to refer the job to the Joint FAO/WHO Expert Committee on Food Additives (JECFA), whose members are independent scientists serving as individuals, not as representatives of their governments or other organizations.[43]

At the first meeting of the CCRVDF in 1986, the United States formally proposed that JECFA examine the hormones used in beef production. "Had the Germans been in the chair, I don't know if the job would have been assigned to JECFA," says one observer. Crawford agrees: "Had [the vote] gone the other way, there could have been a lot of trouble for the US." At the recommendation of the CCRVDF, the Codex Secretariat referred the hormone issue for independent review to JECFA. During 1987, JECFA examined the safety of five of the six hormones at issue.[44]

---

42. Also in 1985, the United Nations passed Resolution 39/248, which advised: "Governments should take into account the need of all consumers for food security and should support and, as far as possible, adopt standards from the . . . Codex Alimentarius." Interestingly, the United States had adopted few Codex standards.

43. JECFA was established in 1955 as a scientific advisory committee to the FAO, WHO, member governments, and the Codex. JECFA's mission is to assess the human health risks associated with the consumption of additives to food and to recommend acceptable daily intake (ADI) levels, tolerable limits for environmental and industrial chemical contaminants in food, and maximum residue levels (MRLs) of agricultural chemical inputs in food such as veterinary drug residues in meat and meat products (see www.fao.org).

44. Data on melengestrol acetate (MGA), which was banned throughout Europe, were not submitted.

Hormones at the GATT

Meanwhile, the United States also sought to challenge the EC ban at an international trade forum. Until the WTO came into being in 1995, the international institution that dealt with trade quarrels was the GATT.

In March 1987 the United States lodged a complaint at the GATT against the EC directive, claiming that the ban violated Article 7 of the Agreement on Technical Barriers to Trade (TBT). Article 7 stipulated that certification systems should not obstruct trade of similar products from other TBT signatories. The EC responded that the use of hormones was a process and production method (PPM) and thus not covered by the TBT code, which applied only to the characteristics of a final product. The United States countered that the EC had deliberately drafted its directive to address only PPMs in order to circumvent the code. Furthermore, the United States argued that the use of hormones in cattle was safe and submitted scientific reports as proof. The European delegation asserted that the ban was aimed at protecting health (and therefore consistent with GATT Article XX) and "doubted the usefulness of relying on current scientific findings because there had been past mistakes in judging the safety of chemical products."[45] The United States favored the appointment of a technical expert group to determine whether the ban was really necessary to protect health, but the EC blocked the formation of the group (see GATT 1988, 80). In short, the ban on hormones went unresolved at the GATT. No action would be taken to settle the dispute.

Meanwhile, Back at Codex

As the date of the ban approached, JECFA—the committee commissioned by Codex to look at the hormone question—published its findings. The 1988 JECFA report concluded that residues of four of the growth-promoting hormones did not create a safety hazard to humans, provided that proper veterinary practice was followed; later, the same findings were released for the fifth. Acceptable daily intake levels (ADIs) and maximum residue levels (MRLs) were established for synthetic hormones. The committee found that the levels of natural hormones in treated meat were so low compared with the hormones present in the human body that there was no need to set an ADI.

JECFA sent its report to the Codex committee. The CCRVDF then recommended draft standards to the Codex Commission. Even if standards were adopted, however, there was no obligation for the European Com-

---

45. GATT 1988, 80. GATT Article XX stipulates that "nothing in this Agreement shall be construed to prevent the adoption or enforcement by any contracting party of measures: (a) necessary to protect public morals; (b) necessary to protect human, animal or plant life or health."

mission to act on Codex findings. "At that point we were operating under the GATT, and there was no connection between GATT and Codex," Lester Crawford explains. "Having Codex on your side was helpful, but there was no legal requirement at that point to do what Codex told you to do." The role of Codex was not yet as significant as it would later become.

Internal Politics and a Failure to Ease Tensions

As the January 1988 implementation date for the ban approached, efforts were made to ease the dispute. EC Farm Commissioner Frans Andriessen proposed to delay the ban on trade of hormone-treated meat by 18 months. In November 1987, EC agricultural ministers adopted a 12-month delay after West Germany, France, and the Netherlands dropped their objections.[46] The ban on the use of hormones in Europe took effect as scheduled, but meat already containing hormones could be traded until January 1, 1989.[47]

The vote on the delay took place within the context of intense US efforts to persuade the EC to completely overturn the hormone directive. The European press reported that the United States was threatening a transatlantic trade war over the ban. Despite the agriculture ministers' decision to delay implementation for a year, the Reagan administration announced that it was preparing to raise tariffs on millions of dollars of EC food imports if the Community proceeded with the ban; President Reagan ordered hearings to determine which products would be subject to the punitive levies. The US action was called "regrettable and unjustified" by Andriessen and by Willy de Clercq, the foreign relations commissioner.[48] EC officials were surprised and angry that the United States was still undertaking offensive maneuvers after their delay of the ban.

---

46. Belgium, Spain, Greece, and Ireland voted against the 12-month transition period. The *Financial Times* reported that discussions were complicated by French concerns that the transition period would discriminate against French producers, who were still treating beef cattle with growth-promoting hormones. The French agricultural minister promised that French meat would be hormone-free by April 1, 1988, and West Germany and Italy pledged that French beef exports would have easier access to their markets (Tim Dickson, "EC to Delay Effect of Beef Hormone Ban," *The Financial Times*, November 19, 1987, 4).

47. In February 1988, the European Court of Justice annulled the beef ban legislation in a case brought by Britain and Denmark, ruling that the EC legislation was "invalid" because the member states had not followed the correct technical procedures when adopting the law at the end of 1985. More importantly, the court rejected the complaint by the United Kingdom that the decision should have been taken unanimously instead of by a qualified majority. On March 7, therefore, the ban was simply readopted by the EC Council of Ministers under the correct procedures.

48. Andriessen and de Clercq, quoted in Bruce Barnard, "EC Threatens Sanctions if US Acts on Beef Ban," *Journal of Commerce*, November 25, 1987, 3A.

The Reagan administration's threats to retaliate under section 301 of the 1974 Trade Act were not motivated solely by the beef dispute. Its public posturing was also intended to send a message to Congress, which was considering legislation to restrict the president's discretionary authority to decide how to respond to complaints of unfair trade practices. The sponsors of a huge omnibus trade bill contended that Reagan had not been tough enough. The White House hoped that taking strong action in the beef dispute would head off congressional efforts to force the administration's hand. "Congress may wish to review this and other effective uses of Section 301," the White House suggested, "before considering any changes in law that would attempt to force the president to retaliate at times when it would be counterproductive."[49]

In the end, however, the United States agreed to defer retaliatory sanctions for a year. As one US negotiator put it, "Europe held their effective date in advance for a year, and we held our effective date in advance for a year so we could spend that time trying to work out a solution." In informal negotiations over the next few months, US sources say, Europeans suggested that the United States sign a document testifying that hormones in US beef production were being used for therapeutic reasons, not the promotion of growth. Such a move would solve the entire problem, the Europeans held, since the directive allowed for therapeutic use of hormones. The Americans did not agree to do so.[50] Len Condon explains why: "When hormones are used therapeutically, they are primarily used for reproduction purposes—synchronization of estrus, for example. We said, 'Well look, 50 percent of the animals we give hormones to and slaughter are steers, so how could we claim we're using hormones therapeutically with these animals?'"

Negotiations intensified amid reports of a growing European black market for hormones. In August 1988, West German inspectors found 15,000 illegally injected calves. An underground network of veterinarians giving hormone shots was uncovered in the Netherlands and Belgium. The drug company lobby FEDESA noted that the illegal use of uncontrolled hormone mixtures only strengthened the case for allowing use of the "five entirely safe hormones." As Michael Leathes, FEDESA's secretary general,

---

49. Quoted in Clyde Farnsworth, "The US Plans to Punish Europe," *The New York Times*, November 27, 1987, D2.

50. As discussions were taking place, a fungicide called procymidon was discovered in French wine being imported to the United States. "A lot of people now think if we had banned French wine in 1988, we would have solved the hormone dispute right then," Crawford says. "We stopped shipments of French wine only for what amounted to a long weekend. We could have banned it because it was going to be years before they got all the procymidon out. But a risk assessment showed that the amount of procymidon found in the wine was not injurious to human health. So we said, 'No, we won't do that.'" Crawford believes that a ban on the wine might have put enough political pressure on Europe to end the beef ban.

observed, "It is not surprising that a black market has mushroomed."[51] Condon remembers the impact of the discoveries on the US-EU negotiations: "In a number of European countries, the press uncovered illegal use of hormones. That led to a recommitment on the part of the Community that they were not going to allow these hormones to be used. It created a public furor, and so the Community was no longer in the position to be able to discuss any kind of exemptions with us. They lost all their flexibility."

At the same time, a group of US senators were pressing US Agriculture Secretary Richard Lyng to recommend that President Reagan declare a complete embargo on all European beef imports. (Lyng had served as president of the American Meat Institute from 1973 until 1979.) The 14 senators who urged this action included Senate Agriculture Committee Chairman Patrick Leahy (D-VT) and Senate Finance Committee Chairman Lloyd Bentsen (D-TX).[52] An embargo, which would affect $450 million worth of products, was made possible by a section of the new Trade and Competitiveness Act of 1988. The act authorized reprisals against countries that restricted imports of US meat for reasons that could not be "substantiated by reliable analytical methods."[53]

Many observers point out that the timing of the impending ban was unfortunate. For one thing, new administrations were moving into place in both Brussels and Washington. In addition, the transatlantic trade relationship had already been soured by the breakdown of the Uruguay Round of trade talks in early December 1988. They had ground to a halt when Europe and the United States failed to agree on appropriate levels for agricultural supports. Observers were concerned that the hormone spat would deepen divisions during a delicate period.

European MP Ken Collins, a member of the Labour Party, observed that the whole beef hormone episode demonstrated the need for a European equivalent of the FDA, with comparable status and independence. "At the moment we've got 12 different licensing systems, with only the doctrine of the internal market to hold them together," Collins noted. Britain and Denmark reportedly continued to lobby for restraint, though any reversal was seen as unlikely. The United Kingdom's foreign minister, among oth-

---

51. Leathes, quoted in Tim Dickson, "US Takes Moral High Grounds on Hormones," *The Financial Times*, November 16, 1988, 7.

52. Richard Lawrence, "US Spells Out Reprisal in Hormone Ban Dispute," *Journal of Commerce*, December 28, 1988, 1A.

53. Omnibus Trade and Competitiveness Act of 1988, §4604. According to this "Reciprocal Meat Inspection Requirement," if the secretary of agriculture determines that "a particular foreign country applies standards for the importation of meat articles from the United States that are not related to public health concerns about end-product quality that can be substantiated by reliable analytical methods," he or she, together with the USTR, may recommend that the president "prohibit imports into the United States of any meat articles produced in such foreign country unless it is determined that the meat articles produced in that country meet the standards applicable to meat articles in commerce within the United States."

ers, proposed another delay on the ban in hopes of giving the new incoming European Commission and Bush administration a chance to work through the dispute. "There's little we can do now, apart from register our lack of support for the directive," admitted a spokeswoman for the British Ministry of Agriculture, Fisheries, and Food.[54]

As European and US officials traded jabs, the lead-up to the implementation of the ban was closely followed by the press. European supporters argued that the blanket ban was a legitimate, nondiscriminatory response to consumer concerns. "Any country, and this includes the European Community, is entitled to take whatever measures it judges necessary to protect the health of consumers, provided this is done in a nondiscriminatory way," declared EC External Relations Commissioner de Clercq.[55] "[The ban] isn't based on a trade barrier," added a spokeswoman for the EC Washington office. "It's based on what consumers want to eat."[56] Sir Roy Denman, head of the Washington delegation, noted that for years, Americans had banned European products made from unpasteurized milk, including many cheeses. "In the Community, we have accepted this and not threatened retaliation," he said. "So what's sauce for the goose is sauce for the gander."[57]

The Europeans did make the concession of exempting meat used as pet food from the ban. The United States responded by committing to reduce trade retaliation from $125 million to $100 million. But US officials were frustrated by the European Union's unwillingness to lift the ban completely. "We have tried repeatedly to bring this issue to a scientific dispute-settlement panel under the GATT in order to have it resolved," USTR Clayton Yeutter was widely quoted as saying. "However, our European counterparts have consistently blocked our efforts. The EC has yet to present any evidence that proper application of the growth-promoting hormones in question poses any threat to human health."[58]

The United States announced that $100 million in sanctions would go into effect on January 1, one minute after the implementation of the beef ban. One hundred percent tariffs would be levied on a range of EC agricultural products. Pork products dominated the list, which also included

---

54. Collins and the spokeswoman, quoted in Hugo Davenport, "Beefing About Trade: The View from Europe," *The Daily Telegraph*, December 29, 1988, 15.

55. De Clercq, quoted in Tim Dickson, "EC Attacks US for Curb on Food Imports," *The Financial Times*, December 29, 1988, 1.

56. Ella Krucoff, quoted in Elizabeth Ross, "US Challenges EC Plan to Ban Treated Beef," *The Christian Science Monitor*, November 21, 1988, 3.

57. Denman, quoted in Charles Laurence, "US Prepares for Tariff War over EEC Beef Ban," *The Daily Telegraph*, December 28, 1988, 1.

58. Yeutter's statement was quoted in articles in the *Los Angeles Times*, *New York Times*, *Financial Times*, and *Journal of Commerce* (e.g., see Lionel Barber, "US to Impose Sanction on EC Over Meat Ban," *The Financial Times*, December 28, 1988, 2).

boneless beef, canned tomatoes, fruit juice, packaged pet food, some fermented beverages, and instant coffee. The sanctions would mainly punish Denmark, Italy, and Spain. A front-page editorial in the French daily *Le Monde* accused the United States of attempting to "divide Europe so as to better impose its views. . . . The use of force reveals one more time the importance of unity among the Twelve."[59] European ministers drew up a list of American exports as targets for potential counterretaliation, including honey, walnuts, dried fruit, and hormones.

USTR Yeutter and Agriculture Secretary Lyng of the United States met with Farm Commissioner Andriessen and Commissioner for External Relations de Clercq of the EC in mid-November 1988 to try to work out a solution. Last-minute negotiations continued as 1989 approached, but officials were pessimistic. "We will suffer damage by this ban and we will have to retaliate," said Yeutter. "The Community legislation cannot be modified and will not be modified," countered de Clercq.[60]

The Ban Goes into Effect and the United States Retaliates

When the January 1, 1989, ban went into effect, it blocked European imports of about $100 million worth of American beef. As expected, the Reagan administration retaliated by imposing 100 percent tariffs on $100 million worth of European exports under section 301 of US trade law. US officials continued to emphasize the safety of hormone use in beef production. Gerald Guest, director of the FDA-CVM and chairman of the CCRVDF, the Codex committee, declared that when the hormones were used properly, any remaining traces in meat were so slight that "a man himself would manufacture 1,500 times more estrogen a day than he would get if he consumed a pound of beef every day, and a pregnant woman would manufacture several million times more estrogen every day than if she ate a pound of beef each day."[61]

Because the United States did not have GATT approval to retaliate, Europe brought a case against the United States at the GATT. But it went nowhere. "When the US had challenged the Community's directive in the GATT standards code, the EC blocked us from doing that. When the Community brought a case against us for retaliating, we blocked their case," recalls Len Condon. "So in terms of GATT action, we sort of reached a standoff." However, the United States was criticized for imposing sanc-

59. Quoted in Michael Balter, "US Picks a Beef That May Unify Europe Fast," *Los Angeles Times*, December 6, 1988, 7.

60. Yeutter and de Clercq, quoted in Paul Montgomery, "US and Europe Near Trade War over Hormone Use in Beef Cattle," *The New York Times*, November 20, 1988, 22.

61. Guest, quoted in Gina Kolata, "Hormone-Treated Beef Termed Generally Safe," *The New York Times*, January 1, 1989, 22.

tions without permission. GATT Director-General Arthur Dunkel, while not naming the United States explicitly, said that discriminatory import tariffs went against the General Agreement.[62]

When the United States imposed its duties, the EC threatened to counterretaliate if the dispute was not resolved by the end of January. But when President George H. W. Bush took office, he reiterated the Reagan administration's stance on the hormone ban. Press response to the ban was generally critical of continuing escalation of the transatlantic wrangle, blaming both sides. "The US and the European Common Market are celebrating New Year's Day by marching into a trade war with each other," observed an editorial in the *Washington Post*. "It's a stupid idea, reflecting—on both sides—a failure of common sense[,] . . . [with] hysteria on one side and, on the other, a bullying insistence that American health practices have to be the world's standard."[63] The *Financial Times* was similarly unimpressed: "The story of the EC hormone ban combines human tragedy, rampant consumerism, murky politics, and, to put it at its most polite, a trail of stumbling diplomacy."[64]

The four-person US negotiation team of scientists and regulators was dismantled when the ban was formally implemented. The hormone debate "had become a trade and diplomatic issue, and no longer a scientific issue," explains Lester Crawford: "We really didn't need any more science, because we had tried that. It was clear that even though everyone else adopted our [scientific] position, including the European Society of Toxicology, the EC wasn't looking for science. It was clear to us it was a nontariff trade barrier. Therefore, it was really not in our interest to continue playing the science card."

Some US officials believed that in addition to the technical criteria of effectiveness, safety, and reliability, Europe was developing a "fourth criterion" for deciding if it would adopt a particular technology—the technology's economic and social impact. Officials worried that this criterion would become an excuse for protecting other agricultural markets (Josling, Roberts, and Orden 2004, 119).

In mid-February 1989, the United States and the EC agreed to a 75-day cooling-off period during which neither side would impose new tariffs. Meanwhile the players were shuffled as the incoming Bush administration and a new five-year rotation of the European Commission settled in. Carla Hills became the USTR; the outgoing USTR, Clayton Yeutter, became secretary of agriculture. (When President Bush appointed Yeutter, he did so saying he was determined to "crack" European agriculture mar-

---

62. William Dullforce, "EC Wins Support Against US Trade Measures in GATT," *The Financial Times*, February 9, 1989, 8.

63. "Where's the Hormone-Free Beef?" editorial, *The Washington Post*, January 1, 1989, B6.

64. Tim Dickson, "US Takes Moral High Grounds on Hormones," *The Financial Times*, November 16, 1988, 7.

kets for American farmers.) On the European side, Frans Andriessen, the outgoing agricultural commissioner, became the commissioner for external affairs, a trade position. The new agricultural commissioner was Raymond MacSharry.

The key European and US officials promptly met to reassess the state of play of the hormone dispute. Len Condon recalls, "There had been three years of trade war, and so this was the biggest issue facing the new teams on both sides. So MacSharry, Andriessen, Hills, and Yeutter decided to have this meeting over at USTR one Saturday. At this point, it became clear to Carla Hills that this wasn't a simple problem—it was a huge problem with many different principles and issues. The EC couldn't back down and the United States couldn't back down."

The participants at this meeting decided to create a US-EC Hormone Task Force. The US participants would be Lester Crawford and Ann Veneman from the USDA and Len Condon and Joshua Bolten from USTR.[65] The European side included Fernando Mansito from the Commission's Directorate General–Agriculture and Jean-Pierre Lang from Directorate General–Trade. They had little hope of achieving great breakthroughs, according to Len Condon: "I think all of the political people in the room knew that this Hormone Task Force wasn't going to be able to come up with any solution, but it was a way of saying the problem was being addressed. I think the hope was that the Task Force would spend a few months meeting, but at the end of the day people would gradually forget about this."

Some observers characterize the US-EC Task Force and the "truce" called over hormones as part of an effort to improve trade relations after the breakdown of the Uruguay Round over agriculture. In February 1989, the United States also presented European Uruguay Round negotiators with a position paper in which US insistence that Europe set a target date for complete elimination of farm subsidies was abandoned. In his first address to Congress, President Bush said that the major industrial democracies needed "to rise above fighting about beef hormones to building a better future, to move from protectionism to progress."[66]

The Hormone Task Force met frequently. "We spent a lot of time in meetings," one participant recalls. "Brussels and Washington, Brussels and Washington, Brussels and Washington." Substance was not the only challenge, as Lester Crawford explains: "Here's a ludicrous thing. There was never anybody on the American negotiating teams who smoked. There was never anyone on the European teams who didn't. And so the big bat-

---

65. Ann Veneman served as secretary of agriculture from 2001 to 2004. She became the executive director of the United Nations Children's Fund (UNICEF) in 2005. Joshua Bolten became director of the Office of Management and Budget in June 2003 after serving as assistant to the president and deputy chief of staff for policy at the White House from January 2001 onward.

66. Stuart Auerbach, "US Seeks to End European Beef Trade War," *The Washington Post*, February 10, 1989, F3.

tle, which sometimes took half a day, was whether or not we would allow smoking in the room. I can't tell you how important that was."

Also during this period, the conclusions of the European Committee of Enquiry into the Problem of Quality in the Meat Sector were published in a document known as the Pimenta Report, which endorsed the ban on the use of growth-promoting hormones. On March 29, 1989, the European Parliament, which had established the committee in 1988 after illegal hormone use was reported in the European press, adopted its recommendations to maintain and expand the ban.

The Hormone-Free Proposal

Europeans on the Hormone Task Force hoped to interest the US side in instituting a "hormone-free" program whereby the United States would produce beef without hormones to sell to Europe. Lester Crawford explains:

> It became very clear when the Hormone Task Force sat down that the Europeans' whole plan was to get a lot of this hormone-free beef flowing in. Then, they hoped, ultimately the US would get all of our market back and the retaliation would stop. You see, the political problem was that the US had retaliated against Europe. The EC argued it was an unjustifiable retaliation, and their member states were saying, "Well then, do something about it." The Commission had to have something to tell the member states. So I think they were telling the member states that they had a plan where the US would send hormone-free beef to Europe and we would no longer have a basis for retaliation and the problem would be solved.

Initially, neither the US beef industry nor US government officials were interested in the hormone-free plan. For one, the USDA did not have an inspection program to certify beef as meeting European hormone-free standards, a prerequisite for export.[67] And even if the USDA could satisfy the certification requirement, "it will by no means resolve the principles that are involved here," said Yeutter.[68]

The situation was further complicated by a maverick initiative undertaken by Texas Agriculture Commissioner Jim Hightower. Hightower, a charismatic, controversial populist Democrat and former journalist, approached the EC directly with an offer to sell its members hormone-free beef from Texas. The proposal earned him national publicity—and the resentment of some in the beef industry, who felt that Hightower's offer implied that other US beef was unsafe. At a time when Americans had already reduced their average beef consumption (by 18 percent between

---

67. "Consumer Groups Back Europe's Ban of Hormone-Treated Beef," *Associated Press*, January 30, 1989.

68. "Yeutter Blasts Texan in EC Beef Dispute," *Reuter News*, February 2, 1989.

1971 and 1989), beef producers did not want questions raised about the healthfulness of their product.[69] The Bush administration, for its part, objected to Hightower's offer as undercutting the administration's position. Hightower reported that Agriculture Secretary Yeutter threatened legal action if he tried to sell hormone-free beef to the Europeans. Yeutter "fumed darkly that I was consorting with the enemy and possibly violating the Logan Act of 1800," Hightower later wrote, "which can get a citizen thrown in the federal pokey for engaging in unauthorized diplomacy with a foreign government" (1999, 246).

Other states were also eager to serve Europe's niche market for hormone-free beef offal. Mark Ritchie, then the trade policy staff member of the Minnesota Department of Agriculture and later co-founder and executive director of a nonprofit advocacy and research organization, the Institute for Agriculture and Trade Policy,[70] says that Minnesota beef producers (as well as producers in Idaho) made plans to send hormone-free products to Europe: "The ban was good news to Minnesota because we were a beef-producing state that at the time did not use many hormones." But the federal government was less than enthusiastic. According to Ritchie, "The US Department of Agriculture threatened us and imposed an embargo against us shipping hormone-free beef. This alerted me to what was going on. I pursued this issue, and my conclusion was that this was an attempt to promote the interests of the handful of companies that produced these drugs and had nothing to do with the kind of fight that was portrayed in public. It resulted in discrimination against US beef producers that did not use hormones."[71]

The companies that produced the implants did not want hormone-free products sent to Europe, Ritchie explains, out of fear that consumers in the United States and elsewhere might also demand hormone-free beef. "There was already such a negative reaction to hormones in the US, with regards to DES and with regards to unrelated issues like steroid treatments for athletes, which were seen as dangerous and unethical," he says. "Drug-producing companies were worried that this issue would catch on in the US and elsewhere."

---

69. "At 65 pounds per capita in 1989, beef use was 14 pounds below 1971's total and 24 pounds less than the high of 89 pounds in 1976 when beef supplies reached record levels as ranchers reduced the size of the nation's beef herd. The current forecast for 1990 indicates beef consumption will be at the lowest level since 1962" (Putnam 1990, 1).

70. "The Institute for Agriculture and Trade Policy promotes resilient family farms, rural communities and ecosystems around the world through research and education, science and technology, and advocacy" (see www.iatp.org).

71. Unless otherwise noted, all quotes from Mark Ritchie are from a May 2000 interview with the author; at that time, Ritchie was executive director of the Institute for Agriculture and Trade Policy.

The IATP's Ritchie and others emphasize that the National Cattlemen's Beef Association does not necessarily represent the interests of all beef producers. "Feedlots and other industrial agricultural interests dominate the National Cattlemen's Beef Association," Ritchie notes. Producers that do not use industrial techniques are not as influential, he says. "If you were to do a case study of [the NCBA], you would find that some of the state-based cattlemen's associations have dropped out in frustration."

In the end, officials reached an agreement allowing small amounts of high-grade US hormone-free beef to be exported to Europe and certified by the EC (not the USDA).[72] But soon after, Europe banned US beef and pork imports due to concerns about hygiene in American slaughterhouses. In a letter to USTR Carla Hills, Agriculture Commissioner Raymond Mac-Sharry said that the state of US slaughterhouses "is potentially dangerous to the health of European consumers."[73] Hills called the EC's actions protectionist and Yeutter called the ban "absurd."[74] Some US observers noted that the Commission's decision was primarily aimed at helping European producers reduce their pork and beef surpluses.

In brief, the period between 1989 and 1996 was characterized by continuing debate on the hormone dispute but little activity. Europe decided not to impose sanctions on the United States. US tariffs on European goods did not appear to exert much pressure on the EC to change its position. The punitive sanctions affected only a few industries in the European countries most responsible for the ban. Len Condon recalls, "We identified Italy as the core of the problem and we retaliated mostly on Italian products. At that time, there were 12 European member states. The other 11 member states just breathed a sigh of relief and said, 'Well, hey, why should we change anything?' So nothing changed."

Affected businesses also made adjustments to compensate for the sanctions. For example, European alcoholic beverages containing less than 7 percent alcohol were subject to 100 percent tariffs. The US company Riunite imported wine coolers from Italy that fell into that category. For a time, Riunite hoped that the dispute would be resolved and the duties would be removed, but eventually the company simply adjusted the product so that it would be classified differently.

As a result, according to Condon, "The hormone dispute sort of died out toward the end of 1989, and then we remained in a standoff until 1996. The only major relevant thing that happened in between was we negotiated the SPS agreement." Negotiation of the SPS agreement took place as a part of the Uruguay Round of multilateral trade negotiations.

---

72. "US-EC Fight on Beef is Partly Settled," *The Washington Post*, May 4, 1989, E5.

73. "Community Frontiers Closed to US Pork and Beef," *Agence Europe*, November 1, 1990.

74. "EC Ban on US Meat Called Absurd," *Supermarket News*, November 26, 1990, 33.

Changing the Rules

The United States Moves to Strengthen International Institutions

The United States had not had much luck in relying on international rules and institutions to end the European ban. However, the playing field was changing at the international level. Many of these changes occurred during the Uruguay Round (1986–94), a 96-nation negotiation under the auspices of the GATT.

As noted earlier, US officials—especially Agriculture Secretary Richard Lyng—hoped to make the Uruguay Round the "agriculture round." According to US negotiators, a key problem in agricultural trade was the use of what they viewed as bogus health regulations by many countries to protect their own markets; the beef dispute was a prime example. They worried that if the Uruguay Round further constrained a government's ability to protect and subsidize its agricultural producers, the result would be even more so-called health-centered restrictions as a way to protect domestic markets. As one negotiator put it, "We had to plug that hole."

In December 1987 Dan Amstutz, ambassador-at-large for agriculture at the State Department, paid a visit to the USDA meat inspection program headed by Lester Crawford. Crawford and his staff were asked to write a paper exploring how health-centered "nontariff trade barriers" could be avoided. Crawford recalls: "Secretary Lyng wanted to make the Uruguay Round the agriculture round, but it didn't look like they were going to get anywhere because of all the disputes. For one, there were these nontariff trade barriers about health that were developing. I was asked to write a paper on how you might solve these problems." Theoretically, the GATT would address such concerns, but the United States had not seen satisfactory results with the hormone issue at the GATT. "They weren't doing anything except listening to us testify," Crawford says. Crawford and other USDA officials assembled a report called *The Sanitary and Phytosanitary Dispute Settlement Paper*.

Negotiating the SPS Agreement

Achieving an agreement on SPS measures became a key element of the US agenda for agricultural trade negotiations. Within the United States, the hormone case was often cited to explain the need for an SPS agreement and to build support for the Uruguay Round. "The hormone case was one of the most notable ones, as far as the US was concerned," says Len Condon. "During the Uruguay Round negotiations, as we publicly discussed our objectives, we said that we needed the SPS agreement to prevent something like the hormone dispute from happening again."

Some say that the hormone dispute was also pivotal in selling Congress on the notion that the Uruguay Round should be the agriculture round. For Democrats, who controlled both houses of Congress, the idea of reducing agricultural subsidies was unpopular, but they largely supported ending the European ban. Because there was widespread agreement with the US position in the case and little sympathy for the European position, some say the hormone dispute became the spoonful of sugar that helped the medicine go down.

Some participants even contend that the SPS agreement was negotiated as a result of the US-EU hormone dispute. "The SPS agreement would have never happened if it hadn't been for the hormone dispute," asserts Lester Crawford. "If it hadn't been for the persistence of the hormone dispute, no one would have ever said, 'Let's figure out this sanitary and phytosanitary problem.'" Other observers agree. According to one analyst, "a serious disagreements between the United States and the European Union over hormone-treated beef, nearly a decade in duration, motivated much of [the SPS] text" (Wirth 1994, 824).

Len Condon (then at the USTR) was part of the small group that hammered out the US agricultural position. Unlike many other issues in the Uruguay Round, he says, the SPS talks were a "classical negotiation," involving many countries and a search for common ground. The negotiations proceeded smoothly, without the gridlock that occurred in other agricultural areas. "The SPS agreement was really negotiated separately from other issues," remembers Condon. "It proceeded very differently, and the dynamics were very different, from the rest of the Uruguay Round negotiation. The other three agricultural areas were much more controversial and were much less a classical negotiation. Instead, they primarily occurred between the US and the EC and were accomplished in fits and starts."

EC negotiators did not object to the SPS negotiations. In fact, some say that Europe was not a major player in the SPS talks at all. One reason was the relatively small role of the European Parliament in the Uruguay Round negotiations—in marked contrast to its prominent involvement in the beef hormones ban, which was framed as a public health issue. While the parliament had the authority to act on public health issues, it did not have the same power over trade and agriculture. One analyst notes that in the Uruguay Round, "Parliamentarians did not have the authority to influence the negotiation mandate or the conduct of negotiations, and they could not veto any individual part of the Uruguay Round Agreement. Whereas the hormone directive had occupied the full attention of the Council and Parliament as a single issue, the negotiations for the SPS agreement had little political intervention. Framed as a trade issue within the Uruguay Round, the SPS agreement fell outside of the jurisdiction of the European Parliament and was overshadowed by the Agriculture Agreement" (Davis 2003, 329).

According to some observers, the only major player in the SPS talks was the United States. "The SPS agreement was written by the United States," remarks the Community Nutrition Institute's Rod Leonard. Leonard organized a group of US nonprofit organizations that lobbied to influence the outcome of the SPS negotiations. This coalition of consumer and environmental groups—including the Institute for Agriculture and Trade Policy, Public Voice,[75] the World Wildlife Fund, the National Wildlife Federation, the Sierra Club, Defenders of Wildlife, the Humane Society, and the Environmental Defense Fund—met with officials at the USDA, USTR, FDA, State Department, and Commerce Department. Leonard summarizes their position: "We tried to get the US government to incorporate within the SPS agreement the understanding that if a country's standards were set to be more protective than Codex standards, or if they were adopted for reasons that the public in those countries felt was appropriate, then the country could not be taken before the WTO and charged with a trade violation."[76]

The final SPS agreement did acknowledge the sovereign right of members to take measures to protect health and life within their territories, but it held that they could do so only if such measures were not arbitrary or unjustifiably discriminatory (thereby constituting disguised restrictions on international trade) and if they were science-based. According to annex A(3) of the SPS agreement, the international standards, guidelines, and recommendations governing food safety would be those established by the Codex Alimentarius Commission. Unlike in the earlier GATT process, in other words, Codex standards were to play an official role in solving disputes at the new WTO. While members could set standards higher than the international standard, they needed scientific justification to do so. WTO members also agreed that in disputes over whether a member's domestic regulatory measures were inconsistent with the SPS agreement, the WTO Dispute Settlement Body would be the final arbiter.

Codex Votes

While the SPS agreement was being negotiated, the United States continued to press the hormone question at Codex. An important vote took

75. Public Voice for Food and Health Policy, a US consumer advocacy organization headquartered in Washington, DC, was active in the hormones debate. According to the New York Times, the group also campaigned for expanded seafood inspections, better fat labeling, reduced use of pesticides, healthier school lunches, and better nutrition for the rural poor (Judith Blake, "Pulling the Strings: Here Are Some of the Major Players Behind America's Food Fights," The New York Times, May 20, 1992, D1).

76. Unless otherwise noted, all quotes from Rod Leonard are from a May 2000 interview with the author.

place at the 1991 Codex conference in Rome. At issue was whether Codex should adopt standards for four of the hormones used in beef production, based on the JECFA evaluation. Creating such standards would essentially affirm that residues of these hormones in food posed no risk to health.

The Codex vote was the last step in the eight-step process required to create a Codex standard. To no one's surprise, the United States pushed for adoption of the standard, while EEC members expressed opposition to the proposal. The EEC position was supported by the International Organization of Consumer Unions (IOCU); the US position was supported by COMISA (Confédération Mondiale de l'Industrie de la Sante Animale, the World Federation of the Animal Health Industry), the international federation representing manufacturers of veterinary medicines, vaccines, and other products (Codex Alimentarius Commission 1991, paras. 155–59).

It was the US delegation's prerogative to call for a secret ballot. Though expected to exercise that option to lessen political pressure on Codex delegates to side with the EEC, the United States chose not to do so. In open voting, Codex representatives defeated the call to adopt a Codex standard, 27–12 (nine countries abstained). The status of the hormones was put on hold (Codex Alimentarius Commission 1991, paras. 160–61).

Some observers wonder why the United States acted as it did. Lester Crawford, later the head of the US delegation to Codex, makes clear the logic of the US decision:

> The reason we didn't call for the secret ballot in 1991 was to support the Uruguay Round. The main opposition to GATT considered the GATT to be a secret cabal plotting against the civilized world. In the US, that opposition, led by groups like Public Voice, was particularly strong and pernicious. They were winning the popularity contest in the US by claiming that these international institutions were all too secretive. We could not call for a secret ballot in that atmosphere. Had the US done so, the worst news of all would be that we won the hormone vote. They would have had press conferences all over the country the next day. You can see the way they would spin it. They'd say, "The only way the US ever got this odious hormone thing passed was by secret ballot, and no one knows what pressure or bribery the US used in order to win." That is why we made that call. A lot of people have a hard time understanding it. We had to lose the vote in the open in order to support the GATT.

After the vote, Crawford was made vice chairman of Codex, which he described as "a consolation prize because the US lost the vote on hormones" (also see Codex Alimentarius Commission 1991, para. 5).

At its next meeting, in 1993, Codex considered the fifth growth-promoting hormone, trenbolone acetate, which had not been addressed in 1991. The Commission decided to put a hold on determining standards for trenbolone acetate at step 8, along with those for the other growth-promoting hormones. The draft maximum residue levels for all five hormones would not be set "until such time as guidance was obtained from the [Codex] Committee on General Principles on the status of science in Codex policies and procedures" (Codex Alimentarius Commission 1993, para. 157). What exactly was meant by "the status of science in Codex"? What else would enter into the decision?

According to the Codex proceedings, the hormone review would have to take into account "other factors"—including legitimate consumer concerns, animal welfare, fraudulent or unfair trading practices, labeling, and other ethical and cultural considerations—while stressing the preeminence of science in Codex procedures (Codex Alimentarius Commission 1993, para. 159). Industry was unhappy about the "other factors," and about the new delay on MRLs. The representative of the trade group for the animal medicine industry, COMISA, noted that in light of the Codex Commission's decision, it would not recommend that its members place a high priority on participating in the Codex process for establishing residue standards for veterinary drugs (Codex Alimentarius Commission 1993, para. 161).

Questions were also arising about who should participate in the Codex process and in what capacity. In 1993, the International Organization of Consumer Unions presented a paper to Codex representatives on consumer involvement in decision making about food standards. The IOCU asserted that because industry groups had more resources, their interests were more strongly represented than those of consumer organizations. There was also a call for greater press access to Codex meetings to improve transparency, and the Codex Commission suggested that the guidelines governing public and press attendance at Codex sessions be revised (Codex Alimentarius Commission 1993, paras. 50–51; summary and conclusions, iv).

Clearly, changes were afoot at Codex. In light of its new role in the evolving international trade system, Codex was facing questions about the who, what, why, and how of decision making and standard setting. According to the Codex Commission itself, the 1993 Codex meeting "highlight[ed] changes adopted by the Commission which respond to its new role in the context of the GATT Uruguay Round of Trade Negotiations on SPS and on technical barriers to trade." The assistant director-general of the WHO also noted that the SPS agreement would "change the status of Codex recommendations, especially related to food safety[;] . . . knowing the role of such recommendations in international trade it may become more difficult to formulate new Codex standards, and their formulation may be subject to greater political pressure."[77]

At its 1995 meeting, the Codex Commission engaged in "lengthy and exhaustive" debate on four principles drafted by the Executive Committee that "confirmed the pre-eminent role of science in Codex decision-

---

77. These opening remarks were delivered by Dr. Fernando S. Antezana on behalf of Dr. Hiroshi Nakajima, the WHO's director-general (Codex Alimentarius Commission 1993, 108).

making processes while allowing for other factors to be taken into account." The European member countries submitted a proposal to amend the statements, but after intensive discussion the Commission adopted all four as originally drafted, and the EU member countries made known their opposition to the decision (Codex Alimentarius Commission 1995, paras. 23–25).

Codex Votes Again

The 1995 Codex meeting also held another vote on the hormone issue. This time, Codex voted by secret ballot to adopt the JECFA MRLs on growth-promoting hormones. The vote was 33–29, with seven countries abstaining. (A proposal to postpone a decision pending further study had earlier been defeated by a similar margin.) The official observer of the European Community expressed regret that this far-reaching decision was made by secret ballot—a move that, he said, was at odds with the Commission's decision to increase transparency and cast doubt on the "validity and value of Codex work and standards." The consequences would be grave, he predicted, "including the European Community's rethinking of participation in Codex work" (Codex Alimentarius Commission 1995, para. 46).[78]

Lester Crawford, who recalls the vote as a victory for the United States, credits "brilliant work by Steve Sundlof at FDA-CVM." The vote, Crawford says, "marginalized the Europeans for sure. They had staked a lot of political and Codex capital in their position. And once they lost that, then their side went into retreat and it was immediately referred to the WTO."

Not everyone in the United States celebrated the Codex results. According to Global Trade Watch's Lori Wallach, "The Codex action was extremely controversial, not only because Codex procedures allow for undue industry influence in rule-making, but because a four-year debate on the safety of these chemicals led to a highly unusual occurrence of voting in the Codex, which typically operated by consensus."[79] The Sierra Club Legal Defense Fund's Patti Goldman adds that "a nearly split Codex vote hardly indicates a general consensus concerning a purportedly scientific question." Goldman also points to the political nature of making decisions, even those said to be based on science. "Turning science into action is an inherently political endeavor," she observes. "Conflicting evidence must be weighed and risks and benefits must be balanced before action can be taken. These are political decisions that must be made by govern-

---

78. The delegations of the Netherlands, Sweden, Finland, Spain, and the United Kingdom dissociated themselves from part or all of the observer's statement.

79. Lori Wallach, Global Trade Watch, prepared statement before the House Ways and Means Subcommittee on Trade, 106th Congress, 1st session, *US Negotiating Objectives for the WTO Seattle Ministerial Meeting*, August 5, 1999.

ments which are responsible to the people who are directly affected by the outcome of the decisions" (Goldman and Wagner 1996: 8–9).

The United States Tries Again

A Case at the WTO

With a new set of international rules in place, the United States considered another challenge to the EU beef ban. The new WTO, which opened its doors on January 1, 1995, also had a new system for resolving disputes. According to WTO Director-General Renato Ruggiero, the WTO's dispute settlement system was "in many ways the central pillar of the multilateral trading system and the WTO's most individual contribution to the stability of the global economy" (WTO 1999, 38). The system was designed to be stronger, more predictable, and more credible than its GATT predecessor. In the GATT system, there was no fixed timetable, rulings were easy to block, and many cases dragged on without ever reaching a conclusion. The WTO process was more structured, with clearly defined stages (see appendix 1B). WTO members agreed to use the dispute settlement system instead of taking action unilaterally.

In May 1995, the new European agriculture commissioner, Franz Fischler, made his first official visit to the United States, where he addressed the World Meat Congress in Denver, Colorado. Fischler also visited the USDA to meet with its new secretary, Dan Glickman, and USTR Mickey Kantor. Glickman devoted most of the meeting to the hormone issue, essentially giving Fischler until the end of the year to "fix" the situation.

Eight months later a dissatisfied Glickman reportedly called Fischler to say that time was up, and the United States was taking the dispute to the WTO. The United States, joined by Australia, New Zealand, and Canada, requested consultations with the European Union at the WTO in January 1996. That same month, the European Parliament voted unanimously "steadfastly to oppose the import of hormone-treated meat in the EU."[80]

In April 1996, the United States filed its formal complaint—the first SPS case brought to the WTO. A panel of three WTO officials was assigned to the beef dispute in July 1996. Some Commission officials and representatives of US consumer groups questioned the appropriateness of designating a lawyer and two trade diplomats to evaluate what they viewed as a public-health measure. ("Three trade officials who knew nothing about health or science," notes Mark Ritchie of the nonprofit Institute for Agriculture and Trade Policy.) The panel met with the parties in October and November. Later in November, the panel chairman informed the Dispute

---

80. "EU Votes to Continue Hormone Ban on Beef," *Journal of Commerce*, January 19, 1996, 3A.

Settlement Body that the panel would not be able to issue its report within the standard six-month time period.

In arguments before the WTO panel, the United States claimed that the EC hormone ban was inconsistent with a number of international trade agreements, including GATT Articles I and III and the SPS and the TBT agreements.[81] European officials argued that the hormone ban did not violate any provision of the SPS agreement, because Europe satisfied all its conditions: The ban was based on scientific principles, as required by SPS Article 2.2, and a risk assessment had established the scientific basis for regulatory action. Moreover, the Europeans emphasized that the ban was based on the precautionary principle. Finally, they claimed that no arguments were needed pertaining to the TBT agreement, because the ban was an SPS issue.[82] The European Union also requested a WTO panel to review the legitimacy of the $100 million in US retaliatory tariffs. But the United States promptly rescinded its tariffs in July 1996.

Some US consumer and environmental groups shared European concerns about the health hazards of growth-promoting hormones. "There was more to this from a medical/scientific perspective than our government was telling us," says Mark Ritchie. "Our organization helped compile information about the danger posed to consumers by hormones, and we submitted a brief to the original WTO panel and to the appellate body." A group of US nonprofits, including Public Citizen, the Cancer Prevention Coalition, and the Sierra Club Legal Defense Fund, prepared a paper on hormones for the WTO. While the WTO allowed panelists to read such outside briefs, it did not mandate that they do so. However, four scientists of different nationalities had also appeared before the panel in February 1997, each answering more than 30 questions about the safety of the hormones in question.

Reflecting on the procedures for WTO dispute resolution, observers said that the process resembled that of a courtroom. Some Europeans blamed the litigious nature of the WTO proceedings on US influence. One European official remarked, "The US has brought a new style to dispute settlement that did not exist before. In the GATT, dispute settlement was not meant to bear any similarity whatsoever to a court system. It was a negotiation mechanism. At the GATT there wasn't this confrontational style. Clearly something has changed. I firmly believe this is entirely the doing of the US."

---

81. The United States claimed that the EC measures appeared to be inconsistent with agreements, including (1) the GATT 1994 Articles I, III, and XI; (2) the Agreement on the Application of Sanitary and Phytosanitary Measures, Articles 2.2, 2.3, 3.1, 5.1, 5.6, and 5.7; (3) the Agreement on Technical Barriers to Trade, Articles 2.1, 2.2, 5.1.1, and 5.1.2; and (4) the Agreement on Agriculture, Article 4.

82. "EC Measures Concerning Meat and Meat Products (Hormones), Complaint by the United States," Report of the WTO Panel, WT/DS26/R/USA, August 18, 1997, 3:4–6.

Business and Trade in the United States

Soon after the United States filed its formal WTO complaint about the beef ban, USTR Mickey Kantor brought another WTO case against Europe. This case, initiated in April 1996, was filed on behalf of US-based Chiquita Brands International. Chiquita complained that Europe had changed its trade rules in 1993 to favor bananas grown by Britain's former Caribbean colonies over bananas from Latin America. Because Chiquita grew most of its fruit in Latin America, this shift left the company—which previously had been Europe's largest supplier of bananas—at a disadvantage.

The banana case was quickly linked in the press to the beef case, since both pitted the United States against Europe. Perhaps the most-discussed facet of the banana case was Chiquita CEO Carl Lindner's vast political contribution. Some say that although relatively few US jobs were at stake (most of Chiquita's 45,000 employees were in Honduras and Guatemala), Lindner managed to position his banana problem at the top of the US trade agenda. After donating nothing to the Democrats in 1992—traditionally, he gave to Republicans—Lindner contributed $250,000 in December 1993.[83] In September 1994, Chiquita filed a petition asking the United States to impose trade sanctions against Europe. Shortly thereafter, Lindner and his interests made $580,000 in soft money contributions: $275,000 to the Democrats, $250,000 to the Republicans, and $55,000 to GOPAC, the political action committee of Newt Gingrich (R-GA).[84]

On November 17, 1994, House Speaker–designate Gingrich, new Senate Majority Leader Bob Dole (R-KS), new House Minority Leader Richard Gephardt (D-MO), and Senator John Glenn (D-OH) sent a letter to the Clinton administration in support of Lindner's position on banana trade. *Time* magazine reported that on April 12, 1996, the day after the banana case went to the WTO, Lindner and his executives began sending more than $500,000 to two dozen less-examined Democrat state party accounts.[85] The company's officials emphasized that there was nothing wrong with lobbying the government. "Who else are we going to turn to to save our business?" asked Joseph Hagin, Chiquita's vice president for corporate affairs.[86]

A number of US observers note that the case against Europe over bananas was sound regardless of any political contributions—after all, the

---

83. Michael Isikoff and Brook Larmer, "And Now Bananagate?" *Newsweek*, April 28, 1997, 20.

84. Common Cause press release, "Banana Republic: Carl Lindner and Affiliates Give Huge Soft Money Contributions While Seeking and Obtaining Key Congressional and Administrative Aid; Democrats Raise $40 Million in Soft Money in '94 Election Cycle, Common Cause Study Finds," March 8, 1995.

85. Michael Weisskopf, "The Busy Back-Door Men," *Time*, March 31, 1997, 40.

86. Hagin, quoted in Isikoff and Larmer, "And Now Bananagate?" 20. Hagin became deputy chief of staff to President George W. Bush in 2001.

WTO ultimately ruled in favor of the United States. However, many Europeans point out that the beef and banana cases represented examples of big business's influence on decision making in US trade policy. "The perception is certainly that USTR is sensitive to lobbies," says one European official, "and will sometimes pursue the interests of lobbies to the detriment of more general interests of the US." In a nutshell, the beef case became so politically important in the United States "simply because of the influence lobbying groups representing specific interests can have in the American political system." He adds,

> I think the European Commission is more able than USTR to say, "What is the strategic importance of a given case?" Whereas, the way USTR has come to work is more or less like a law firm acting on behalf of clients. If they have a client like the beef producers, there is no way for USTR to send these people home. They cannot say, "This case is worth $100 million dollars and we have a trade-and-investment relationship with the EU that is in the trillions. This is just not worth ruining our good relations with the EU." They can't do that because they are in a lawyer–client relationship.

Others counter that little outside influence was needed to convince USTR of the merits of the beef case. Leonard Condon notes, "From my perspective as a mid-level bureaucrat at USTR from 1981 to 1997, I can say that not a lot of pressure was necessary from the US beef industry to motivate the government to initiate and pursue this case. It was clear to all of us from the start that the EU had no scientific basis for the ban."[87] From the beginning, the real issue was not industry influence, but the fact that Europe would not change its policy. As Condon remembers, "When Commissioner Andriessen made the decision to refuse to cooperate in the case we had taken in the GATT Standards Code, the US Government had no choice, we all believed, but to respond with retaliation, which we did."

The WTO Rules

In its interim decision on the hormone case, distributed on May 7, 1997, the WTO panel sided with the United States: It ruled that Europe had violated international obligations negotiated in the SPS agreement by establishing a ban on beef raised with growth hormones without undertaking a scientific assessment of risk. The interim report was followed by a separate ruling on the similar Canadian complaint, which also went against the European Union. The final report of the WTO dispute settlement panel on the hormone issue was released in August 1997. As expected, the report found the European Union in violation of its international obligations.

---

87. Comments made to author, January 2006.

The European Union could not impose rules on hormone exposure that were stricter than existing international (Codex) standards, the panel reasoned, because the necessary scientific evidence had not been provided. In the judgment of the panel, none of the scientific evidence presented by the European Union on growth-promoting hormones "indicates that an identifiable risk arises for human health from such use of those hormones if good practice is followed."[88] In response, the European Commission charged that "the panel has failed to properly take into account the large body of scientific [evidence] brought forward by the EU in support of its legislation." The European Union also argued that the ruling undermined a nation's right to determine the level of protection appropriate for its own consumers.[89]

European officials also noted that the ruling flew in the face of what was known as the "precautionary principle," which they claimed entitled the European Union to prohibit or restrict products that were suspected, but not proven, to be hazardous. Commission officials later explained that the precautionary principle was not "a politicization of science or the acceptance of zero risk"; instead, it enabled countries to take action when science was unable to provide a clear answer.[90] Many US observers pointed out that the SPS agreement only allowed import bans on a "provisional" basis while scientific information was being gathered, not open-ended bans on precautionary grounds (see Article 5.7 of the SPS agreement, in appendix 1C).

Unsurprisingly, the European Union quickly appealed the WTO ruling, taking advantage of a process that had not been available under the GATT's dispute settlement mechanism. At the WTO, three people were assigned through an internal rotation process to handle an appeal. If the European Union was unsuccessful in its appeal, there would be repercussions: Europe would have to open its market to US beef, pay compensation, or allow the United States to retaliate against its exports in an amount equivalent to the value of the banned meat. "We would prefer not to see compensation," US Agriculture Secretary Dan Glickman testified at a June 1997 hearing of the Senate Agriculture Committee.[91] The United States did not want to create the precedent that the European Union could buy its way out of WTO-determined violations of trade rules, observers said.

---

88. "EC Measures Concerning Meat and Meat Products (Hormones), Complaint by the United States," Report of the WTO Panel, WT/DS26/R/USA, August 18, 1997, 8:124.

89. EU statement, quoted in "EU Announces It Will Appeal WTO Panel Ruling on Hormone Ban," *Inside US Trade*, July 4, 1997.

90. "EU Cements Policy on Food, Health Precautionary Principle," *Dow Jones Industrial News*, February 2, 2000.

91. Glickman, quoted in "EU Announces It Will Appeal WTO Panel Ruling on Hormone Ban," *Inside US Trade*, July 4, 1997.

In January 1998, the appellate body released its report. Though it overruled the original panel on several points, it affirmed the key finding that Europe's beef ban was inconsistent with the SPS agreement. The WTO adopted the appellate report and the report of the original panel in February 1998.

Implementing the Ruling

The European Union requested four years to implement the WTO ruling, in part because it hoped to conduct a risk assessment of the hormones in question. However, a WTO arbiter allowed only 15 months for implementation, with a deadline of May 13, 1999. Many US participants commented on the European Union's intention to undertake a risk-assessment study. "That is the most intriguing thing that happened, because it means they had never done a risk-assessment study—never evaluated whether or not the compounds were safe," Crawford says. "So that was the most stunning indictment you could get. They admitted publicly, repeatedly, that they had never evaluated the safety of hormones." The Europeans commissioned two independent committees of scientists, including several Americans, to conduct a series of 17 risk assessments. The result, said the *Wall Street Journal*, was "a scientific process that resembles an open-ended academic project."[92]

Meanwhile, different alternatives were considered. One possible compromise was for Europe to accept US beef as long as it was "properly labeled." But what did it mean to be properly labeled? According to a US proposal, the United States would agree to a label such as "product of the US" that would identify the source of the beef "thereby giving EU consumers the choice about whether to purchase US beef."[93] But the European Union insisted that any label must include the word "hormone." As EU External Relations Commissioner Leon Brittan put it, indicating that the product came from the US was not sufficient "because that doesn't meet the concern." He added, "We certainly don't want a label which casts doubt on the safety of the product. We just want to make certain that it indicates that it does or may contain hormones."[94] The United States did not agree, arguing that such a label could mislead consumers (Josling, Roberts, and Orden 2004, 121). Therefore, the labeling idea was rejected.

Congressional allies of the Cattlemen's Association and Chiquita were making known their views on the US-EU trade disputes. In October 1998,

---

92. Geoff Winestock, "Column One: EU Beef Battle with US Began in a Rare Event—Italian Boys Grew Breasts; Ministers Banned Hormones—But Scientific Evidence Was Always Lacking," *The Wall Street Journal Europe*, March 2, 2000, 1.

93. "Text: US Proposal on Beef Labeling," *Inside US Trade*, February 19, 1999.

94. "EU Considers New Beef Ban As US, EU Try to Resolve Hormone Dispute," *Inside US Trade*, April 23, 1999.

House Speaker Gingrich and Majority Leader Trent Lott (R-MS) wrote to President Clinton about the WTO rulings on beef and bananas, pressing the White House to "spell out a specific timetable the Administration will take to ensure compliance with the WTO's ruling." They warned, "If the Administration will not take action to protect trade agreements, Congress will have no choice but to take action of its own."[95]

In March 1999, the administration announced that if the European Union did not comply with the WTO ruling on the EU beef ban, it would exercise its right to impose 100 percent duties on a variety of European products. The USTR created a preliminary list of 81 products that included beef, pork, poultry, Roquefort cheese, flowers, and chocolate truffles;[96] the goods targeted would be drawn from this group. In hearings in Washington, many importers of European delicacies argued that they were unfairly trapped in the middle of a trade war.

In April, the European Union threatened to ban all American beef imports unless the United States could guarantee that beef labeled "hormone-free" was indeed free of hormones. The European Union claimed that in product tests, 12 percent of all certified "hormone-free" beef contained residues of growth promotants. Also in April, an interim scientific report commissioned by the European Union was released to the public. The report claimed that one of the hormones in question—oestradiol-17β—could cause cancer: "Even small additional doses of residues of this hormone in meat arising from its use as a growth promoter in cattle has an inherent risk of causing cancer."[97] "We now have a scientific basis to defend our position," declared EU Consumer Policy Commissioner Emma Bonino (Hurd 1999).

The US government was not impressed. "The EU, having failed in every step of the WTO process, appears to be once again searching for a way to avoid its international obligations," Agriculture Secretary Dan Glickman and USTR Charlene Barshefsky declared in a joint statement. "This latest report is not a risk assessment. It repeats the same unsubstantiated arguments that the European Union has already made before the WTO panel of experts, which were flatly rejected by the panel."[98] In addition, the WHO/FAO Joint Expert Committee on Food Additives had reexamined and reconfirmed the safety of three of the hormones (oestradiol, progesterone, and testosterone) when properly administered to animals.

---

95. "October 7, 1998 Gingrich, Lott Letter to Clinton," reprinted in *Inside US Trade*, October 9, 1998.

96. The full list of products was published in the *Federal Register*, March 25, 1999.

97. Barry James, "Hormone in US Beef Causes Cancer, EU Scientists Conclude," *International Herald Tribune*, May 4, 1999, 5.

98. Foreign Agriculture Service, "Joint Statement by Secretary of Agriculture Dan Glickman and United States Trade Representative Charlene Barshefsky on the EU Hormone Report," May 3, 1999 (available at www.usda.gov).

The Deadline Passes

Continuing to hold to its position, Commission officials explained that scientific study was ongoing—past May 13, 1999, the date set by the WTO for compliance. "We are ready to pay the price," said Henrik Dam Kristensen, Denmark's minister for foodstuffs. "We want to examine the consequences for consumers of hormone meat."[99] The United States continued to condemn the European Union. "The EU should meet its WTO obligations, including those resulting from adverse rulings against it. To do anything less is to jeopardize the credibility and integrity of the WTO," noted Charlene Barshefsky in a May 14 statement.[100] Agriculture Secretary Dan Glickman concurred, "When the EU became a WTO member, it agreed to abide by all WTO rules."[101]

On May 17, the United States sought WTO authorization to impose tariffs on EU products at a level equivalent to lost US beef exports. "The actions that we are taking here are 100-percent consistent with our WTO rights," said Barshefsky. "We take this course as a last resort."[102] The United States estimated its annual loss at $202 million (industry analysts had put the figure at about $500 million). The EU countered that the annual cost to US exports was only $53 million and requested WTO arbitration. The total of $202 million was "grossly excessive," said European Trade Commissioner Sir Leon Brittan.[103]

Food and Fear

As the beef dispute headed back to the WTO yet again, food-related concerns continued to hold the spotlight in Europe. Indeed, a panic had erupted over food safety. In 1996 the European Commission had banned all exports of British beef, in an effort to protect consumers from a deadly brain disease called new-variant Creutzfeldt-Jakob Disease (nvCJD) (the United States had banned British beef in 1989). Experts believed nvCJD to be contracted by eating the nervous tissue of cattle afflicted with a similar condition called bovine spongiform encephalopathy (BSE), commonly

---

99. Kristensen, quoted in Peter Ford, "US to Up Prices of EU Goods," *The Christian Science Monitor,* July 26, 1999, 1.

100. Office of the USTR, "United States to Request WTO Authorization to Retaliate in the Amount of $202 Million," May 14, 1999.

101. Foreign Agriculture Service, "Statement by Agriculture Secretary Dan Glickman on the EU's Failure to Comply with WTO Rulings on the Beef Hormone Ban," May 14, 1999 (available at www.usda.gov).

102. Office of the USTR, "United States to Request WTO Authorization to Retaliate."

103. Brittan, quoted in Elizabeth Olson, "$253 Million Sanctions Sought in Beef Fight with Europe," *The New York Times,* June 4, 1999, C4.

known as mad cow disease. The disease, first identified in the mid-1980s, had spread through British herds from processed cattle feed containing the ground-up remains of already-infected animals, and hundreds of thousands of cattle had to be slaughtered. The mad cow crisis magnified distrust in the government's ability to monitor food safety.

Debate and protest were also heating up over genetically modified (GM) crops, grown mostly in the United States. These new field crops, which utilized recombinant DNA technology to assist in pest and weed control, had been released for large-scale commercial use in 1996. By 1999, roughly half of the US soybean crop and one-third of the corn crop were genetically modified. Observers noted that GM crops created new possibilities for higher yields, lower pesticide use, greater food security in the developing world, more profits for farmers, and more nutritional food. European farmers, however, generally did not adopt GM crops and protesters questioned the safety of GM technology. By April 1998, Europe had stopped approving new GM crop varieties for use or import.

Other food-related issues were coming to a head in Europe. In May 1999, following a TV report on contaminated animal feed in Belgium, European retailers began yanking potentially dioxin-tainted foods from their shelves. At the order of the Commission, Belgium destroyed huge quantities of possibly contaminated chicken, dairy products, eggs, baked goods, and some beef products. The contamination likely resulted from a batch of animal feed tainted with motor oil. Belgian government officials had reportedly known about the tainted feed, and popular outrage first led to the resignations of Belgium's farm and health ministers and ultimately toppled the incumbent Belgian government. The incident ended up costing more than $750 million, and thousands of farmers converged on Brussels to demand compensation.[104] In response to the crisis, the United States held up all EU poultry and pork imports, an action that some observers criticized as based more on fear than on fact. One editorial described the move as "ironic" in light of US diplomats' concurrent efforts to convince Europe that its fears about genetically modified crops and growth hormones were grounded in emotion rather than science.[105]

The food scares did not end. In June, more than 250 people (including children) in Belgium and France reported stomachaches, dizziness, and nausea after drinking Coca-Cola products. In the company's largest-ever product recall, 17 million cases of Coke, Fanta, and Sprite were pulled from the shelves. Belgian and French authorities banned the sale of Coke products for 10 days.

---

104. Julie Wolf, Brandon Mitchener, and Konstantin Richter, "Cost Mounts in Belgium's Food Crisis—Poultry Sales Are Delayed in Blow to Government as Election Approaches," *The Wall Street Journal*, June 10, 1999, A21.

105. "Global Food Panic," editorial, *Journal of Commerce*, June 9, 1999, 7.

Still reeling from the effects of the mad cow outbreak, some European Commission officials attributed the spate of food-related incidents to a series of random accidents rather than to a flawed regulatory system. "We have an awful lot of legislation, from the stable to the table, but that doesn't stop someone from breaking the rules, and it's not going to stop an accident," said one European Commission spokesman. Others wondered if a new, independent agency was needed to oversee food safety. "It is worth considering whether some functions of an overall food policy could be more effectively carried out by an agency," noted EU Agriculture Commissioner Franz Fischler.

A number of groups suggested that industrial food production was partly to blame for the recent scares. Though European farms were traditionally small and family-owned, American-style agribusiness was establishing a presence. "I am very concerned that it's the accountants now that are getting hold of the [food] business, and that there is a continuous effort to drive down prices and to maximize profit," said one small-scale British sheep farmer, "Inevitably, in doing so, corners are going to be cut."[106]

Back to the Future—Retaliatory Tariffs and a Stalemate

Before the WTO arbitrators reached a decision, US and EU scientists met to discuss the hormone issue one more time. On June 21, 1999, ten US regulators—led by Stephen Sundlof, the head of FDA-CVM—sat down with a group of EU scientists and officials at the National Institutes of Health (NIH) outside Washington, DC.[107] The European representatives included the chair of the EU scientific committee that had issued the April interim report. The mood was chilly, and the meeting ended without agreement on how to move forward.

On July 12, WTO arbitrators assessed the annual cost of the beef ban at $116.8 million for the United States and $11.3 million for Canada (Canada had requested $51 million in sanctions). This decision permitted the United States and Canada to impose 100 percent duties on a list of EU products of comparable value. Only months before, the United States had imposed $191 million in duties on European products as the result of a ruling in the WTO banana case. "This retaliation will stay in place until the EU has lifted its ban," announced US Special Trade Negotiator Peter Scher. "This is now the second time this year in a WTO dispute that the EU has failed to honor its WTO obligations. To put a finer point on it, the EU has

---

106. European Commission spokesman Gerry Kiely and sheep farmer Sandy Boyd, quoted in "Food Scares Mount Up, Perplexing Europeans," *The New York Times*, June 20, 1999, 15; Fischler, quoted in "EU's Fischler sees Role for New Food Safety Agency," Reuters News, August 16, 1999.

107. Geoff Winestock, "Column One: EU Beef Battle with US Began in a Rare Event—Italian Boys Grew Breasts; Ministers Banned Hormones—But Scientific Evidence Was Always Lacking," *The Wall Street Journal Europe*, March 2, 2000, 1.

now become the only member of the 134-nation membership of the WTO to fail to respect rulings of the dispute settlement panel."[108]

Rita Hayes, US ambassador to the WTO, called the decision a victory: "We now have a combination of more than $300 million in beef and bananas retaliation against the European Union," she pointed out. The French farm minister, Jean Glavany, countered that the United States had "the worst food in the world."[109] The American Meat Institute, the American Farm Bureau Federation, the National Cattlemen's Beef Association, and the US Meat Export Federation released a joint statement charging that "EU intransigence has forced the least desirable conclusion to this trade dispute."[110]

The final list of products targeted in the US retaliatory action was determined by an interagency process involving the Departments of State and Commerce, USDA, and USTR. Scher said that the list of EU products was crafted to exert "maximum pressure" on the Europeans while inflicting "minimum economic impact" on American business.[111] France, Germany, Italy, and Denmark were the countries most deeply affected by the tariffs because they were the largest countries within the European Union—with the exception of Denmark, chosen because it was the European Union's largest meat exporter. US officials indicated that these countries had played the most decisive role in preserving the beef ban and would also wield the most influence on future EU decisions. When the retaliation went into effect on July 29, affected products included Danish ham; German pork; French goose-liver pâté, mustard, and Roquefort cheese; and Italian truffles and canned tomatoes.[112] The most heavily targeted of these goods was European pork. Reportedly, the US National Pork Producers Council had urged President Clinton to put EU pork products on the list. Facing low prices, pork producers in the United States were competing with $247 million of EU exports per year.[113] In the end, pork accounted for $30 million of US retaliation.

---

108. Scher, American Farm Bureau Federation Press Conference, National Press Club, July 13, 1999 (unofficial transcript available at www.useu.be).

109. Hayes, quoted in Frances Williams, "US Wins Approval for Beef Sanctions," *The Financial Times* London, July 27, 1999, 8; Glavany, quoted in Peter Ford, "US to Up Prices of EU Goods," *The Christian Science Monitor*, July 26, 1999, 1.

110. "Statement by the American Meat Institute, the American Farm Bureau Federation, the National Cattlemen's Beef Association, and the US Meat Export Federation Regarding US Retaliation List Against EU Products," July 19, 1999 (on file with author).

111. USTR Telebriefing, Special US Trade Negotiator Peter Scher on the EU Beef Hormone Dispute, July 19, 1999 (unofficial transcript available at www.usembassy.it).

112. Among the other products affected were glues and adhesives from France, Germany, and Italy, as well as chocolate and foie gras. France was hit with tariffs of 24 percent of the total value; Germany, 24 percent; Italy, 21 percent; and Denmark, 15 percent. The remainder was divided among the other 10 EU countries, excluding the United Kingdom.

113. "Extra Tariff on Pork as US Reacts," *Farmers Guardian*, July 16, 1999, 7.

Both the United States and Canada excluded UK agricultural and food exports from trade sanctions because the British government had generally opposed the ban.[114] British Agriculture Minister Nick Brown welcomed the US decision, pointing out that "The UK government has consistently worked for a constructive solution to the trade dispute with Canada and the USA over the EU's beef hormones ban." Brown added, "We will continue to base our approach on the science and to work within the EU for a settlement which results in the trade sanctions being lifted."[115] Britain was the only EU nation to escape penalties.[116]

Targeting the US Food Industry

Some French farmers, particularly incensed by the punitive levy on Roquefort cheese, reacted angrily to the US tariffs. In retaliation, manure and rotten fruit were dumped outside of McDonald's restaurants in the southern towns of Montauban, Arles, Martigues, and Nîmes. In Noyon, farmers lured customers away from McDonald's with gifts of fresh baguettes and French cheese.[117] Going a step further, in the heart of the Roquefort region in southwest France, farmers did $65,000 worth of damage to a McDonald's site under construction in Millau. Charged with willful destruction, Jose Bové and four other farmers were imprisoned.

When Bové refused to accept release on bond, preferring to stay in jail until trial, his name became a household word in France. The founder of the farmers' group Confédération Paysanne, Bové declared that he would resist GM foods, hormone-raised beef, and anything else he considered *sale bouffe* (dirty grub). Some trade unions, farmers, and Green Party members rallied around Bové, dubbing him "the Robin Hood of the Larzac" (his native region); others criticized his record of violent protest, citing his recent role in the destruction of GM crops on experimental plantations. "Jose Bové uses violence as a media tool," said Jacques Godfrain, a former Gaullist minister and mayor of Millau.[118]

In an attempt to defuse the situation, Jean Glavany expressed sympathy for the farmers' plight. The agriculture minister also called Bové's de-

---

114. Canada's list of products included Danish pork, French and Austrian beef, and Spanish gherkins and cucumbers.

115. Brown, quoted in "Ministerial Welcome to Sanction Exceptions," *Farmers Guardian*, August 6, 1999, 2.

116. The UK pork industry, whose exports to the United States totaled more than £8 million annually, was especially relieved. Don Curry, British Meat and Livestock Commission chairman, had urged the Clinton administration not to impose tariffs on British pork exports ("UK Escapes US Penalties," *Farmers Guardian*, July 23, 1999, 8).

117. Patricia Ochs, "Trade Fight Has Flavor of France," *The Boston Globe*, September 9, 1999, A2.

118. Bové and Godfrain, quoted in Julian Nundy, "The Raider of Roquefort Rallies French," *The Scotsman*, September 4, 1999, 11.

tention "regrettable," but warned farmers that any protests should be kept within the law. While admitting "a crisis that we have to deal with," he cautioned against "giv[ing] the impression that there is a civil war in our countryside."[119] Eric Boutry, head of the Roquefort producers' association, said that his organization would pay Bové's bail whether he liked it or not.

McDonald's French subsidiary launched a national media campaign to counter the negative publicity. Full-page ads in 60 regional daily newspapers positioned the company as "Born in the USA but made in France." The campaign emphasized that the 750 French McDonald's restaurants purchased French products.[120] "Today, 80 percent of the products we serve are made in France," said Stephanie Biais, a spokeswoman for McDonald's France in Paris. "As a longstanding purchaser of French agriculture, we deplore the violence used in these instances."[121]

Other American icons were also targeted by protesters. In Dijon, France, where local mustard was affected by the US tariffs, some café owners increased prices on Coca-Cola to more than $100 a bottle.[122] The small town of St. Pierre-de-Trivisy in the Roquefort region imposed a 100 percent tax on Coca-Cola. "We feel there's a piling-on going on with respect to the Coca-Cola Co.," one company executive said. "This may or may not have to do with sanctions. But we definitely feel we've become a target."[123]

The United States had deliberately imposed tariffs on foods that were symbols of European culture, and the French protest was also rich in symbolism. According to protesters, McDonald's and Coca-Cola were emblems of world commerce, the corporatization of food production. "We led this action, which we know was against the law," Bové announced from jail. "But we are the legitimate victims of a global market economy."[124] Other farmers expressed fear of losing the French culture and way of life.

---

119. Glavany, quoted in Samer Iskandar, "Farm Protester Refuses to Leave French Jail Cell," *The Financial Times*, September 3, 1999, 3.

120. "McDonald's Launches Ad Campaign to Counter French Farmers' Anti-US Protests," *Euromarketing*, September 10, 1999.

121. Biais, quoted in Patricia Ochs, "Trade Fight Has Flavor of France," *The Boston Globe*, September 9, 1999, A2.

122. Stephen H. Dunphy, "The WTO: A Case of Washington Meat and French Mustard—How One Big Beef in World Trade Trickles Down to Folks on the Farm," *The Seattle Times*, Sunday, September 19, 1999, A1.

123. Executive quoted in John-Thor Dahlburg, "Soft-Drink Giant Coca-Cola Is Downing a Case of Criticism in Europe Trade: Some Wonder Whether the Firm, Plagued by Recalls and Raids There, Is Being Singled Out as a Symbol of American Capitalism," *Los Angeles Times*, July 31, 1999, C1.

124. Bové, quoted in Ochs, "Trade Fight Has Flavor of France," A2.

US Industry Increases Pressure

The beef industry urged the US government to increase pressure on Europe to comply with the WTO. An industry representative conceived of a tool known as "carousel retaliation," which would require the US government to regularly rotate the list of products subject to sanctions. Changing the list would increase the number of affected European industries, and it was believed that these industries would push to end the ban on hormone-treated beef. Chuck Lambert of the National Beef Cattlemen's Association explains:

> Once retaliation goes into effect, the affected industries adjust or governments shift their subsidies. And once those shifts are made, everyone becomes comfortable again and life goes on. For example, the US retaliated against Italian tomatoes from 1980 to 1995, and didn't gain anything. So our viewpoint is that every six months, you review the existing commodities. If you aren't getting any movement, any political pressure for change, you shift retaliation to other products in order to generate additional pressure. There are 15 EU countries, but initially we only retaliated on products from 4 countries. So 11 European countries were breathing easy.

The American Meat Institute contacted a Chiquita representative in the spring of 1999 to elicit support for carousel retaliation. Initially, there was little interest in the idea but later—after no movement from the EU on bananas—Chiquita and other banana interests saw value in the concept and worked with the American Meat Institute, American Farm Bureau Federation, and National Cattlemen's Beef Association to lobby the Administration and Congress to support carousel (a former beef industry representative notes that this was the first time the beef and banana groups worked together to forward their interests related to the WTO cases).

The European Union called the carousel approach "a no-no."[125] In a review of the WTO's Dispute Settlement Understanding (DSU), European officials demanded language that would prohibit any rotation of retaliation lists.[126] In addition, not all US officials were completely enthusiastic about the tactic. Testifying before the House Ways and Means subcommittee on trade, USTR Barshefsky said that an interagency panel was weighing two concerns: whether changing the retaliation list could harm negotiations with the European Union, and what impact a change would have on US consumers and business.[127] Sources said that the other de-

---

125. "EU Floats Provisional Implementation of DSU Review," *Inside US Trade*, December 2, 1999.

126. The United States continued to oppose the EU proposal on prohibiting changes in retaliation lists. There was hope the issue would be resolved during the December 1999 Seattle WTO ministerial, but the ministerial failed.

127. Charlene Barshefsky, testimony before the Trade Subcommittee of the House Committee on Ways and Means, Subject: World Trade Organization, 106th Congress, 2nd session, February 8, 2000.

partments were concerned about rotating the retaliation lists—the Treasury Department feared that the move would harm the overall US-EU relationship, and the Commerce Department worried that it would hear complaints from affected domestic businesses.[128] In addition, the USTR wanted to maintain the ability to revise the lists as it saw fit and was suspicious of any congressional legislation that would force its hand.

Beef and banana industry representatives were finding allies in Congress. In September 1999, US farmers and food groups backed a Senate carousel retaliation bill (S. 1619) introduced by Senator Mike DeWine (R-OH). In the House, Agriculture Committee Chairman Larry Combest (R-TX) introduced a similar bill, H.R. 2991. But some companies opposed such legislation, fearing that the European Union would use a similar approach against the United States in future trade disputes—and that US business would suffer for it.

Carousel Retaliation Is Passed

In May 2000, US cattle and banana interests won a long-sought victory when Congress passed carousel retaliation as section 407 of the Trade and Development Act of 2000 (amending the Trade Act of 1974). Section 407 called for the revision of product retaliation lists every 180 days in a manner most likely to induce the targeted country to come into compliance.[129] Exceptions would be made if a resolution to the dispute was imminent, or if the USTR and the affected US industry mutually agreed that such revisions were unnecessary. The first revision of the product list was mandated to come within 30 days of enactment. Soon after President Clinton signed the legislation, a coalition of beef interests wrote to USTR Barshefsky supporting substantial revision of the list of products subject to retaliatory duties. "This issue has always been about re-opening the EU market to US beef," they declared. "It should not be about increasing protection for opportunistic US interests."[130] However, the administration failed to rotate the product list as mandated.

---

128. "Administration Conducts Review of Beef, Banana Retaliation," *Inside US Trade*, February 11, 2000.

129. "In revising any list or action against a country or countries under this subsection, the Trade Representative shall act in a manner that is most likely to result in the country or countries implementing the recommendations adopted in the dispute settlement proceeding or in achieving a mutually satisfactory solution to the issue that gave rise to the dispute settlement proceeding. The Trade Representative shall consult with the petitioner, if any, involved in the initial investigation under this chapter" (Trade and Development Act of 2000, §407(d)).

130. The American Farm Bureau, the American Meat Institute, the National Meat Association, the National Cattlemen's Beef Association, and the US Meat Export Federation, letter to USTR Charlene Barshefsky, June 12, 2000 (on file with author).

The European Union charged that carousel retaliation was illegal since it would affect a larger volume of trade than the WTO had authorized. "The EU believes that such type of shotgun legislation is fundamentally at odds with the basic principles of the Dispute Settlement Understanding," stated one Commission report (European Commission 2000, 13). Other Europeans felt it was time to soften the adversarial nature of the beef dispute. The rhetoric of trade talks should be toned down, said EU Commission President Romano Prodi at a US-EU summit press conference. "We decided that megaphone diplomacy will be replaced by telephone diplomacy," Prodi told reporters. "It's more constructive even though less sexy."[131]

But some say that the bad blood created by the beef and bananas cases was apparent in the European Union's decision to bring a new billion-dollar WTO case against the United States. Europe objected to a provision of the US tax code that in 1984 created a new entity, the foreign sales corporation (FSC), which allowed US companies like Microsoft and Boeing to avoid paying taxes on some overseas sales by channeling them through offshore subsidiaries. International trade rules explicitly prohibited export subsidies such as rebates of direct taxes, but FSC supporters argued that the provision leveled a playing field made uneven by different approaches to corporate income: The United States taxed it directly, while European countries taxed it indirectly through a value-added tax. "The FSC is simply an attempt by the US to allow its exporters to compete against foreign competitors that have long enjoyed far bigger tax breaks," wrote Bob Dole, who originally introduced the act in the Senate.[132]

But in February 2000, the WTO ruled against the United States on the FSC. A front-page *New York Times* article declared it the United States' "largest defeat ever in a trade battle."[133] Some wondered if the United States would ease its demands on beef and bananas trade as a part of a settlement deal, but at a Senate hearing, USTR Charlene Barshefsky committed not to link the bananas, beef, and FSC cases, calling them "separate matters; they need to be handled separately." Barshefsky also agreed with Senate Majority Leader Trent Lott that Europe had initiated the FSC case to deflect attention from beef and bananas. "I think the FSC decision, apart from being incorrectly decided . . . was largely put forward by the EU as . . . a means to try and even the litigation scorecard," she said.

---

131. Prodi, quoted in Alex Keto, "Clinton Turns Attention to Mideast," Dow Jones Newswires, May 31, 2000. Also see Erik T. Burns, "EurOpinion: Top Bananas Don't Talk Bananas," Dow Jones Newswires, June 1, 2000.

132. Bob Dole, "Comment and Analysis: Upsetting the World's Trade Balance," *The Financial Times*, February 22, 2000, 21.

133. Joseph Kahn, "US Loses Dispute on Export Sales," *The New York Times*, February 24, 2000, A1.

"Nonetheless, we will work with the Congress, work with the EU, with respect to our obligations under that decision."[134]

Despite the launching of the FSC case at the WTO, there were some signs of transatlantic cooperation. In April 2001, the banana battle between the United States and the European Union moved toward settlement after months of negotiations when the European Commission agreed to shift the European Union's banana import regime to a tariff-only system by 2006. In return, the United States agreed to suspend $191 million in annual sanctions on the European Union. In addition, the George W. Bush administration decided not to rotate its sanctions list in the beef dispute as required by the carousel law. "Implementation of carousel would likely kill an agreement with the European Union on low-key handling of the Foreign Sales Corporation dispute, triggering earlier steps toward retaliation in the $4 billion fight," noted *Inside US Trade*.[135] But the beef industry was frustrated that both the Clinton and Bush administrations had chosen to ignore the law.

A new head of the WTO, Thailand's former commerce minister, Supachai Panitchpakdi, took office in September 2002. Supachai told reporters that one of his priorities would be to attempt to address trade disputes before they became major crises. "We should be able to interpret the rules in a way that would help resolve conflicts," he said, expressing the hope that more disputes could be settled early, by mutual agreement, as opposed to relying on legal rulings, appeals, and sanctions.[136]

The Standoff Continues

Despite such sentiments, the US-EU standoff over the beef ban continued. Though the European Union offered to lower tariffs or raise import quotas on US hormone-free beef exports as compensation for the ban, no

---

134. Charlene Barshefsky, testimony before the Senate Finance Committee, Upcoming World Trade Organization Agriculture Negotiations, 106th Congress, 2nd session, March 7, 2000.

Later that year, President Clinton signed the Extraterritorial Income Exclusion Act (ETI) into law, intended to replace the FSC and comply with the WTO decision. But in August 2001, a WTO compliance panel found that the new law also constituted a prohibited export subsidy and violated WTO trade rules—a decision upheld by an appellate panel. In August 2002, WTO arbitrators authorized $4.043 billion in countermeasures against the United States, by far the largest total sanctions ever permitted by the WTO, but the European Commission held off on putting them into effect.

135. "US Seeks to Restart Compensation Talks with EU in Beef Dispute," *Inside US Trade*, June 15, 2001.

136. Supachai, quoted in Naomi Koppel, "New WTO Head Sets Out His Priorities," Associated Press, September 2, 2002.

agreement was reached. Thus, after years of negotiations, new trade agreements, a new system for resolving trade disputes, and long debates at Codex, the ban remained.

In one last twist, after passing legislation in 2003, Europe argued that its ban on hormone-treated beef now complied with the WTO's ruling. The ban on five of the growth hormones was made "provisional" pending further scientific research, while a new risk assessment allowed the ban on the sixth hormone, oestradiol-17β, to be permanent. Under the SPS agreement, WTO members could take provisional measures in the face of uncertain science and work to provide additional information within a "reasonable period of time." The European Union notified the WTO of its new legislation and reported that it had now implemented the WTO's ruling. The United States argued that Europe was still in violation—making a ban provisional while keeping it in place indefinitely did not meet the WTO's obligation. "The EU ban remains in place and is still unsupported by any scientific rationale," said USTR spokesman Richard Mills.[137] But in November 2004, the European Union requested WTO consultations on the grounds that the United States had failed to remove its retaliatory tariffs related to the beef hormones case despite Europe's having come into compliance. A WTO panel was established in February 2005.[138] Interestingly, for the first time, the United States, Canada, and the European Union agreed to open the panel proceedings to the public despite objections from other members. Closed-circuit television cameras would be allowed in the courtroom. Whether such transparency would contribute to greater public understanding or a mutually acceptable resolution to the dispute remained to be seen.

As the beef ban heated up again, tensions were also on the rise over the bananas dispute and FSC as well as a new US case against Europe's de facto moratorium on approving GM crops. Some experts wondered if these high-profile cases put too much pressure on the WTO dispute resolution system. Could WTO panels be expected to solve such politically charged disputes? Would such cases undermine the WTO's legitimacy? Others emphasized that while the contentious disputes got all the attention, the majority of WTO cases were successfully resolved through negotiation. "We've had several hundred cases," trade scholar Claude Barfield has noted, "and most have not created a problem."[139]

---

137. Mills, quoted in Scott Miller, "EU Renews Fight over Hormones in Beef Products," *The Wall Street Journal*, November 9, 2004, A2.

138. Third parties to the beef case were Australia, Brazil, Canada, China, Chinese Taipei, India, Mexico, New Zealand, and Norway.

139. Barfield, quoted in Edward Alden and Raphael Minder, "Tough Decisions Ahead on World Trade Rules," *The Financial Times*, December 31, 2004, 6.

Case Analysis

Regulation and markets are often seen as antagonists, but in the absence of adequate confidence in regulation, some markets are unable to operate. Lack of such confidence can be particularly damaging when there are concerns about safety and health. We have seen the results in Europe with respect to food, particularly after the mad cow food scares, and in the United States with respect to nuclear power after the 1979 accident at Three Mile Island. Though all perceive the need for regulation, nations may diverge markedly in their regulatory decisions. These decisions may reflect societies' differences in the interpretation of available information, in the internal distribution of power, in the availability of resources for regulatory activities, or in cultural preferences as articulated through political and regulatory institutions.

In this case we learn how the United States and the European Union responded to six hormones that promote growth in cattle by enacting very different regulations. In the United States, where such decisions are made by an independent regulatory agency, the FDA, use of the hormones in question was allowed; another hormone (DES, or diethylstilbestrol) was banned as harmful. In Europe, by contrast, though a commission of scientists found no evidence that the hormones had ill effects on humans, the European Council of Ministers banned their use. The 1989 ban covered all beef—including meat imported from the United States, where growth-enhancing hormones were widely used. This decision was unquestionably influenced by concerns voiced by European farm and consumer groups and by the European Parliament.

What accounts for these differences? Some interpret the European actions as based in cultural attitudes, reflecting a lower tolerance for risk or less faith in the statements of scientists. They see such behavior as perfectly appropriate and laud this approach as sensitive to consumer concerns. To others, the ban on hormone use demonstrates flaws in the European decision-making process that hold it captive to agricultural and consumer interests. Critics also see the ban as a symptom of Europe's failure to persuade the public that government officials are able to guarantee food safety. Opinions about the US position are likewise divided. Some assert that the US decision was more influenced by scientific opinion and reflects a more optimistic view of new technologies; others claim that the US system has given producers' interests too much weight while downplaying consumers' worries about safety.

The "truth" remains elusive, but it is clear that their policies separate the Americans and Europeans almost as thoroughly as the Atlantic does. Europeans seek to carve out more scope for a "precautionary principle," the idea that products suspected but not proven to be hazardous can be prohibited or restricted. Americans seek to give greater weight to what has been proven by science. The beef hormones case is thus just one example of the more widespread problems caused by such policy differences within a trading system, problems that are also manifest in the case on genetically modified organisms (GMOs).

Trade Rules

Even if all border barriers are removed, divergent regulations can still impede trade. Indeed, sometimes countries deliberately craft their regulations to protect domestic producers. It is quite natural, therefore, that those concerned with facilitating trade will try to develop mechanisms to deal with the problems created by regulatory diversity. One approach is harmonization: fashioning a single standard agreed on by the trading countries. This option is attractive because it reduces transaction and information costs—but one size may not fit all. Adopting a single international standard may sacrifice the benefits of tailoring rules to local conditions; moreover, deciding which standard should be accepted is itself a knotty problem. An alternative approach is mutual recognition of standards, which the European Union relies on for many regulations. Under this principle, if a product satisfies the regulations of one member state, it can be sold in all members' markets. Mutual recognition avoids the negotiations involved in choosing one standard, but it requires considerable trust in regulations made in other countries. A third approach is tolerance of diversity in regulations so long as they are subject to certain disciplines, such as agreements to follow established scientific standards and methods and commitments not to engage in discrimination simply to further domestic interests.

The SPS agreement in the WTO is a blend of the first and third options: under the SPS, harmonization is promoted and, absent harmonization, disciplines are imposed. The SPS encourages members to base "measures on international standards, guidelines or recommendations, where they exist" (Article 3.1). Indeed, if a country applies international standards, its measures will be presumed to be consistent with WTO rules and it will enjoy safe harbor from challenge. However, WTO member countries may also adopt higher levels of protection if such levels (1) can be scientifically justified or (2) are based on an assessment of risk following rules laid out in Article 5 of the agreement. In these cases, members are also expected to ensure that their measures are not more trade-restrictive than necessary and to avoid discriminating against the products of other members. The SPS agreement also allows a member to provisionally adopt protective measures when it lacks sufficient relevant scientific information to come to a judgment. According to Article 5.7, "In such circumstances, Members shall seek to obtain the additional information necessary for a more objective assessment of risk . . . within a reasonable period of time."

When the European Union decided to ban growth-promoting hormones in the 1980s, the United States tried to bring a challenge at the

GATT under the SPS code that had been negotiated in the Tokyo Round. But since the GATT system required unanimity for the case to proceed, the European Community was able to use its veto power to block the action. The United States also sought to have hormones declared safe at the Codex Alimentarius Commission—the international body responsible for setting food standards—but failed to win enough votes. Stymied, the United States unilaterally imposed sanctions on European exports, but Europe refused to back down.

Because the dispute continued in the 1990s, it allows us to explore the differences and similarities in dispute settlement under the GATT and the WTO. When the United States brought the case under the WTO's DSU, the European Union was unable to stop it, because the new system had a reverse consensus rule: It required unanimity to *prevent* a case from being heard. Therefore, the WTO was able to make a ruling on the dispute; its panel found that Europe had indeed violated the SPS agreement. When Europe failed to come into compliance, the United States was authorized to retaliate against European exports deemed to be of equivalent value to the beef exports it had lost.

In some respects, the WTO has made a difference. It has allowed the case to be heard and for the rules to be clarified through the dispute settlement process. Instead of resorting to unilateral and potentially arbitrary retaliation as in the 1980s, when it had acted as prosecutor, judge, and executioner, in the 1990s the United States was validated by an impartial panel and its retaliation made subject to multilateral scrutiny. On the other hand, Europe continued to maintain the ban. And thus in the end the WTO, like the GATT, was unable to achieve compliance. However, some note that the ruling discouraged other WTO members from banning the hormones in question or US beef.

Noncompliance

A particularly interesting feature of the US-EU clash is that the European Union signed the Uruguay Round agreement despite refusing to follow its requirements under the SPS in the case of beef. Why would a member sign an agreement that it was actually violating? One explanation is that the two actions involved different decision makers. The Uruguay Round agreement was ratified by the European Council of Ministers, most of whom are foreign and trade ministers. In contrast, the ban on beef hormones reflected the views of the European Parliament, which is far more concerned about public health than trade, and of agricultural ministers, who placed a high value on internal integration under a single rule. Indeed, since national governments are ultimately responsible for food safety, the ban could have been reinstituted in some countries but not in others, thereby interfering with the operation of the internal market.

A second explanation is simply that Europe was outmaneuvered. When Europe signed the SPS agreement in 1993, there was no Codex standard on the hormones in question and thus European countries may have felt that their regulations were justified. Only when they lost the vote at Codex in 1995 was the EU case fundamentally weakened. The efforts by the United States to elevate the role of Codex were, in fact, a classic example of a strategy to "change the game." Unable to win the battle through negotiation and dispute resolution efforts aimed at the *substance* of the issues, the United States sought to alter the *process* through which decisions were made. But even though it succeeded in that attempt, the resulting changes in the process did not then lead to a "win," since the European Union continued to refuse imports of US hormone-treated beef.

The continued failure to reach a settlement in part reflects the zero-sum nature of the dispute and the strength of the coalitions on each side. These factors are examples of structural barriers to negotiated agreement. In addition, eliminating the ban would be extremely costly from a political standpoint, given the pervasive public concerns in Europe about food safety. This political bind is an example of an institutional barrier to agreement.

Further complicating the institutional picture, national governments in Europe also regulate food safety; and, as noted above, if the ban were lifted at the European level, some national governments would probably keep the ban in place. Producers in some countries might gain a competitive advantage over those in others, and beef produced in some countries could be banned in others. Thus, Europe is faced with choosing between a unified single market and WTO compliance.

As an alternative to lifting the ban, Europe can come into compliance by meeting the regulatory requirements for justifying the ban. It has attempted to do so; and in 2005 the European Union brought a case at the WTO seeking the elimination of US retaliation on the grounds that it had complied. On the other side, the United States can agree to sell non-hormone-treated beef to Europe. But this decision would mean abandoning the case as a precedent for ensuring that regulation is based on science, something the United States has been unwilling to do. Concerns about precedents and the resulting linkages to future negotiations are further examples of structural barriers to agreement.

How should we view the outcome? As this is being written, the EU ban on hormone-treated beef and the US retaliation remain in place. From one vantage point, the result is disappointing: A member of the WTO has refused to comply with the organization's rulings. In addition, the parties have failed to reach a compromise settlement that might have involved reducing other European trade barriers or allowing US beef to be sold with a distinctive label. On the other hand, the United States has been legally authorized to suspend concessions of equivalent value—thus gaining what some might regard as a form of compensation. In addition, the European Union has not been compelled to alter its regulations in an area in which change would be politically costly. Indeed, one could imagine Europeans being driven to reevaluate the benefits of WTO membership if the organization actually tried to ramp up the sanctions on the European Union to force compliance. In this sense, the continuing impasse has operated as a safety valve. De jure, Europe is obliged to come into compliance, but de facto, it faces no additional measures beyond the US retaliation. The outcome thus falls between the Scylla of the European Union's adopting a regulation that undermines the WTO's legitimacy in Europe and the Charybdis of an escalating trade war.

Appendix 1A
Timeline of Key Events in the Beef Hormones Case

Date	Event
1979	The United States bans diethylstilbestrol (DES) but allows other hormones.
1979–80	Europe experiences hormone scares.
1980	The BEUC, a European consumer group, mobilizes against beef from cattle treated with growth-promoting hormones.
1981	The European Commission establishes the Lamming Group to determine if the use of growth-promoting hormones endangers human health.
1982	The Lamming Group's interim report concludes that the three natural hormones studied "would not present any harmful effects to the health of the consumer when used under the appropriate conditions."
1985	The European Parliament passes a resolution supporting a ban on all growth-promoting hormones.
	The European Council of Ministers bans all beef from cattle treated with growth-promoting hormones. The ban is scheduled to go into effect in 1988.
	The Lamming Group is disbanded, but some of the scientists in it independently publish the group's findings on the safety of the remaining hormones in question in 1987.
	A new Codex Alimentarius group to study hormones is created, the Codex Committee on Residues of Veterinary Drugs in Food, with an FDA regulator as its chair.
1986	A group of European hormone manufacturers form their own lobby (FEDESA) and launch a campaign against the ban. FEDESA challenges the ban at the European Court of Justice, which upholds it in 1990.
1987	The Uruguay Round of trade talks begins. The United States hopes it will be "the agriculture round."
	The United States lodges a complaint against the ban at the GATT, but it is blocked by the EC. Europe extends the implementation date of the ban from January 1988 to January 1989.

Date	Event
	To forestall congressional action, the Reagan administration threatens section 301 action against Europe over the beef hormones issue.
1988	JECFA concludes that residues of four of the growth-promoting hormones do not create a safety hazard to humans, provided that proper veterinary practice was followed; later, the same findings are released for the fifth.
	The ban on the use of hormones in Europe goes into effect.
	The European press reports illegal use of hormones and a growing black market.
1989	The ban on trade in beef from cattle treated with hormones goes into effect, and the United States imposes $100 million in sanctions against Europe.
	The United States and Europe create the Hormone Task Force.
	Europe advocates for hormone-free beef imports.
	Texas Agriculture Commissioner Jim Hightower offers to sell hormone-free beef to Europe, but is discouraged by the US Department of Agriculture.
1991	The United States loses a public Codex vote to adopt standards for four of the hormones used in beef production, based on the JECFA evaluation. The Codex Committee on General Principles is asked to consider "the status of science in Codex."
1993	The SPS agreement becomes part of the Uruguay Round of GATT negotiations and Codex is given a major role in setting international health standards for food.
1995	Codex votes by secret ballot to adopt the JECFA MRLs on growth-promoting hormones.
1996	The United States brings a WTO case against Europe over the beef ban.
	The United States brings a WTO case against Europe over bananas.

(timeline continues next page)

Timeline of Key Events   *(continued)*

Date	Event
	The European Commission bans all exports of British beef after mad cow disease spreads through British herds.
1997	The United States wins its WTO beef case and Europe and appeals the ruling.
1998	A WTO appellate body upholds the ruling on the beef case. Europe requests four years to implement it. A WTO arbiter allows only 15 months.
1999	Europe does not lift the ban by the imposed deadline. The United States imposes $117 million in sanctions, as authorized by the WTO.
	US and EU scientists meet at the National Institute of Health in the United States, but no resolution is reached on the hormones issue.
	French farmers target McDonald's, and Jose Bové is jailed.
2000	The European Union wins the FSC case against the United States at the WTO.
	Carousel legislation passes in the US Congress. Both the Clinton and Bush administrations ignore the law.
2003	Europe revises its position on five of its six hormones, making the bans "provisional," and notifies the WTO that it is now in compliance.
2004	The European Communities request WTO consultations, arguing that the United States should remove its retaliatory measures related to the beef hormone case.
2005	The WTO establishes a panel.

Appendix 1B
The WTO Panel Process

At all stages of dispute resolution in the WTO (figure 1B.1), the countries involved are encouraged to consult each other in order to settle "out of court." At all stages, the WTO director-general is available to offer his good offices, to mediate, or to help achieve conciliation.

Figure 1B.1   WTO dispute settlement procedure

60 days	**Consultations** (Article 4)	**During all stages** good offices, conciliation, or mediation (Article 5)
	↓	
	Panel established by Dispute Settlement Body (DSB) (Article 6)	
By 2nd DSB meeting	↓	Note: A panel can be composed (i.e., panelists
0–20 days for terms of reference	**Terms of Reference** (Article 7) **Composition** (Article 8)	chosen) up to about 50 days after its establishment (i.e., DSB's
0–20 days for composition (+10 if the director-general is asked to pick the panel)	**Panel examination:** Normally two meetings with parties (Article 12) and one meeting with third parties (Article 10)	decision to have a panel)
		→ **Expert review group** (Article 13; Appendix 4)
	Interim review stage: Descriptive part of report sent to parties for comment (Article 15.1). Interim report sent to parties for comment (Article 15.2)	→ **Review meeting with panel** upon request (Article 15.2)
6 months from panel's composition, 3 months if urgent	**Panel report** issued to parties (Article 12.9; Appendix 3, part 12(j))	
Up to 9 months from panel's establishment	**Panel report** circulated to DSB (Article 12.9; Appendix 3, part 12(k))	→ **Appellate review** (Articles 16.4 and 17) maximum 90 days
60 days for panel report, unless appealed	**DSB adopts panel/appellate report[s]** including any changes to panel report made by appellate report (Articles 16.1, 16.4, and 17.14)	30 days for appellate report
"Reasonable period of time" determined by: member proposes, DSB agrees; or parties in dispute agree; or arbitra- tor (approx. 15 months if by arbitrator)	**Implementation report** by losing part of proposed implementation within a "reasonable period of time" (Article 21.3)	**Possibility of proceedings** including referral to the initial panel on proposed implementation (Article 21.5)
	In cases of nonimplementation parties negotiate compensation pending full implementation (Article 22.2)	
30 days after "reasonable period" expires	**Retaliation** if no agreement on compensation, DSB authorizes retaliation pending full imple- mentation (Articles 22.2 and 22.6). **Cross-retaliation** same sector, other sectors, other agreements (Article 22.3)	**Possibility of arbitration** on level of suspension procedures and principles of retaliation (Articles 22.6 and 22.7)

Source: WTO (1999, 42).

Appendix 1C
WTO Agreement on the Application of Sanitary and Phytosanitary Measures (1994), Selected Articles

Members,

Reaffirming that no Member should be prevented from adopting or enforcing measures necessary to protect human, animal or plant life or health, subject to the requirement that these measures are not applied in a manner which would constitute a means of arbitrary or unjustifiable discrimination between Members where the same conditions prevail or a disguised restriction on international trade;

Desiring to improve the human health, animal health and phytosanitary situation in all Members;

Noting that sanitary and phytosanitary measures are often applied on the basis of bilateral agreements or protocols;

Desiring the establishment of a multilateral framework of rules and disciplines to guide the development, adoption and enforcement of sanitary and phytosanitary measures in order to minimize their negative effects on trade;

Recognizing the important contribution that international standards, guidelines and recommendations can make in this regard;

Desiring to further the use of harmonized sanitary and phytosanitary measures between Members, on the basis of international standards, guidelines and recommendations developed by the relevant international organizations, including the Codex Alimentarius Commission, the International Office of Epizootics, and the relevant international and regional organizations operating within the framework of the International Plant Protection Convention, without requiring Members to change their appropriate level of protection of human, animal or plant life or health;

Recognizing that developing country Members may encounter special difficulties in complying with the sanitary or phytosanitary measures of importing Members, and as a consequence in access to markets, and also in the formulation and application of sanitary or phytosanitary measures in their own territories, and desiring to assist them in their endeavors in this regard;

Desiring therefore to elaborate rules for the application of the provisions of GATT 1994 which relate to the use of sanitary or phytosanitary measures, in particular the provisions of Article XX(b); [1]

Hereby agree as follows:

---

1. In this Agreement, reference to Article XX(b) includes also the chapeau of that Article.

Article 1
General Provisions

1. This Agreement applies to all sanitary and phytosanitary measures which may, directly or indirectly, affect international trade. Such measures shall be developed and applied in accordance with the provisions of this Agreement.
2. For the purposes of this Agreement, the definitions provided in Annex A shall apply.
3. The annexes are an integral part of this Agreement.
4. Nothing in this Agreement shall affect the rights of Members under the Agreement on Technical Barriers to Trade with respect to measures not within the scope of this Agreement.

Article 2
Basic Rights and Obligations

1. Members have the right to take sanitary and phytosanitary measures necessary for the protection of human, animal or plant life or health, provided that such measures are not inconsistent with the provisions of this Agreement.
2. Members shall ensure that any sanitary or phytosanitary measure is applied only to the extent necessary to protect human, animal or plant life or health, is based on scientific principles and is not maintained without sufficient scientific evidence, except as provided for in paragraph 7 of Article 5.
3. Members shall ensure that their sanitary and phytosanitary measures do not arbitrarily or unjustifiably discriminate between Members where identical or similar conditions prevail, including between their own territory and that of other Members. Sanitary and phytosanitary measures shall not be applied in a manner which would constitute a disguised restriction on international trade.
4. Sanitary or phytosanitary measures which conform to the relevant provisions of this Agreement shall be presumed to be in accordance with the obligations of the Members under the provisions of GATT 1994 which relate to the use of sanitary or phytosanitary measures, in particular the provisions of Article XX(b).

Article 3
Harmonization

1. To harmonize sanitary and phytosanitary measures on as wide a basis as possible, Members shall base their sanitary or phytosanitary measures on international standards, guidelines or recommendations, where they exist, except as otherwise provided for in this Agreement, and in particular in paragraph 3.

2. Sanitary or phytosanitary measures which conform to international standards, guidelines or recommendations shall be deemed to be necessary to protect human, animal or plant life or health, and presumed to be consistent with the relevant provisions of this Agreement and of GATT 1994.

3. Members may introduce or maintain sanitary or phytosanitary measures which result in a higher level of sanitary or phytosanitary protection than would be achieved by measures based on the relevant international standards, guidelines or recommendations, if there is a scientific justification, or as a consequence of the level of sanitary or phytosanitary protection a Member determines to be appropriate in accordance with the relevant provisions of paragraphs 1 through 8 of Article 5.[2] Notwithstanding the above, all measures which result in a level of sanitary or phytosanitary protection different from that which would be achieved by measures based on international standards, guidelines or recommendations shall not be inconsistent with any other provision of this Agreement.

4. Members shall play a full part, within the limits of their resources, in the relevant international organizations and their subsidiary bodies, in particular the Codex Alimentarius Commission, the International Office of Epizootics, and the international and regional organizations operating within the framework of the International Plant Protection Convention, to promote within these organizations the development and periodic review of standards, guidelines and recommendations with respect to all aspects of sanitary and phytosanitary measures.

5. The Committee on Sanitary and Phytosanitary Measures provided for in paragraphs 1 and 4 of Article 12 (referred to in this Agreement as the "Committee") shall develop a procedure to monitor the process of international harmonization and coordinate efforts in this regard with the relevant international organizations.

Article 5
Assessment of Risk and Determination of the Appropriate Level of Sanitary or Phytosanitary Protection

1. Members shall ensure that their sanitary or phytosanitary measures are based on an assessment, as appropriate to the circumstances, of the risks to human, animal or plant life or health, taking into account risk assessment techniques developed by the relevant international organizations.

2. In the assessment of risks, Members shall take into account available scientific evidence; relevant processes and production methods; relevant

---

2. For the purposes of paragraph 3 of Article 3, there is a scientific justification if, on the basis of an examination and evaluation of available scientific information in conformity with the relevant provisions of this Agreement, a Member determines that the relevant international standards, guidelines or recommendations are not sufficient to achieve its appropriate level of sanitary or phytosanitary protection.

inspection, sampling and testing methods; prevalence of specific diseases or pests; existence of pest- or disease-free areas; relevant ecological and environmental conditions; and quarantine or other treatment.

3. In assessing the risk to animal or plant life or health and determining the measure to be applied for achieving the appropriate level of sanitary or phytosanitary protection from such risk, Members shall take into account as relevant economic factors: the potential damage in terms of loss of production or sales in the event of the entry, establishment or spread of a pest or disease; the costs of control or eradication in the territory of the importing Member; and the relative cost-effectiveness of alternative approaches to limiting risks.

4. Members should, when determining the appropriate level of sanitary or phytosanitary protection, take into account the objective of minimizing negative trade effects.

5. With the objective of achieving consistency in the application of the concept of appropriate level of sanitary or phytosanitary protection against risks to human life or health, or to animal and plant life or health, each Member shall avoid arbitrary or unjustifiable distinctions in the levels it considers to be appropriate in different situations, if such distinctions result in discrimination or a disguised restriction on international trade. Members shall cooperate in the Committee, in accordance with paragraphs 1, 2 and 3 of Article 12, to develop guidelines to further the practical implementation of this provision. In developing the guidelines, the Committee shall take into account all relevant factors, including the exceptional character of human health risks to which people voluntarily expose themselves.

6. Without prejudice to paragraph 2 of Article 3, when establishing or maintaining sanitary or phytosanitary measures to achieve the appropriate level of sanitary or phytosanitary protection, Members shall ensure that such measures are not more trade-restrictive than required to achieve their appropriate level of sanitary or phytosanitary protection, taking into account technical and economic feasibility.[3]

7. In cases where relevant scientific evidence is insufficient, a Member may provisionally adopt sanitary or phytosanitary measures on the basis of available pertinent information, including that from the relevant international organizations as well as from sanitary or phytosanitary measures applied by other Members. In such circumstances, Members shall seek to obtain the additional information necessary for a more objective assessment of risk and review the sanitary or phytosanitary measure accordingly within a reasonable period of time.

---

3. For purposes of paragraph 6 of Article 5, a measure is not more trade-restrictive than required unless there is another measure, reasonably available taking into account technical and economic feasibility, that achieves the appropriate level of sanitary or phytosanitary protection and is significantly less restrictive to trade.

8. When a Member has reason to believe that a specific sanitary or phytosanitary measure introduced or maintained by another Member is constraining, or has the potential to constrain, its exports and the measure is not based on the relevant international standards, guidelines or recommendations, or such standards, guidelines or recommendations do not exist, an explanation of the reasons for such sanitary or phytosanitary measure may be requested and shall be provided by the Member maintaining the measure.

Annex A
Definitions[4]

1. *Sanitary or phytosanitary measure*—Any measure applied:
    (a) to protect animal or plant life or health within the territory of the Member from risks arising from the entry, establishment or spread of pests, diseases, disease-carrying organisms or disease-causing organisms;
    (b) to protect human or animal life or health within the territory of the Member from risks arising from additives, contaminants, toxins or disease-causing organisms in foods, beverages or feedstuffs;
    (c) to protect human life or health within the territory of the Member from risks arising from diseases carried by animals, plants or products thereof, or from the entry, establishment or spread of pests; or
    (d) to prevent or limit other damage within the territory of the Member from the entry, establishment or spread of pests.

Sanitary or phytosanitary measures include all relevant laws, decrees, regulations, requirements and procedures including, *inter alia*, end product criteria; processes and production methods; testing, inspection, certification and approval procedures; quarantine treatments including relevant requirements associated with the transport of animals or plants, or with the materials necessary for their survival during transport; provisions on relevant statistical methods, sampling procedures and methods of risk assessment; and packaging and labelling requirements directly related to food safety.

2. *Harmonization*—The establishment, recognition and application of common sanitary and phytosanitary measures by different Members.

3. *International standards, guidelines and recommendations*
    (a) for food safety, the standards, guidelines and recommendations established by the Codex Alimentarius Commission relating to food additives, veterinary drug and pesticide residues, contaminants, methods of analysis and sampling, and codes and guidelines of hygienic practice;

---

4. For the purpose of these definitions, "animal" includes fish and wild fauna; "plant" includes forests and wild flora; "pests" include weeds; and "contaminants" include pesticide and veterinary drug residues and extraneous matter.

(b) for animal health and zoonoses, the standards, guidelines and recommendations developed under the auspices of the International Office of Epizootics;

(c) for plant health, the international standards, guidelines and recommendations developed under the auspices of the Secretariat of the International Plant Protection Convention in cooperation with regional organizations operating within the framework of the International Plant Protection Convention; and

(d) for matters not covered by the above organizations, appropriate standards, guidelines and recommendations promulgated by other relevant international organizations open for membership to all Members, as identified by the Committee.

4. *Risk assessment*—The evaluation of the likelihood of entry, establishment or spread of a pest or disease within the territory of an importing Member according to the sanitary or phytosanitary measures which might be applied, and of the associated potential biological and economic consequences; or the evaluation of the potential for adverse effects on human or animal health arising from the presence of additives, contaminants, toxins or disease-causing organisms in food, beverages or feedstuffs.

5. *Appropriate level of sanitary or phytosanitary protection*—The level of protection deemed appropriate by the Member establishing a sanitary or phytosanitary measure to protect human, animal or plant life or health within its territory.

NOTE: Many Members otherwise refer to this concept as the "acceptable level of risk."

6. *Pest- or disease-free area*—An area, whether all of a country, part of a country, or all or parts of several countries, as identified by the competent authorities, in which a specific pest or disease does not occur.

NOTE: A pest- or disease-free area may surround, be surrounded by, or be adjacent to an area—whether within part of a country or in a geographic region which includes parts of or all of several countries—in which a specific pest or disease is known to occur but is subject to regional control measures such as the establishment of protection, surveillance and buffer zones which will confine or eradicate the pest or disease in question.

7. *Area of low pest or disease prevalence*—An area, whether all of a country, part of a country, or all or parts of several countries, as identified by the competent authorities, in which a specific pest or disease occurs at low levels and which is subject to effective surveillance, control or eradication measures.

Banana Wars: Challenges to the European Union's Banana Regime

In April 1999, a six-year-old dispute between the United States and the European Union over the latter's banana import policies erupted into a trade war. The European banana trade policies had been under attack since 1993, when the European Union instituted its first single-market agricultural regime. According to the European Union, the banana regime, which granted preferential treatment to fruit imported from former colonies, was necessary to honor existing trade obligations to the ex-colonies and to help them to compete against the cheaper Latin American bananas that dominated the world marketplace. But according to the United States and a group of Central and South American banana-producing countries, the complex import system discriminated against Latin American bananas and US and Latin American distribution companies in violation of international trade rules.

Latin American banana growers brought the first challenges against the regime. But by 1994, following a request by the US multinational Chiquita Brands International, Inc. and the Hawaii Banana Industry Association, the Office of the United States Trade Representative (USTR) had entered the fray, ultimately bringing the case before the recently formed World Trade Organization (WTO). The resultant WTO ruling favoring the United

Banana Wars: Challenges to the European Union's Banana Regime is an edited and revised version of the case with the same name originally written by Susan Rosegrant, a case writer at the Case Program at the John F. Kennedy School of Government. For copies or permission to reproduce the unabridged case please refer to www.ksgcase.harvard.edu or send a written request to Case Program, John F. Kennedy School of Government, Harvard University, 79 John F. Kennedy Street, Cambridge, MA 02138.

States and its Latin American allies did not end the dispute, however. When the European Union adopted a modified regime in 1998, US and Latin American critics insisted that the new version was no better than the old. The European Union's continued refusal to discuss further changes led to threats of US retaliation, followed by EU countercharges that US actions were themselves a violation of international trade rules. In April 1999, immediately after two simultaneous WTO rulings backing the US position, the United States brought punitive tariffs against almost $200 million in EU exports.

The sanctions did not bring a quick or easy resolution. Over the next two years, as the United States and the European Union struggled to reach a settlement, the banana dispute became intertwined with other trade disagreements, and political repercussions, both domestic and international, grew. The uproar raised questions about international obligations, interpretations of WTO dispute settlement mechanisms, and even whether the banana dispute was a case the United States ever should have fought at all.

A Fruit of Historic Importance

That policies regulating banana imports could be both so complex and apparently worth fighting for was actually not surprising, given the economic and political importance of the fruit within the European Union and throughout the developing world. Although each country had a different set of interests at stake, for most EU members, bananas had taken on a significance that went beyond a mere agricultural commodity.

The banana industry itself was unusual, having evolved to include just a handful of major companies that operated with a high degree of vertical integration. Because the fruit was so fragile, not only easily damaged by bad weather and disease while growing but also extremely perishable after harvest, the pioneers of the banana trade—particularly in Latin America—had become experts in the entire process, from preparing the land, managing the workers, and growing the fruit to transporting the time-sensitive cargo from equatorial growing regions to key consumer markets in Europe, the United States, and Asia. With banana landholdings in some cases dating back to the 1800s, capital-intensive communications and transportation networks already in place, and marketing relationships well-established, a mere six companies had come to dominate the industry. In addition to the US multinationals Chiquita Brands International and Dole Food Co., Inc., the industry's lead companies were Geest Ltd. of the United Kingdom and Fyffes Ltd. of Ireland, Ecuador's Noboa Group, and Fresh Del Monte Produce, Inc., also of the United States.

In contrast with the relatively straightforward framework supporting the production of bananas, the fruit's distribution and marketing in some instances had become intertwined with political and economic agendas.

Colonial powers such as Britain and France, for example, had encouraged banana production in certain of their Caribbean and African colonies for decades, in part so that they would not to have to rely on imports of the Latin American "dollar bananas" sold by the dominant US multinationals, Chiquita and Dole.[1] After the colonies became independent, they continued to get special access for their bananas under the Lomé Convention, an agreement forged in 1975 whereby what is now the European Union provided aid, duty-free access, and other forms of commercial assistance to its African, Caribbean, and Pacific (ACP) former colonies.[2] EU representatives say that such support was necessary, because the 12 traditional banana-producing ACP countries could not grow the fruit as cheaply as their Latin American counterparts or compete effectively in the open market.[3] The trade with ACP countries was substantial, making up about 20 percent of the EU banana market.

Other EU members had very different concerns, however. Some countries had their own banana production to protect, and did not want cheaper imports to harm domestic growers and traders. Such domestic production supplied almost another 20 percent of EU consumption. Still other countries wanted banana imports to be entirely free of restrictions. For example, Germany, one of the world's leaders in per capita banana consumption and the largest consumer of the fruit in the European Union, saw bananas as a symbol of postwar prosperity and rejected all barriers to its free trade.[4] By 1992, the strong demand for dollar bananas in Germany and other more northern European nations had given Latin American bananas a 60 percent share of the total EU market, thereby helping to propel them to a 67 percent share of the world market (see table 2.1 for banana exports by country in 1991 and 1992).

A jumble of trade measures had resulted from these varied priorities. Spain allowed no imports, relying on domestic production from the Canary Islands. France bought most of its bananas from its territories of Guadeloupe and Martinique, and also gave special preference to Côte d'Ivoire and Cameroon, its former colonies. The United Kingdom was essentially closed to Latin American bananas, buying instead from its former colonies, Jamaica, the Windward Islands, Belize, and Suriname. By

---

1. Central and South American bananas became known as "dollar bananas" because historically most were produced and marketed by US companies.

2. As of 1998, there were 70 ACP members. Between 1967 and 1993, the European Union (the name used here throughout, for convenience) was known as the European Community.

3. The main suppliers of ACP bananas to the European Union were Cameroon, Côte d'Ivoire, St. Lucia, Jamaica, Belize, and Dominica. Principal Latin American banana suppliers were Costa Rica, Ecuador, Colombia, Panama, and Honduras.

4. As chancellor, Helmut Kohl brought bunches of bananas with him to the former East Germany during the postreunification campaign as a sign of the wealth he pledged to bring to the recently united country.

Table 2.1 World trade in bananas: Exports, 1991–92

Region	Volume (thousands of metric tons)				Value (millions of dollars)			
	1991	Percent of total	1992	Percent of total	1991	Percent of total	1992	Percent of total
World	10,513	100	10,765	100	3,110	100	3,122	100
Latin America	8,036	77	8,188	76	2,132	69	2,089	69
Ecuador	2,714	26	2,557	24	716	23	655	21
Costa Rica	1,550	15	1,769	16	384	12	495	16
Colombia	1,473	14	1,500	14	405	13	400	13
Honduras	727	7	800	7	315	10	203	7
Panama	707	7	719	7	87	3	91	3
Guatemala	378	4	446	4	85	3	113	4
Mexico	238	2	180	2	81	3	84	3
Other	249	2	217	2	59	2	48	2
ACP	612	6	715	7	291	9	312	10
European Union	176	2	210	2	121	4	139	4
EU territories	241	2	301	3	117	4	165	5
United States	356	3	378	4	198	6	190	6
Asia (non-ACP)	1,087	10	970	9	250	8	226	7
All other	5	0	3	0	1	0	1	0

ACP = African, Caribbean, and Pacific countries

Note: Percentage figures may not add to 100 percent because of rounding.

Source: UNCTAD, *Commodity Yearbook*, 1994.

contrast, Germany, with no banana-producing former colonies and no domestic production, had no tariffs or restrictions on imports, and Belgium, Denmark, Luxembourg, Ireland, and the Netherlands imposed only a 20 percent tariff on Latin American bananas.

Strong consumer preferences that had developed over time further reinforced these historic trading patterns. Although most of the imports were the same species—Cavendish bananas—those from the Caribbean were generally more curved and smaller than dollar bananas, often half the size. Caribbean bananas were the favored fruit of the average British shopper, who claimed that their diminutive size made them cheaper on a per banana basis and easier to slip into a lunchbox. But German consumers preferred dollar bananas, and most German grocers stocked only the larger, more uniform fruit.

In 1992, as the European Union prepared to institute a single market for trade the following year, representatives of the 12 EU members met to transform the fragmented set of trade arrangements into a unified banana regime.[5] Because the banana trade system was so controversial, it was the last item addressed. Not surprisingly, given the mix of concerns involved, negotiations within the European Commission (the European Union's executive body and the lead agency in this effort) dragged on for months, with particular clashes between Germany's free trade position and the insistence of France and Britain on honoring the Lomé Convention—the agreement designed, in part, to increase trade between ACP countries and the European Union by providing preferential access to ACP products.

In fact, the Fourth Lomé Convention, signed in December 1989, had included a separate banana protocol providing a guarantee by the European Union on behalf of its member states that ACP banana exporters would not be harmed by the shift from member-state regimes to a single market regime. Countries such as France and Britain, though, claimed a sense of responsibility toward their former colonies that went beyond mere legal obligations to encompass an almost moral duty to protect them and ensure their economic stability.

As the debate in the European Union continued, Latin American and US interests closely followed the evolving negotiations. The European Union was the world's largest importer of bananas in 1992, purchasing about 48 percent of the more than $5 billion global total (for a breakdown of 1991–92 world banana imports by country, see table 2.2). If the European Union followed the German model, the new regime could be a bonanza for both the producers and the marketers of Latin American bananas, as significant new markets opened for trade. On the other hand, a system modeled on the British or French approach, imposing restrictive measures EU-wide, could prove devastating for the dollar banana industry.

Unfortunately for US and Latin American interests, the new regime announced in December 1992 favored the latter pattern. Known as Regulation 404 (in full, Regulation (EEC) 404/93), it created a complex system of quotas and licenses that, according to US and Latin American critics, constituted serious barriers to entry in violation of international trade regulations. As the different sides staked out their positions, it was clear that the trade policies would face serious opposition. Probably few predicted that six years later, the controversy over the EU banana regime would still be unresolved.

---

5. Since the end of World War II, the European Community had been gradually moving toward a single market that would allow the free movement of goods, services, people, and capital without regard to country borders. Agricultural policy was the final area to be negotiated.

Table 2.2   World trade in bananas: Imports, 1991–92

Region	Volume (thousands of metric tons)				Value (millions of dollars)			
	1991	Percent of total	1992	Percent of total	1991	Percent of total	1992	Percent of total
World	10,095	100	10,443	100	5,229	100	5,132	100
United States	3,382	34	3,690	35	1,234	24	1,339	26
European Union	3,798	37	3,976	38	2,571	48	2,487	48
Germany	1,355	13	1,378	13	853	16	784	15
United Kingdom	489	5	545	5	384	7	418	8
France	503	5	533	5	424	8	418	8
Italy	574	6	475	5	370	7	273	5
Belgium-Luxembourg	206	2	302	3	107	2	144	3
Netherlands	148	1	201	2	77	1	109	2
Other	523	5	542	5	356	7	341	7
Japan	803	8	777	7	466	9	523	10
Other Asia	687	7	618	6	347	7	249	5
Latin America	317	3	377	4	63	1	83	2
All other	1,108	11	1,005	10	548	10	451	9

Note: Percentage figures may not add to 100 percent because of rounding.

Source: UNCTAD, Commodity Yearbook, 1994.

Regulation 404

The European Union enacted Regulation 404 in July 1993, for the first time establishing a single European market for bananas. Within this extremely complex regulation, US and Latin American critics focused on certain key aspects.

To begin with, the regime broke the EU market into three distinct sectors: domestic production, ACP bananas from the former colonies, and "third country"—essentially Latin American—bananas.[6] The provisions on subsidies for domestic production were within reason, observers say,

---

6. The actual sector designations were slightly more complicated, including within the category of third-country bananas an allowance for "nontraditional" ACP bananas—that is, ACP bananas imported in excess of historical levels, as well as bananas imported from ACP members that were not traditional suppliers.

and did not spur significant external challenges.[7] But US and Latin American industry representatives charged that the regulations governing ACP and Latin American bananas were highly discriminatory. ACP bananas, like domestic bananas, faced no duty: The European Union gave each of the 12 countries its own duty-free tariff quota based on its best export year up to 1991. These individual quotas totaled 857,700 metric tons, US officials say, well above what the countries as a group had ever exported to the European Union in any given year.

Even more troubling from the US and Latin American perspective were the tariff-rate quota (TRQ, the application of a reduced tariff rate for a specified quantity of imported goods) and the licensing restrictions imposed on third-country bananas. To limit the supply of Latin American bananas, the European Union set the TRQ at 2 million metric tons, with a tariff of 75 European currency units (ECU) per metric ton for bananas brought in under the main quota, and 822 ECU per metric ton for bananas in excess of the quota.[8] Because the tariff rate for bananas imported in excess of the quota was so high, the TRQ effectively limited imports to 2 million metric tons a year. According to US trade officials, this level would not only end the average 9 percent annual growth that Latin American banana imports to the European Union had enjoyed over the previous decade but would freeze imports at a level well below Latin America's existing 60 percent share of the EU market. In 1992, for example, Latin American countries had shipped more than 2.4 million metric tons of bananas to the European Union.

And the TRQ was just the beginning. The chunk of the EU market set aside for Latin American bananas was further segmented by a complex licensing system that created three categories of licensed importers and gave each group a specific percentage of the Latin American TRQ. Category A operators—historical traders of Latin American bananas, such as Chiquita, Dole, and Ecuador's Noboa Group—were assigned 66.5 percent of the volume. Category B operators—historical importers of ACP and EU bananas—got 30 percent, and Category C operators, the newcomers, received 3.5 percent.

According to EU representatives, the different importer categories worked hand in hand with the TRQ, providing a necessary cross-subsidy to ensure that ACP bananas made it to market. Caribbean bananas—in part because many were grown on small farms, as opposed to the large mechanized plantations common in Latin America—cost much more to harvest (up to $500 a ton versus $160 a ton in Latin America). But by

---

7. Domestic producers faced no tariffs and no access limitations, and they received some compensation for loss of income resulting from price reductions due to the banana regime.

8. To accommodate market growth, the European Union later increased the TRQ to 2.1 million metric tons in 1994 and 2.2 million metric tons in 1995.

granting Category B operators a guaranteed percentage of the cheaper Latin American production, the theory went, these operators could afford to sell the higher-cost ACP bananas. Without this edge, EU representatives argued, the quotas and tariff alone were not enough to make trade in ACP bananas profitable.

But according to US and Ecuadorian banana traders, who had historically dominated Latin American banana exports to the European Union, ACP farmers were not the sole—or necessarily even the principal—beneficiaries of the plan. For one thing, distributors of bananas grown in EU countries received half of the Category B licenses. Moreover, because most Category B operators were EU firms, such as Ireland's Fyffes and the United Kingdom's Geest, the licensing system effectively handed over to these EU firms almost a third of the Latin American volume previously marketed by US and Ecuadorian or other Latin American companies.[9] It therefore deprived US multinationals like Chiquita, which had already had their European access cut by the quota, of an additional share of the market. "The European Union just wrapped itself in the flag of the ACP," says one US trade official. "You'd never know that they were doing anything for their own farmers or for their own companies."

Moreover, the new licensing regime had yet another layer of classification. The Category A and B operators were divided into three further subfunctions. Within both A and B, 57 percent of licenses went to "primary importers" (companies such as Fyffes and Chiquita); 15 percent went to "secondary importers" (smaller companies handling customs clearance within the European Union that might or might not be affiliated with one of the primary importers); and 28 percent went to ripeners.[10] Typically, a country imposed a quota by distributing licenses to importers based on historical trading patterns. But in the view of US trade officials, the European Union's licensing regime created entirely new categories of operators with no historic precedents. The only justification for the new categories, critics said, was to build EU support for the regime, particularly in countries such as Germany that lacked primary operators or producers who could benefit from the other licensing controls. German ripeners who suddenly had been granted licenses to import bananas, for example, could either expand their businesses into importing or sell the licenses to a company like Chiquita.

According to US trade estimates, the licensing changes automatically transferred about 50 percent of US companies' EU business to EU and ACP firms that had never before distributed Latin American bananas. "There is

---

9. Geest later sold its banana business to a consortium that included Fyffes and the Windward Islands Banana Development and Exporting Companies.

10. In the United States, large supermarkets usually ripened their own bananas; in Europe, many stores relied on designated ripeners who stored the green bananas until they were ready for market.

the feeling," said one US trade specialist, "that the EU agriculture people are incapable of doing anything that isn't discriminatory." A chart prepared by the USTR comparing the tariff, quota, and licensing arrangements for EU, ACP, and Latin American bananas, appeared to support the claim (see appendix figure 2A.1).

A paper funded and published by the World Bank in December 1994 was almost equally critical, maintaining that the EU regime cost EU consumers an estimated $2.3 billion a year; shoppers in countries such as Germany, where trade had been unrestricted, were particularly hard-hit (Borrell 1994). Moreover, most of the so-called quota rents—the excess profits generated as the result of higher prices paid by consumers and others due to the restrictions on competition imposed by a quota system—were flowing not to the ACP banana producers but to the EU firms that were marketing ACP bananas. Either EU policymakers did not understand the impact of their policies, the report concluded, or they intended to "protect (and expand) the vested interests of EU-based marketing companies. This group is clearly the main beneficiary of the policy. EU consumers, other marketers and Latin American suppliers are clearly big losers" (Borrell 1994).

International Reactions

The international community did not accept the new EU regime without a fight. Just months before the European Union enacted Regulation 404, five banana-producing Latin American countries brought a challenge in the General Agreement on Tariffs and Trade (GATT) against the banana regimes of several individual EU member states, charging that they violated international trade rules. By bringing the GATT challenge when they did, Colombia, Costa Rica, Guatemala, Nicaragua, and Venezuela hoped to increase their chances of winning a subsequent case against the soon-to-be-implemented single-market regime. In fact, in June 1993, before the first GATT panel had even ruled on the original complaint, the same countries requested a second panel to evaluate the new regime going into effect the following month.

The Latin American countries were vindicated. In July, the first panel ruled that the former regimes were GATT-incompatible; a few months later, the second panel found that Regulation 404 violated the GATT by, among other things, giving a preferential tariff to ACP countries, imposing a tariff quota on Latin American producers whose overquota rate was above the tariff level that had been negotiated, and imposing licensing requirements that discriminated against new traders. But this victory for the Latin American complainants brought them little satisfaction, for the rulings had no teeth. Because GATT proceedings required a consensus, it was always possible for a losing party in a trade dispute (in this case the European Union) to block adoption of a panel report, a limitation—and in the minds of some, a flaw—that often transformed GATT rulings into diplomatic tools rather than legal proceedings.

US companies had not participated directly in the two GATT challenges. According to industry sources, the Latin American complainants had not wanted direct US involvement, fearing it would transform the case into a US versus EU fight. Instead, representatives of Chiquita and Dole had worked as advisors, providing assistance and support to their Latin American suppliers behind the scenes.

The US multinationals were also busy at home. In the months before Regulation 404 took effect, representatives of both companies met quietly with officials at the Office of the USTR, the government agency responsible for developing and coordinating US international trade policy, to discuss the possibility of filing a section 301 case. Section 301, created by Congress as part of the 1974 Trade Act, provided a formal mechanism by which companies that felt they were being harmed by discriminatory trade practices could ask the US government to intervene. If an investigation found that a country had imposed unfair trade measures, the USTR had the power under US law to retaliate in an amount equivalent to the damage estimated to have been done to US commerce. Either the USTR or a company could initiate a section 301 case, but a company typically would not ask for an investigation unless the USTR had indicated that it would accept the case.

According to one industry source, however, the USTR, which accepted only about 14 cases a year, made it clear that it was not interested. "You had the reality of a trade complaint that didn't necessarily strike one as being crucial to American interests," he admits. In particular, he says, the fact that the United States was not exporting bananas meant the complaint was not "automatically recognizable as something that needed the immediate attention and action of USTR."

The Framework Agreement

Although the USTR had not filed a formal complaint when the European Union first enacted Regulation 404, USTR Mickey Kantor began to speak out against the banana regime in January 1994. Kantor was particularly concerned by news that the European Union was trying to negotiate an agreement with the Latin American GATT complainants that would settle the banana dispute and make it unlikely that they would bring future complaints against the regime.

In March 1994, as the United States had feared, the European Union and four of the five Latin American countries announced a new framework agreement (of the original petitioners, only Guatemala refused to take part). The agreement, which the European Union was to institute in January 1995, provided two important concessions to the Latin American signatories.[11] First, each of the four received a set percentage of the third-country quota: 23.4 percent for Costa Rica, 21 percent for Colombia, 3 percent for Nicaragua, and 2 percent for Venezuela. Taken together, these new quotas represented almost half of the third-country market and, according to US trade officials, gave these countries a disproportionate share of the quota. In fact, US officials estimated that the non-framework Latin American countries—Ecuador, Guatemala, Honduras, and Mexico—lost 27 percent of their access to the EU market because of the double whammy of Regulation 404 and the agreement.

Second, the agreement created a system of export certificates that essentially mirrored the import certificates on the other side of the ocean. Category B operators—traders that sold ACP or EU bananas—did not need them. But Category A operators such as Chiquita now had to obtain these export licenses, usually buying them either from local producers or from government offices, in order to be eligible for import licenses for the EU market.

The agreement addressed many of the complaints of the framework countries. The quotas provided guaranteed access to the EU market, and the special export certificates provided a new form of revenue for local producers, since producers who had been granted more certificates than they needed could sell them to outside traders like Chiquita. "The EU was not willing to adopt the recommendations of the GATT panel, but they knew that they had to do something," explains Irene Arguedas, minister counselor for economic affairs at the Embassy of Costa Rica in Washington, DC. "The Framework Agreement was the something they were willing to do."[12]

For a multinational marketer like Chiquita, however, the Framework Agreement was anathema. Panama, Honduras, and Guatemala, countries where Chiquita produced bananas, were expected to lose EU market share because they had no guaranteed quotas. In addition, the country-specific quotas and need for export certificates made it impossible for Chiquita to optimize the performance of the larger shipping fleet it had recently launched by buying from whichever country was the lowest-cost provider at any given time. Finally, the company feared that independent producers in the framework countries would receive a disproportionate share of the licenses, forcing Chiquita to buy extra export certificates, just as it had had to invest in extra import licenses for Europe.

"What you have here is something that was discriminatory to begin with, and then each new level of discrimination gets added as the Euro-

---

11. Although no formal investigation was ever conducted, some US trade officials believed that the European Union had bribed Latin American representatives to ensure their cooperation with the agreement.

12. Unless otherwise noted, all quotes from Irene Arguedas are from a December 1998 interview with the author.

pean Union seeks to pay off another constituent," says a USTR official. "We realize it has difficult domestic problems, but they can't be handled at the expense of its WTO obligations." A US banana industry representative agrees. "The Framework Agreement obviously imposed an additional obligation in terms of coming up with the special export certificates that had to match the licenses granted in Europe," he notes. "To the extent that a company had lots of licenses in Europe and an imbalance in the amount of export certificates they obtained, they were terribly hurt by that. That's what happened with Chiquita."

US Section 301

Dole Food, like Chiquita, had opposed Regulation 404 from the start. Even as Dole spoke out against the new regime, though, it was positioning itself to operate within its constraints. After Regulation 404 was adopted, the company invested in banana production in Africa and the Canary Islands and formed joint ventures with EU importers, thereby qualifying as a Category B importer of ACP bananas and marketer of EU fruit. Dole also bought ripeners in Europe to qualify for an additional share of import licenses. Dole's preferred status thus allowed it to avoid many of the most restrictive aspects of the regime.

Chiquita, in contrast, was not well-positioned financially to undertake such diversification, despite its long history of industry leadership. The company's predecessor, United Fruit Company Limited (established in 1899), had been a dominant—and controversial—presence in Latin America throughout much of the twentieth century, with an unprecedented degree of economic and political clout that extended through Guatemala, Honduras, Costa Rica, Panama, Colombia, and Ecuador. By the middle of the century, United Fruit owned more than 1.7 million acres of land in Latin America. Its 1955 net profits of $33 million were greater than the central government revenues of Honduras, and it was bigger than any other single landowner, company, or corporate employer of labor in Guatemala, Honduras, or Costa Rica.[13]

The company's fortunes remained strong over the next few decades. A new owner had renamed the company United Brands in 1970 and multimillionaire businessman Carl Lindner bought a controlling share in 1984, changing the name to Chiquita Brands International five years later.[14] Chairman and CEO Lindner changed the company's direction as well, adopting a new, more aggressive strategy. During the 1980s, the company

---

13. For more information on Chiquita's history, see Mulligan (1999).

14. Lindner's holding company, American Financial Group, Inc., acquired a majority interest, and Lindner later moved the company to Cincinnati.

Table 2.3 World banana prices, 1985–92
(dollars per metric ton)

Year	Current	Constant, 1990
1985	378	551
1986	382	472
1987	393	442
1988	478	502
1989	547	578
1990	541	541
1991	560	548
1992	473	444

Note: Data refer to Central and South American first-class quality tropical pack of bananas, importer's price to jobber or processor, f.o.b. US ports.

Sources: World Bank, *Price Prospects for Major Primary Commodities, 1990–2005,* including *Quarterly Review of Commodity Markets,* third and fourth quarters 1992; *Commodity Markets and the Developing Countries: A World Bank Quarterly,* May 1996; *Commodity Price Data,* July 1996 (see also www.worldbank.org/pink.html); and US Bureau of Labor Statistics.

divested its Caribbean holdings, decreased banana production, and diversified into other crops. Heading into the 1990s, however, Lindner instead increased Chiquita's land under cultivation and made major investments in new shipping capacity, apparently with the expectation that the European Union would adopt an open banana regime and that the emerging Eastern European market would greatly boost demand for the company's dollar bananas.

At first, Lindner's strategy looked sound. In 1990 and 1991, Chiquita's fresh food sales grew an impressive 18 percent. But in 1992, as a worldwide oversupply of fruit helped to precipitate a sudden drop in banana prices, Chiquita found itself with too many ships and bananas, as well as substantial debt (for world banana prices from 1985 through 1992, see table 2.3). Contributing to the company's problems was the growing economic chaos in the countries of the former Soviet Union—an area that Chiquita had targeted as a key new market. Indeed, critics of the company primarily faulted bad business decisions for its difficulties. Chiquita, however, blamed its faltering bottom line on changes in anticipation of the restrictive single-market EU regime. Either way, the results were dramatic. In 1992, the year before the regime took effect, the company reported net losses of $284 million—a stark contrast to the $128 million earned the previous year.

Chiquita's and Dole's initial talks with the USTR about bringing a case against the regime had not been productive, but the looming implementation of the Framework Agreement impelled Chiquita to further action.

Lindner had long given generously to Republican campaigns, and with the Framework Agreement looming, he stepped up his contributions to both parties. According to a study by the nonpartisan public interest group Common Cause, Lindner, his company, its subsidiaries, and their executives donated almost $1 million to the Democratic and Republican national party committees in 1993 and 1994, making him one of the nation's largest contributors of soft money during that election cycle.[15] "The signals were becoming pretty clear that USTR was not going to pursue this, and I think it was probably about that time when Chiquita realized that raising the interest in this case politically would have an effect on the reaction of USTR as an executive branch agency," says a banana industry representative. "The results speak for themselves."

In the summer of 1994, Chiquita's Washington, DC–based trade attorney and lobbyist, Carolyn Gleason, became a regular visitor and informal consultant to the USTR, providing policy recommendations as well as detailed trade information regarding Chiquita's estimates of damage done to US industry by the EU regime. Chiquita alone was estimated to have lost as much as 50 percent of its EU market share—falling from 40 percent of the total to less than 20 percent between 1992 and 1993. Gleason also began arranging meetings between Carl Lindner and key politicians and government officials. USTR Mickey Kantor held three meetings with Lindner, two of them hosted by Senate Majority Leader Bob Dole (R-KS).[16]

The effort was well spent. In August, a group of 12 senators, including Bob Dole, wrote Kantor urging that a formal investigation under section 301 be undertaken of both the banana regime and the Framework Agreement; in September, a coalition of 50 members of the House sent a similar letter. "The express intent of the new export quota and licensing authority is to inflict additional revenue and market share loss on American companies," the House letter read in part. "US companies have suffered a 50 percent decline in EU market share; a substantial loss of customers and associate growers; job losses; massive increases in operational costs, including transport costs; major additional reorganization costs; and significant price-depression in third country markets."

On September 2, the same day that the House letter went out, Chiquita and the Hawaii Banana Industry Association petitioned the Clinton administration to file a section 301 case against the European Union, as well as separate 301 cases against the four Latin American signatories to the Framework Agreement. As is customary with a 301 petition, the USTR had already informally indicated its willingness to take on the case and, in fact,

---

15. After giving no money to the Democrats in 1992, Lindner donated $525,000 to the party during the 1993–94 cycle. Soft money contributions, or donations to political parties, were not subject to the same restrictions as donations to individual candidates.

16. Brook Larmer with Michael Isikoff, "Brawl over Bananas," *Newsweek*, April 28, 1997, 43–44. Senator Dole had no family ties or affiliation with Dole Food.

had helped Chiquita to prepare the petition. According to the petition, the European Union's practices were "unreasonable and discriminatory," restricted US commerce, and threatened the "survivability" of US production.[17] It was Chiquita's hope, says a USTR official, that a fast USTR investigation followed by threats of retaliation could stop the Framework Agreement from going into effect in January.

On October 17, 1994, Mickey Kantor announced that the USTR would initiate a section 301 investigation against the European Union, claiming that Regulation 404 discriminated against Chiquita's ability to market and distribute Latin American bananas. The investigation triggered immediate protests on the part of Kantor's counterpart, EU Commissioner Sir Leon Brittan. Not surprisingly, the 13 Caribbean Community (Caricom) nations and the Caribbean Banana Exporters Association (CBEA) also decried the section 301 complaint. According to Caricom, the EU banana regime did not discriminate against US companies; instead, it simply guaranteed market access and adequate prices for the less efficiently produced Caribbean bananas in accordance with Lomé Convention obligations. The economies of such nations as Dominica and St. Lucia of the Windward Islands would be particularly devastated without Regulation 404, the groups argued, because their production expenses were so much higher than those of Latin American countries, and they had no other agricultural or industrial product to take the place of bananas. "Populations on the USA's own doorstep would be transformed from hard-working family farmers into mendicant unemployed," declared a Caricom release. Caribbean representatives also stressed the likelihood that a drop-off in banana production would lead directly to an increase in illegal drug trading.

In January 1995, as the Framework Agreement went into effect, the USTR brought similar 301 cases against Colombia and Costa Rica.[18] The US action raised alarm in the two countries, since if the United States decided to retaliate, it would likely withdraw concessions granted under such key programs as the Caribbean Basin Initiative and the Generalized System of Preferences. According to Irene Arguedas of the Costa Rican embassy, the politically and economically susceptible Latin American countries were caught in the middle. If they did not implement the Framework Agreement, their years of struggle to win better access to the EU market, including the two GATT cases, would be for naught. But if they did implement it, they faced the real threat of US retaliation. "It was ridiculous,"

17. According to data from the US government, Statistics of Hawaiian Agriculture, and the Puerto Rican Department of Agriculture, US production of bananas (in metric tons) was 63,143 in 1992, 59,684 in 1993, and 54,550 in 1994—all for domestic consumption. Because the restricted EU market had created a banana surplus outside of the European Union, the Hawaiian banana industry argued, prices in the US domestic market had been forced down.

18. The USTR did not challenge Nicaragua or Venezuela, as their banana exports were too small to affect Chiquita significantly.

declares Arguedas. "The US does not produce any bananas. It was very obvious that the US was enacting this case because of [Lindner]. There were not substantial interests involved."

Indeed, the USTR action, taken on the heels of Lindner's large campaign contributions, raised eyebrows in the United States as well as abroad. It was particularly suspect, critics claimed, because the USTR had rarely if ever taken on a case with so few US jobs at stake. Also significant, noted some observers, was the fact that Dole Food did not participate in the section 301 complaint.[19] "The driving force behind the case is Chiquita," says a US lawyer who backed the Caribbean cause. "Not the governments of any of the countries, but Chiquita, and Carl Lindner in particular."

Taking the Case to the WTO

Even as Kantor was launching the section 301 case, the arena for resolving international trade disputes was shifting dramatically. Since the GATT's drafting in 1948, members periodically had refined the agreement and made it more liberal through a series of negotiations known as trade rounds. In the Uruguay Round, the latest negotiation begun in 1986, members had taken up an ambitious and controversial roster of changes that resulted in the creation of the WTO on January 1, 1995. In contrast to the provisional GATT, the WTO was an official international body formed to help promote free trade, serve as a forum for trade negotiations, and settle international trade disputes. GATT rules were amended and incorporated into the new body, whose scope was considerably broader: The WTO's agreements covered not only trade in goods but also trade in services and intellectual property.

During January 1995, in the weeks after the WTO's founding, USTR Mickey Kantor pressed forward on the section 301 case, declaring that a preliminary investigation showed that the EU regime was costing US companies "hundreds of millions of dollars." Indeed, although Chiquita's banana sales were still far greater than those of any other marketer, the company had remained in the red in 1994, with a net loss of $72 million (see table 2.4 for total sales, banana sales, and net income in 1994 for the six major banana companies). But although Kantor wrote EU Commissioner Sir Leon Brittan to threaten retaliatory measures if the European Union and United States could not reach a compromise, several bilateral consultations between US and EU representatives made no headway. The European Union, one USTR official says, showed no interest in making changes.

---

19. A USTR staff member notes that Dole was extremely cooperative whenever the USTR requested technical support. However, the company had practical reasons for not taking part, since it had invested heavily in ACP and EU operations, and probably hoped to amortize its investments before the regime came to an end.

Table 2.4 Global banana companies, 1994 (thousands of dollars)

Company	Total sales	Sales of bananas	Net income
Chiquita	3,961,720	2,377,032	71,540
Dole	3,841,566	960,400	67,883
Fyffes	1,408,309	563,324	39,398
Geest	1,057,437	528,719	14,867
Noboa	700,000	280,000	21,000
Del Monte Produce	600,000	240,000	18,000

Source: Mulligan (1999); figures are drawn from company financial reports and own estimates.

Undoubtedly, playing a role in the European Union's unwillingness to craft a compromise were the deep divisions over Regulation 404 that still existed within the Community. As recently as October 1994, the European Court of Justice had upheld the regime against a challenge to the licensing provisions brought by Germany, the Netherlands, and Belgium. Indeed, seven EU members, including the recently acceded countries of Austria, Finland, and Sweden, openly opposed the regime. If the European Commission tried to revise Regulation 404, it would have to again engage with strong disagreements among members over the regulation's fundamental design.

Many EU members who backed the regime, moreover, believed that the European Union had already taken a necessary step toward coming into compliance with international agreements. In December 1994, during the last month of the GATT's existence, the EU and the ACP nations had requested—and been granted—a waiver from international trade rules covering some of the Lomé Convention trade preferences.[20] Specifically, the waiver covered the most favored nation clause of GATT Article I, which dealt, in part, with rules governing the imposition of tariffs. From the EU and ACP perspective, the Lomé waiver legitimized the preferential treatment of former colonies. But while USTR officials were willing to concede that the waiver sanctioned the tariff on Latin American imports, they insisted that it left many additional trade violations unresolved.

Finally, some EU representatives say they bristled at the idea of changing Regulation 404 just to satisfy Chiquita. "There was a perception that Chiquita's losses may not have been purely due to the restrictions of the regime," says Alison Mable of the United Kingdom's Trade Policy and Tropical Foods Division, Ministry of Agriculture, Fisheries and Food.[21] "Many people later came to feel, for example, that Dole, who bought into

---

20. The GATT panels that ruled against the EU regimes in 1993 had advised the European Union to obtain such a waiver.

21. Unless otherwise noted, all quotes from Alison Mable are from a January 1999 interview with the author.

the B license system and worked within the system, had done okay with the regime."

Although the deadline for the section 301 case was October 17, 1995, one year after the USTR initiated the investigation, at midsummer the EU Commission still could not agree on how to respond. Dole Food had been lobbying all sides for a compromise, but in July the Commission finally decided not to seek from member states the mandate it needed to negotiate with the United States. With the Commission at a standstill, the USTR faced two choices: forge ahead with a section 301 retaliation or bring the case instead to the fledgling WTO.

In some respects, a decision to go to the WTO might seem to have been preordained. After all, the two GATT panels had already set a precedent in finding the EU banana regime incompatible with international trade rules. Yet no one could be sure what proceedings under the WTO would be like. Historically, complainants had won most GATT cases. But under the WTO, dispute settlement rules were different. While most decisions still had to be reached by member consensus, panel reports could not be blocked unless there was a reverse consensus—in other words, unless all members voted against adoption. Now that rulings could no longer be blocked, it was possible that the WTO dispute panels would be more cautious about finding a country to be out of compliance.

Moreover, the GATT cases had been brought by banana producers, and many observers, including some in the United States, believed that the United States, as a banana marketer, did not have a strong GATT case. Instead, the United States would probably have to rely on a novel interpretation of the new, and still untested, General Agreement on Trade in Services (GATS). In addition, political pressure was building domestically for quick section 301 action, as Senate Majority Leader Bob Dole, among others, pushed for legislation that would threaten retaliation against Colombia and Costa Rica for their participation in the Framework Agreement.[22]

The USTR, however, was reluctant to launch a unilateral challenge right after the WTO had gone into effect. The international community had always hated section 301 for the ability it gave the United States to impose unilateral retaliations, even though the United States had done so in only 15 out of the 91 cases brought between 1974 and 1994 (Bayard and Elliott 1994, 66). Now, with the advent of the WTO and its new dispute settlement procedures, many critics of the policy asserted that section 301 was no longer a legitimate response in disputes involving WTO members. The USTR insisted it was, and, in fact, noted that the United States would never have approved the Uruguay Round leading up to the WTO if it had not believed its ability to bring 301 cases to be still intact. Nevertheless, to

---

22. During 1995, then-presidential candidate Dole flew a dozen times in planes made available by the Lindner family's corporate interests (as reported to the Federal Election Commission).

retaliate under section 301 when the ink on the WTO agreement was barely dry, USTR officials conceded, could make the United States appear to be thumbing its nose at the new international trade dispute mechanisms. "If we had gone with unilateral sanctions, all we would have done was raised the ire of all the other WTO members, including the member states in the European Community who favored our position," remarks one USTR official. "You can't have the Community and the Commission united by antipathy to the United States and their unilateral action. You always need some people on the inside helping to bring about change."

A final consideration clinched the decision. The Latin American countries that had not signed the Framework Agreement, such as Honduras and Guatemala, were facing the same set of restrictions that were affecting Chiquita. If these banana-producing nations became co-complainants, USTR officials reasoned, the case before the WTO would be stronger. Moreover, a possible ruling in their favor by the WTO panel would not only show that the United States was respecting and acting within the new dispute settlement process but also put pressure on the European Union to do the same. "Presumably," says one USTR official, "the EU would feel shamed into complying with its international obligations."

In September 1995, almost one year after first launching the section 301 investigation, USTR ended the section 301 case without a formal finding and, together with Mexico, Honduras, and Guatemala, initiated a WTO investigation of the EU regime.[23] "We have repeatedly sought changes in the European banana regime to address the discrimination against US companies, but unfortunately the EU has been inflexible," Kantor's statement announcing the action read in part. "We think it is appropriate at this time to resort to WTO dispute settlement procedures and we are pleased that other countries in our region that are also adversely affected by the regime are joining us."[24] In February 1996, Ecuador, which had just become a WTO member (and which had not been a party to the earlier GATT cases because it was not a GATT member), joined the challenge. Ecuador's involvement was particularly key since it was the only Latin American participant with substantial sales to the EU market.

There were reports that the United States had needed to persuade Honduras and Guatemala to participate in the WTO case. Ecuador, whose special circumstances made it perhaps the hardest hit of the Latin American countries, needed no such urging. Because it had refused to take part in the Framework Agreement, Ecuador had no specific country allocation, even though it had some 5,000 independent growers and was the world's largest banana exporter. Moreover, unlike Guatemala or Honduras, most of whose

23. The United States did not drop its separate 301 claims against Colombia and Costa Rica, however.

24. Kantor, quoted in "US Requests WTO Consultations on EU Banana Import Restrictions," *Inside US Trade*, September 29, 1995.

exports were handled by US multinationals, Ecuadorian traders—in particular the prominent Noboa Group—handled 80 percent of the country's exports. Yet because Noboa only sold Ecuadorian bananas, it—like Chiquita—could not qualify as a Category B operator, and therefore had to buy many of the licenses it needed to import into the EU market.[25] "I want to be very clear on this—we didn't join in this action because of the US," asserts Teodoro Maldonado, counselor for economic affairs at the embassy of Ecuador in Washington, and formerly secretary for trade responsible for the banana case in the WTO. "We had our own legitimate concerns."[26]

In January 1996, faced with the imminent threat of US retaliation, Colombia and Costa Rica signed a memorandum of understanding with the United States in exchange for an end to the section 301 case. As part of the agreement, the two countries pledged support for an open EU market for bananas and promised to begin distributing their export licenses in a manner more favorable to US multinationals. According to Irene Arguedas at the Costa Rican embassy, both Costa Rica and Colombia continued to be caught between the jockeying of the United States and the European Union, unable themselves to influence events. "The countries that suffered the most in the end were the small countries," she declares.

On February 5, 1996, the four complainants, along with new WTO member Ecuador, filed a fresh request for WTO consultations. In retrospect, one USTR official reflects, EU officials should have realized that if they had negotiated a compromise during the section 301 phase, the United States would have been willing to settle for less. "We wanted some improvement to help US companies out of the worst of it," he says. "That is what we were looking for—some quick relief."

The Case in the WTO

The WTO process got off to a slow and contentious start. The European Union wanted bilateral consultations in order to deal with each country's complaints individually and to isolate the United States—its most powerful adversary, but the one whose case appeared to be the weakest because it was not a banana exporter. The complainants, for their part, wanted one multilateral consultation to combine their charges and to ensure that the WTO would appoint only one dispute settlement panel rather than five.

---

25. While joining the Framework Agreement would have won Ecuador a quota, it would not have resolved the licensing issues that were critical to Ecuador as a major banana trader. Indeed, under the regime, the Ecuadorian government estimated that the country's traders were granted licenses for only about one-third of the bananas they imported into the European Union, forcing them to buy licenses for the other two-thirds.

26. Unless otherwise noted, all quotes from Teodoro Maldonado are from a December 1998 interview with the author.

In mid-March, a compromise was approved. The European Union got its bilateral meetings, but the challengers made the same presentations and posed nearly identical questions. In addition, the WTO convened only one panel, as the complainants had desired.

In a typical WTO case, the countries involved in the dispute selected the three panelists together, drawing from a permanent list of trade experts who served as individual consultants rather than country representatives. After the two sides were unable to agree on a panel, however, in June WTO Director-General Renato Ruggiero selected Stuart Harbinson, Hong Kong's permanent representative to the WTO; Kym Anderson, a University of Adelaide economist; and Christian Haeberli, an international trade expert from the Swiss economics ministry.[27] On July 9, the United States and the four Latin American countries submitted their first briefs laying out their challenges to the regime.

In an attempt to get maximum leverage, a USTR official says, the United States filed as many different claims against the EU regime as possible. While the Latin American countries, as banana producers, focused primarily on trade in goods, USTR claims covered both goods and services.[28] Under the GATT segment of the claims relating to goods, the USTR challenged both the quotas and the licensing systems imposed by Regulation 404 and the Framework Agreement. The services claims brought under the General Agreement on Trade in Services (GATS) concentrated on how the regime's licensing requirements had, in the words of the brief, "drastically reallocated, reconfigured, and restricted" the Latin American banana service market.

USTR officials say they felt fairly confident on the goods side, particularly on the issue of Category B licenses, since the GATT already had ruled twice on that issue. They were less certain about the services claims, however. Not only was this a new area of the regulations, but services traditionally had been construed as marketable activities such as legal or accounting services rather than the transfer of goods, and it was unclear if the WTO would accept the US interpretation.

In a July 30 panel submission, and again at the first dispute settlement panel meeting in mid-September 1996, the European Union attacked the US brief on several key points. The European Union argued that as a non–banana exporter, the United States not only had no right to bring a WTO case also should not be allowed to press claims on behalf of other nations.[29]

---

27. "Top WTO Official Picks Panel to Settle Dispute over EU Banana Regime," *Inside US Trade*, June 14, 1996.

28. Ecuador, as a banana marketer, also brought claims under services rules.

29. "Fortunately that was defeated," notes a USTR official. "They wanted us out because we were helping the other countries. They figured they might be able to buy out the other countries, I suppose."

The US argument that the regime had hurt the ability of its companies to supply services was also faulty, the European Union said, because the rules cited dealt with trade in goods, and trade in services was not intended to include the marketing of goods as a service. In addition, the European Union defended its preferential treatment of ACP countries, noting that the GATT waiver it had obtained protected precisely the policies that the complainants were challenging.

Because the ACP countries had not been designated as defending parties, representatives of the Caribbean banana-producing nations were relegated to third-party status in the WTO proceedings and thus could not participate fully in the debates. But they could make their wishes known in the United States, and supporters of preferential trade policies for the Caribbean became more vocal as the WTO process went forward. For example, a public relations campaign, organized on behalf of the CBEA, bombarded White House and Capitol Hill politicians with stories about Carl Lindner's large donations in an attempt to counterbalance the pressure that Chiquita was exerting. "From the ACP perspective, Chiquita made a bad corporate decision and didn't like the results, so it glommed on to a legal challenge to try to undo the damage," explains a lawyer involved with the effort.

In addition, representatives of the Caribbean nations spoke out whenever possible on the potentially tragic consequences of US efforts to end the preferential EU regime, including the likelihood that drug trafficking on the United States' southern flank would increase dramatically. Caribbean bananas were a small factor in world trade, accounting for only 3 percent of the world market and about 9 percent of the EU market, notes Dame Eugenia Charles, prime minister of the Windward Island of Dominica from 1980 to 1995. But for many fragile Caribbean economies, she says, bananas were key—accounting for 70 percent of Dominica's export earnings, for example. "With the little bit that we grow, we couldn't put any other country out of jobs," she says, "but it could make all the difference in the world to the Caribbean."[30]

Richard Bernal, Jamaica's ambassador to the United States, agrees. "Every country, including the United States, realizes that in a free market you make allowances for certain vulnerable participants," he argues. "It doesn't affect the operation of the market if a small percentage of the participants are given some kind of specialized treatment."[31] David Christy, senior associate in the Washington office of Winthrop, Stimson, Putnam & Roberts and a member of the CBEA's legal team assembled to fight the

30. Unless otherwise noted, all quotes from Eugenia Charles are from an April 1998 interview with the author.

31. Unless otherwise noted, all quotes from Richard Bernal are from a January 1999 interview with the author.

WTO case, adds: "The importance economically of banana trade to many of these countries cannot be overstated, because the boats coming in are bringing in supplies and taking out not just bananas but other goods, so it's really a lifeline. It's the core economic activity that allows all other economic activities to occur."[32]

Kantor tried to placate domestic critics, such as the Congressional Black Caucus, a group of about 40 African American representatives whose members often supported Caribbean causes. In a memo to Maxine Waters (D-CA) responding to her concerns over the US challenge to the EU regime, Kantor wrote in part, "I would also like to stress that the United States supports EU tariff preferences for products, like bananas, from African, Caribbean and Pacific (ACP) nations under the Lomé Convention." But he pointed out as well that "the Lomé Convention does not require the European Union to discriminate in favor of EU firms over US companies. The United States cannot tolerate the EU's licensing system which took away American business and gave it to a few EU firms."

Indeed, the USTR stayed firm in its stance that the EU regime was the wrong way to assist the struggling Caribbean economies. According to the agency, the European Union's discriminatory policies—supposedly put in place to help the 20 percent of bananas that came from ACP producers—in fact gave preferential treatment to almost 40 percent of bananas sold in the European Union, many of which came from relatively affluent EU territories, as well as from countries, such as Côte d'Ivoire and Belize, where production was almost as efficient as in Latin America. Moreover, American officials argued, while some ACP countries undoubtedly needed some form of support, research had shown that the EU regime was an extremely inefficient means of providing it. A World Bank study frequently cited by the USTR, for example, had found that the EU regime only returned 7.5 cents to ACP countries for every dollar it cost. In addition, the USTR noted, although import taxes on Latin American bananas had brought in more than $300 million annually, the European Union was spending only about $30 million a year to aid ACP banana production. "We really do believe that there are better ways to help the Caribbean and not hurt Latin America and not hurt our companies," says a USTR official. "That's the basis on which we're operating."

The WTO Panel Reports

On March 18, 1997, slightly more than a year after Ecuador had joined in asking for WTO consultations, the WTO dispute settlement panel issued a confidential report that represented a resounding victory for the United

---

32. Unless otherwise noted, all quotes from David Christy are from a December 1998 interview with the author.

States and its co-complainants (the public report was released on May 22, 1997). According to the interim decision, the European Union had violated WTO agreements—including the GATT, the GATS, and the Agreement on Import Licensing Procedures—on 16 counts. Among the specific EU measures ruled to be breaches of trade rules were the establishment of Category B operator licenses; the granting of individual country allocations to nonsubstantial suppliers, such as Nicaragua and Venezuela; and the requirement that export certificates from framework countries be matched with EU import licenses. Although the panel also found the country-specific quotas for ACP countries to be in contravention of the GATT, it concluded that the violation was covered by the European Union's Lomé Convention waiver.

Particularly significant was the panel's interpretation of the GATS, which agreed with the US argument: It allowed the services agreement to apply not only to marketable services, such as accounting, but also to service aspects of goods transactions, such as wholesale marketing. Thus a single trade measure could be found to be incompatible with both the GATT and the GATS. The panel also ruled that a country did not have to be an exporter in order to bring a case involving GATT violations. According to a USTR official, the WTO ruling was a striking validation of the US position. EU officials were reportedly stunned.

Although the European Union appealed most of the findings in June, the WTO Appellate Body report released in September 1997 was another win for the United States. Indeed, the appeals panel went beyond upholding most of the findings against the European Union and overruled the original panel's finding that the ACP country quotas were allowable under the European Union's Lomé Convention waiver.

While EU officials were disappointed by the WTO rulings, ACP representatives were shattered, according to a lawyer affiliated with the Caribbean defense: "What you have from the perspective of the ACP countries is a clash of two international obligations," he explains. "You have the treaty commitment between the EU and the ACP promising them no diminution in treatment from the past with regard to their banana exports, and then second, you have the arguably conflicting obligations that the EU and its member states have under the GATT and the WTO not to discriminate." He adds: "I think that the WTO—the panel and the appellate body—should have been, and could legally have been, more sensitive to the obligations flowing from the Lomé Convention. The focus that we are the WTO, we focus only on WTO issues and everything else is either irrelevant or of tertiary importance, I think that's wrong."

In the wake of the WTO Appellate Body report, USTR officials announced their intent to meet with Caribbean banana producers, and informally put forward a proposal for a new preferential regime. The European Union, the USTR suggested, could set a higher though not restrictive tariff on non-ACP bananas. For those most vulnerable ACP producers, meanwhile, the European Union could provide additional assistance—for example, in the form of income support, giving farmers the difference between the price they could get in the EU market and a targeted income level. But most Caribbean representatives flatly rejected the US suggestion. Christopher Parlin of Winthrop, Stimson, Putnam & Roberts, another member of the CBEA's legal team, points out that what the United States was suggesting was basically a welfare regime for the Caribbean, "which no government in its right mind wants." He says, "There is a recognition among the Caribbean elites that they will have to find alternatives to banana production, and that bananas are not the long-term solution. What you're talking about is the transition mechanism."[33]

The Road to Compliance

During the first few months after the appeal, the European Union continued to refuse to discuss plans for a new regime and the USTR kept up its constant prodding. By December, the only commitment the European Union had made was to comply by January 1, 1999, the end of the standard 15-month period allowed by the WTO, and to respect its "international obligations"—a statement the United States considered suspect, since it could be taken to refer not just to the WTO panel ruling but also to the European Union's Lomé Convention obligations. "We tried to go in there and say, 'Look, can we talk about the WTO-consistent alternatives, what the reports mean, what your options are?'" says one USTR official, "and they said, 'Oh no, we can't because it's internal, and we can't talk to any countries while it's still within the Commission because we haven't even talked to the member states yet.'" Although USTR officials met periodically with individual EU member states, the meetings appeared to have little impact.

The USTR was alarmed by preliminary reports about EU plans, but officials continued to harbor hopes about the makeup of new regulations. Best, says one official, would have been a tariff-only regime, which would have imposed duties on non-ACP countries but otherwise allowed an unrestricted market. If the European Union concluded that a TRQ was necessary to provide additional protection for ACP producers, the official continues, the European Union could have given the largest suppliers—Ecuador, Costa Rica, Colombia, and Panama—allocations of the entire market consistent with their shares in the past, and then allowed all the smaller providers—including Guatemala, Honduras, and ACP nations such as the Windward Islands—to compete for the rest. Licenses, meanwhile, could be distributed on the basis of importing practices in the period prior to Regu-

33. Unless otherwise noted, all quotes from Christopher Parlin are from a December 1998 interview with the author.

lation 404. While this system would not be ideal from Chiquita's point of view, the official says, it would at least be WTO-consistent.

But the first round of proposed regulations that the European Commission made public in January 1998 bore little resemblance to these speculations, and the United States and its Latin American co-complainants immediately protested at the WTO. The biggest EU concession, USTR officials say, was the promise to get rid of Category B and ripener licenses. The European Union would set up a new licensing system consistent with WTO rules, the Commission announced, but it declined to offer specifics, delaying that portion of the regime until later in the year. In addition, the European Union dropped individual country quotas for Venezuela, Nicaragua, and the ACP countries, since WTO regulations permitted the granting of such specific quotas to smaller countries only if it gave a quota to every single banana exporter. As substantial suppliers, Ecuador, Costa Rica, Colombia, and Panama would receive individual allotments of the Latin American quota, although the Commission had not yet said how those country quotas would be determined.[34]

Much to USTR's dismay, however, the Commission proposal kept its two-quota system, set at the same levels: a tariff-free quota of 857,700 metric tons for ACP countries and a tariff-rate quota for Latin American bananas of 2.2 million metric tons at 75 ECU per metric ton.[35] The USTR and its co-complainants charged in a joint statement issued February 5, 1998, that this system violated the WTO: By assigning two separate quotas based on the country of origin, the European Union had created restrictions for Latin American countries that were not "similar" to those faced by ACP countries. In addition, they claimed, the regime did not reflect trade in the absence of restrictions, since it gave ACP bananas a market share that was 40 percent higher than that justified by historic imports, at the expense of Latin American imports. "I think they decided at the outset that they simply didn't want to come into compliance," says a USTR official. "They tried to do the minimal amount."

The Commission proposal was almost as unpopular within the European Union as it was in the United States. In discussions leading up to a June 1998 vote by the Agriculture Council, whose approval was needed for the proposal to become law, Sweden, Germany, the Netherlands, Belgium, Luxembourg, and Italy all favored a system similar to that suggested by the United States, one that would rely on tariffs only, rather than on quotas. Denmark felt that the Latin American quota was too small, and

---

34. Such "substantial supplier" quotas were WTO-compatible as long as they were based on a reference period free of restrictions.

35. An additional allotment of 353,000 metric tons had been tacked on to the TRQ each year since 1995 to account for demand from the three new members that joined the European Union that year.

should be boosted to 3 million tons. For their part, France, Spain, and Portugal asserted that the proposal did not include enough protection for domestic growers, such as those in Martinique and the Canary Islands. Only the United Kingdom and Ireland seemed solidly behind the plan.[36]

Some US observers speculated that the Commission had postponed the licensing portion of the regime in order to delay USTR opposition. In June, with details on the licensing regulations still unknown, the new USTR, Charlene Barshefsky, sent out strongly worded letters to all EU trade ministers, warning that without changes in the proposal, "the United States will not hesitate to exercise its full rights under the WTO and take all available actions."[37] Barshefsky was under pressure herself from Senate Majority Leader Trent Lott (R-MS), who wanted the USTR—before the Agriculture Council vote—to publish a specific list of EU agricultural products that would be subject to retaliation if the European Union did not make changes to the proposed regime.

In fact, says one British official, the decision to break the proposal into two pieces had more to do with concerns about getting Agriculture Council approval than with thwarting the United States. Proposal supporters wanted to get the main structure of the regime through the Council in June while the United Kingdom, the plan's staunchest supporter, still held the rotating EU presidency. Passage of the first part of the regulations would bolster support for the licensing segment, which, since it directly affected the fate of many EU companies, was the most controversial portion of the regime domestically. In addition, under Council regulations, the licensing portion could be decided by a different committee, the Bananas Management Committee, whose rules made approval more likely.

At the end of June, the Agriculture Council finally approved the plan, and in October, the Commission announced its licensing proposal. Although the Commission abolished the categories of primary importer, secondary importer, and ripener, as promised, it announced that both licenses and country quotas would be based on imports during 1994 to 1996, a decision that the United States immediately denounced. Because the preferential regime giving licenses to ripeners and other new operators was already in effect during that time, USTR officials declared, the new system would simply perpetuate the wrongs of the previous preferential regime, including giving licenses to companies that had never imported in the past.[38] According to an EU Commission representative, however, winning

---

36. "EU Members Attack Commission Banana Proposal to Settle WTO Fight," *Inside US Trade*, February 13, 1998.

37. Letter from Barshefsky, quoted in "US, EU Set to Clash Over Banana Regime with Threats of Retaliation," *Inside US Trade*, June 19, 1998.

38. Had the Commission awarded licenses determined by a base period of 1990–92, a USTR official says, the United States would have accepted the licensing plan.

EU support would have been impossible without the reference period chosen. If the regime had been based on some span of years before 1993, she says, "you would have had endless litigation from all the [EU] companies that had been quite happily trading with legitimate expectations between 1993 and 1998."

The Battle Lines Are Drawn

As the EU proposal moved forward during the summer of 1998, Dole Food, which over the previous five years had increased its EU market share as Chiquita's share fell, continued to call for a negotiated solution. "What Dole was trying to do was to broker a solution, to find the common ground and build on that," explains Frank Samolis, a partner in the Washington law firm of Patton Boggs, which represented Dole on a variety of legal and regulatory issues. "A legal victory on paper in the WTO is one thing, but actually coming up with a change in the system is another, and we thought the chances of doing that were going to be far better under some sort of compromise proposal."[39]

No compromise appeared likely, however. The first part of the plan, approved in June 1998, had already led the USTR to conclude that the new EU regime was out of compliance. In July and September, the United States and its co-complainants sought an expedited WTO dispute settlement panel to rule on the validity of the plan, but the European Union blocked both requests, claiming that the regime could not be judged until the licensing portion was approved. Nor did the European Union respond to US calls to reconfigure the regime in accordance with the USTR's interpretation of the WTO ruling.

In July, USTR had warned the European Union that unless it brought the new regime into compliance, the United States planned to retaliate. According to Article 22 of the WTO's dispute settlement rules, the USTR maintained, the time frame during which a complainant could ask the WTO Dispute Settlement Body for permission to withdraw concessions was very limited. In this case, to make such a request and take advantage of the reverse consensus rule—which would prevent the EU and ACP countries from blocking the request unless all members were opposed—the United States would have had to act within 30 days of the new regime's implementation, or by January 31. The Dispute Settlement Body would then have to grant the US request within 30 days of the regime's implementation, or by February 1, 1999, unless the European Union requested

---

39. Unless otherwise noted, all quotes from Frank Samolis are from a December 1998 interview with the author.

arbitration to negotiate the amount of the retaliation. The 30 days allowed for that process would delay US retaliation until March 3, 1999.

On the other side, the European Union insisted that the US interpretation was dead wrong. Article 21.5 of the new regulations, EU officials said, clearly stated that for a complainant to withdraw concessions, the WTO first had to rule that a trade measure was out of compliance. Because the WTO had made no such ruling, they claimed, any US retaliation would constitute a unilateral action taken outside the jurisdiction of the WTO— an action that the European Union would then challenge in the WTO.

USTR officials countered that this reading of the rules was flawed because it could result in an endless loop of litigation, an eventuality that WTO members had never intended. If the European Union made only minor changes, for example, but refused an expedited panel, the entire dispute settlement process could start again, including consultations, panel hearings, rulings, appeals, and another 15 months in which to comply. At the end of the two to three years required to work through these stages, if the European Union instituted a third regime that was still out of compliance, the process might begin yet again.[40]

By October, the impasse had drawn Congress back into the fray, with several members calling for the USTR to publish for public comment a list of products that would be subject to retaliation if the United States decided to withdraw concessions—the first step toward such an action, as required by law. "We sold the Uruguay Round to Congress on the basis of our automatic ability to retaliate at the end," says one USTR official. "There's no way any business or exporter in the United States could consider the WTO an efficient process if all it is is endless litigation. Why should we do any trade agreements if nobody complies with them and all they do is use up US government resources?" A group including House Speaker Newt Gingrich (R-GA) met with Carl Lindner on October 2, and less than a week later Gingrich and Senate Majority Leader Lott wrote President Clinton to warn him of Congress's plan to pass legislation forcing the United States to withdraw concessions from the European Union unless the regime had been proven to be WTO-compatible.[41] The House debated such a bill on October 10, but chose not to take action after White House Chief of Staff Erskine Bowles delivered a letter to Congress pledging to retaliate under section 301 if the European Union did not meet its WTO obligations.

---

40. At the time, WTO members were planning to take up the apparent contradiction between Articles 22 and 21.5 as part of a review of the Dispute Settlement Understanding to be initiated during 1999; as of late 2005, the controversy still had not been settled.

41. Lindner's generous contributions to both parties had continued. Lindner and his wife were fourth on the *Mother Jones* magazine's 1998 list of top contributors to political parties, having donated $536,000 from January 1997 through August 1998.

According to a Republican House staff member who helped to draft the bill, while Lindner's involvement was clearly key, the case's significance went beyond Chiquita.[42] "Considering that the administration is supposed to submit a report on the WTO to Congress in the year 2000, and that there's an opportunity for Congress to vote to back out of the WTO," she says, "it's pretty important to make sure that we are on record as having not only won cases, but gotten a fair implementation as a result." More immediately, the aide notes, the outcome of the banana dispute was viewed as likely to affect EU behavior concerning a second WTO decision that favored the United States, a ruling against the European Union's ban on beef raised with growth hormones. The USTR needed to set a strong precedent in bananas, officials believed, to ensure that the European Union would comply in the beef hormones case, a dispute that had a direct impact on the United States as a major beef exporter.

In mid-December, the European Union requested a new WTO panel, in essence to judge whether the United States would be violating trade rules if it retaliated against the European Union without the WTO having found the banana regime to be out of compliance. However, no such panel was immediately convened. At the same time, USTR officials were keeping a close eye on Ecuador, fearing that the country might strike a side deal with the European Union for a larger share of the Latin American market, thereby hurting Chiquita and splintering the complainants' united front.[43] On December 21 the USTR published a retaliation list that would place tariffs on about $520 million worth of EU imports, concentrating on goods that would not disrupt American commercial interests, that would have a minimal impact on US consumers, and that originated in those countries most supportive of the regime. Products that would be subjected to a 100 percent tariff, effectively doubling the price of the goods, included pecorino cheese, sweet biscuits, handbags, cashmere sweaters, and Christmas ornaments. "Everyone loves to rail against the US's so-called unilateralism," says a USTR official. "But you know what? We didn't get the EU's attention until we put that list up. How many years has it been? It's unfortunate, but that's the way it works."

---

42. It had not been an easy year for Chiquita. On May 3, 1998, the *Cincinnati Enquirer* ran a damning 18-page series outlining a number of improper business practices and questionable dealings on the part of Chiquita in Latin America. However, after learning that the lead reporter had allegedly stolen voice mail messages from Chiquita while researching the series, and facing a likely Chiquita lawsuit, the *Enquirer* ran front-page apologies repudiating the articles for three consecutive days (beginning June 28). In addition to firing the reporter, whom Chiquita also sued, the *Enquirer* paid the company a sum reportedly in excess of $10 million. Despite the *Enquirer* retraction, the Securities and Exchange Commission continued its investigation of some Chiquita practices.

43. Although the European Union had given Ecuador 26.17 percent of the TRQ, the largest share, Ecuador considered the allotment restrictive and unrepresentative of its actual imports to the EU market over the previous three years.

The $520 million figure, meant to represent the annual export revenues lost by Chiquita and Dole because of the regime, was well below what Chiquita alone had sought, but it was at the high end of estimates prepared by an interagency team of government economists charged with the unenviable task of assessing damages in the highly complex case. Among the factors complicating the calculations were the many different ways in which the European Union could conceivably make its regime legal, as well as the lack of any recent period during which a free market had existed in the European Union to use as a basis for comparison. According to a staff economist at the Council of Economic Advisers who helped to come up with the damage estimate, the USTR and the team were also constrained by political pressures. If the estimate was much higher than what the WTO ultimately approved, US companies would probably feel let down by USTR's performance. If, on the other hand, the estimate was too low, Congress might question the usefulness of the WTO or press for more direct involvement in international trade disputes. "One of the things we were very aware of throughout the whole process was whether this was going to be okay for the people who were putting the political heat on in the first place," the economist recalls.

Retaliation Begins

As the new year began, observers were mystified as to how the dispute would ultimately end. On January 12, 1999, the WTO Dispute Settlement Body convened a new panel, in response to requests by Ecuador and the European Union, to determine whether the new EU banana regime complied with the WTO judgment, but a ruling was not expected until April.[44] On January 20, the United States, Honduras, Mexico, Guatemala, and Panama requested consultations with the European Union to discuss a last-minute compromise, but no immediate date was set.[45] Meanwhile, the two Windward Islands of St. Lucia and Dominica—claiming their economies would be devastated if the EU regime ended—blocked the agenda for the WTO Dispute Settlement Body's planned January 25 meeting, thus temporarily stopping the United States from requesting permis-

---

44. The United States opposed the panel, fearing that the European Union could use an ongoing evaluation of the banana regime's WTO consistency as an additional argument against US retaliation. It was also unclear whether the European Union would try to use the panel to evaluate compliance, or to rule on the legitimacy of the planned US retaliation. But Ecuador, hoping to protect its relationship with the European Union, was apparently trying to avoid further escalation of the dispute ("US to Request WTO Consultations with EU to Resolve Banana Fight," *Inside US Trade*, January 15, 1999).

45. Panama, which joined the WTO in September 1997, was not a member when the original complaint was filed. Ecuador asked to join the consultations a few days later.

sion to retaliate against the European Union for noncompliance. The meeting took place on the 29th, however, and the United States made its official request. An official says, the USTR "was not budging on our right to go and get a reverse consensus on the request for retaliation. That was fundamental to us."

When the European Union asked for arbitration on the amount of retaliation, the WTO sent the question to the same three-member panel that was already considering the request of Ecuador and the European Union to rule on whether the regime was WTO-compliant. Although the compliance decision was not due until April, the United States still hoped that the WTO would deliver a report on March 2 authorizing it to begin imposing sanctions on EU products a day later.

As the dispute dragged on and a trade war appeared increasingly likely, some critics of US policy began to question why the trade wrangle had ever begun. "On one hand, I concede that there's a legal case here," says a lawyer who supported the Caribbean position. "I just don't believe that every legal case was meant to be brought. This is a case study in the abuse of the WTO process by private interests, namely Chiquita. And I think the United States and the system are going to pay dearly for it."

US trade and government representatives could not disagree more. "There was a discriminatory regime, and the US went to the WTO—as it should have—and won," says one banana company representative. "It's hard to argue with the judgment that this was a case worth taking on." Peter Scher, USTR's chief negotiator on agricultural issues, agrees. "What's at stake here is the credibility of the World Trade Organization," Scher declared after the USTR published its retaliation list in December. "This is the first case in which any country has essentially refused to comply with rulings of the WTO."[46] Indeed, another USTR official notes, a US failure to insist that the European Union comply on the banana regime would not only weaken all US trade agreements but also call into question the power and legitimacy of the entire WTO. "We've got something big on the line," the official says. "It's way beyond bananas."

In early 1999, the protracted case finally moved a significant step closer to resolution. In lieu of a negotiated settlement, USTR had hoped to begin imposing sanctions against the European Union on March 3. But to the disappointment of US government and industry officials, the WTO did not determine the figure in time. Instead, on March 2, the WTO arbitrator reported that it could not address the amount of US retaliation until it had ruled on the consistency of the regime.[47]

---

46. Scher, quoted in David Sanger, "U.S.-Europe Trade War Looms Over Bananas," *The New York Times*, December 22, 1998, A1.

47. The United States immediately suspended liquidation on a list of EU products worth $520 million, meaning that the US Customs Service refrained from assessing final tariffs and left open the possibility of punitive tariff increases if the WTO later approved retaliation. The

But the European Union had been given only a temporary reprieve. On April 6, the three-member WTO group announced two important rulings. In its role as a dispute settlement panel, the three WTO representatives found the EU banana regime to be out of compliance with WTO rules. At the same time, having concluded that the regime was inconsistent, the group as arbitrator delivered the WTO's first retaliation decision, allowing the United States to impose against the European Union sanctions worth $191.4 million, the panel's estimate of the EU banana regime's impact on the import of US goods and services.[48] "This is the fifth time in six years that an international trade panel has found the EU's banana policies to be in violation of international trade rules," USTR Charlene Barshefsky declared in a triumphant statement.[49]

Although the almost $200 million in sanctions was the highest retaliation ever approved by an international organization in a trade dispute, it was far below the United States' original $520 million request. EU representatives quickly trumpeted the reduced damages as proof that the United States had been overstating the regime's harm to US companies all along.[50] But one US economist who had helped calculate the original damage estimate says that simply getting a decision at that time was a major victory for the United States. He points out that a delay by the WTO in addressing the entire question of retaliation until after it had reached a ruling on compliance could have stalled the sanctions process for at least months, if not more than a year, allowing the European Union to continue its discriminatory practices without international reprisal and exacerbating tensions within the United States over how to manage trade disputes.

On April 9, the United States published a new pared-down retaliation list of European products that would be subjected to 100 percent tariffs. While pecorino cheese and cashmere sweaters had been dropped from the list, items slated for retaliation still included French high-fashion handbags, English bed linens, and German coffeemakers, as well as more pedestrian items such as lead-acid storage batteries and felt paper. Products from England and France, the two countries seen as most supportive of the discredited regime, were hit hardest, while the Netherlands and

European Union challenged the move, insisting that sanctions should not have begun until retaliation became official. One year later, a WTO panel ruled against the United States, concluding that its action constituted an illegal trade restriction.

48. The banana ruling failed to resolve the debate between the United States and the European Union over the contradictory language in Articles 21.5 and 22 of the WTO's dispute settlement rules regarding the time frame during which a country can ask to impose sanctions, and the need for the WTO to reevaluate any new trade regime before approving a retaliation amount.

49. Barshefsky, quoted in David E. Sanger, "Ruling Allows Tariffs by US over Bananas," *The New York Times*, April 7, 1999, C1.

50. The WTO used a different and more conservative set of assumptions to calculate damages, including a smaller quota for non-ACP bananas under a hypothetical free market.

Denmark, opponents of the regime, escaped all sanctions. "The United States has paid the cost of the EU's discrimination for six years," said Peter Scher. "Now the EU must pay the price."[51] Ecuador was likely to make its own demand for compensation, which had the potential to be larger than the claim won by the United States.

As the US retaliation began, Scher announced the willingness of the United States to end sanctions as soon as the European Union implemented acceptable changes in its banana regime, and on April 20, Roderick Abbott, EU trade ambassador, declared the European Union's intention to "comply fully" with the WTO ruling. The WTO panel had suggested three ways in which the European Union might comply: a tariff-only regime that would not require special import licenses, a TRQ that would need a waiver from WTO rules, or a quota that did not rely on country-specific limits or that was done with the support of banana suppliers.

An Elusive Resolution

Many in the United States saw the WTO ruling as a critical breakthrough in addressing unfair EU trade policies. But early efforts to settle the banana regime impasse proved futile, as the European Union failed to make substantive alterations in its built-in protections for European marketers and ACP banana producers, and the United States continued to push for a new system that would comply with WTO rules and restore much of Chiquita's lost European market share. As the dispute remained unresolved, international and domestic developments ratcheted up the pressure on the USTR to settle the issue at the same time that they heightened the difficulty of negotiating an agreement.

In July 1999 the United States imposed WTO-approved sanctions of $117 million a year against EU products in a long-running case against the European Union's ban on imports of hormone-treated beef. This second trade retaliation only worsened cross-Atlantic relations. At the same time, the European Union had been pursuing a case in the WTO against the US foreign sales corporation (FSC) provision, a component of US tax law that allowed US companies with foreign subsidiaries to shield part of their income from US income taxes. USTR officials claimed the European Union brought the case in large part to retaliate against the United States for its successful beef and banana cases; previously, European countries had accepted the FSC provision as part of a 1981 understanding among GATT members regarding tax policies. In any event, a WTO panel ruled in 1999 that the FSC tax provision constituted an illegal export subsidy; in Febru-

---

51. Scher, quoted in Michael M. Phillips, "WTO Supports US in Dispute over Bananas," *The Wall Street Journal*, April 7, 1999, A3.

ary 2000, a WTO Appellate Body upheld that ruling, opening the way for the European Union to impose punitive sanctions against the United States that could top $2.5 billion.

The ruling stirred immediate fears among representatives of US banana and beef companies that USTR officials might compromise in the two cases affecting those industries to gain a satisfactory resolution of the potentially costly FSC case. Senate Majority Leader Trent Lott, who had backed strong retaliation against the European Union for its banana and beef trade policies all along, asked for and got reassurance from USTR Barshefsky that the cases would be kept separate.

But in early 2000, many members of Congress remained frustrated that almost a full year after the United States had first imposed sanctions, the European Union still had not proposed a nondiscriminatory trade regime for bananas. For months, Congress had been debating trade legislation—known as the carousel provision—that would mandate regular rotation of products subject to retaliation in trade disputes, in order to increase pressure on those countries out of compliance. The USTR, which already had the ability to change sanctioned products when it deemed such action prudent, opposed the legislation as weakening its ability to manage trade disputes. Nevertheless, in May 2000 the House and Senate approved the carousel provision as part of a larger trade bill expanding certain trade benefits to sub-Saharan Africa and the Caribbean. Under the provision, the USTR was to rotate retaliation lists every six months once a list had been in place for 120 days.[52] EU representatives immediately declared that such a unilateral change in the retaliation list, without the approval of a WTO Dispute Settlement Body, would violate WTO rules.

Over the next few months, the trade tumult continued. EU member states, sharply divided over proposed revisions to the European Union's banana trade regime, were unable to come to any agreement. The USTR, for its part, while still denying any linkage between the beef and banana settlements and the FSC tax case, delayed rotating the retaliation lists for fear of upsetting ongoing talks with the European Union regarding the trade disputes. Moreover, the Clinton administration still hoped to resolve either the beef or the banana case before leaving office in January 2001, and the imminence of a settlement could justify the deferral of product changes.

In October Senator Lott proposed legislation requiring industry petitioners in trade cases such as the banana dispute to approve US-negotiated trade deals before punitive sanctions could be lifted, as well as mandating fast implementation of the carousel provision. Lott eventually dropped the amendment after critics in the administration and both houses of Con-

---

52. The rotation was not required if a settlement was pending or if the USTR and the industry that sought the action agreed it was not needed ("House Approves Africa-CBI Conference Report with Carousel," *Inside US Trade*, May 5, 2000).

gress claimed it would give industry undue control over trade policy generally, and would specifically grant Chiquita veto power over any potential resolution of the banana dispute. Meanwhile, although some administration officials believed that the carousel law required the USTR to rotate products subject to punitive tariffs within six months of the law's passing—in this case, by November 18—the USTR ignored that deadline in the face of European Union warnings that any unilateral rotation could trigger aggressive retaliatory measures against the United States in the FSC case.[53]

At a US-EU trade summit in December 2000, the European Union finally put forward a tentative banana trade policy that it had been debating for months. The system would retain TRQs, but they would be administered on a first-come, first-served basis rather than under a licensing scheme, an approach that many trade experts agreed would be WTO-compatible. Dole and Noboa of Ecuador quickly announced their support for the scheme since both, as relative newcomers to the EU market, were likely to fare poorly under most historical licensing plans.

But the Clinton administration declared that this approach, which ignored historical licensing data and gave no preference to traditional importers, would be too complex to manage fairly and would benefit new marketing firms at the expense of companies like Chiquita. The USTR argued instead for a larger Latin American quota and for a system that would base its allocation of licenses on an agreed-on reference period—ideally a time before the 1993 regime took effect. In addition, the USTR said the European Union should give most of those licenses to major importers rather than reserving a significant share for ripeners and other smaller companies that the current regime had allowed into the market.

In mid-January 2001, pressure on the USTR to resolve the trade dispute only increased. Financially ailing Chiquita—declaring that the European Union's discriminatory regime had cost it $200 million a year since 1992—announced that it could not meet its payments on its outstanding public debt of $862 million and would likely file for bankruptcy. While industry analysts noted other causes for Chiquita's fiscal woes—its earlier overambitious expansion; the devastation of 1998's Hurricane Mitch, which had leveled company plantations in Honduras and Guatemala; rising interest rates; and the devaluation of the euro—the company held the banana regime primarily culpable. "The direct blame for today's actions should be put on the bureaucrats in Brussels who have manifested this ongoing illegality," declared Steven Warshaw, Chiquita's president and chief operating

---

53. Although the US House of Representatives had passed a bill that fashioned an alternative to the FSC on November 14, and US and EU officials had negotiated a procedural agreement to delay possible EU trade sanctions until the following year, the European Union threatened to suspend that agreement if the United States changed the products subject to retaliation.

officer. "If not for the European Union, we wouldn't be going through this today."[54] About a week later, Chiquita sued the European Commission for $525 million in damages, the amount the company claimed that the latest EU banana regime had cost it since taking effect in January 1999.[55]

Striking a Deal

As the new administration of President George W. Bush settled in, banana industry representatives and members of Congress lost no time in bringing their concerns forward. A source close to Chiquita said that sponsors of the still-to-be-implemented carousel provision saw it as the "law of the land and it must be honored."[56] Senator Lott, meanwhile, called on the new USTR, Robert Zoellick, to aggressively enforce US laws, including the carousel law, or to expect congressional action. "I do not think our trading partners are dealing with us fairly right now," Lott declared.[57]

During March, staff officials under Zoellick and European Trade Commissioner Pascal Lamy held a flurry of meetings to resolve the banana standoff. Lamy, like Zoellick, was feeling pressure to settle. The European Union had to implement a WTO-compatible regime by July 1—and thus the plan had to be circulated by late April to allow banana producers and marketers sufficient time to conform to the new rules. But if the European Union planned to implement its proposed first-come, first-served approach in defiance of US wishes, Zoellick warned, an impatient Congress would probably insist that the USTR rotate the European products subject to sanctions, a move that would spur additional discord and likely set off EU retaliations against US exports that could reach $4 billion. And the position of Ecuador—which had favored first-come, first-served—also had to be considered, or trade officials there might initiate a new WTO challenge.

On April 11, after officials had worked through the night, Zoellick and Lamy finally announced a compromise acceptable to both sides. To satisfy the United States, the European Union dropped the first-come, first-served approach and agreed instead to award licenses according to import levels from 1994 to 1996. The European Union also abandoned the country-

---

54. Warshaw, quoted in Anthony DePalma, "Citing European Banana Quotas, Chiquita Says Bankruptcy Looms," *The New York Times*, January 17, 2001, A1.

55. Dole Food had already brought a number of similar suits against the European Commission, and even some European governments had challenged the regime in court.

56. Source quoted in "Chiquita Vows to Fight on Against EU Rules Despite Financial Trouble," *Inside US Trade*, January 19, 2001.

57. Lott, quoted in "Lott Warns Zoellick to Take a Tough Stance on Trading Partners," *Inside US Trade*, February 9, 2001.

specific allocations that had further segmented the Latin American quota under the previous regime. The European Union would keep a TRQ system in place temporarily, but 83 percent of licenses for Latin American banana imports would go to primary importers—companies such as Chiquita and Noboa that owned or bought bananas in the country of origin and brought them to the first point of sale in Europe. In addition, the European Union promised soon to increase the Latin American quota by 100,000 tons while reducing the ACP quota by the same amount.[58]

The United States also made significant concessions to win EU support. Although the USTR had earlier argued that 88—rather than 83—percent of licenses should go to primary importers, it agreed to let the European Union set aside 17 percent of licenses for a "newcomers" category. Along with encompassing actual new entrants, the category would allow European ripeners and other companies that were not traditional importers to continue to market bananas. Though the United States had originally asked for an immediate end to quotas, TRQ would remain in effect for a four-and-a-half-year transition period, finally switching to tariff-only in 2006. When the new regime took effect July 1, the United States would suspend its retaliatory tariffs. At the same time, the United States promised to support a waiver for the European Union from GATT Article XIII, to allow the European Union to offer an exclusive quota for ACP bananas.[59] Once that waiver was granted, the punitive sanctions would officially end.

Although some critics charged that the agreement failed to meet acceptable free trade standards, Zoellick defended the compromise as the best possible deal that both the United States and European Union could accept. "The banana disputes of the past nine years have been disruptive for all the parties involved," Zoellick, Lamy, and European Agriculture Commissioner Franz Fischler said in a joint statement. The new agreement, they declared, "will end the past friction and move us toward a better basis for the banana trade."[60]

For Chiquita, which had continued to make generous donations to both Democrats and Republicans throughout the trade war, the banana agreement's new quota and licensing provisions promised an immediate improvement in EU market share.[61] Given allocations based on the 1994 to 1996 reference period, Chiquita and Dole would receive import licenses for

---

58. The quota change would not go into effect until its approval by the Council of Ministers and the European Parliament, which was to occur sometime before January 1, 2002.

59. Article XIII banned discrimination in the use of import or export quotas, and also required that any quota applied should roughly match the expected share that a supplier country would have if no quota existed.

60. Joint statement, quoted in Anthony DePalma, "U.S. and Europeans Agree on Deal to End Banana Trade War," *The New York Times*, April 12, 2001, C1.

about 44 percent of Latin American bananas, industry experts predicted, with two-thirds of that share going to Chiquita.[62] Although Chiquita had lobbied for the European Union to use a pre-1993 period when its market share was even higher, in awarding licenses, the company still praised the accord. "We are pleased with this positive development for Chiquita and Latin American banana interests," company president Steven Warshaw said in a prepared statement.[63]

Dole, however, whose total contributions to both political parties during the recent campaign cycle totaled only $159,750, came away from the agreement a loser, according to company officials.[64] David Murdock, chairman and chief executive of Dole, described the plan as "inconsistent with the American free enterprise system." He added, "All American agriculture exporters will be deeply disappointed by the action."[65] Because Dole had not had a strong European presence during the two-year period beginning in 1994, it would not benefit from the historical licensing approach. Moreover, Dole's entire strategy over the previous nine years, unlike Chiquita's, had been to operate within the restrictions of the European Union's single-market banana regime. Thus, Dole had built up its European business primarily by buying or establishing joint ventures with smaller European and Ecuadorian companies—the kinds of firms that were now excluded from the 83 percent of licenses designated for primary importers. According to one Dole official, USTR's actions showed that "the real issue was simply to get a system that would take care of Chiquita."[66]

With the long-running banana war finally at an end, US trade officials breathed a sigh of relief. Yet other trade issues still remained unresolved, including the battle over the European Union's ban on imports of hormone-treated beef and a fight over EU approval of US genetically modified crops

---

61. Chiquita had donated $1.7 million to the two parties during the previous election cycle—$1.03 million to Republicans and $676,750 to Democrats (Helene Cooper, "Dole Fails to Find Much Appeal in Accord to End Banana War," *The Wall Street Journal*, April 13, 2001, A12).

62. "Banana Deal Effectively Locks in U.S. Share of EU Market," *Inside US Trade*, April 13, 2001.

63. Warshaw, quoted in Paul Blustein, "US, EU Reach Pact on Bananas," *The Washington Post*, April 12, 2001, E1.

64. Ecuador also questioned the accord, but the country's concerns appeared to have been met in late April, after the European Union granted more access to Ecuador's companies and growers within the 17 percent "newcomer" category, which favored operators in producing countries over banana marketers in the European Union.

65. Murdock, quoted in Anthony DePalma, "Dole Says Trade Accord on Bananas Favors Rival," *The New York Times*, April 14, 2001, C2.

66. Dole official, quoted in Cooper, "Dole Fails to Find Much Appeal in Accord to End Banana War," A12.

that also appeared headed for the WTO. Indeed, the clashes over bananas and beef exemplified the increasingly complex nature of international trade disputes, involving not just the United States and the European Union but most nations, as simple quota and tariff conflicts were joined by murkier and less easily resolved disagreements encompassing social policies as well as medical and environmental concerns. In the eyes of many observers, such issues merely underscored the importance of supporting a strong and effective WTO, as it appeared almost certain that the organization's dispute settlement mechanisms would be called on and tested with increasing frequency in the years to come.

Case Analysis

This case concerns the operation of a traditional border barrier—the European quota system for imported bananas. At its heart, it describes a clash between a multilateral trading system based on principles of non-discrimination and selective preferential arrangements in which certain trading partners are treated differently. The case demonstrates how complex the political economy of trade policy can become, and it reveals the barriers to resolving disputes that such complexity can create. The case also explores issues in the enforceability of the rulings of the WTO. In particular, the banana dispute highlights problems in determining compliance and authorizing retaliation.

In the 1980s, as the European Union implemented its initiative to complete a single-market regime by 1992, some expressed concerns that it might use the opportunity to become more protectionist—concerns encapsulated in the phrase "fortress Europe." For the most part, these fears proved to be misplaced—but not in the case of bananas. European countries had come to the table with distinctly different regimes on the fruit. They ranged from the liberal in Germany (no tariffs), to fairly liberal regimes in other northern European countries, to highly regulated systems in Spain, France, and the United Kingdom that reflected a desire to protect producers in the Canary Islands (on the part of Spain) and in Africa and the Caribbean (on the part of the United Kingdom and France, wishing to give special consideration to their former colonies, collectively known as the ACP, or African, Caribbean, and Pacific, countries). When Europe finally came together in a single system in 1993, the more protectionist countries gained the upper hand. The result was a new distribution of winners and losers.

Winners and Losers

The WTO is an intergovernmental association in which each member is treated as a single actor. In reality, however, as the banana case illustrates, the costs and benefits in WTO disputes may not neatly accrue to those directly involved in the conflicts. Here, the United States, which brought the case, was primarily defending the interests of a US multinational that was not producing bananas in the United States. And while the offending measure was European and the main defendant was Europe, those whose interests were most involved were Caribbean nations that could participate only as third parties. The European framing of the issue highlighted the benefits to these poor, disadvantaged producers. But the system that the European Union implemented conferred new benefits on major European distributors such as Geest and Fyffe, as well as other local distributors and ripeners, and dealt losses to poor developing countries in the Western Hemisphere.

Gains and losses occurred within the parties to the dispute, too. Northern European consuming countries were major losers, and Germany actually challenged the measure in European courts. When we talk of winners and losers in trade we often think only of producers and consumers, but this case reminds us that distributors may have significant interests. European distributors were big winners; Chiquita and Dole, both American, and Noboa, from Ecuador, stood to lose a great deal.

The case is also notable for showcasing how relatively small players in the trading system can have disproportionate impacts if they focus their energy and organize to create alliances. Deciding that its interests were being prejudiced, Chiquita successfully put bananas on the agenda of the Office of the USTR and built the coalitions necessary to launch a section 301 investigation against the European Union—that is, an intervention by the US government on the grounds that companies were being harmed by discriminatory trade practices.

Moreover, the banana dispute underscores that firms do not all respond in the same way—even when facing similar challenges. Dole was better able than Chiquita to mitigate the damage caused by the EU Framework deal. It therefore preferred a nonconfrontational strategy of accommodation, positioning itself to take advantage of the new system. Here, too, we see how zero-sum issues and complex institutional dynamics—in this case, competition among firms within a domestic industry—can act as barriers to agreement, or even as drivers of international trade disputes.

The case also exposes underlying strengths and weaknesses in the WTO dispute settlement system. The strengths lie in its ability to channel conflict into a multilateral setting and produce findings. For example, rather than acting unilaterally under its own section 301, the United States brought the dispute to the WTO. Both the GATT and WTO panels found that Europe had clearly violated the agreements. (More violations were found by the latter, including breaches of the GATS.) At the same time, however, the banana wars reveal some weaknesses of the WTO system, especially concerning compliance. Under the GATT, the European Union had been able to simply veto implementation, an outcome that the WTO no longer allowed. But implementation remained problematic. Despite losing the case, the European Union moved very slowly and then adopted measures that failed to bring it into compliance.

Determining Compliance

The United States sought authorization to retaliate before the European Union actually implemented its measures and before the WTO had a chance to rule whether the new measures remained noncompliant. In pressing its case, the United States invoked Article 22.6 of the Dispute Settlement Understanding (DSU) which states that if a member fails to come into compliance within a reasonable period, the Dispute Settlement Body will grant authorization to suspend concessions within 30 days or—if there are objections to its action—will refer the matter to arbitration, to be completed within 60 days. For its part, the European Union argued that the United States needed to resubmit its case and that a new finding of noncompliance had to be made prior to authorizing retaliation. In making this claim, the European Union invoked Article 21.5–6: "Where there is disagreement as to the existence or consistency with a covered agreement of measures taken to comply with the recommendations and rulings such dispute shall be decided through recourse to these dispute settlement procedures." This conflict exposes contradictions in the DSU that have become the subject of negotiations in the Doha Round. Eventually, the United States received the necessary authorization to retaliate. But the case shows that retaliation does not always work well: Retaliatory tariffs remained in place for a long time before a settlement was reached.

Article 3.7 of the DSU states that "the aim of the dispute settlement mechanism is to secure a positive solution to a dispute. A solution mutually acceptable to the parties to a dispute and consistent with the covered agreements is clearly to be preferred." In this particular case, that goal was never fully achieved. Viewed narrowly, the proceedings were successful, in that they averted a full-blown trade war. However, the European Union was provoked by its losses into making an effort to get even: It brought a case to the WTO against the foreign sales corporation provision of US tax law.

Postscript

At Doha, the WTO granted the European Union the Cotonou Waiver. This allowed the European Union to extend nonreciprocal preferences to the ACP group until December 31, 2007, when the two sides are scheduled to move toward WTO-consistent economic partnership agreements based on mutual concessions. At the time, it was believed that the European Union would replace its quota- and license-based banana import regime with a system relying on tariffs in 2006. But as of late 2005, negotiations for such a regime had yet to bear fruit. The beneficiaries of the current system have insisted on a high most favored nation (MFN) tariff to preserve their preferences. Latin and Central American producers, by contrast, want much lower tariffs. In September 2005, the European Union proposed giving ACP countries a quota of 775,000 tons—a reversal of its commitment for a tariff-only regime. The issue was submitted for arbitration at the WTO. If the EU proposal is rejected by the WTO, the Cotonou Waiver will cease to apply to bananas as of January 1, 2006. And so the conflict continues.

Appendix 2A

Figure 2A.1   Regulation 404

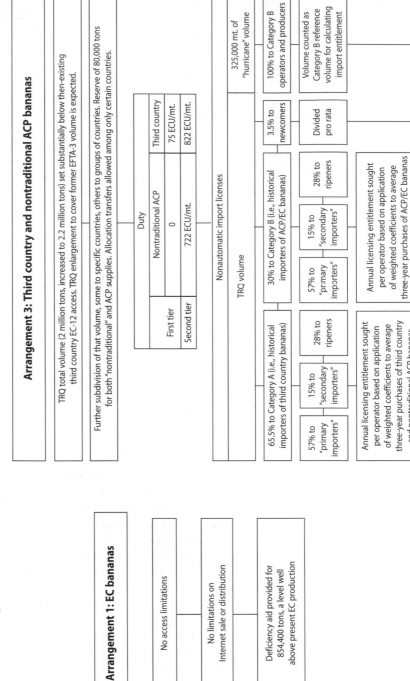

Arrangement 3: Third country and nontraditional ACP bananas

TRQ total volume (2 million tons, increased to 2.2 million tons) set substantially below then-existing third country EC-12 access. TRQ enlargement to cover former EFTA-3 volume is expected.

Further subdivision of that volume, some to specific countries, others to groups of countries. Reserve of 80,000 tons for both "nontraditional" and ACP supplies. Allocation transfers allowed among only certain countries.

	Duty	
	Nontraditional ACP	Third country
First tier	0	75 ECU/mt.
Second tier	722 ECU/mt.	822 ECU/mt.

Nonautomatic import licenses

TRQ volume

325,000 mt. of "hurricane" volume

65.5% to Category A (i.e., historical importers of third country bananas)

30% to Category B (i.e., historical importers of ACP/EC bananas)

3.5% to newcomers

100% to Category B operators and producers

57% to "primary importers"

15% to "secondary importers"

28% to ripeners

57% to "primary importers"

15% to "secondary importers"

28% to ripeners

Divided pro rata

Volume counted as Category B reference volume for calculating import entitlement

Annual licensing entitlement sought per operator based on application of weighted coefficients to average three-year purchases of third country and nontraditional ACP bananas

Annual licensing entitlement sought per operator based on application of weighted coefficients to average three-year purchases of ACP/EC bananas

Arrangement 1: EC bananas

No access limitations

No limitations on Internet sale or distribution

Deficiency aid provided for 854,400 tons, a level well above present EC production

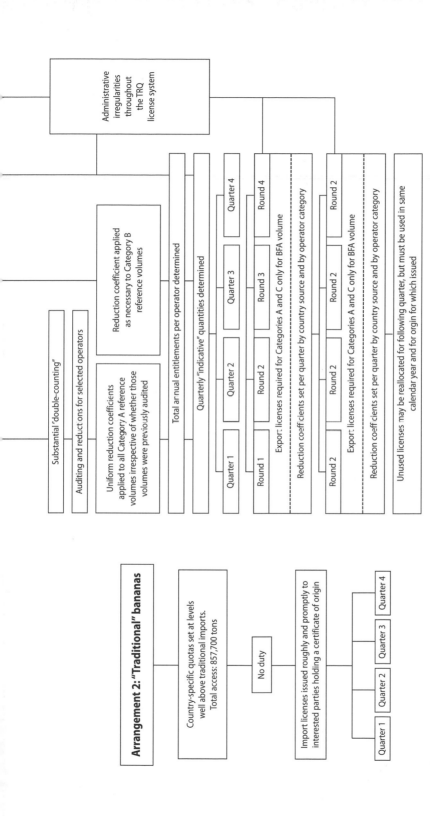

Arrangement 2: "Traditional" bananas

Country-specific quotas set at levels well above traditional imports.
Total access: 857,700 tons

No duty

Import licenses issued roughly and promptly to interested parties holding a certificate of origin

| Quarter 1 | Quarter 2 | Quarter 3 | Quarter 4 |

Administrative irregularities throughout the TRQ license system

Substantial "double-counting"

Auditing and reductions for selected operators

Uniform reduction coefficients applied to all Category A reference volumes irrespective of whether those volumes were previously audited

Reduction coefficient applied as necessary to Category B reference volumes

Total annual entitlements per operator determined

Quarterly "indicative" quantities determined

| Quarter 1 | Quarter 2 | Quarter 3 | Quarter 4 |

| Round 1 | Round 2 | Round 3 | Round 4 |

Export licenses required for Categories A and C only for BFA volume

Reduction coefficients set per quarter by country source and by operator category

| Round 2 | Round 2 | Round 2 | Round 2 |

Export licenses required for Categories A and C only for BFA volume

Reduction coefficients set per quarter by country source and by operator category

Unused licenses may be reallocated for following quarter, but must be used in same calendar year and for orgin for which issued

BFA = Banana Framework Agreement
EFTA = European Free Trade Association
TRQ = tariff-rate quota
ECU/mt = European currency units per metric tons

3

Snapshot: Kodak v. Fuji

On May 18, 1995, the Eastman Kodak Company of Rochester, New York, filed a complaint with the US government under section 301 of the 1974 Trade Act, claiming that its archrival, the Fuji Photo Film Company of Japan, in collusion with the Japanese government, had denied it fair access to the Japanese market. In fact, Kodak estimated that it had lost at least $5.6 billion in potential revenues in Japan over the previous 20 years, in a market now worth an estimated $2.8 billion a year.[1]

The Clinton administration, reeling from the political setback of the 1994 midterm elections, was determined to show a hostile Congress that international trade agreements such as the North American Free Trade Agreement and the General Agreement on Tariffs and Trade (GATT) would in no way compromise the trading position of US companies.[2] With most conventional cross-border trade barriers, such as tariffs and quotas, significantly lowered or eliminated by international agreements, attention had shifted to domestic policy instruments as sources of trade friction between

---

Snapshot: Kodak v. Fuji is an edited and revised version of the case with the same name originally written by Samuel Passow for the Case Program at the John F. Kennedy School of Government. For copies or permission to reproduce the unabridged case please refer to www.ksgcase.harvard.edu or send a written request to Case Program, John F. Kennedy School of Government, Harvard University, 79 John F. Kennedy Street, Cambridge, MA 02138. Support for an update of this case was provided by the Kansai Keizai Doyukai.

1. Obtained from Alan Wolff and Thomas Howell at Dewey Ballantine, 1996.

2. The Republican Party had gained control of Congress for the first time in 40 years in the midterm elections of 1994. Organized labor (specifically, the AFL-CIO), which bitterly opposed the free trade treaties that it believed would lead to US job losses, not only withheld its traditional financial support of the Democratic Party but even campaigned against those Democratic members of Congress who had voted for the free trade bills. As a result of the Republican victory, New York's Senator Alfonse D'Amato became chairman of the Senate Banking Committee.

countries. The policies of the government of Japan as well as the private practices of Japanese firms had long been an irritation in trade talks with the United States. Not only did the Japanese government tightly regulate many aspects of the economy—a government permit was needed in some 10,760 circumstances[3]—but also myriad "private barriers," alleged to arise from certain practices or arrangements between local firms, stifled foreign access to the Japanese economy.

For its part, the Japanese government complained that the US government used bilateral negotiations combined with the threat of unilateral sanctions as a way of guaranteeing market share for US companies doing business in Japan, a practice more commonly called "managed trade." In response to the frictions over semiconductors, the Japanese had made it a cornerstone of their trade policy to use international forums like the World Trade Organization (WTO) to resolve trade disputes in ways that emphasized solutions that emerged from changing the rules.

Acting United States Trade Representative (USTR) Charlene Barshefsky hoped that the Kodak case could accomplish what she and her staff had laboriously sought in 23 sectoral agreements with Japan over the previous four years. After almost a year of investigation of and often intense deliberation about Kodak's claims, as well as several failed negotiations with the Japanese government, Barshefsky and her staff had to decide whether to resolve a broader version of Kodak's claim before the WTO or take unilateral action against the Japanese photographic industry. The management of Kodak had billed this suit to the USTR "as the trade case of the century," claiming that "this would be the case that would finally allow the US to nail Japan."[4]

At its core, the dispute centered on the question of whether the lack of enforcement by a government of its competition laws provided advantages to domestic firms in their home markets. A ruling by the WTO Dispute Settlement Body (DSB) could well set the precedent for broadening the definition of competition policy to include consideration of whether laws of a sovereign nation that are neutral on their face but administratively abused by that government contributed to problems of market access for foreign suppliers.

The case was also highly politically charged. It brought into question the deep issues of sovereignty, first defined in the 1648 Treaty of Westphalia (which brought an end to Europe's Thirty Years' War) and jealously guarded by governments ever since, by challenging whether an external organization, such as the WTO, was empowered to intervene and force a sovereign nation to abrogate or amend a domestic law intended to protect

---

3. Obtained from Alan Wolff and Thomas Howell at Dewey Ballantine.

4. Kodak manager, quoted in Helene Cooper and Wendy Bounds, "Kodak Chief and Capital Lawyer, Heavy Hitters on Trade Matters, May Strike Out in Fuji Case," *The Wall Street Journal*, May 24, 1996, A12.

the rights of its citizens or the cultural heritage of that nation. Many in the United States who were concerned about ceding power to international organizations would watch this case and USTR's handling of it carefully.

Background on Kodak and Fuji

For decades, Eastman Kodak Company was the world's preeminent manufacturer of photographic imaging materials. In its global brand-name recognition, it was surpassed only by the likes of McDonald's, Coca-Cola, and Disney.[5] In 1995 the firm was the 247th largest company in the world, with sales exceeding $14.9 billion.[6] The company, which employed more than 96,600 people worldwide, had net earnings that year of $1.25 billion; it had 70 percent of the US market and 36 percent of the global market in color film.[7] Over the years, the company had spent tens of millions of dollars on a warm and fuzzy advertising campaign promoting that special "Kodak moment."

Kodak has had other moments, too. The company had been the subject of investigation and prosecution by the Justice Department since the turn of the century. From its founding in 1878 until 1915, George Eastman's company managed to get a lock on 98 percent of the total photographic market in the United States through various methods of price control and a combination of vertical and horizontal market restraints. In 1921, following an appeal to the US Supreme Court of a case brought by the Justice Department in 1915, Kodak entered into a consent decree that, among other things, required the company to divest itself of a number of factories, a photographic paper and supply company, and a dry-plate company. Kodak was ordered to refrain from engaging in resale price maintenance or employing "terms of sale." The company was also enjoined from monopolizing through mergers and acquisitions and from purchasing downstream distribution businesses without disclosure.[8]

In the 1940s and 1950s, Kodak engaged in a practice of tying its film sales to its photo-finishing services. Film was sold at a minimum unit price, set by Kodak, which included the cost of photo finishing. At that time, Kodak had a 95 percent market share of the color film market. By bundling the cost of film and processing, Kodak effectively monopolized the photo-processing industry as well. In 1954, the Justice Department was forced to add additional claims to its original 1915 suit in an attempt

---

5. "The World's Best Brands," *The Economist*, November 16, 1996, 108.

6. "Global 500 Poll," *Fortune Magazine*, August 15, 1996, F5.

7. Eastman Kodak, *Annual Report*, 1995.

8. *United States v. Eastman Kodak*, 226 F. 26, 63 (W.D. NY, 1915); appeal dismissed, 225 US 578 (1921).

to curtail Kodak's market behavior. This resulted in another consent decree prohibiting resale price maintenance and tying. The decree also required Kodak to divest itself of some of its photo-finishing labs. Both consent decrees were in force until 1994, when they were terminated by the US District Court in Rochester at the request of Kodak, which argued that various changes that had occurred in the photographic industry rendered the restraints obsolete.[9] The US government took the case to the court of appeals, which affirmed the lower court's decision.

Fuji Photo Film, founded in 1934, was by 1995 the 338th largest company in the world with sales of $10.2 billion. The company, the largest manufacturer of film products in Japan, employed 29,903 people worldwide and had net earnings of $685 million. It controlled about 70 percent of the Japanese market and 33 percent of the global market.[10] Though Fuji had been competing head-on with Kodak since its inception, it was not until the mid-1980s that the Japanese firm became a threat to Kodak's worldwide market domination. By then, according to Fuji's president and CEO Minoru Ohnishi, the stakes of global competition with the American firm were very clear: "We were in a race for survival with Kodak. We could almost see their numbers" (i.e., the numbers on the backs of the runners in a road race) (quoted in Sieg 1994, 18).

Kodak and Fuji battled each other relentlessly around the globe. In both their successes and failures, they seemed to be mirror images. In the United States, Kodak had approximately a 70 percent market share in color film to Fuji's 10 percent, while in Japan the reverse was true: Fuji had a 70 to 10 percent advantage over Kodak. The similarities persisted even when viewed globally, as these two titans could each lay claim to a third of worldwide market share.

Kodak began selling its products in Japan in 1889; by the 1930s, it had established a thriving operation and developed long-term relationships with the major Japanese wholesalers (Kashimura, Ohmiya, Asanuma, and Misuzu), or *tokuyakuten*, and was successfully using their extensive distribution system throughout Japan. After World War II, the Japanese government erected a wall of tariffs and quotas on all products, including photographic supplies, severely restricting the US firm's ability either to maintain its market share or to penetrate the market further. In the early 1950s, Kodak was limited to using only two distributors. In the official

---

9. *United States v. Eastman Kodak Company,* 853 F. Supp. 1454 (W.D. NY, 1994). In his opinion, Judge Telesca agreed with Kodak's argument that the relevant market for film was global. Given Kodak's worldwide share of 36 percent and the technological innovativeness of all the major competitors, he found that Kodak did not have monopoly market power. Even if the relevant market were limited to the United States, where Kodak's share was much higher (70 percent), Telesca found that Kodak did not possess monopoly power, because consumers were price-sensitive and because other suppliers could increase their capacity if Kodak restricted output or raised its prices.

10. "Global 500 Poll," *Fortune Magazine,* August 15, 1996, F7.

parlance of the Japanese bureaucracy at the time, the action was taken to "end confusion" in the importing business (Sieg 1994,102).

By 1960, Kodak was selling its products in Japan through a single intermediary trading house, Nagase & Co. The other *tokuyakuten* became the main distributors for Fuji Photo Film. Kodak's former president for Japan (1984–91), Dr. Albert Sieg, noted: "In effect, we taught the distribution company that was to become our main competitor how to move film throughout the country's retail stores" (Sieg 1994, 102).

Kodak's decision to run its business through a single trading house upset a number of Japanese. The management of Asanuma, the third-largest *tokuyakuten* in Japan, had a prior relationship with Kodak dating back to 1890 and did not like going through its rival, Nagase, for its supply of US film (Asanuma 1971).[11] Until World War II, the US firm accounted for nearly half of Asanuma's business.

In 1973, the top management of Asanuma claims to have visited Rochester to reestablish direct dealings but was allegedly rebuffed.[12] Kodak declares that it has no records of those meetings, and for that reason doubts that they took place. Two years later, Asanuma stopped buying the US firm's film product, a move that the Kodak management seemingly did nothing to reverse. But whether the meetings occurred or not, Sieg recalled in his memoirs, "Those distributors (the ones abandoned by Kodak) never forgave us, even after the government eased restrictions and we attempted to expand our network; many told us in no uncertain terms that they would never work with us because of the way we treated them in the past. Indeed, they stuck with Fuji and became part of one of Japan's most successful alliances" (Sieg 1994, 102).

In addition to running its business through a single Japanese trading house, Kodak also sold technology to Japanese companies. "Like most American companies [in the 1950s and 1960s], we were content to sell technology to the Japanese and make money. And we did," said Dr. Sieg. "We sold technology to Fuji Photo Film and Konica and anybody that came to our door. That was the way we decided we could make money in Asia. It was also a judgment—obviously not right—that we didn't need to worry about the Japanese as a competitor."[13]

---

11. In 1920, when George Eastman came to Japan for the first time, Tokichi Asanuma, the founder of the firm, hosted him with a lavish geisha party in Kyoto. Eastman commented at the time, "In thinking back on the growth of this industry, the credit that I allot myself is for always getting good men to join us." ("Asanuma—A Commemorative History of the First Hundred Years," Japan, 1971)

12. Asanuma professes to have made several trips to Rochester that year to meet with the Kodak management as part of its process of strategically reevaluating the film distribution market in Japan following the liberalization of the market (Interviews with company directors, November 14-15, 1996).

13. Sieg, quoted in Scott Lathan, "Manager's Journal: Kodak's Self-Inflicted Wound," *The Wall Street Journal*, August 14, 1995, A10.

Between 1971 and 1976, the Japanese government progressively dismantled its tariffs on photographic goods, which earlier were as high as 40 percent. In 1979, it also ended the prohibition on direct foreign investment in the sector, including in distributors and photo-processing facilities. With legal barriers to direct investment gone, Kodak established a local subsidiary to provide technical and marketing support to its exclusive distributor. The American managers were confident that Nagase's network of 33 distributors and dealers was sufficient to compensate for the loss of Asanuma.[14]

In fact, by 1983, Kodak's sales soared and its market share of consumer color film reached an all-time high of 15.8 percent. This success was primarily attributed to Kodak's decision not to raise prices in response to the increased market cost in 1980 of silver, a major component in the manufacture of film, and the resulting wide price differential between its product and Fuji's. Other contributing factors were Kodak's introduction of the highly popular 110 cartridge film two years earlier than its Japanese competitors and the decline of import quotas, which enabled the company to bring more film into Japan.

But it was not until 1984 that Kodak made its major push into the Japanese market by creating a joint venture, Kodak Japan Ltd., which absorbed Nagase's division of Kodak products. Starting with only 11 people, Kodak set up a technical center in Tokyo and hired Japanese salespeople, managers, and advertising and marketing experts.[15] In 1986, Kodak listed its shares on the Tokyo Stock Exchange to allow for greater local participation in the company. To bolster marketing efforts in Japan, Kodak undercut its competition by selling its film at an average rate of 100 yen (90 US cents) less per roll, even though its product was imported. In addition, it sold its film in Japan under a private label for the Japanese Consumer Cooperative Movement, a group of 2,500 retail outlets, at an estimated 38 percent discount off the price of its own brand in Japan.[16]

Fuji and Kodak ruthlessly attacked and counterattacked each other. Both firms introduced new products in quick succession, advertising them with outrageously large colored neon signs in major metropolitan areas in order to capture that all-important market share. In addition to fighting

---

14. Kodak had built direct distribution systems in the United States, Canada, the United Kingdom, France, Spain, Sweden, Switzerland, Taiwan, Singapore, Indonesia, Thailand, Chile, Peru, South Africa, Australia, and New Zealand.

15. Kodak also opened a state-of-the-art research and development facility in Yokohama to develop goods tailor-made for the Japanese market; its products, such as the Weekend 35 single-use camera, which could be used under water, and the Panorama single-use camera for wide-angle prints, had no competitive counterpart.

16. Wendy Bounds, "Kodak Pursues A Greater Market Share in Japan with New Private-Label Film," *The Asian Wall Street Journal*, March 7, 1995, B9.

Figure 3.1 Kodak's market share in Japan in consumer color film roll, 1965–95

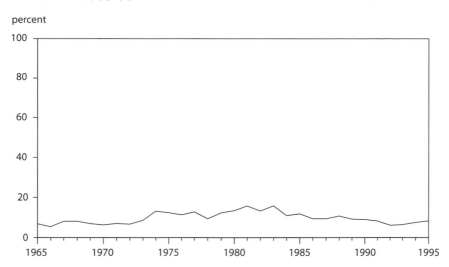

percent

Source: Dewey Ballantine (1995).

over photographic film and paper, they also went head-to-head in the photocopier and clinical blood analyzer markets.

While Fuji had always held an overwhelming advantage over Kodak in Japan, it seemed to solidify its hold of about 70 percent of market share when it became the first company there to introduce the single-use camera (in 1987) and ISO 400 fast film (in 1989).[17] Kodak lagged a year behind Fuji in producing a single-use camera for the Japanese market, and two years behind with the highly popular faster film. The marketing war in Japan became so intense that Kodak had its blimp with "Go Kodak" printed on it buzz the Fuji Tower in Tokyo just to rile the company's management.

By 1995, Kodak had more than 4,300 employees in Japan and had built its own network of affiliated photo-processing laboratories by acquiring an equity position in several Japanese firms. It accounted for 8.3 percent of the local market in color film. But less than half of Kodak's more than $1 billion total annual revenues in Japan was from consumer film products. The company also stopped trading its shares on the Tokyo Stock Exchange (see figure 3.1).

Kodak claimed that by the time the Japanese government had lifted all trading restrictions in the photographic sector in 1979, Fuji Photo Film

---

17. After the film in the plastic single-use camera is developed, the photo finisher returns the camera to the company for reuse. This innovation was considered the brainchild of Minoru Ohnishi, the president of Fuji.

had already created the closed distribution system that has acted to the present day to protect its business in Japan and its 70 percent market share (see appendix figure 3A.1).

Antitrust and Trade Frameworks

The United States

The United States has one of the world's oldest and the most comprehensive system of antitrust regulations, embodied in such laws as the Sherman Act (1890), the Clayton Act (1914), the Robinson-Patman Act (1936), and the Celler-Kefauver Act of 1950 (the latter two being amendments to the Clayton Act). Under the US system, antitrust laws are articulated and enforced by the courts; the final arbiter of this case-by-case adjudication is the Supreme Court. While US antitrust doctrine is premised on ensuring that the quality of competition generally is not injured, noncompetitive behavior is more often than not interpreted as causing harm to specific individuals or business firms.

In the American legal system, individuals or corporations can bring private antitrust lawsuits before the courts. From 1980 to 1989, 10,018 private antitrust cases were filed in the United States, compared to 1,001 government-initiated cases (First 1995, 163). The goal of these private litigants was not to maximize the economic welfare of the country nor to establish public policy by providing guidance to other business firms, but to gain financial compensation. Private litigants sought the "treble-damage remedy": triple the actual damage incurred was awarded if the plaintiff could prove the fact of injury and the amount.

The president's primary vehicle for negotiating and implementing international trade policy is the Office of the USTR, a cabinet-level agency within the Executive Office of the President. While the US trade representative is not a cabinet member per se, the official holds the title of ambassador and is directly responsible to both the president and Congress, which must confirm his or her appointment.

Internationally, the USTR has at its disposal a number of enforcement tools approved by Congress to help break down foreign trade barriers. The most important of these methods of dealing with trade cases are section 301 of the Trade Act of 1974 and the dispute settlement procedures of the WTO.

Section 301 is the principal statute for addressing unfair foreign practices affecting US exports of goods and services. It can be used to enforce US rights under international trade agreements and also to respond to unreasonable, unjustifiable, or discriminatory foreign government practices that burden or restrict US commerce. Under section 301 the USTR can take action, subject to direction from the president, against such practices as withdrawing trade agreement concessions and imposing duties, fees, or restrictions on imports.

Throughout the 1980s and early 1990s, successive US administrations actively used the unilateral threat of retaliatory measures under section 301 to improve market access for US exporters in both emerging markets and developed economies. In most cases, the one-year investigation conducted by the USTR, combined with a 30-day notice period for imposing tariffs or quotas required under the legislation, helped to catalyze an agreement, as well as provide a face-saving period during which both sides in a dispute could back away from a trade war.

Japan

Modern Japan's main legal framework for anticompetitive conduct was originally put in place by US General Douglas MacArthur, who as Supreme Commander for the Allied Powers (SCAP) of Japan headed the victorious Allied occupation from 1945 to 1951. As part of his effort to "democratize" Japan, MacArthur quickly introduced antitrust principles by dismantling the *zaibatsu*, the large family-owned conglomerates that dominated the Japanese economy before and during World War II through their cross-ownership of banks, manufacturing, and distribution. The four major firms—Mitsubishi, Mitsui, Sumitomo, and Yasuda—were, in effect, the military-industrial complex of imperial Japan.

Under SCAP's autocratic direction, in 1947 the Japanese Diet (Parliament) approved the Anti-Monopoly Law (AML) that established the Japan Fair Trade Commission (JFTC) to ensure the existence of competitive conditions by destroying cartels and preventing the reemergence of large, single-firm monopolies. The JFTC was empowered to eliminate "substantial disparities" in economic power—by divestiture, if necessary—and to prevent various devices for monopolization such as interlocking directorates, intercorporate stockholding, and holding companies.[18] The Diet also passed the Trade Association Act of 1948, which prohibited groups of firms from restrictive operating practices.

After the peace treaty of September 1951 returned full sovereignty to Japan, the Diet wasted little time in modifying the US-imposed antitrust laws. An amendment to the AML in 1953 permitted groups of domestic manufacturing firms in "depressed industries" to form cartels in order to rationalize production, improve technology, assess quality, and increase

---

18. In 1949 and 1950, before the end of the occupation, the AML's prohibition of interlocking directorates, stockholding, and mergers was modified, as SCAP was concerned that the economy was not developing fast enough. At a time when communists had gained control of China and North Korea, the United States worried that a weakened Japan could undercut the region's defense.

business efficiency (Ito 1992, 204).[19] In addition, the practice of maintaining resale price through linked relationships called *keiretsu* was reinstituted, and the Trade Association Act was repealed. The constituent firms of the old *zaibatsu* were drawn together again; but now, instead of being centrally controlled by a holding company, relations between the various entities were looser and often indeterminate (Allen 1981, 41).[20]

The AML, which was amended again in 1977 and 1991, empowers the JFTC to monitor all oligopolistic industries and investigate violations reported by any person.[21] If it finds any price-fixing or other market-rigging measures, it can order the payment of fines or "administrative surcharges" against a cartel. If the matter involved is criminal, the JFTC can refer the case to the prosecuting authority who would try the case in court. Convictions rarely result in penal sentences. In the 10-year period from 1985 to 1994, the JFTC conducted only 109 cases, handing out penalties totaling $223.3 million (Willkie, Farr & Gallagher 1995). While Articles 25 and 26 of the AML allow courts to rule on private action in antitrust cases, the JFTC must first determine that there was unlawful conduct. If the matter is then taken to court, the plaintiff need only prove linkage between the damage and the illegal conduct. According to Harry First of New York University Law School, an expert on Japanese law, "This takes on great significance because the JFTC has always preferred to act informally, disposing of the large bulk of its cases through warnings or guidance" (First 1995, 147). Under the AML, plaintiffs can recover only single damages, and there is no provision for the additional recovery of attorney fees. In 1989, the Japanese Supreme Court held that plaintiffs could use Article 709 of the Civil Code, the general tort provision, to recover damages caused by antitrust violations, but the plaintiff had to first prove unlawful conduct before establishing a linkage to the damages; not until 1993 was any private plaintiff successful in recovering damages under the AML.[22]

---

19. Industries designated "depressed" by the Ministry of International Trade and Industry (MITI) were then approved by the JFTC under Article 24-3 of the AML; "after such a cartel was formed, production and investment schedules were coordinated by MITI." Thus, at times during the 1970s and 1980s the coal mining, aluminum, and shipbuilding industries were legal cartels.

20. After 1953, the ability of the JFTC to curb monopoly and restrictive practices was further weakened by special enactments sponsored by MITI, which made it possible for the law to be bypassed in particular industries. Moreover, firms brought under scrutiny by the commission sometimes pleaded successfully that they had acted under "administrative guidance."

21. The 1977 amendments limited a bank's shareholding of a company to 5 percent of the company's equity and introduced an "administrative surcharge" against cartels affecting prices. The 1991 reforms, which followed the 1989–90 Structural Impediments Initiative talks between the United States and Japan, raised the amount of surcharge to be imposed by the JFTC.

22. Professor Mitsuo Matsushita of Seikei University, "Private Enforcement of Competition Law" (speech, 1996). In the breakthrough case, upheld by the Osaka High Court, a Japanese

Rather than viewing antitrust regulations as a legal mechanism for protecting the quality of competition, the Japanese saw them as a bureaucratic approach to managing the economy through "administrative guidance." The former chairman of the JFTC, Masami Kogayu, conceded that "even though 48 years have passed since the AML was established in Japan, it had not really taken root in Japanese society."[23]

This attitude is explained in part by the strong tendency in Japanese society to value cooperation over competition, perhaps best illustrated in the wording in the first article of the 1947 AML. After setting out the law's intent to promote "free and fair competition," it concluded by stating the law's overall purpose: "to protect the democratic and wholesome development of the national economy as well as assure the interests of consumers in general" (quoted in First 1995, 144). This phrasing would later provide US negotiators with an insight into how Japan's government then viewed the proper place for antitrust legislation. Of paramount concern was protecting not the consumer, the individual, but rather the national economic interest. The Japanese cultural aversion to litigation also stunted any significant doctrinal development of the AML, as legal precedents were scarce. Without the practical guidance offered by court cases, enforcing the highly detailed piece of legislation was not feasible.

US influence on Japan's antitrust enforcement surfaced again in the late 1980s during the Structural Impediments Initiative (SII), a bilateral negotiation aimed at setting a new framework for getting negotiations between the two countries back on track after the Market-Oriented Sector-Specific (MOSS) talks had broken down over importation in particular areas that the Japanese considered to be strategic industries underpinning their economy, such as rice and lumber. As First notes, "The fact that the United States focused on antitrust as a critical trade issue made antitrust into an important economic policy for Japan's government. It was irrelevant whether Japan's government believed, as a general matter, that antitrust laws were good economic policy. Doing something about antitrust laws became vital national policy simply because it was necessary for managing the trade relationship with the United States" (First 1995, 174).

As a result of the SII discussions, the JFTC published *The Antimonopoly Act Guidelines Concerning Distribution Systems and Business Practices* in 1991. This 93-page document, written in English, spelled out in detail where, in

---

small elevator service company using Article 709 proved that Toshiba, which manufactured elevators, illegally used anticompetitive tie-in clauses to favor its own service subsidiary and that its refusal to sell spare parts prevented the independent maintenance contractor from working in buildings with Toshiba elevators. Among other arguments, both sides cited legal precedents from Kodak antitrust cases in the United States.

23. Michiyo Nakamoto, "The Watchdog that Refuses to Bite—Japan's Anti-Cartel Agency," *The Financial Times*, February 23, 1996, 4.

its view, the line between legality and illegality falls in such practices as boycotts, exclusive dealing arrangements, full-line forcing, reciprocal dealing, sales territory restrictions, rebates, resale price maintenance, acquisition of ownership interests in vertical trading partners, and the abuse of a dominant bargaining position by retailers (Scherer 1995, 2). Enforcement of the AML was also increased.

The World Trade Organization

The WTO was established in April 1994 when the ministers from 112 nations gathered in Morocco and signed the Final Act Embodying the Results of the Uruguay Round of Multilateral Trade Negotiations. The legal texts in this 550-page document spell out the results of the round's negotiations, which began in Punta del Este, Uruguay, in September 1986.

The forerunner of the WTO was the GATT, established following World War II to provide a mechanism for setting international trade standards and providing a voluntary forum for resolving disputes. The WTO went a step further. Article III of the agreement, the Dispute Settlement Understanding (DSU), defines an arrangement for a new "trade court," known as the Dispute Settlement Body. For the first time, a dispute settlement mechanism's text and procedures constituted treaty obligations (as opposed to "interpretations" or "understanding of practices"), and its use was mandatory (see appendix figure 1B.1 in chapter 1).

As soon as the WTO began operating in January 1995, the USTR in the Clinton administration, under the direction first of Ambassador Mickey Kantor and later of Ambassador Barshefsky, made vigorous use of the dispute settlement provisions of the Geneva-based international monitoring body, filing 20 cases in a 21-month period.[24] In 1996 alone, the United States invoked the dispute settlement procedure 14 times, compared with eight cases brought by Canada and seven by the European Union.[25]

---

24. Mickey Kantor was the USTR from January 1993 until April 1996, when he became secretary of commerce following the death of Ron Brown. Charlene Barshefsky, designated acting USTR by President Clinton in April 1996, was officially appointed to the position in January 1997.

25. The United States won the first case that it took to the WTO involving Japan's taxes on liquor imports. It signed a settlement agreement in another case involving European Union imports of grain. In a third case, the defending party, Portugal, changed its practice regarding the protection of patents as a result of the US complaint. The USTR settled on two other issues, one involving Japan's protection for sound recordings and the other, Turkey's discriminatory box-office tax on foreign films.

Kodak Takes Action

In December 1993, Kodak hired George Fisher from Motorola to be its president and CEO. Fisher, a dynamic, results-oriented executive, came to the job with a well-earned reputation as an unrelenting fighter in developing market share.[26] Fisher was adamant in his belief that closed foreign markets were one of corporate America's major obstacles to global success. He unabashedly claimed, "I don't see anything wrong in getting the help of our government to help us be successful."[27]

Fisher's mandate at Kodak was to restructure and revitalize the ailing company. He stripped some $7.9 billion in tangential businesses away from Kodak and revamped those that remained into seven profit centers. Kodak stock was trading on the New York Stock Exchange at $40 a share when Fisher took over. By December 1996, it was trading at $82 a share.[28]

Yet Fisher had inherited a major problem. Despite its worldwide success, its considerable investment in the Japanese market, and a brand name that had been recognized for generations, Kodak could manage to carve out only about 10 percent of the market share in Japan. On May 18, 1995, Kodak filed a 280-page petition with the USTR under section 301 of the 1974 Trade Act, claiming that it was being denied full access to the consumer photographic film and paper market in Japan.[29] The entire submission, which took two years to produce, was prepared entirely by Dewey Ballantine's Washington office. Lacking an office in Japan, the international firm did not seek assistance from Japanese lawyers; its research was conducted with the help of several local marketing firms. The report, titled *Privatizing Protection: Japanese Market Barriers in Consumer Photographic Film and Paper*, claimed that the wholesale price of a roll of color film in Japan was 3.1 times higher than in the United States, 3.6 times higher than in the United Kingdom, and 4.1 times higher than in Switzerland. It further claimed that even in the stores where Kodak film could be found, in four out of five purchases Japan's consumers were denied the benefit of Kodak's competitive wholesale price.[30]

---

26. Neil Weinberg, "Calling the Competition," *Forbes*, November 4, 1996, 146. As Motorola's CEO, Fisher successfully lobbied the US government to use threats of trade sanctions, under section 301 of the 1974 Trade Act, to open up the fast-growing cellular telephone market in Japan to his and other US firms. At the time (1994) Motorola was doing a thriving business in cell phones. Also see Matthew Fletcher, "Film Fight—Fuji vs. Kodak," *Asia Week Magazine*, July 5, 1996, www.asiaweek.com.

27. Fisher, quoted in Cooper and Bounds, "Kodak Chief and Capital Lawyer," A12.

28. New York Stock Exchange listing, *The International Herald Tribune*, December 3, 1996.

29. USTR press release, June 13, 1996.

30. Kodak's legal brief took a shotgun approach to possible trade violations by Japan; one of its claims was that Japan's actions were not only "unjustifiable" practices inconsistent with international trade law but a breach of the 1953 US-Japan Friendship, Commerce and Navigation Treaty and the 1961 OECD Code of Liberalization of Capital Movements.

Kodak's section 301 case focused mainly on Japan's "vertical market restraints," which are the impediments encountered by importers seeking access to the wholesale and retail distribution channels needed to convey their products to the end consumer (Scherer 1995, 2–3). The complaints by Kodak included the following:

- Fuji controlled and enjoyed an exclusive relationship with all the leading wholesalers (*tokuyakuten*) of consumer photographic products, who in turn strongly influenced the distribution channels for consumer film down to the retail level.[31] Kodak claimed that the *tokuyakuten* were essential for doing business in Japan, but that the costs of setting up its own distribution network on the same level in order to compete fairly would be so high that doing business in Japan would be uneconomical. Because it was closed off from the existing distribution system, Kodak claimed that Fuji's 70 percent market share of film in Japan was the equivalent of a monopolistic market.

- Fuji controlled a network of photo-processing laboratories that served as a captive market for consumer photographic paper.

- The Fuji system was reinforced by a web of financial ties with the Mitsui Group of banks, one of the major lenders in the Japanese economy.[32]

- To maintain stable, high prices—up to four times higher than those in other major markets—Fuji and its affiliated dealers used a variety of anticompetitive practices, including resale price maintenance; horizontal coordination of pricing; opaque and discriminatory volume-based rebates; and reliance on its trade association, the Zenren, to monitor and enforce discipline on maverick retailers who discounted prices. (figure 3.2)[33]

---

31. According to the USTR's *National Trade Estimate Report on Foreign Trade Barriers—Japan* (March 1996), film is sold at 279,000 outlets in Japan. About half of all sales are made through photo-specialty stores (as compared with 3 percent in the United States). Another 23 percent are sold through supermarkets and department stores, 8 percent at tourist resorts and parks, 7 percent at convenience stores, 2 percent at drug stores, and the rest through kiosks and other channels. At the retail level, foreign film is available in only about 36 percent of all outlets and only about half the photo-specialty stores.

32. Mitsui was one of the traditional *zaibatsu* until the end of World War II, and Kodak claimed that its involvement exceeded the guidelines of the AML with the tacit approval of the JFTC. Mitsui is today part of a *keiretsu*, and it financed Fuji's interlocking financial ties with processing labs around the country.

33. Kodak alleged that it was through the Zenren and other trade associations that horizontal pressure (i.e., down the chain from manufacturer to wholesaler to retailer) was applied to maintain the retail price suggested by Fuji, thus preventing price reductions for consumers. A survey commissioned by Kodak in November 1995 concluded that the average price of film at a Zenren store was higher than at other stores.

Figure 3.2   Indexed film prices in Japan, 1986–95

index (1986 = 100)

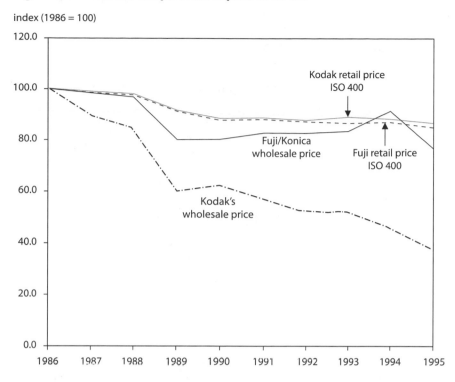

Price stability was indirectly reinforced by the government of Japan through the JFTC, which "flexibly" interpreted and enforced the antimonopoly laws and used its authority to administer an industry competition code that prohibited a range of promotional activities at the retail level.

Kodak claimed that it simply sought access to retail shelf space in Japan and an end to anticompetitive price stabilization activity in that market. Fisher was adamant that he did not desire the US government to fight for guaranteed market share for imports or to impose trade sanctions on Japanese products. In the company's words, all it wanted was "to get on the shelves, get off the shelves and get on more shelves."[34] The remedies that Kodak urged the USTR to suggest would require extensive intervention by the Japanese government to change Fuji's practices and to force the JFTC into acting more aggressively against anticompetitive and monopolistic practices, including directing Fuji to terminate

---

34. Alan Wolff; unless otherwise noted, all quotes from Wolff are from a November 1, 1996, interview with the author.

- all practices that promoted horizontal and vertical price fixing;

- the exclusive distribution of Fuji film by primary and secondary wholesalers and ensuring that the wholesalers were free of any coercion restricting their willingness to distribute Kodak and other competitors' products; and

- rebates that illegally excluded competitors and induced resale price maintenance.

Also in May 1995, Kodak hired Ira Wolf, a former assistant USTR responsible for Japan and China (1992–95), to be its vice president and director of Japan relations at its Tokyo office. Wolf, who spoke Japanese, was the government liaison officer for Motorola in Japan (1990–92) when Fisher was its CEO.

Kodak's lead lawyer at Dewey Ballantine in Washington was Alan Wolff, who had helped to write section 301 of the 1974 Trade Act while he was deputy general counsel at the USTR. Wolff emphasized the importance of getting Kodak's products on the shelves: "It's the consumer who determines the level of trade. If we could get access to the Japanese distribution system and be able to price competitively, we would capture our fair share of the market." Indeed, Kodak's research showed that in Tokyo, where it had the strongest market presence (its film could be found in 54 percent of the retail outlets surveyed), it enjoyed twice the market share it had in Japan as a whole (Kodak claimed that its product was wholly absent from two-thirds of the Japanese market) (Alan Wolff at Dewey Ballantine, 1995).

The Kodak action coincided with a period of growing trade friction between the United States and Japan caused by contentious negotiations over the sale of US autos and auto parts in Japan. The US ambassador to Japan, former vice president Walter Mondale, who was very much involved in those negotiations, reportedly said to one American businessman in Tokyo, "I'm used to a system where elected leaders make decisions and bureaucrats implement them, but this place has it turned upside down."[35]

On July 2, 1995, the USTR initiated an investigation into Kodak's allegations under section 301 of the Trade Act of 1974, independently verifying them through the US Embassy in Tokyo and other sources. Eleven months later, it concluded that the US firm did have a substantial case, on the following evidence:

- When, under international pressure between 1964 and 1976, Japan dismantled its formal restrictions on imports and inward investment

---

35. Teresa Watanabe, "In Mondale, U.S. Firms Found an Adept Envoy; Diplomacy: Ambassador's Quick, Clear Understanding of Japan Helped American Business, Executives Say," *Daily Yomiuri Newspaper*, Japan, November 10, 1996 (syndicated article originally published in the *Los Angeles Times*).

in the industry, it simultaneously created an anticompetitive market structure as a "liberalization countermeasure" to restrict foreign producers' effective participation in the market.

- This restrictive market that the Ministry for International Trade and Industry (MITI) established under the liberalization countermeasures in the 1970s was still in place, maintained and tolerated by the government of Japan despite Japan's commitments to the United States regarding structural adjustments to the economy.

- The industrial policy of the Japanese government—a major component being the lukewarm enforcement of its AML—permitted anticompetitive practices by domestic manufacturers and trade associations that were serious violations of Japan's own laws on competition.

Fuji Responds

In Tokyo, the top managers of Fuji Photo Film were not only stunned by the scope of the Kodak complaint but also offended by what they thought were outright malicious lies. They feared the harm those lies would do, not so much in Japan as in markets around the world where Fuji was spending enormous amounts of time and money cultivating an image and a reputation as a dynamic and innovative firm. Fuji's president, Minoru Ohnishi, complained that

> Kodak has violated all the standards of business ethics. It has shamelessly made false allegations against Fuji in a self-serving attempt to use political pressure to accomplish what its own lack of managerial effort and failed marketing strategies have not been able to accomplish. What is most troubling about Kodak's action is not that it attempted to tarnish Fuji with false allegations of anticompetitive practices, but that it attempted to exploit growing tensions between the US and Japan on trade issues to the detriment of a crucial bilateral relationship.[36]

Fuji wasted little time in huddling with their two key international strategists. Willkie Farr & Gallagher, a US-based law firm, had a long history of working for foreign firms, including work as counsel to the Japanese auto industry during the US-Japan auto talks. Edelman, an international public relations firm founded in the United States, had offices all over the world; its Washington office boasted Mike Deaver, the communications wizard of the Reagan White House, and used the lobbying firm of Downey Chandler, whose principals were a former Democratic congressman from New York (Tom Downey) and was a former Republican congressman from Washington state (Rod Chandler).

---

36. Fuji Film press release, May 1995.

During their brainstorming, they concluded that the small staff at the USTR would never have the time to investigate the case properly; they therefore resolved to neutralize Kodak's home court advantage by over-whelming the trade representative's office with documents refuting Kodak's evidence. "George Fisher understood the system and the built-in advantages any US company would have playing the [section 301] game," said Rob Rehg, senior vice president of Edelman. "We decided we would match them pound for pound in terms of paper."[37] They produced *Rewriting History,* their own 535-page rebuttal of Kodak's 280-page study.

The Fuji side spent millions of dollars creating a rapid response team that not only rebutted Kodak's claims but often "pre-butted" them. Between July 1995 and June 1996, Fuji representatives made 17 submissions to the American government, compared with Kodak's 9. After conducting three market surveys to Kodak's one, Fuji argued that more than three-fourths of the four primary film wholesalers that sell Fuji products purchased Kodak film or had relationships with Kodak film suppliers, claimed that Kodak had never approached the four major *tokuyakuten* (which Fuji was not preventing from carrying Kodak film), and blamed Kodak's low market share on its own failings, pointing out the far greater success of Konica, a film manufacturer that used two of its own distributors (Willkie Farr & Gallagher 1995). Over the months, journalists around the globe were showered with documents, letters, briefs, and even videotapes showing Kodak film being sold in Japan.

The Agencies Take Action

MITI Gets Involved

The Kodak case was filed at a time when MITI was working to formulate a new strategy for dealing with the United States on trade. In the spring of 1995, the US government threatened Japan with more than $6 billion in punitive duties under section 301 if it did not open up its home market to allow more US cars and car parts to be sold in Japan and to Japanese car companies overseas. Although this dispute was eventually settled, the government of Japan quietly decided it had had enough.[38] The next time

---

37. Rob Rehg, interview with author, Washington, DC, October 22, 1996.

38. Yataka Osada (professor of international law, Surugadai University, Japan), interview with the author, May 17, 1997. The Japanese attitude toward bilateral negotiations began to shift after a new five-year accord on semiconductors was reached in the summer of 1991. Both sides signed a document that called for a 20 percent target for US market access in Japan by the end of 1992. While Japan insisted that the deal's language explicitly noted that the target was neither a guarantee, a ceiling, nor a floor on foreign market share, the Americans publicly declared it a commitment.

the US government invoked section 301, Japan would simply refuse to negotiate on those terms.

On March 15, 1996, Japan's top trade negotiator, Yoshihiro Sakamoto, who was vice minister for international affairs at MITI, fired the first shot across the Americans' bow. Speaking in English so that there would be no misunderstanding, he told an audience at the Foreign Correspondents' Club of Japan that "the era of 'bilateralism' is over. . . . This was not to say that bilateral frictions would disappear. But any such friction from now on would have to be solved in accordance with the WTO and other international rules and by following market mechanisms."[39]

MITI felt that for the first time, it had been given the perfect cover for not having to engage the USTR in bilateral negotiations under section 301. The film industry was not regulated by the government. There were no import restrictions, and all the companies operating in that industry were private and independent.[40] MITI maintained it was not a party in the section 301 dispute, contending that any allegations of anticompetitive business practices came under the jurisdiction of the JFTC, a quasi-judicial body that was a distinct branch of government. It also realized that Kodak Japan Ltd., a registered Japanese company, had never filed an official complaint with the JFTC alleging any anticompetitive practices. Nor, for that matter, had Kodak ever sought to resolve the matter by approaching Fuji or any other participants in the industry. The Japanese officials believed that eventually the case could end up before the WTO, which was their preference all along. It seized the opportunity to sit back and appear to take a tough stance against the United States.

Adding to tensions between the countries was the months-long trial of three US soldiers, who in March were found guilty of raping a schoolgirl in Okinawa. The public furor in Japan over the case pressured the United States to reduce its sizable military presence on the island; more broadly, it threatened the stability of the US-Japan security relationship, the touchstone to which the nations had always returned in eventually resolving disputes. Although Washington was keen to delink issues of security and trade, in Japan the Okinawa incident translated symbolically into a behind-the-stage power struggle, exacerbated by earlier suggestions from officials in the Clinton administration that trade and economic policy, rather than defense and regional security, would be the basis for a new US-Japan relationship.

---

39. Text of speech supplied by MITI.

40. Fact sheet supplied by MITI through Willkie Farr & Gallagher, November 1996. Japan had no tariffs on photographic color film and paper, unlike the United States (3.7 percent duty on imports) and the European Union (5.3 percent duty on film, and 7.6 percent on photographic paper). In 1995, the share of imports in the Japanese market was 18.7 percent for consumer color film and 29.6 percent for photographic paper.

On February 21, 1996, the JFTC announced it would look into possible anticompetitive business practices in the Japanese markets for color film and photographic paper.[41] The probe, conducted through the voluntary submissions of material and information by the concerned parties, would focus mainly on market structures and corporate interactions. The findings would be issued in a report by March 1997. This survey, undertaken by the JFTC's Economic Department, was separate from the Kodak private-party complaint made in August 1996 under Article 45-1 of the AML, which was being looked into by the Investigation Department. The JFTC survey was not itself an investigation, though the JFTC could take action against any problematic practices that it found. According to Kodak's vice president in Japan, Ira Wolf, "We were cooperating with the JFTC. They asked us questions and we gave them answers; but we did not volunteer any information."[42]

Three months later, Hashimoto attempted to bolster the JFTC's international image as a reliable regulatory body by appointing Yasuchika Negoro, the former head of the Tokyo High Prosecutor's Office, to chair its five-member executive council. All previous heads of the commission had been drawn either from MITI or from the Ministry of Finance. The weakness of its antimonopoly enforcement had earned the JFTC the not-undeserved reputation in its own country of being a watchdog without teeth. The commission had conducted 13 similar surveys since 1990, including one on the film industry in 1992,[43] without recommending that a single company be prosecuted for breach of the AML.

Either because of or despite its extensive experience and knowledge of conducting business in Japan, the management of Kodak Japan never formally submitted a request to the JFTC to investigate the alleged anticompetitive conditions in the Japanese photographic film and paper market, or brought any formal charges against Fuji in Japanese court or with a government agency. One option was to lodge complaints with the Office of Trade and Investment, part of an ombudsman system created to mediate market-opening disputes. Kodak's Fisher said bluntly, "We did not feel that the JFTC was the proper investigation forum. The JFTC had been part of the problem."[44]

---

41. The JFTC's announcement came two days before the first scheduled meeting between President Bill Clinton and Prime Minister Ryutaro Hashimoto, who had been heading a shaky coalition government for just over a month. As trade minister, prior to becoming prime minister, Hashimoto steadfastly fought US demands for "managed trade" during the auto and auto parts negotiations concluded in June 1995.

42. Unless otherwise noted, all quotes from Ira Wolf are from a November 15, 1996, interview with the author.

43. *The Highly Oligopolistic Industries Report* (1992), a study that included the film industry, examined the question of vertical market restraints and how they suppressed price competition.

44. Fisher, quoted in Nikkei News Service, August 12, 1996 (statement made in 1995).

Alan Wolff, the company's lead counsel, speculates that Kodak's lack of trust in the JFTC could be traced to an earlier experience: A Kodak executive in Japan who submitted documents to the commission in 1977 later discovered that it had leaked proprietary information to Japanese film companies. Wolff also contends that part of the Kodak strategy was to "engage the Japanese government so that any JFTC review would not be conducted in a vacuum" and delayed interminably.

Barshefsky's Decision

To USTR Barshefsky and her dedicated team, the Kodak case was important because it put a spotlight on alleged anticompetitive practices in Japan that extended to other areas of the Japanese economy and all types of foreign consumer products. As she noted, "We see in this sector [photographic paper and film] the same market barriers that are present in sector after sector in Japan. These are systematic structural barriers, such as closed distribution systems and excessive regulation that we have been discussing with Japan for years. With the detailed evidence uncovered in this investigation, we now have a clear understanding of how these barriers have interacted to keep out competitive foreign products in a particular sector."[45]

The USTR saw the strategic advantages of this case: If the WTO Dispute Settlement Body ruled in favor of the United States, the office would accomplish at one stroke in an international forum what had taken four laborious years to achieve in 23 US-Japan sectoral agreements, negotiated using the threat of unilateral sanctions under section 301. Though hundreds of companies ask Washington to investigate unfair trade practices, the USTR accepts only about 14 cases per year, and even fewer are taken to Geneva for resolution by the WTO.

But there was certainly a downside to pursuing the matter. "If we lost, the fallout would not be predictable and scientific, it would be political," commented a USTR lawyer. She added, "It would be bad for the WTO if we lost because it would play to the skeptics in the Congress." To some American legislators, the GATT agreement was not a treaty but a statute, under which US law should not be subordinated to that of another body (Horlick 1995).[46]

Barshefsky was the target of political pressure from all sides. Kodak had spent millions of dollars in legal fees and lobbying efforts to see this

---

45. Barshefsky, quoted in the USTR press release, June 13, 1996.

46. In June 1995, Senate Majority Leader Robert Dole (R-KS) unsuccessfully proposed legislation that would have created a commission to review all adopted reports of WTO dispute settlement panels and the Appellate Body considered adverse to the United States; three such judgments in a five-year period would trigger a process leading to a possible congressional vote on withdrawing from the WTO.

complaint through as a section 301 case.[47] The company clearly wanted action. On March 28, 1996, testifying at a hearing of the House Ways and Means trade subcommittee, Fisher argued that "while certain discrete actions of Japan's government could be presented to a WTO panel for adjudication, its toleration of systematic anti-competitive activities that block market access is not covered by WTO rules."[48] At the same time, officials in the Clinton administration were pointing out to the USTR that a decision to put this case before the WTO would ensure that they would not have to deal with the potentially sensitive issue until after the president's November 1996 reelection bid.[49] "Kodak was fairly powerful politically," noted a USTR official. "They had friends in high places and it was hard to think that there wouldn't be a strong reaction if we lost. It wasn't a wonderful thing for us because it raised the stakes higher."

The USTR began to carefully examine its options. In the process, officials distilled Kodak's list of grievances to two core issues that could form the basis for either acting unilaterally under section 301 or seeking a broader consensus. If it chose to go before the WTO panel, the United States would first cite alleged violations by the government of Japan of the 1994 GATT agreement, pointing to nullification and impairment of GATT benefits arising from the full panoply of "liberalization countermeasures" that were put in place and maintained to thwart imports in this sector.[50] In making this argument, it would cite Articles II, III, X, and XXIII:1(b) of the GATT. Moreover, though the WTO was empowered to rule only on current practices, the USTR would claim that the liberalization countermeasures put in place by MITI in the 1970s were still in effect in the photographic industry and that while the Japanese laws were on their face neutral, they were being abused administratively.

---

47. "US Cites New Distribution Measures under Expanded Film Complaint," *Inside US Trade*, September 1997.

48. Fisher, quoted in "Kodak Steps Up Pressure for Bilateral Resolution of Film Dispute," *Inside US Trade*, March 29, 1996.

49. The wish to keep international trade from becoming a major issue in the November 1996 elections helps to explain President Clinton's decision in August 1996 to delay by six months the implementation of the Helms-Burton Act, which imposed sanctions on foreign firms that trade with Cuba. Though Clinton was reelected, the Republicans retained control of Congress; their party platform called for US law to supersede all trade agreements whenever disputes arose.

50. USTR press release, October 15, 1996. Specifically, the USTR claimed that (1) the government of Japan, under cover of investment restrictions, limited Kodak's access to the existing distribution system, which handled about 95 percent of the film sold in Japan; (2) the government of Japan restricted the use of marketing incentives through implementation of the 1962 Premiums Law (amended in 1977), which limited the types of premiums and promotional offers a firm could use to generate sales; (3) the Premiums Law regulated the content of advertising; and (4) the Premiums Law deputized local groups of competitors to set and enforce standards of competition.

MITI could be expected to present three counterclaims:

- The US charges were overly broad and vague as to which specific measures constituted a violation of which specific obligation under the GATT and what positive solution it was seeking.

- The theory of a government and business conspiracy was a myth, since the film industry had not been regulated for almost 20 years. The US position was purely historical and unfairly implied that the present government of Japan should be held accountable for the possible abusive behavior of previous administrations.

- If the US allegation that the government of Japan instituted effective "liberalization countermeasures" to block market access in the early 1970s were accepted, how then could one account for Kodak's dramatic rise in market share from about 8 percent in 1970 to almost 18 percent in 1983—a year before Kodak Japan set up its own formal distribution system, still in operation?

In essence, the Japanese argument would attempt to drive home the problematic implications of bringing such claims to the dispute settlement process at the WTO.[51]

The second case the United States might put before another WTO panel concerned the alleged violations by the government of Japan of the 1994 General Agreement on Trade in Services (GATS) arising from the requirements and operations of the Large-Scale Retail Stores Law[52] and measures such as the Guidelines for Rationalizing Terms of Trade for Photo Film and the Basic Policy for Distribution Systematization. The United States claimed that these constituted a serious barrier to foreign service suppliers as well as to importers of film and other consumer products, citing Articles III, VI, XVI, XVII, and XXIII:3 of the GATS. A USTR official observed, "We could bring this GATS case anytime. In effect, the GATS case was simply a backup to the GATT case. Even if the film case was resolved in the first panel, we would probably pursue this because it affects other trade problems."

The Japanese could argue that the Large-Scale Retail Store Law was no different from many building and zoning regulations in the United States

---

51. Official at MITI, interview with the author, Tokyo, November 14, 1996.

52. USTR press release, October 15, 1996. The Americans viewed this 1976 law as placing onerous requirements on prospective store owners, who had to complete lengthy and cumbersome negotiations with local authorities, merchants, and consumers, as well as MITI, before opening a store. The USTR contended that because large stores tended to carry more imported products than small stores, government limitations on their numbers severely constricted foreign manufacturers' access to the Japanese market—though large retail stores made up only 17 percent of the 279,000 retail outlets that sold film in Japan, they handled three-quarters of all sales.

or other countries. Moreover, the law itself did not regulate particular products like film. The USTR believed that MITI might further assert that its "administrative guidelines" did not hamper the distribution or sale of specific products, defending itself against the US argument that there was a "causal connection" between the distribution of film and paper and the "adjustments recommended" to private firms in an unregulated industry. While the Japanese government's "recommendations" did not carry an obligation under the law, considerable literature on the subject suggested that in the cultural context of Japanese society, they did in fact carry the same weight as law.

At the same time as the GATT and GATS questions were before the WTO, the US government could also request talks with the Japanese government under the 1960 GATT decision concerning consultations on restrictive business practices (RBP). Through this mechanism, according to a USTR official, the United States could bring forward the significant evidence of anticompetitive activities it had uncovered in this sector and ask the government of Japan to take appropriate action. In effect, this was a potential second track in the Kodak-Fuji dispute, which could take place either during or after the WTO panel hearings. Barshefsky expected the Japanese to counter, as they had done in earlier negotiations on this issue, with the "mirror image" argument and insist that business practices in both markets be examined simultaneously. A precedent of sorts for using the 1960 GATT decision as an alternative mechanism for substantive discussion was set in the auto talks in 1993–95, when the United States and Japan resorted to what was called the Auto Basket of Framework Negotiations as a way to circumvent the deadlock surrounding the Americans' section 301 claim. It had been the first major initiative by the Clinton administration in a trade dispute with Japan.

Barshefsky knew that unlike the unilateral action of section 301, such an approach would keep alive the possibility of a face-saving compromise right up to the public announcement of any WTO findings, as both sides would be shown the panel's recommendations and legal justifications and asked for their comments before a final verdict was rendered. While she felt that the case mounted by the USTR was strong, it was certainly not as clear-cut as Kodak had originally insisted. She had to answer a basic question: Which option would give the US government the most leverage in opening up the Japanese market?

Influenced in part by knowledge that the sanctions on imports threatened by a section 301 action would hardly be effective against Fuji, which has a major film manufacturing plant in Greenwood, South Carolina, and 30 other facilities across the United States; by fear that sanctions on Fuji would harm Polaroid (a major US firm that sells Fuji film in the United States under its own name); and by reluctance to escalate the trade conflict by imposing sanctions on other industries, Ambassador Barshefsky decided on June 13, 1996, to initiate dispute settlement proceedings against the government of Japan through the WTO (see appendix 3B). "This case is about increasing leverage against Japan in a WTO world," said a USTR official. "We are not as reluctant to take unilateral action as the Japanese think, and they will find there was no refuge in the WTO."[53]

The decision to refer this case to the WTO rather than proceed with it under section 301 was made after weeks of exchanging internal position papers that offered a spectrum of options. At one end were the "activist" policymakers who insisted that it was essential to establish quotas and timetables for market share. At the other end were those who favored a pure rules-based approach: change the rule, make discrimination illegal, and then sit back and see what happens. Tempering both of these groups were those who held what might be called an "affirmative action" view, not necessarily demanding specific outcomes but seeking to ensure that minority members (or foreign products or firms) received adequate consideration.

"This was a case of policy being determined from the bottom up, and there are a lot of questions out there that were all being posed for the first time," said a high-level source in the USTR. "Kantor and Barshefsky were pretty open-minded about the whole issue, but after a while, a consensus began to develop that Kodak had provided us with a level of detail we never had before to put to a neutral body. It was that level of proof which influenced our decision."

"This was the appropriate course of action for this case," said Dr. Laura Tyson, head of the president's National Economic Council. "It should allay any concerns that the US was turning away from the multilateral process."[54] Making sure the US government dotted its i's and crossed its t's in its submission to the WTO, Barshefsky requested that Kodak a submit a complaint to the JFTC concerning anticompetitive practices in its industry sector. Kodak did so but in very specific and narrow terms, presenting only a small part of the panoply of grievances it had lodged with the USTR. According to Ira Wolf, "It was a test to see if the JFTC would take any action. Kodak is also using this as a test to see if the JFTC will keep the investigation confidential." Former USTR Mickey Kantor insisted that while the United States has a strong case, "Trade is not a zero-sum game. It can be a win-win situation for everyone."[55]

Turning away from Japan to the other side of a different ocean, Kodak hired former deputy USTR Rufus Yerxa, then working at the Brussels law

---

53. At the time the original story was written in 1996, the case was still pending before the WTO, so the interviewee was talking in the future tense.

54. Tyson, quoted in Helene Cooper and Wendy Bounds, "US Choosing a Mild Course Shifts Kodak's Complaint Over Japan to WTO," *The Asian Wall Street Journal*, June 14, 1996, B5.

55. Mickey Kantor, speaking at the Arco Forum, Kennedy School of Government, Harvard University, October 17, 1996.

firm of Akin, Grump, Strauss, Hauer & Feld, to lobby the European Union to endorse the US case against Japan. Kodak had also been urging the German film producer Agfa-Gevaert to express interest in the case and to exert pressure on local politicians. Fuji tried to counter this move by hiring Frieder Roessler, the former head of the GATT legal affairs division, to drum up support for its position in Europe.[56]

During the summer and fall of 1996, there briefly appeared to be an opportunity for the governments of the two countries to find a way to settle out of court. Concurrent with the GATT consultations, a frustrated team at the USTR tried a new and separate initiative to engage MITI in bilateral talks, invoking a 1960 ruling by the GATT that called on members to be willing to have consultations on restrictive business practices. During the previous year, when the issue was being investigated under section 301, the Japanese had refused to negotiate. Once the matter was referred to the WTO, the two sides met in Geneva only twice, for a half day each time, during the 60 days allowed for "official consultations." US negotiators felt that the talks were going nowhere. One recalled, "We presented our side of the case and they just listened without any intention of responding."[57]

As Japan interpreted the 1960 RBP decision, however, consultations would not amount to an admission by Japan that restrictive practices existed, and any talks that did take place would concern only activities of private companies and not government measures. Furthermore, the Japanese wanted the Americans to agree in advance that if the two sides saw that harmful practices did exist, remedial action should be determined by the Japanese government to decide what action to take; moreover, the newly formed WTO should have no control over the agreement or ability to investigate it.[58]

On October 16, 1996, just as the WTO announced that the Dispute Resolution Body had agreed to form a panel to hear the US complaint against Japan, the Japanese government agreed to allow the European Union to join the talks only if the United States accepted the Japanese request for the talks to include discussions on restrictive practices in the American market. Two days later, the European Union and Mexico announced that they would join the US challenge against the Japanese trade barriers. The Commission declared in an official statement: "The EU is a significant player in

---

56. "EU to Be Third Party in US Film Case in World Trade Organization," *Inside US Trade*, October 18, 1996.

57. The USTR was under the impression that by the end of the decade Japan would be removing barriers like the Large Retail Store Law, which it eased during the 1989–90 SII talks, allowing US companies like Toys"R"Us to enter the Japanese market and do well. The USTR claims that the Japanese government's published deregulation plans committed to phasing out the law by 1991.

58. Japanese WTO Ambassador Minoru Endo, letter to Deputy USTR Booth Gardner, August 9, 1996, Office of the United States Trade Representative.

the Japanese consumer film market. Apart from this economic interest we also have a systemic interest in the operation of the Japanese distribution system and improved market access to the Japanese market, as well as the international dimension of competition raised by this case."[59]

While the United States acceded to two Japanese preconditions—that the talks would not be considered an admission of anything, and any agreement would be limited to areas of government responsibility—it balked at the idea of including restrictive trade practices in the US market and of limiting discussions on the Japanese market to the activities of the private sector. "It would be appropriate to discuss factors and conditions (such as market structure and government measures) relating to the structural and competitive environment in which business practices take place," noted Deputy USTR Booth Gardner.[60] The US interpretation of the RBP decision also did not rule out the WTO's later engaging in oversight of an agreement reached between the two parties. From a tactical point of view, a USTR official pointed out, US negotiators opposed the linkage in the talks because it would establish "equivalency" issues, thereby creating what has been termed a "mirror image" problem.

The RBP talks never took place. Although consultations under the 1960 GATT decision were hardly commonplace—indeed, none had ever been held—US trade officials were exasperated by the Japanese intransigence. Only a year earlier, the two countries had managed at the eleventh hour to end a decade-old dispute over automobiles with an agreement that addressed a range of barriers to market access affecting the sales of foreign autos and auto parts, both to buyers in Japan and to Japanese companies outside Japan. The film dispute was the first time that the Japanese had ever refused to discuss a matter bilaterally, deciding to force the issue rather than to concede or compromise. "We've not even been able to agree on the shape of the table,"[61] noted a USTR official. "So we've told the Japanese government, 'See you in court!'"

Judgment in Geneva

It took three months to form a panel for the WTO dispute resolution procedure. In mid-November 1996, the Japanese delegation submitted the names of candidates from Switzerland, Brazil, and New Zealand. The

---

59. Statement quoted in "EU to Be Third Party in US Film Case in World Trade Organization," *Inside US Trade*, October 18, 1996.

60. Deputy USTR Booth Gardner, letter to Japanese WTO Ambassador Minoru Endo, August 21, 1996, Office of the United States Trade Representative.

61. This metaphor alludes to the six-month stalemate in the opening round of the 1968 Paris peace talks between the United States and North Vietnam.

United States agreed to all three, but the Swiss and the Brazilians both said they were unavailable. The two countries resumed their search.

After vainly going through almost 60 names, the two countries turned in frustration to WTO Director-General Renato Ruggiero and asked him to impose a panel. On December 17, 1996, Ruggiero persuaded the originally agreed-on Swiss and Brazilian candidates to accept the appointment. All three panel members had previous experience with the WTO: William Rossier of Switzerland had served as ambassador to the WTO and chairman of the WTO General Council; Victor Luiz DoPrado of Brazil was first secretary in the WTO delegation; and Adrian Macy of New Zealand, ambassador to Thailand, was formerly ambassador to the WTO.

Once the panel was formed, the chairman quickly realized that the complexity of this case—which would require that the panel consider 21 specific measures by the United States and wade through nearly 20,000 pages of documentation that both sides had presented as evidence— would make it impossible to render a judgment in the usual six months, as set out in the Uruguay Round Dispute Settlement Understanding.[62] A further six months would be needed.

The panel faced the difficult problem of making a ruling under the so-called nonviolation provisions of the GATT 1994 and the GATS. While most WTO disputes involve claims that a member has failed to carry out its obligations under a particular agreement, a matter that is relatively easy to assess, nonviolation complaints arise (under GATT Article XXIII:1, for example) when a member applies "any measure, whether or not it conflicts with the provisions of this Agreement" that denies another member benefits that it expects to obtain.

On December 5, 1997, the WTO panel issued its interim ruling. It concluded that (1) the United States *did not* demonstrate that the Japanese "measures" it cited individually or collectively nullified or impaired benefits to the United States within the meaning of GATT Article XXIII:1(b); (2) the United States *did not* demonstrate that the Japanese distribution "measures" it cited accorded less favorable treatment to imported photographic film and paper within the meaning of GATT Article III:4; and (3) the United States *did not* demonstrate that Japan failed to publish administrative rulings of general application in violation of GATT Article X:1.[63] The final report was issued to the parties on January 30, 1998, and was circulated to WTO members on March 31, 1998. It was adopted by the Dispute Settlement Body on April 22, 1998.

Minoru Ohnishi, Fuji's president and CEO, said that that WTO "prove[d] its mettle" by ruling on the facts. It was an outcome, he claimed, that

---

62. *Inside US Trade*, June 13, 1997.

63. "Japan—Measures Affecting Consumer Photographic Film and Paper," Report of the WTO Panel, WT/DS44/R, March 31, 1998.

"most experts predicted." But a disappointed USTR Barshefsky faulted the ruling for "sidestep[ping] the real issues in this case and instead focus[ing] on narrow, technical issues."[64] Despite such sentiments, the United States chose to forgo an appeal out of its reluctance, according to US officials, to upset legal precedents established by the panel's final report. In particular, uncertainty over whether actions taken by the private sector (and officially tolerated by a domestic government) could be considered "measures" that would be actionable under Article XXX:1 was removed by the case: The panel said that such measures could indeed be actionable, and validation of this principle was regarded as a victory by the United States in its war against Japanese barriers, even if it had lost this particular battle.

The US decision did not stop Kodak from firing its own broadside at the WTO. Without hesitation, Fisher called the verdict "totally unacceptable" and demanded that the US government "define a concrete plan to open the Japanese market."[65] Almost immediately, members of the House and Senate from both sides of the aisle renewed the call for action against Japan under section 301. Within two weeks of the final report's issuance, the Clinton administration announced a new effort to monitor the Japanese film and photographic paper sector to ensure that it was as open as Japan claimed. This initiative was backed by 218 members of the House of Representatives, who signed a letter warning the Japanese ambassador in Washington, Kunihiko Saito, that Congress was ready to put further pressure on Japan.[66]

Despite these strong statements, the United States did not threaten Japan with additional 301 action over market access in the film industry. In fact, some view the Kodak-Fuji case as signaling the end of two decades of fierce market-opening disputes between Japan and the United States. Beginning in the early 1990s, Japan's economic problems and the resurgence of the US economy muted US concerns about competing in Japan.

---

64. Ohnishi, quoted in "Fuji Statement on Film Case," *Inside US Trade*, December 8, 1997. Barshefsky, quoted in "USTR Statement on Film Case," *Inside US Trade*, December 8, 1997.

65. Fisher, quoted in "Kodak Statement on Film Case," *Inside US Trade*, December 8, 1997. In a June 25, 1998, submission to the USTR, Kodak continued its attack on the WTO, complaining that "most of the decisions in the film case were not made by the panelists, who were largely absent from the process, but by WTO Secretariat staffers, who lacked both the competence and the mandate to do so"; it viewed this "inordinate role" as "wholly inappropriate and a serious breach of the organization's responsibility" (Kodak made the comments in a June 25 submission to the Office of USTR dealing with the year's review of the WTO Dispute Settlement Understanding. "Kodak Charges WTO Secretariat with Unfair Intervention in the Film Case," *Inside US Trade*, July 3, 1998).

66. "Text: House Letter on Japan Film," letter and signatures reprinted in *Inside US Trade*, February 20, 1998.

At the same time, the emergence of China as an economic power captured US attention. As less effort was devoted to US trade relations with Japan, the focus of US policy shifted to the security relationship and Japan's major macroeconomic problems.

Some observers add that the Kodak-Fuji case also marked a change in US threats of unilateral action under section 301. In the 1980s and early 1990s, the United States had turned increasingly to unilateral measures under section 301 as a way of resolving trade disputes. While Kodak had initially filed a 301 complaint against Japan, the USTR chose to take the case to the WTO instead. From this point forward, the United States increasingly used the WTO route rather than unilateral action to deal with trade disputes. Indeed, since the Kodak case, the United States has not resorted to retaliation under section 301 without first going through the WTO. One USTR official noted that as a result, industry was no longer filing as many section 301 complaints. For example, from 1995 to 2002, the private sector filed only six section 301 petitions (Iida 2004, 207).

Robert Zoellick, who headed the USTR in the Bush administration (2000–2005), cautioned those in Congress who believed that success in defending US trade interests was now measured by the number of WTO cases litigated at the WTO. While "the Administration does not shy away from bringing WTO cases to advance US trade interests," he noted, "it is important to recognize that losing offensive WTO cases does not necessarily advance US interests or produce meaningful results for affected US companies—as Kodak painfully learned in the last Administration."[67]

Finally, the Kodak-Fuji case was also significant because it established that WTO rules were not well suited for dealing with problems related to weak national enforcement of competition policy. The ruling also demonstrated the great difficulty of proving nonviolation complaints. It was clear that for the WTO to encompass matters of competition policy, international rules would have to be explicitly negotiated. In 1996, Europe proposed putting competition policy on the WTO agenda, including it in a list of four new areas known as the "Singapore issues." The United States was less than enthusiastic, however. Some Americans worried that a WTO competition policy regime would weaken domestic antitrust rules. Also raising concerns were jurisdictional complications between the US Justice Department and the Federal Trade Commission, which administered US antitrust policy, and the USTR, which was in charge of antidumping policies.

Eight years on from the Kodak-Fuji decision, the film and photographic paper market has been overtaken by digital imaging. Technology, not politics, proved to be the catalyst for change. Some argue that their preoccupation with the WTO case caused Kodak's managers to take their eye off what was really happening in the marketplace. As a result, Kodak, despite

---

67. "Text: Zoellick Letter to House Democrats," *Inside US Trade*, April 23, 2004.

its famed research and development capabilities, lagged behind new and more agile competitors. Although the company developed the first digital camera for sale to retail consumers in 1994 and holds 1,000 digital photography patents,[68] it is no longer leading the market in photographic products in the United States or around the world. By 2005, the value of Kodak's stock had dropped 70 percent from its high under George Fisher.[69]

---

68. Saul Hansell, "Kodak's New Image," *The International Herald Tribune*, December 28, 2004.

69. Claudia H. Deutsch, "Kodak Misses Targets But Says Its Digital Moment Will Come," *The International Herald Tribune*, September 29, 2005, 2. Kodak was removed from the Dow Jones Industrial Average in April 2004 after its market value sank to $7.8 billion from $26.6 billion in 1996.

Case Analysis

The rules of the WTO focus on border barriers that inhibit market access and on policies that explicitly discriminate between domestic and foreign goods and services. But what happens if the barriers to trade are imposed by private practices that are tolerated (or encouraged) by the government? Are such practices actually covered by WTO rules? If they are covered, is the existing dispute settlement system an effective mechanism for dealing with them? If they are not covered, do new agreements on competition policy need to be negotiated? The trade conflicts between Japan and the United States over photographic film serve as a vehicle for exploring these questions.

Policies and Private Behavior

American firms have long complained of facing unusual problems when they try to sell and invest in Japan. These problems were not due to traditional barriers, such as high tariffs or restrictive quotas, or for that matter policies that were explicitly discriminatory. US companies alleged, rather, that structural barriers such as the close ties and loyalties among Japanese firms and between the Japanese government and private sector—sometimes labeled "Japan Inc."—made market entry particularly difficult.

In Japan, transactions based on the invisible handshakes of tradition, mutual understanding, and implicit contracts between associates of long standing are more common than in most other developed economies. Examples range from labor relations, in which large firms offer employment guarantees, to supplier relationships, in which long-term business relationships between firms and their customers and between suppliers and distributors commonly are formalized through an exchange of equity, to long-term relationships between firms and their lead banks. These links form networks to which newcomers (be they Japanese or foreign) find entry difficult.

However, there may also be advantages to these structures, which combine some of the flexibility of markets with the security of transactions that occur within firms. Indeed, many pointed to Japan's extraordinary economic performance prior to 1990 as evidence of its superiority. In any case, should (or could) WTO rules regulate the behavior of private actors? Should it be considered a trade barrier if Japanese consumers prefer domestic products or if Japanese firms prefer to deal with one another?

Rules or Managed Trade?

Some Americans came to the conclusion that Japanese business practices made intergovernmental agreements that focus on regulations and rules be ineffective in opening the Japanese market. Instead, they called for trade to be managed so that foreigners would be guaranteed a minimum market share. Others preferred to seek changes in rules. In the 1980s the United States had employed both rules (e.g., the Structural Impediments Initiative) and managed trade tactics (e.g., the semiconductor agreement) in its market-opening negotiations with Japan, and in the early 1990s the debate over these approaches continued.

A side letter to the semiconductor agreement signed in 1986 had set as a goal that 20 percent of the Japanese semiconductor market should go to foreign firms. Between 1986 and 1991, the share of foreign semiconductors actually increased from 9 to 30 percent. Many Americans therefore concluded that results-oriented approaches worked, and when the Clinton administration came into office in 1993 it sought to apply this approach to other sectors. The Japanese authorities drew the opposite conclusions from their experience with the semiconductor agreement: They felt that the government's agreement to control private-sector outcomes was a great mistake.

Bilateral or Multilateral Challenges?

A second strategic issue was whether the United States should deal with Japan bilaterally or multilaterally. Although the United States had had some success in challenging Japan at the GATT on its policies relating to beef, citrus, and rice, for the most part it had used bilateral negotiations in its efforts to pry open Japan's markets. Americans pursued this approach in part because many of the concerns were not covered by WTO rules and in part because they felt that Japan's strategic dependence on the United States would lead it to be more forthcoming in a bilateral setting. The Japanese had acquiesced to these negotiations until the mid-1990s, but thereafter sought to insist that disputes be dealt with through the WTO.

Like the bananas case, the Kodak-Fuji dispute highlights the ways in which companies pursue competition with key rivals through nonmarket means and the methods that they use to get their grievances onto the trade agenda. In May 1995, Kodak filed a petition asking the Office of the USTR to initiate a section 301 action (an intervention against restrictions on US exports) against Japan, claiming that its sales had been impeded in Japan by the anticompetitive actions taken by the Japanese authorities. This filing had been preceded by an orchestrated public relations and lobbying effort in Congress and by the president's National Economic Council, which aimed at laying the groundwork for acceptance of the case by the USTR. A year later, the USTR chose to pursue the case at the WTO. It was significant that the Clinton administration chose not to implement this 301 case bilaterally and instead brought the case to the WTO.

The case was innovative because many of the US claims rested on Article XXIII:1(b) of the GATT. Under this provision, a WTO member can bring a case if a benefit to which it was entitled has been denied it as a result of the application by another member of any measure—even one that does not conflict with the agreement. This provision protects parties if, after signing an agreement, a member adopts another policy that has the effect of denying others the benefits they might have expected from the agreement. Thus, for example, a country would be barred from subsidizing competing domestic products after lowering a tariff on imports.

The United States argued that Japan had nullified and impaired trade concessions it had granted to the United States by adopting a number of measures that affected the distribution and sale of imported photographic film and paper. In particular, it claimed that the Japanese government had adopted (1) distribution measures that allegedly created a market structure by which imports were excluded from traditional distribution channels, (2) restrictions on large retail stores that allegedly limited the growth of alternative distribution systems for imported film, and (3) measures that allegedly disadvantaged imports by restricting the use of sales promotion techniques. From the US perspective, the case presented an opportunity to explore if bringing a dispute under the WTO's DSU could be an effective way of resolving a conflict over nontariff barriers not covered under the rules. From the Japanese perspective, the case presented an opportunity to escape the bilateral pressures to which it had been vulnerable.

The WTO panel made clear that winning under this provision is not easy. It found that Japan's distribution measures, restrictions on large stores, and promotion measures did not nullify or impair US benefits. It also rejected claims that the distribution measures resulted in less favorable treatment for imported products under GATT Article III (National Treatment). Significantly, the United States did not appeal the ruling.

This case study reveals how private actors in the US system can take the initiative in pressuring Washington to bring a case. Under the 301 legislation, any interested person can petition the USTR to take action (or the USTR can self-initiate such a case). In this instance, Kodak and its lawyers were the principal source of the information on which the USTR relied to pursue the case. It was a collaborative effort (much like the cotton case brought by Brazil). Here too we see how WTO cases may reflect deliberate corporate initiatives.

The case study allows us to think about the factors considered by government officials as they decide whether to bring a case. The most straightforward is the wish to change a particular foreign policy, but trade authorities might sometimes have other reasons: This dispute suggests that bringing a case and losing it might be preferred to rebuffing a domestic constituent seeking assistance. Thus cases can act as institutional safety valves.

Cases might also be used strategically to expose weaknesses in the existing rules and influence the trade agenda, thereby setting the stage for future negotiations. In this way, a short-term defeat for Kodak could lead to a longer-term victory enjoyed by a much broader set of players. Indeed, the Kodak-Fuji case was significant because it established that as they stood, the WTO rules were not well suited to deal with problems growing out of the weak enforcement of competition policy. WTO panels have sometimes been accused of judicial activism, but in this case the panel was clearly reluctant to interpret Article XXIII:1(b) very broadly. The panel stressed that this remedy "should be approached with caution and treated as an exceptional remedy."

The film case suggests that rules on competition policy will have to be explicitly negotiated if such issues are to be effectively covered by the WTO. Indeed, the European Union has tried to introduce competition rules into the WTO, but it was eventually rebuffed at the WTO minister-ial held in Cancún in 2003. Resistance was particularly strong from de-veloping countries, which argued that accepting additional obligations would be too burdensome. Moreover, support from the United States was only lukewarm. In part this lack of enthusiasm reflected the wariness of many US experts on antitrust issues, who were concerned about how these rules might be enforced in a highly politicized trade regime.

Appendix 3A

Figure 3A.1 Changes in film distribution in Japan as a result of liberalization countermeasures

Organization of distribution (pre-1963)

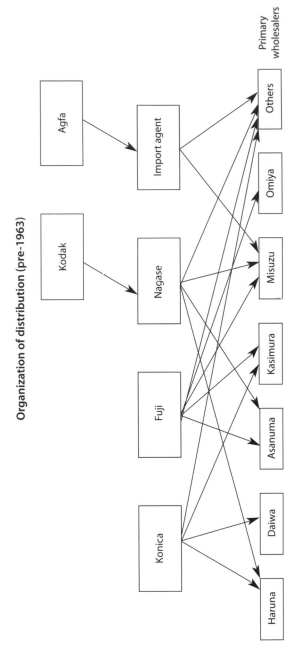

Organization of distribution (as of 1977)

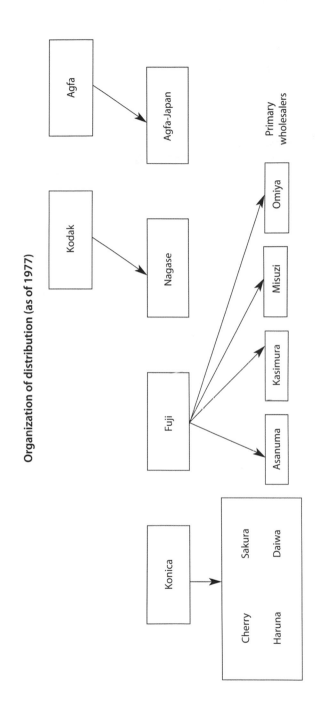

Figure 3A.1 Changes in film distribution in Japan as a result of liberalization countermeasures *(continued)*

Photo Market's description of film distribution in Japan after Kodak filed complaint

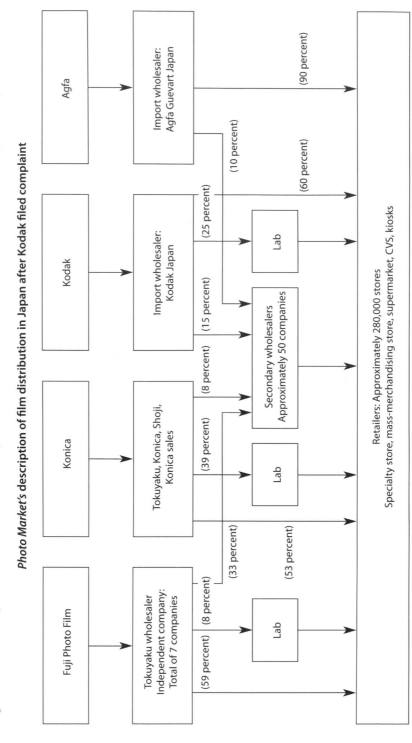

Source: Dewey Ballantine (1995).

Appendix 3B
Japan—Measures Affecting Photographic Film and Paper
First Submission of the United States of America,
February 20, 1997

III. LEGAL ARGUMENT

A. Summary of Argument

1. Nullification or Impairment (Articles II and XXIII:1(b))

377. The United States negotiated for and received concessions from Japan on photographic film and paper over a period of 30 years and three successive rounds of multilateral trade negotiations: the Kennedy Round in 1967, the Tokyo Round in 1979, and the Uruguay Round in 1994. Through laws, regulations, and other measures, including administrative guidance, the Government of Japan has upset the competitive relationship between imports and domestic products. Through its application of distribution countermeasures, the restrictions on large retail stores, and promotion countermeasures, the Government of Japan has frustrated the United States' reasonable expectations of improved market access for imported film and paper that accompanied each round of negotiations, thus nullifying or impairing benefits accruing to the United States. Japan's actions could not have been reasonably anticipated at the time the United States negotiated for the tariff concessions in each round of multilateral tariff negotiations.

378. The text of the GATT 1994 incorporated all of the protocols and certifications relating to tariff concessions that had entered into force under the GATT 1947 before the effective date of the WTO Agreement—including Japan's tariff concessions in the Kennedy and Tokyo Rounds. Thus, the benefits accruing to the United States under these concessions, as well as the concessions arising from Japan's schedule attached to the Marrakesh Protocol, are GATT 1994 benefits. As demonstrated below, the competitive relationship between imported and domestic photographic materials has been, and continues to be, upset as a result of Japan's measures.

379. The combination of measures implemented by the Government of Japan represents a systematic and elaborate plan to obstruct the market access that Japan's trading partners reasonably expected from the tariff concessions they received. The United States asks the panel to conclude that the Government of Japan has applied measures that have nullified or impaired benefits accruing to the United States within the meaning of Article XXIII:1(b) of the GATT 1994, impairing the benefits of tariff conces-

sions granted to the United States under Article II in three successive rounds.

2. National Treatment (Article III)

380. The Government of Japan designed and applied distribution countermeasures "so as to afford protection" to Japanese photographic film and paper after Japan eliminated its import restrictions, lowered tariffs, and liberalized investment restrictions. The distribution countermeasures are requirements directly affecting the internal sale, offering for sale, and distribution of imported photographic film and paper products, within the meaning of Article III:4. Through the application of these requirements, the Government of Japan has not fulfilled its obligation to accord "treatment no less favorable" to like products of national origin. The United States asks the panel to conclude that the Government of Japan has applied measures which impair the opportunities of foreign firms to distribute and sell imported products and, as a result, that those measures are inconsistent with Japan's obligations under Article III.

3. Publication and Administration of Laws (Article X)

381. In designing and implementing the various measures that comprised its liberalization countermeasures plan, the Government of Japan generally made it extremely difficult for its trading partners—or private businesses attempting to compete in Japan's market—to understand the precise nature of the Government's actions or their consequences. Throughout the period during which the liberalization countermeasures were developed, and continuing to the present, the Government of Japan has relied heavily on non-transparent forms of administrative action, and has promoted and used a web of public-private sector relationships to implement its protectionist measures.

382. The United States asks the Panel to conclude that the Government of Japan's actions in implementing and maintaining its liberalization countermeasures are inconsistent with Japan's obligations under Article X:1 of the GATT 1994 to publish "laws, regulations, judicial decisions and administrative rulings of general application . . . promptly in such a manner as to enable governments and traders to become acquainted with them."

THE GENERAL AGREEMENT ON TARIFFS AND TRADE

Article II
Schedules of Concessions

1. (*a*) Each contracting party shall accord to the commerce of the other contracting parties treatment no less favourable than that provided for in the appropriate Part of the appropriate Schedule annexed to this Agreement.

(*b*) The products described in Part I of the Schedule relating to any contracting party, which are the products of territories of other contracting parties, shall, on their importation into the territory to which the Schedule relates, and subject to the terms, conditions or qualifications set forth in that Schedule, be exempt from ordinary customs duties in excess of those set forth and provided therein. Such products shall also be exempt from all other duties or charges of any kind imposed on or in connection with the importation in excess of those imposed on the date of this Agreement or those directly and mandatorily required to be imposed thereafter by legislation in force in the importing territory on that date.

(*c*) The products described in Part II of the Schedule relating to any contracting party which are the products of territories entitled under Article I to receive preferential treatment upon importation into the territory to which the Schedule relates shall, on their importation into such territory, and subject to the terms, conditions or qualifications set forth in that Schedule, be exempt from ordinary customs duties in excess of those set forth and provided for in Part II of that Schedule. Such products shall also be exempt from all other duties or charges of any kind imposed on or in connection with importation in excess of those imposed on the date of this Agreement or those directly or mandatorily required to be imposed thereafter by legislation in force in the importing territory on that date. Nothing in this Article shall prevent any contracting party from maintaining its requirements existing on the date of this Agreement as to the eligibility of goods for entry at preferential rates of duty.

2. Nothing in this Article shall prevent any contracting party from imposing at any time on the importation of any product:

(*a*) a charge equivalent to an internal tax imposed consistently with the provisions of paragraph 2 of Article III in respect of the like domestic product or in respect of an article from which the imported product has been manufactured or produced in whole or in part;
(*b*) any anti-dumping or countervailing duty applied consistently with the provisions of Article VI;

(*c*)   fees or other charges commensurate with the cost of services rendered.

3. No contracting party shall alter its method of determining dutiable value or of converting currencies so as to impair the value of any of the concessions provided for in the appropriate Schedule annexed to this Agreement.

4. If any contracting party establishes, maintains or authorizes, formally or in effect, a monopoly of the importation of any product described in the appropriate Schedule annexed to this Agreement, such monopoly shall not, except as provided for in that Schedule or as otherwise agreed between the parties which initially negotiated the concession, operate so as to afford protection on the average in excess of the amount of protection provided for in that Schedule. The provisions of this paragraph shall not limit the use by contracting parties of any form of assistance to domestic producers permitted by other provisions of this Agreement.

5. If any contracting party considers that a product is not receiving from another contracting party the treatment which the first contracting party believes to have been contemplated by a concession provided for in the appropriate Schedule annexed to this Agreement, it shall bring the matter directly to the attention of the other contracting party. If the latter agrees that the treatment contemplated was that claimed by the first contracting party, but declares that such treatment cannot be accorded because a court or other proper authority has ruled to the effect that the product involved cannot be classified under the tariff laws of such contracting party so as to permit the treatment contemplated in this Agreement, the two contracting parties, together with any other contracting parties substantially interested, shall enter promptly into further negotiations with a view to a compensatory adjustment of the matter.

6. (*a*) The specific duties and charges included in the Schedules relating to contracting parties members of the International Monetary Fund, and margins of preference in specific duties and charges maintained by such contracting parties, are expressed in the appropriate currency at the par value accepted or provisionally recognized by the Fund at the date of this Agreement. Accordingly, in case this par value is reduced consistently with the Articles of Agreement of the International Monetary Fund by more than twenty per centum, such specific duties and charges and margins of preference may be adjusted to take account of such reduction; *provided* that the CONTRACTING PARTIES (*i.e.*, the contracting parties acting jointly as provided for in Article XXV) concur that such adjustments will not impair the value of the concessions provided for in the appropriate Schedule or

elsewhere in this Agreement, due account being taken of all factors which may influence the need for, or urgency of, such adjustments.

(b) Similar provisions shall apply to any contracting party not a member of the Fund, as from the date on which such contracting party becomes a member of the Fund or enters into a special exchange agreement in pursuance of Article XV.

7. The Schedules annexed to this Agreement are hereby made an integral part of Part I of this Agreement.

Article III
National Treatment on Internal Taxation and Regulation

1. The contracting parties recognize that internal taxes and other internal charges, and laws, regulations and requirements affecting the internal sale, offering for sale, purchase, transportation, distribution or use of products, and internal quantitative regulations requiring the mixture, processing or use of products in specified amounts or proportions, should not be applied to imported or domestic products so as to afford protection to domestic production.

2. The products of the territory of any contracting party imported into the territory of any other contracting party shall not be subject, directly or indirectly, to internal taxes or other internal charges of any kind in excess of those applied, directly or indirectly, to like domestic products. Moreover, no contracting party shall otherwise apply internal taxes or other internal charges to imported or domestic products in a manner contrary to the principles set forth in paragraph 1.

3. With respect to any existing internal tax which is inconsistent with the provisions of paragraph 2, but which is specifically authorized under a trade agreement, in force on April 10, 1947, in which the import duty on the taxed product is bound against increase, the contracting party imposing the tax shall be free to postpone the application of the provisions of paragraph 2 to such tax until such time as it can obtain release from the obligations of such trade agreement in order to permit the increase of such duty to the extent necessary to compensate for the elimination of the protective element of the tax.

4. The products of the territory of any contracting party imported into the territory of any other contracting party shall be accorded treatment no less favourable than that accorded to like products of national origin in respect of all laws, regulations and requirements affecting their internal sale, offer-

ing for sale, purchase, transportation, distribution or use. The provisions of this paragraph shall not prevent the application of differential internal transportation charges which are based exclusively on the economic operation of the means of transport and not on the nationality of the product.

5. No contracting party shall establish or maintain any internal quantitative regulation relating to the mixture, processing or use of products in specified amounts or proportions which requires, directly or indirectly, that any specified amount or proportion of any product which is the subject of the regulation must be supplied from domestic sources. Moreover, no contracting party shall otherwise apply internal quantitative regulations in a manner contrary to the principles set forth in paragraph 1.

6. The provisions of paragraph 5 shall not apply to any internal quantitative regulation in force in the territory of any contracting party on July 1, 1939, April 10, 1947, or March 24, 1948, at the option of that contracting party; *Provided* that any such regulation which is contrary to the provisions of paragraph 5 shall not be modified to the detriment of imports and shall be treated as a customs duty for the purpose of negotiation.

7. No internal quantitative regulation relating to the mixture, processing or use of products in specified amounts or proportions shall be applied in such a manner as to allocate any such amount or proportion among external sources of supply.

8. (*a*) The provisions of this Article shall not apply to laws, regulations or requirements governing the procurement by governmental agencies of products purchased for governmental purposes and not with a view to commercial resale or with a view to use in the production of goods for commercial sale.

(*b*) The provisions of this Article shall not prevent the payment of subsidies exclusively to domestic producers, including payments to domestic producers derived from the proceeds of internal taxes or charges applied consistently with the provisions of this Article and subsidies effected through governmental purchases of domestic products.

9. The contracting parties recognize that internal maximum price control measures, even though conforming to the other provisions of this Article, can have effects prejudicial to the interests of contracting parties supplying imported products. Accordingly, contracting parties applying such measures shall take account of the interests of exporting contracting parties with a view to avoiding to the fullest practicable extent such prejudicial effects.

10. The provisions of this Article shall not prevent any contracting party from establishing or maintaining internal quantitative regulations relating to exposed cinematograph films and meeting the requirements of Article IV.

Article IX
Marks of Origin

1. Each contracting party shall accord to the products of the territories of other contracting parties treatment with regard to marking requirements no less favourable than the treatment accorded to like products of any third country.

2. The contracting parties recognize that, in adopting and enforcing laws and regulations relating to marks of origin, the difficulties and inconveniences which such measures may cause to the commerce and industry of exporting countries should be reduced to a minimum, due regard being had to the necessity of protecting consumers against fraudulent or misleading indications.

3. Whenever it is administratively practicable to do so, contracting parties should permit required marks of origin to be affixed at the time of importation.

4. The laws and regulations of contracting parties relating to the marking of imported products shall be such as to permit compliance without seriously damaging the products, or materially reducing their value, or unreasonably increasing their cost.

5. As a general rule, no special duty or penalty should be imposed by any contracting party for failure to comply with marking requirements prior to importation unless corrective marking is unreasonably delayed or deceptive marks have been affixed or the required marking has been intentionally omitted.

6. The contracting parties shall co-operate with each other with a view to preventing the use of trade names in such manner as to misrepresent the true origin of a product, to the detriment of such distinctive regional or geographical names of products of the territory of a contracting party as are protected by its legislation. Each contracting party shall accord full and sympathetic consideration to such requests or representations as may be made by any other contracting party regarding the application of the undertaking set forth in the preceding sentence to names of products which have been communicated to it by the other contracting party.

Article X
Publication and Administration of Trade Regulations

1. Laws, regulations, judicial decisions and administrative rulings of general application, made effective by any contracting party, pertaining to the classification or the valuation of products for customs purposes, or to rates of duty, taxes or other charges, or to requirements, restrictions or prohibitions on imports or exports or on the transfer of payments thereof, or affecting their sale, distribution, transportation, insurance, warehousing inspection, exhibition, processing, mixing or other use, shall be published promptly in such a manner as to enable governments and traders to become acquainted with them. Agreements affecting international trade policy which are in force between the government or a governmental agency of any contracting party and the government or governmental agency of any other contracting party shall also be published. The provisions of this paragraph shall not require any contracting party to disclose confidential information which would impede law enforcement or otherwise be contrary to the public interest or would prejudice the legitimate commercial interests of particular enterprises, public or private.

2. No measure of general application taken by any contracting party effecting an advance in a rate of duty or other charge on imports under an established and uniform practice, or imposing a new or more burdensome requirement, restriction or prohibition on imports, or on the transfer of payments therefor, shall be enforced before such measure has been officially published.

3. (a) Each contracting party shall administer in a uniform, impartial and reasonable manner all its laws, regulations, decisions and rulings of the kind described in paragraph 1 of this Article.

(b) Each contracting party shall maintain, or institute as soon as practicable, judicial, arbitral or administrative tribunals or procedures for the purpose, *inter alia*, of the prompt review and correction of administrative action relating to customs matters. Such tribunals or procedures shall be independent of the agencies entrusted with administrative enforcement and their decisions shall be implemented by, and shall govern the practice of, such agencies unless an appeal is lodged with a court or tribunal of superior jurisdiction within the time prescribed for appeals to be lodged by importers; *Provided* that the central administration of such agency may take steps to obtain a review of the matter in another proceeding if there is good cause to believe that the decision is inconsistent with established principles of law or the actual facts.

(c) The provisions of subparagraph (b) of this paragraph shall not require the elimination or substitution of procedures in force in the territory of a contracting party on the date of this Agreement which in fact provide for an objective and impartial review of administrative action even though such procedures are not fully or formally independent of the agencies entrusted with administrative enforcement. Any contracting party employing such procedures shall, upon request, furnish the contracting parties with full information thereon in order that they may determine whether such procedures conform to the requirements of this subparagraph.

Article XIII
Non-discriminatory Administration of Quantitative Restrictions

1. No prohibition or restriction shall be applied by any contracting party on the importation of any product of the territory of any other contracting party or on the exportation of any product destined for the territory of any other contracting party, unless the importation of the like product of all third countries or the exportation of the like product to all third countries is similarly prohibited or restricted.

2. In applying import restrictions to any product, contracting parties shall aim at a distribution of trade in such product approaching as closely as possible the shares which the various contracting parties might be expected to obtain in the absence of such restrictions and to this end shall observe the following provisions:

(a) Wherever practicable, quotas representing the total amount of permitted imports (whether allocated among supplying countries or not) shall be fixed, and notice given of their amount in accordance with paragraph 3 (b) of this Article;

(b) In cases in which quotas are not practicable, the restrictions may be applied by means of import licences or permits without a quota;

(c) Contracting parties shall not, except for purposes of operating quotas allocated in accordance with subparagraph (d) of this paragraph, require that import licences or permits be utilized for the importation of the product concerned from a particular country or source;

(d) In cases in which a quota is allocated among supplying countries the contracting party applying the restrictions may seek agreement with respect to the allocation of shares in the quota with all other contracting parties having a substantial interest in supplying the product concerned. In cases in which this method is not reasonably practicable, the contracting party concerned shall allot to contracting parties having a substantial interest in supplying the product shares based upon the proportions, supplied by such contracting parties during a previous representative period, of the total quantity or value of imports of the product, due account being taken of any special factors which may have affected or may be affecting the trade in the product. No conditions or formalities shall be imposed which would prevent any contracting party from utilizing fully the share of any such total quantity or value which has been allotted to it, subject to importation being made within any prescribed period to which the quota may relate.

3. (*a*) In cases in which import licences are issued in connection with import restrictions, the contracting party applying the restrictions shall provide, upon the request of any contracting party having an interest in the trade in the product concerned, all relevant information concerning the administration of the restrictions, the import licences granted over a recent period and the distribution of such licences among supplying countries; *Provided* that there shall be no obligation to supply information as to the names of importing or supplying enterprises.

(*b*) In the case of import restrictions involving the fixing of quotas, the contracting party applying the restrictions shall give public notice of the total quantity or value of the product or products which will be permitted to be imported during a specified future period and of any change in such quantity or value. Any supplies of the product in question which were *en route* at the time at which public notice was given shall not be excluded from entry; *Provided* that they may be counted so far as practicable, against the quantity permitted to be imported in the period in question, and also, where necessary, against the quantities permitted to be imported in the next following period or periods; and *Provided* further that if any contracting party customarily exempts from such restrictions products entered for consumption or withdrawn from warehouse for consumption during a period of thirty days after the day of such public notice, such practice shall be considered full compliance with this subparagraph.

(*c*) In the case of quotas allocated among supplying countries, the contracting party applying the restrictions shall promptly inform all other contracting parties having an interest in supplying the product concerned of the shares in the quota currently allocated, by quantity or value, to the various supplying countries and shall give public notice thereof.

4. With regard to restrictions applied in accordance with paragraph 2 (*d*) of this Article or under paragraph 2 (*c*) of Article XI, the selection of a representative period for any product and the appraisal of any special fac-

tors affecting the trade in the product shall be made initially by the contracting party applying the restriction; *Provided* that such contracting party shall, upon the request of any other contracting party having a substantial interest in supplying that product or upon the request of the contracting parties, consult promptly with the other contracting party or the contracting parties regarding the need for an adjustment of the proportion determined or of the base period selected, or for the reappraisal of the special factors involved, or for the elimination of conditions, formalities or any other provisions established unilaterally relating to the allocation of an adequate quota or its unrestricted utilization.

5. The provisions of this Article shall apply to any tariff quota instituted or maintained by any contracting party, and, in so far as applicable, the principles of this Article shall also extend to export restrictions.

4

Standing Up for Steel

When President George W. Bush took office in January 2001, a messy trade issue landed on his desk that had bedeviled the administration of President Bill Clinton for the previous three years. Since 1998, the domestic steel industry had experienced two distinct downturns, resulting in depressed prices, falling profits, a stream of bankruptcies, and job losses numbering in the tens of thousands. According to the United Steelworkers of America (USWA), a coalition of powerful members of Congress, and most US steelmakers, unfairly priced foreign imports had caused the alarming declines. To restore the industry's profitability, steel representatives repeatedly called for the Clinton administration to seek a trade ruling—known as a section 201 action—that, if successful, would allow the president to impose a steel quota or other form of far-reaching relief.

But a range of critics claimed that such a measure would be misplaced and that the relief it would bring was unjustified. Foreign steelmakers insisted that US firms were struggling because of increasing domestic competition and a lack of consolidation at home; many steel analysts said that falling steel profits were the inevitable result of excess capacity worldwide, including in the United States; and a number of US steel consumers and economists argued that cheap foreign steel was actually good for the country, and that quotas would inevitably spur trade retaliation. If the government imposed a steel quota, many observers agreed, it would unnecessarily harm foreign countries dependent on steel exports, while benefiting one narrow product sector at the expense of the broader US economy.

Standing Up for Steel is an edited and revised version of the case with the same name originally written by Susan Rosegrant, a case writer at the Case Program at the John F. Kennedy School of Government. For copies or permission to reproduce the unabridged case please refer to www.ksgcase.harvard.edu or send a written request to Case Program, John F. Kennedy School of Government, Harvard University, 79 John F. Kennedy Street, Cambridge, MA 02138.

The Clinton administration ultimately left office without bringing a section 201 case. But as the health of the domestic steel industry continued to deteriorate in 2001, the Bush administration faced increasingly urgent pleas to open a comprehensive 201 trade investigation. Whatever Bush decided would likely have far-reaching consequences for the domestic steel industry, the US economy, and the nation's relationships with its foreign trading partners.

A History of Trade Remedies

The steel industry's quest for trade relief was not new. For much of the 20th century, the US steel industry had served as the nation's industrial backbone; it had provided jobs for generations of workers and in the process it became a potent symbol of the country's industrial might. But since the 1960s, when foreign steel first entered the US market in significant quantities, domestic companies and steelworkers had complained of unfairly priced imports and an uneven playing field.

While market conditions had changed over the years, and the number of steel-producing countries had grown, many of the fundamental issues remained the same. According to US industry, domestic companies could not compete effectively against most imported steel because of pervasive market-distorting practices overseas. These practices included closed markets that permitted few imports, such as Japan's protected domestic market; nonmarket economies in which steel enterprises were state-owned and supported, such as in the former Soviet Union; and reliance on government subsidies, such as the assumption of pension costs by European governments to aid restructuring during the 1980s and 1990s. In addition, US steelmakers said, production costs in the United States were generally higher owing to more stringent regulation of labor and the environment.

Because foreign steelmakers enjoyed such home-market advantages, US companies claimed, they often could afford to sell steel in the United States at prices well below what US steelmakers needed to charge to remain profitable. To be sure, domestic steelmakers did not compete directly with imports for all their business. Large steel consumers, such as the major auto manufacturers, met most of their steel needs through contracts with US companies. By contrast, most foreign steel was imported by metal-trading companies or steel service centers that sold the steel on the so-called commodity-grade spot market. But even the large contract sales were affected when cheap imports forced down overall prices, industry representatives said.

In order to protect profitability and market share, the US steel industry and its workers had repeatedly appealed to the government for protection from foreign imports, claiming that without relief the domestic industry would be unable to compete. The government had been unusually responsive, in large part because of the clout of the steelworkers' union, the United Steelworkers of America, and the strength of the Congressional Steel Caucus, a powerful bipartisan group of lawmakers who represented districts and states containing steel manufacturers.

Four administrations in a row imposed import restraints, beginning with President Richard Nixon, who in 1969 established quota-like voluntary restraint agreements that lasted five years and affected steel from Japan and Europe. In the late 1970s, Jimmy Carter's administration devised a "trigger price mechanism" that allowed a certain amount of steel imports into the country if sold at or above a set price. After that expired, President Ronald Reagan negotiated a new round of voluntary restraint agreements (later renewed by President George H. W. Bush) that apportioned shares of a limited import pool among foreign steel-producing countries. Many critics pointed to this series of import restraints as evidence of undue government protectionism. "Beginning with import quotas in 1969, protection has been the rule rather than the exception for the steel industry," according to Daniel Griswold, associate director of the Cato Institute's Center for Trade Policy Studies.[1]

By the time Bill Clinton assumed the presidency in 1993, the voluntary restraint agreements of the Reagan and Bush era had expired. Domestic steelmakers continued to make aggressive use of the US trade laws at their disposal, however.

Antidumping and Countervailing Duty Laws

The antidumping and countervailing duty laws dealt specifically with unfair trade. Most frequently brought were antidumping cases, often referred to simply as dumping cases. If a union or group of domestic steel companies believed that a steel product was being imported at an unfair price, or "dumped," it could request that the US Commerce Department initiate an investigation.[2] If Commerce concluded that unfair pricing had occurred, by finding that the import price was lower than the home-market price or than the cost of production, it then determined the margin of dumping (that is, the difference between the chosen basis of comparison and the US

---

1. Daniel Griswold, "Counting the Cost of Steel Protection," House Committee on Ways and Means, Subcommittee on Trade, Hearing on Steel Trade Issues, 106th Congress, 1st session, February 25, 1999, www.freetrade.org.

2. The Treasury Department had originally overseen dumping cases but Commerce assumed responsibility in 1979, a move that most observers agree has contributed to the process becoming more responsive to industry.

import price). Finally, the petitioners went before the International Trade Commission (ITC), an independent, quasi-judicial federal agency,[3] to try to prove that the dumping had caused injury or threat of injury to the industry. If the ITC reached a positive finding, the importer had to pay duties equal to the dumping margin. Issuance of a final ruling could take 12 to 18 months, but importers had to post a bond to cover estimated duties as soon as a preliminary positive finding had been reached, a process typically completed within about six months.

Countervailing duty cases were brought when domestic companies believed a government subsidy in a foreign country was giving a foreign industry an unfair advantage. Unfair government subsidies could include the granting of interest-free loans and the assumption of pension and health care costs. If the ITC found injury, Commerce would have the US Customs Service impose a "countervailing" or offsetting duty on the imports equal to the estimated subsidy.

Section 201 of the Trade Act of 1974

Unlike antidumping and countervailing duty investigations, a Section 201 case did not rely on proof of unfair trade practices. Rather, if the ITC determined that the volume of a particular import constituted a substantial cause or threat of serious injury to a domestic industry, the president could impose temporary import relief without violating the rules of the World Trade Organization (WTO). Once initiated, usually by the industry in question, the case went straight to the ITC, which ruled on the case and, if it found for the industry, made a recommendation to the president, all within six months. The president then had 60 days to come up with a remedy, which could be no action at all, a tariff, a quota, a tariff-rate quota, or some form of trade adjustment assistance.

Section 201 actions had the potential to provide a more comprehensive remedy than did dumping investigations. In the case of steel, for example, a 201 investigation could target all steel imports from all countries, while a dumping or countervailing duty investigation dealt only with one product and one country at a time (e.g., hot-rolled steel from Japan). But in part because the injury standard was higher for a 201 than for a dumping or countervailing duty case, and thus harder to prove, and in part because the outcome was entirely at the president's discretion, 201 cases were far less common.

Critics of the dumping laws insisted that they were too plaintiff-friendly. Indeed, from 1980 to 1997, 80 percent of all dumping cases brought in the

---

3. ITC regulations require that no more than three of the six commissioners be of the same political party. In practice, this has usually resulted in a commission split between Democrats and Republicans.

United States—including steel actions—were successful. According to William Barringer, a partner at Willkie Farr & Gallagher who had long represented Japanese and Brazilian steelmakers, foreign countries were so convinced of the slim chances of prevailing that they often did not even bother to respond to dumping cases.[4] But industry representatives in the United States maintained that the dumping laws were a completely legitimate and necessary tool for combating surges of unfairly priced imported steel. The number of successful cases, they contended, merely demonstrated the prevalence of dumping and subsidization.

In either case, many economists noted that all steelmakers periodically engaged in dumping because in a cyclical and capital-intensive industry it was more profitable to sell below cost during a downturn than not to sell at all, as long as revenues covered variable costs. While it was legal to sell below cost in a home market, something US firms did regularly, to do so overseas was dumping (US steelmakers exported very little steel). "This is completely economically rational behavior in a period of excess capacity," observes one economist, "but it runs afoul of the dumping laws." Because selling below cost was so common in the industry, and because the domestic industry was aggressive in seeking protection, steel companies historically had used the dumping law more than any other industry: They were responsible for about a third of all cases brought between 1980 and 1995.

History of Restructuring

Although the US steel industry continued to seek relief from what it deemed unfair imports, foreign steelmakers and some other industry observers argued that most of the steel industry's problems were the result of internal decisions and conditions at home. US steel companies—loath to make the huge capital investments required—had taken longer than many of their foreign competitors to upgrade their outdated open-hearth blast furnace technology to more cost-efficient basic oxygen furnaces, critics said. Not until the 1980s did serious industry reinvestment begin, and the last open-hearth furnace in the United States did not close until 1991.

The older integrated steel mills—so called because they relied on a vertically integrated process to turn raw inputs such as iron ore into finished carbon flat-rolled steel products—also faced growing competition domestically from mini-mills, many of which began operating in the 1970s. These faster and more flexible companies typically had far lower costs than the integrated mills did: They produced finished steel from abundant scrap

---

4. Unless otherwise noted, all quotes from William Barringer are from a September 2001 interview with the author.

metal melted in highly efficient electric-arc furnaces; their workforces were often non-union; and because they had been in business only a few years, they did not have to pay benefits to large numbers of retired workers. Although the steel produced by the early mini-mills was mostly low-grade, the product improved with the technology. By 1998, the mini-mills were competing directly against the integrated mills in certain product areas, and their share of US production had increased to almost 40 percent.

Some critics also claimed that US companies had not done enough to consolidate, particularly compared to European and Latin American firms. According to Barringer, efforts by the USWA to keep all plants in operation—regardless of their performance—had constrained restructuring and had resuscitated entire companies that should have been allowed to fail. By 1997, Barringer says, the industry could be broken into three distinct segments: the large integrated steelmakers, such as AK Steel, Bethlehem Steel, and U.S. Steel, most or all of whose operations were cost-competitive; globally competitive mini-mills, such as Nucor and Steel Dynamics; and the second-tier integrated mills, such as Weirton, Wheeling-Pittsburgh, and Geneva Steel, which, he claims, were "on the verge of bankruptcy, have been on the verge of bankruptcy, and will continue to be on the verge of bankruptcy."

Consolidation efforts were hampered as well by the so-called legacy costs borne by the older integrated firms. In the 1970s, even as industry and union representatives decried the market incursions of steel from abroad and appealed to government to protect the domestic industry, wages for steelworkers grew more rapidly than wages in any other industrial sector—increasing not only current worker benefits but also the benefits that would be paid out as workers retired or were laid off during subsequent plant closures. Such generous wage policies, negotiated during a period of industry decline, had contributed by the 1990s to soaring legacy costs in the form of pension, health, and severance benefits that drove down company profits, raised the cost of restructuring, and made steel companies unattractive as potential acquisitions.

But US industry and union representatives painted a very different picture. A two-decade period of comprehensive restructuring, they insisted, had by 1997 created a world-class industry characterized by quality, efficiency, and productivity. Dozens of inefficient mills closed, and employment fell from more than 547,000 workers in 1980 to about 236,000 in 1997—a more than 50 percent drop in the labor force. In fact, the very real burden of legacy costs, US steelmakers argued, was painful proof of the industry's aggressive consolidation. Over the same period, domestic steelmakers—with the federal government's encouragement—invested more than $50 billion in updated facilities and equipment, including more than $7 billion in environmental controls. Productivity increased at twice the average rate of all US manufacturing, helped by the more productive mini-mills; indeed, at less than four man-hours per ton of steel, it was among the highest in the world.

However, even some analysts who conceded that US steelmakers had made great strides over the previous two decades questioned whether government policies supporting widespread reinvestment had been wise. The reason steelmakers were struggling both in the United States and abroad, they argued, was global overcapacity, caused by quickly rising worldwide productivity and relatively sluggish growth in demand. Despite the domestic plant closings and layoffs, total shipments of steel products in the United States had risen from about 84 million tons in 1980 to about 105 million tons in 1997. Thus, as more developing nations became steel producers and countries such as the United States increased production, excess global capacity, which in the last few decades had often topped 20 percent of production, would only get worse. "Why would we try to force an industry that is in decline and supposed to be reducing its capacity to actually take money and invest it in the steel industry?" asks one former government official.

In addition, some industry observers questioned whether the US government should protect the domestic steel industry at all. Cheap foreign imports, after all, lowered the cost of steel for downstream users, who by the 1990s far exceeded steel producers in employment and capitalization. Moreover, given the growing strength of the mini-mills and the number of new steel-producing entrants worldwide, the risk of a single foreign country or company driving all US firms out of business, taking control of the steel market, and then raising prices was negligible. "If the United States adjusted out of steel and we ended up producing only 20 percent of our steel needs, would we be in deep trouble, and unable to have our manufacturing sector produce the kind of machinery we need?" asks one economist. "The answer is no."

But most Americans still believed in the importance of a vital US steel industry. While steel-consuming businesses wanted access to imports, they also wanted a reliable and accessible domestic supply. In addition, despite deep layoffs and numerous plant closings, steel was still a highly visible industry, and regional pockets around the country depended on steel mills to keep their economies afloat. Finally, even some economists who considered themselves supporters of free trade argued that simply allowing market forces to work was not fair in a global industry so skewed by foreign subsidies. "It has been distorted by so much government intervention on so many different levels for so long," says Greg Mastel, trade counsel and chief economist for the Senate Finance Committee, "that it's a marketplace where it is hard to say 'Just let the market operate.'"[5]

5. Unless otherwise noted, all quotes from Greg Mastel are from a September 2001 interview with the author.

The 1998 Steel Crisis

Despite ongoing restructuring, the 1990s were a period of recovery for much of the US steel industry. The nation's strong economy created a ready market for steel, as domestic demand increased by about 7 percent a year. Steel imports accounted for 20 percent of the US market in 1997, but much of that was needed, since domestic demand exceeded what US companies could supply by more than 15 percent. Moreover, about a quarter of the imports consisted of semifinished steel brought in by the domestic steel industry itself for further finishing. US steel shipments were at a record level, and domestic steel mill capacity utilization—a key measure of industry health—was above 90 percent.

By the fall of 1997, however, George Becker, president of the United Steelworkers of America, was becoming uneasy about how the domestic industry would be affected by the growing financial crisis in Asia. Demand for steel in Asia had collapsed, making the US market more than usually attractive, and regional currency devaluations in such steel-making countries as South Korea and Japan were resulting in even cheaper foreign steel. Becker met with members of the Clinton administration to voice his concerns, but the data did not yet support his contention that rising imports and falling prices might spiral out of control. After all, the steel industry's 1997 financial results were the best in more than 15 years.

By the summer of 1998, though, the Asian crisis, coupled with an economic collapse in Russia, began to have a serious impact on the global steel market. As there accumulated a backlog of steel, much of which formerly would have gone to Asia, prices fell worldwide and a huge volume of low-priced steel—in particular, hot-rolled steel from Japan, Russia, Korea, and Brazil—poured into the US market.[6] Imports in a few categories rose to nearly 40 percent of the US market, about double what they had been the year before. Despite a booming domestic economy, US steelmakers faced the choice of following prices down or giving up market share. Even Nucor, the mini-mill whose low-cost production had helped to make it the nation's second-largest steelmaker, wrote to Commerce Secretary William Daley in August to warn that unfairly priced imports were taking a dangerous bite out of the US industry's profitability. "When Nucor came and said it was hurting," one former official says, "that got the attention of people in the administration."

To combat the sudden surge of imports, the steelworkers union began to work several fronts simultaneously. In September, it launched "Stand Up for Steel," a $4 million advertising and public relations campaign designed to identify steel imports as the cause of industry disruption and to

---

6. US imports of Japanese hot-rolled steel for the year would eventually show a 381 percent increase over 1997.

exert pressure on political representatives. "In this great economy when everybody else was doing well, we had to penetrate and push through with the message that there was a major American industry and a lot of employees that weren't sharing in the good fortune," says William Klinefelter, legislative and political director for the USWA. "We had to say that we were under attack. We had to get that message home."[7]

That same month, the union began bombarding Congress and the Clinton administration with requests for legislative and executive action.[8] According to Klinefelter, the union was convinced that only a comprehensive solution could provide the quick and far-reaching action that the steel industry needed to avoid plant closures and job losses. While a legislative quota limiting imports was its clear first choice, the union also considered the likely effectiveness of a section 201 trade case. "I think we all realized that the dumping cases were not going to be enough, that we had to shut off more products from every place," Klinefelter explains. "So that's when the idea of the 201 case came up among us." In particular, the union wanted the Clinton administration to self-initiate a 201 case. If the administration brought the case, union officials reasoned, the president would be more likely to grant significant relief should it succeed.[9]

But the US steel industry disagreed with the union position on quotas and 201.[10] Since the end of Reagan- and Bush-imposed voluntary restraint agreements in the early 1990s, dumping cases had become the main remedy for industry. Section 201 cases, while more comprehensive than dumping cases, carried a number of risks, steel representatives say. They were difficult to bring; the injury standard was high; and relief was at the discretion of the president, who was often constrained by foreign policy considerations. "In the last 20 years, no major industry had gotten relief under 201," says Alan Wolff, a partner at Dewey Ballantine who represented a group of major US integrated steel firms.[11]

Industry did not speak out against the union's efforts, since it did not want to sour relations with the union, but it also did not directly support

---

7. Unless otherwise noted, all quotes from William Klinefelter are from a September 2001 interview with the author.

8. Although the crisis had become apparent the previous month, Klinefelter says, the union delayed the letter-writing campaign because "nothing happens in Washington in August."

9. Industries most commonly requested a 201 investigation, but unions, the president, the USTR, the House Committee on Ways and Means, and the Senate Finance Committee were all authorized to initiate one.

10. According to William Barringer, the second-tier firms were the only ones pushing for a 201 action along with the unions because they were desperate for any form of comprehensive relief: "At the end of the day, what they were really looking for was a political solution—a bailout."

11. Unless otherwise noted, all quotes from Alan Wolff are from a September 2001 interview with the author.

them. At the same time, it pursued its preferred course: On September 30 a dozen steel companies filed dumping cases on hot-rolled steel against Japan, Russia, and Brazil, as well as a countervailing duty case against Brazil. The union, which was also hedging its bets, joined in the filings.

Becker and Klinefelter met repeatedly with leading members of the Congressional Steel Caucus through the fall. Although the steel crisis hit late in the year, making it difficult for Congress to react, the House approved a nonbinding resolution calling for a one-year ban on unfair steel imports from 10 countries, including Japan, Russia, and Brazil. In addition, Senators John Rockefeller (D-WV) and Arlen Specter (R-PA) introduced a bill that would make it easier to bring a section 201 case. "What I was trying to tell the administration with these resolutions," says Klinefelter, "was that if you don't do something, don't think that Congress won't act, because the Congress will act."

The administration had its own reasons to take action. "There is a lot of merit to the argument that foreigners have subsidized their steel industries," says one former Clinton official. "While there is a huge amount of latent political support for free trade, the Republicans and the Democrats also compete in being tough against unfair trade."

The Early Clinton Administration Response

During the fall, as the steel crisis worsened, the Clinton administration tried to reduce the onslaught of imports without resorting to market-closing measures. US Trade Representative (USTR) Charlene Barshefsky in October urged the European Union to accept more Russian steel and pressured Japan, which was responsible for almost half the import surge, to begin cutting its steel exports.[12]

In addition, Commerce streamlined its dumping investigations and instituted a new "critical circumstances" policy that allowed it to impose duties retroactively on whatever preliminary margins were eventually determined, rather than waiting until the margins had been assessed for duties to take effect. On November 23, after the ITC found injury in the dumping cases filed against Japan, Russia, and Brazil, Commerce announced that it would apply retroactive duties to affected imports that had entered the United States beginning November 12; this policy helped to stop importers from rushing products targeted by a dumping action into the United States before duties had been assessed and imposed. The threat of dumping duties helped drive December steel imports down by one-third from the previous month.

But such actions did not constitute a policy. Since August there had been frequent interagency meetings of top officials involved in the steel

---

12. Although the EU talks were largely fruitless, imports of Japanese steel fell by almost 50 percent in December in response to the dumping case and administration negotiations.

issue to discuss what to do. In particular, administration representatives debated the wisdom of bringing a 201 case, the only comprehensive import remedy the administration could impose that was WTO-compatible. Principals' meetings—chaired by National Economic Council head Gene Sperling, who coordinated steel trade policy—consisted of cabinet-level officials such as Treasury Secretary Robert Rubin, Commerce Secretary William Daley; USTR Charlene Barshefsky, Chairman of the Council of Economic Advisers (CEA) Janet Yellen, and White House Chief of Staff Erskine Bowles, usually accompanied by their deputies. But much of the real work occurred in the deputies' meetings, chaired by Deputy Assistant to the President for International Economics Lael Brainard. These sessions normally included Deputy Secretary Lawrence Summers; Under Secretary of Commerce for International Trade David Aaron, backed up by Assistant Secretary for Import Administration Robert LaRussa; USTR General Counsel Susan Esserman; State Department Assistant Secretary Alan Larson; Deputy National Security Adviser James Steinberg; and CEA member Robert Lawrence.

According to inside observers, the policy positions of agencies and individuals were largely predictable. Officials at the Commerce Department and the USTR, who were meeting regularly with industry lawyers and officials, wanted to pursue all legal mechanisms that might help the troubled steel industry; they were considering both the union's request for a section 201 action and regulatory changes that might make it easier for the industry to win trade relief. While the USTR thought industry should bring the 201 case, some Commerce officials felt that the administration should consider self-initiating an investigation. "It was an emergency measure—that's what it was designed for," says David Aaron, then commerce undersecretary. "We were in an emergency, and I felt that was the right way to go."[13]

Officials at the White House, meanwhile, including President Clinton; Chief of Staff Bowles, later replaced by John Podesta; and Deputy Assistant to the President Karen Tramantano, were sympathetic to the steelworkers' plight. But the White House was also very concerned about the message that self-initiating a section 201 case would send. "If we did this, it would be interpreted that we had gone protectionist," Aaron explains. "The Democrats felt vulnerable [to that charge] as a national party. They kept saying, 'We have the right to do this, it's accepted in the WTO, and maybe it's even the best solution, but it would send a terrible signal.'" Adds Klinefelter: "We had tremendous access to the administration. But the philosophical mind-set was for free trade. They did not want to send any signal that they were deviating from that."

Not surprisingly, most of the economists—members of the National Economic Council, CEA, and the Office of Management and Budget—and

---

13. Unless otherwise noted, all quotes from David Aaron are from a September 2001 interview with the author.

agencies concerned with foreign policy, such as the State Department and the National Security Council, wanted to support free trade to the greatest extent possible. But the most powerful voice was that of Treasury Secretary Robert Rubin. Rubin's handling of national and international economic issues over the past four years had given him a "stature within the administration that was beyond anything the other members of the cabinet could possibly reach," according to one well-placed observer. In the midst of the deepening Asian financial crisis—considered by many officials to be the world's worst financial crisis in 50 years—Rubin's paramount concern was to avoid any action that could further destabilize financial markets and lead to inevitable repercussions within the US economy. Part of that effort was keeping the United States open to steel. "Any signals we sent that we would be closing our markets could really destabilize the markets, especially in Asia," says one former White House official. "The US was the importer of first and last resort during that time period, so we recognized the problem in steel could have much larger ramifications."

Rubin's conviction that the United States needed to keep accepting steel imports set him solidly against a section 201 action, whether self-initiated by government or filed by industry. "You have to give him credit for the way in which he handled the whole crisis, and the way the people on the Hill and the people overseas had confidence in his ability to handle it," the union's Klinefelter says. "But we were coming to him and saying, 'Mr. Secretary, what you're doing may be good for the overall economy, but it's going to have a flashback on us.'"

The widely differing administration perspectives made reaching consensus on a cohesive steel policy difficult. One official remembers appearing along with USWA head George Becker before the Senate Steel Caucus on November 30 and worrying because the administration did not have a comprehensive strategy to announce, beyond promising a steel action plan by early January, as requested by a congressional resolution. "At the time, we were saying vigorous trade law enforcement, immediate forays with countries around the world, and bilateral initiatives to have them keep down their exports," the official recalls. "I was quite concerned at the time that it wasn't sufficient, but there were a lot of debates within the administration about what to do."

During this time, the union and the second-tier steel companies continued to press for comprehensive relief. According to the American Iron and Steel Institute, the average price per metric ton for all steel imports had dropped more than 20 percent between January and October to $400, the industry had lost 10,000 jobs over the previous year, and steel mill capacity utilization had fallen to 74 percent. Alarmed by the continuing slide, USTR Counsel Susan Esserman called industry representatives into her office. "I said, 'Let's go over a 201 case. If you're interested in a 201 case, we're interested in working with you.'"[14] But the response, she says, was decidedly unenthusiastic. Lawyers for the integrated steelmakers, on the other hand, say they felt that it was up to the Clinton administration to take the lead. "We met with Sue Esserman and our feeling was it's a wholly discretionary statute, and the president can do what the president wants to do," recounts the lawyer Alan Wolff. "If the president was not committed to the notion that relief was warranted, it would be something of a fool's errand to go ahead."

Perhaps more to the point, the steelmakers' lawyers did not believe that a comprehensive 201 case was winnable at the time, both because the import surge was most pronounced in just a few categories, such as hot-rolled steel and wire rod, and because the history of import penetration and injury was not long enough. Although overcapacity had forced prices and profits down, and US steel imports for the year had increased 37 percent over 1997, domestic companies had shipped 102 million tons of steel in 1998 despite lower overall employment—a production level that was topped in the previous 20 years only by the peak year of 1997—and 11 of the top 13 steel companies were still profitable. "If you have diminished profits in a cyclical, capital-intensive industry during the peak of the business cycle, is that injury?" asks Wolff. "The ITC has never found that. So our feeling was that the statutory criteria as interpreted by the ITC could not be met." He adds, however, that had the Clinton administration chosen to self-initiate, it would have improved the case's chances "significantly."

Although the Clinton administration continued to debate the merits of a 201 case through the end of 1998, Rubin's opposition to market restraints carried the day. "Clearly he did not want to send any signals to our Asian trading partners," the union's Klinefelter recalls. "Their economies were in danger of serious collapse. If we could absorb some of that pain, he felt our economy was strong enough and we were robust enough that we could do it." He adds: "I think they felt that we'd weather it. The world economy would stabilize, the imports would go down, and we'd be back to normal."

The January Steel Plan and the Negotiated Agreements

On January 7, 1999, the Clinton administration delivered the steel action plan promised the previous year. Titled *Report to Congress on a Comprehensive Plan for Responding to the Increase in Steel Imports*, the program included a demand that Japan cut steel exports to the United States back to precrisis levels; a system of earlier import monitoring, since, as one former administration official says, "There was the sense that somehow this

---

14. Unless otherwise noted, all quotes from Susan Esserman are from a September 2001 interview with the author.

crisis had occurred and we hadn't known it was happening;" $300 million in tax relief for steelmakers, spread over five years; financial adjustment assistance for out-of-work steelworkers and hard-hit steel mill communities; and a continued commitment to strongly enforce all US trade laws. "The Clinton administration's posture could be characterized as 'We will aggressively implement the laws, but we are not going to go beyond them,'" says Robert Lawrence, then one of two members of the Council of Economic Advisers chaired by Janet Yellen. "We will neither change the laws nor violate them."[15]

Klinefelter, who says the January steel plan "was not considered a bold new way to go," met with John Podesta and Karen Tramantano to reiterate the union's strong support for a 201 action. Although he got no definitive answer, it was clear to him that the administration would not self-initiate.[16] Nor were steelmakers pleased. Instead of better import monitoring, industry for months had been lobbying for a system similar to Canada's, which did not restrict imports but required a license or permit to import, allowing faster and more accurate tracking of products entering the country.

Industry also objected to the import agreements that the Clinton administration announced one month later. Since September 1998, Russian steelmakers and government officials—alarmed by the sharp industrial and economic declines in that country—had been pleading with the administration not to impose dumping orders on Russian steel, even going so far as to publish a full-page letter to Vice President Al Gore in the *Washington Post*. In February, Commerce announced two tentative deals with Russia: an agreement suspending the dumping case on hot-rolled steel, and a comprehensive agreement covering all other steel exports. Hot-rolled imports were to be cut back to 750,000 tons a year, with a minimum price ranging from $255 to $280 per metric ton. Both agreements, which were to remain in effect for five years, returned steel exports to precrisis levels.

Former assistant secretary for import administration Robert LaRussa, who led the Russian negotiations, says the deals were designed to protect US steel companies while still giving Russia more access to the US market—and to much-needed foreign currency—than it would have had under the dumping order.[17] According to foreign steel attorney William Barringer, the US government had another strong motivation in negotiating: "Russia can export three things: weaponry, oil, or steel. There was a lot

---

15. Unless otherwise noted, all quotes from Robert Lawrence are from a September 2001 interview with the author.

16. According to Klinefelter, "The Clinton administration had a way of never saying no, but never saying yes."

17. Unless otherwise noted, all observations by Robert LaRussa are from a September 2001 interview with the author.

of pressure within the administration not to shut the Russians out of this market for fear that they would ship other products."

But the US steel industry saw the agreements as another example of the Clinton administration's willingness to sacrifice steel to some other agenda. "Suspension agreements are always done to help the foreigner," says one US steel lawyer. "They are never done to help the domestic industry." In a May 24 letter to Commerce Secretary Daley, almost two dozen steel executives expressed their opposition to the agreements. "Foreign policy and other objectives do not have a place in the administration of the antidumping laws," they wrote, adding later: "If foreign aid is to be granted to Russia, it should not be at the expense of a single American industry."

Ironically, LaRussa says, because steel prices did not rebound as much as expected after 1998, the minimum prices set as part of the suspension agreement effectively excluded Russian hot-rolled steel from the US market, contrary to administration intentions. Nevertheless, the US steel industry challenged both the Russian agreements and a similar suspension agreement negotiated with Brazil, charging that they allowed imports in at dumped prices and questioning Commerce's commitment to enforcing the dumping laws. The administration's actions apparently pleased almost no one; Russian steelmakers and American steel users also attacked the agreements, calling them too restrictive to allow needed trade.

The 1999 Steel Legislation

As the administration worked with foreign trading partners—negotiating agreements with Russia and Brazil, pressuring Japan and Korea to cut exports and correct market-distorting practices, and appealing again to the European Union to buy more Russian steel—the steelworkers union was tackling a separate set of initiatives. In a January 8 letter to President Clinton, the union's president wrote that given the limitations of the January steel plan, "we now have no choice but to work with our supporters in Congress, of which there are many, to pass into law the absolutely vital relief which the Administration is apparently unwilling to provide—legally binding quantitative restraints which reduce steel imports to their pre-crisis levels."

George Becker could confidently speak of congressional support. Much of the union's clout came from its close ties to the more than 120 House and Senate members of the Congressional Steel Caucus. More important than their numbers was their seniority: Committed caucus members such as Congressmen Peter Visclosky (D-IN), Jack Quinn (R-NY), and Philip English (R-PA), and Senators Arlen Specter, John Rockefeller, and Robert Byrd (D-WV), were in a position to cast swing votes on key pieces of legislation. "We have people in the right places to deliver a message and to deliver members when you have a vote," says Klinefelter. "I talked with Rockefeller's office and Visclosky's office every day. That's how a union with less than 200,000 members could be as effective as we were."

Starting in January, both the House and the Senate debated several pieces of union-backed steel legislation. Key among these was the Steel Recovery Act, introduced by Peter Visclosky and Jack Quinn. While the bill included a number of measures, its main provision was a quota cutting all steel imports over a three-year period to the average monthly volume during the three years preceding July 1997. The administration immediately spoke out in opposition. To impose a quota unilaterally without an injury determination was a violation of the rules of the WTO and, as Commerce's David Aaron says, "was completely antithetical to the administration's philosophy of more liberalized trade." A former White House official adds: "The president and the vice president felt it was important to use the trade remedies we had negotiated assertively, but that we should make it clear that we were operating within WTO consistency, and that we expected other countries to do the same." The House, however, seemed to feel no such compunction. As one former official puts it: "One of the marvels of the American system of government is that we can sign an international agreement, the Congress can implement that agreement, and the Congress can violate that agreement. Domestic law has precedence over international treaties."

In place of the quota bill, the USTR and the White House worked quietly with Representative Sander Levin (D-MI) on legislation that would change section 201—making it easier for petitioners to prove injury—and charge the ITC with addressing the problem of anticompetitive practices in foreign steel markets. The purpose of Levin's bill, says the attorney William Barringer, "was to try to give Congress an alternative to a quota bill, so members could still say, 'We're helping steel.'" The administration was not united in support of the bill, however. According to one insider, some officials argued that the 201 injury standard should be lower, so that dumping cases would not be overused relative to 201; others argued that it was appropriate for dumping standards to be lower, since the standards dealt with unfair trade; and some insisted that "any rewriting of our laws to look less pro-trade would be a very bad thing for world confidence and stability."

While the union supported Levin's bill, it threw its real weight behind the quota legislation, working the issue hard. "We had 1,000 or more members in 150 congressional districts," Klinefelter explains. "If we have 1,000 or more members in any congressional district, we're going to be a factor." Industry, which did not want to support legislation in violation of the WTO, remained quiet.[18] The administration, for its part, spoke out against the quota bill, one official recounts, but did not expect to prevail. Although

---

18. Weirton Steel, a struggling second-tier integrated mill, was one of the only companies to publicly endorse the bill.

the pro–free trade Republican leadership might ordinarily have been expected to block quota legislation, congressional sources say, Speaker Dennis Hastert (R-IL) asked that the act be allowed to come to a vote in order to put Clinton in the awkward position of opposing a union-backed bill.

On March 17 the House passed the quota bill by a vote of 289 to 141, short of the two-thirds majority needed to override a presidential veto. Though Klinefelter calls the vote a significant victory, others describe it as more symbolic than substantive. "The union's hope was that the votes in Congress, especially the House, would push the ITC, the Commerce Department, and others to consider their trade actions more favorably," says Greg Mastel, the Finance Committee's economist. William Barringer observes, "It was a free vote for House members, because they felt it probably would be blocked in the Senate, but if it wasn't blocked in the Senate, it would be vetoed by the president."

As administration officials were quick to point out, however, the last thing President Clinton wanted was to have to veto legislation backed by key Democratic allies and a powerful constituency like the steel union. Democratic Senator John Rockefeller of West Virginia, who had been a close friend of Clinton's since the two were governors, had been pushing the president to self-initiate a 201 case since the previous fall.[19] According to Ellen Doneski, Rockefeller's legislative director, the senator was opposed to WTO-incompatible quotas and had earlier refused to back such legislation. When it became clear that Clinton would not bend on 201, though, Rockefeller introduced a Senate version of the House quota bill.[20]

This time, the administration launched a serious assault, holding press conferences, courting the members of the steel caucus, and meeting with individual senators and lobbyists. "After the vote in the House, the administration was all over the Hill," recalls Klinefelter. In making its case against trade barriers, the administration was joined by free trade advocates in Congress, domestic steel users concerned about quota-induced steel shortages and inflated prices, and even a coalition of farm groups, which sent a letter to the Senate in mid-June warning that a steel quota would likely spur foreign retaliation against US agricultural exports.

Even during the earlier House bill debate, the administration had been poring over import figures, looking for evidence that the already-imposed dumping penalties and bilateral negotiations had ended the import surge, thus making a quota unnecessary. "The questions we kept asking were 'Will the industry recover, and when will the industry recover?'" says then Council of Economic Advisers member Robert Lawrence, "hoping that

19. West Virginia–based Weirton and Wheeling-Pittsburgh, the eighth and ninth largest of the integrateds, were two of the steelmakers most in danger of failing, and Rockefeller believed that only a comprehensive solution could save them.

20. Like the House, the Senate considered several steel bills, including a measure similar to Levin's bill, but the quota bill garnered the most attention.

would take off the political pressure and, indeed, help the industry." Because of a buildup of inventories, Lawrence says, the domestic industry did not bounce back as quickly as some had expected. But by May, Commerce Secretary Daley was able to announce an encouraging drop in imports and an increase in domestic prices. By mid-June, although Klinefelter insists "there was not much truth to it," Daley was declaring at every opportunity that the crisis was over.[21]

On June 22 the Senate effectively killed the quota bill in a procedural vote. Improved import levels were only part of the story. Senators generally were more attuned to foreign policy considerations and less likely to pass this kind of special interest legislation than were representatives, observers say, in part because they had to report to broader constituencies (even senators from strong steel states also typically represented exporting businesses or major steel users). "It is a much more difficult place for us to operate," acknowledges Klinefelter, "because we just don't have enough people in enough states to control the Senate." Indeed, some of the bill's staunchest supporters admit that they never expected it to pass in the Senate. Instead, they say, the attempt was a necessary exercise to show the union and concerned companies that a quota bill was not doable, and that it was time to try something else.

Although the quota effort died and none of the measures proposed in the House or Senate to change section 201 advanced, one piece of legislation went through that summer that pleased the union and at least a segment of the domestic steel industry. Senator Robert Byrd, a senior member of the Appropriations Committee, attached an amendment to an emergency appropriations bill allocating $1 billion to a measure that became known as the Emergency Steel Loan Guarantee Act. Under the act, troubled steelmakers that met certain requirements could obtain loans from private lenders that Treasury would guarantee for up to 85 percent of the loan amount. Critics charged that Byrd's amendment, backed as well by his fellow West Virginia Democrat Senator Rockefeller, was a blatant effort to bail out failing steel mills in West Virginia, particularly Weirton. "Senator Rockefeller has two major steel manufacturers," says his legislative director, Ellen Doneski, "and what he didn't want to have occur was for the steel market to stabilize after one or two bankruptcies in West Virginia."[22]

The Clinton administration did not like the amendment, but it also did not go out of its way to fight it. Ironically, the Byrd amendment may have been most unpopular among segments of industry. The better-performing mini-mills and those companies that had undergone successful restructur-

21. Although import levels had not returned to 1997 levels, they were well below the surge that began in August 1998.

22. Unless otherwise noted, all quotes from Ellen Doneski are from a September 2001 interview with the author.

ing did not want to see uneconomic competitors kept afloat by government subsidies and thereby add to the problem of excess inefficient capacity.

With a recovery in steel apparently under way, calls for a government-launched 201 investigation mostly subsided. A flurry of trade cases worked through the system, as industry had filed dumping cases in cold-rolled steel, steel beams, and two different sizes of pipe, as well as two section 201 cases in pipe and wire rod. Such cases continued to generate friction. Some observers blamed the failure of that fall's WTO ministerial in Seattle in part on the unwillingness of the United States to allow discussion of dumping laws. LaRussa and Aaron of Commerce, however, say that countries opposed to launching a new trade round called for new dumping negotiations, knowing that the United States would refuse and that they could then blame the collapse of the ministerial on US intransigence.

A Brief Recovery—A Further Fall

For the steel industry, the year 2000 began with some promise. Imports had fallen, at least in some key categories, and the US economy was strong. Domestic demand for steel in autos and construction was booming, and steel mill capacity utilization had increased markedly from the 1998 slump. Still, steel industry profits remained low. Prices had not fully recovered, nor did imports drop to their pre-1998 level.

In July, Commerce released the "Global Steel Trade Report," a study of the steel market that had been promised the previous year after the quota legislation failed. Because the report had been modified during an interagency review, with particular care not to include anything that could harm the presidential candidacy of Vice President Gore, the final recommendations were "pretty limp," says David Aaron, who left Commerce in April. "I would have liked to have seen them recommend a 201 and an international initiative. I felt that having talked to some of the foreign steel people and countries that they would not take us seriously without at least starting a 201." He adds: "Once we got to this report, all the easy things we could do ourselves, apart from 201, had been exhausted."

Nevertheless, industry and the union embraced the document, which summarized unfair and uneconomic practices in other countries and described their effects on the US steel industry and the problems of global overcapacity. Klinefelter, who calls the report "an incredibly valuable document," says, "It was the first time that our government had ever laid out what our trading partners were doing to us in a systematic fashion in regard to steel."

By the time the report came out, however, another downturn had begun. In part because of price increases announced by domestic producers earlier in the year, steel imports had risen in early 2000. After the nation's industrial sector began to slow in May, steel buyers cut back on imports, but even so, weakened domestic demand for steel drove down plant capacity utilization rates once again. Excess inventory and flagging sales soon took a toll on prices: By the fall, hot-rolled steel was selling for only $180 a ton, about half what it had gone for in the early spring. Steel company stock prices also plummeted, drying up available sources of capital.[23] The steel slump, coming as it did just two years after the surge of imports in 1998, hit manufacturers particularly hard. "You had them getting absolutely hammered in '98, you had a little bit of a recovery going into 2000, then the bottom fell out, so [the integrated steelmakers] didn't really have any reserves left," says a former Senate Finance Committee staffer.

By the beginning of October, with Gore and Texas Governor George W. Bush running neck-and-neck in their presidential campaigns, and both candidates struggling to lock in key constituencies, the USWA's George Becker began meeting with Karen Tramantano and John Podesta, pleading for the Clinton administration to self-initiate a 201 case.[24] In an October 16 letter to President Clinton, the union and more than 70 representatives of steelmakers and related firms wrote: "We need a clear public recognition that once again there is a crisis devastating the domestic steel industry and that the existing orders affecting the industry must remain in place. We need you to immediately impose meaningful restraints on steel imports from offending non-WTO countries. Finally, given this extraordinary circumstance, we need the Administration to immediately initiate a comprehensive case under Section 201 of our trade laws. Only through these actions can we stop the onslaught we are facing." Members of Congress began working on legislation to support this effort.

The chorus of calls for the administration to self-initiate was understandable. Although some Clinton representatives had insisted all along that a section 201 case brought by industry would have as much chance of success as one brought by government, that view was shared by virtually no one in the union or in industry. Instead, most observers agreed, action by the administration changed the equation in important ways. First, self-initiation demonstrated that the president had already concluded that imports were the cause of serious injury. "It's a signal to the trading partners, it's a signal to the ITC, it's a signal to the courts who may be looking at an appeal," says former ITC commissioner Thelma Askey. "It's a lot dif-

---

23. One former administration official recalls the head of a major steel firm shouting in a meeting that the value of a share of stock had fallen to less than a cup of latte.

24. In an indication of the union's desperation, Becker even appealed to the administration to provide steel industry protection under a national security provision—but that, one official says, "didn't have a chance in hell," since only a fraction of US steel capacity went to the military.

ferent when the administration says, 'We think that given all the considerations of the broader economy, this warrants our backing.'"[25]

Second, if a case brought by the administration was successful, industry presumably could count on the president to use his discretion to impose a significant trade remedy. Finally—and perhaps most important, according to some observers—if the ITC ruled against the 201 action, the president might still feel bound to provide industry with some meaningful relief. "What it all boils down to was putting the president on the hook for a comprehensive solution," says William Corbett, then on the staff of the National Economic Council, "so that regardless of the outcome at the ITC, the president of the United States is responsible for assisting the industry out of its crisis."[26] Given how few comprehensive solutions existed, Corbett notes, any such relief could easily run afoul of WTO rules concerning quotas or subsidies.

The union appeal, coming as it did just weeks before the presidential election, put the administration on the spot—as it was no doubt intended to do.[27] "We could say, 'No, we won't initiate,'" says the former CEA economist Robert Lawrence, "but that would put a big wedge between Gore and the steelworkers. But if we said 'Yes,' we would be labeled protectionists." In mid-October, the principals began meeting again in earnest on the steel issue, and Gene Sperling convened meetings with Becker, various steel industry CEOs, and the major economic policymakers in the administration to further analyze the crisis. In an October 25 letter to Becker, John Podesta assured the union head that the president was still reviewing section 201 relief, and that the USTR was simultaneously consulting with countries including Ukraine, Taiwan, India, and China about moderating their steel exports.

But in a letter to Clinton the following day, the Executive Committee of the Congressional Steel Caucus complained that the time for more studies was over. "As you know, a Section 201 action would result in a comprehensive investigation of steel imports, similar to the investigation you already propose," the letter read in part. "Any remedy proposed at the end of this investigation would be implemented at the discretion of the President. If the next President feels action is unwarranted, he could choose not to act." Yet in another letter to Clinton written on the same day, the Consuming Industries Trade Action Coalition, a group of steel-using

---

25. Unless otherwise noted, all quotes from Thelma Askey are from a September 2001 interview with the author.

26. Unless otherwise noted, all quotes from William Corbett are from a September 2001 interview with the author.

27. The economist Greg Mastel notes that elections had played an important role in past steel trade policy decisions. President Reagan, for example, endorsed voluntary restraint agreements during his reelection campaign. "Unions and companies are both aware in elections that they have some unique influences," Mastel says, "and they use them."

companies formed in 1999, argued that the steel industry had exaggerated the impact of imports, and that severe trade restraints would hurt far more companies and employees than it would help.

According to White House insiders, the ensuing administration debate on immediate self-initiation of a 201 centered on three main areas of concern: the political ramifications of any decision for the upcoming election, the likelihood of the ITC reaching a positive finding, and the broader economic impact—both in the United States and abroad—of such a trade-limiting measure. While those involved say the short-term political effect was given the least attention, administration strategists concluded there was more to lose than gain by initiating. "We had the steelworkers on our side in the campaign already," points out David Aaron, formerly of Commerce, "so we weren't going to get anything out of it, except that we would hand Bush an issue to say that we were protectionist."

A more critical question, insiders say, was whether a 201 case would even be winnable. According to Robert Lawrence, because imports were subsiding, it would be hard to prove they were the major cause of the industry's distress. Moreover, just six months earlier, the ITC had ruled against the industry during the injury part of a dumping case on cold-rolled steel—and the injury standards for a 201 case would be considerably higher.[28] Given that a few steel product areas were still doing reasonably well, that industry had only posted one quarter of bad economic results, and that certain product segments were already protected by dumping orders, winning a comprehensive case appeared unlikely. "It seemed to me that the immediate problems of the steel industry were caused by a combination of too much capacity and a slowdown domestically," Lawrence recalls. "The biggest source of their injury was not imports."

Perhaps most important, however, was that industry had also apparently concluded that the case was not ripe. Despite the steel company signatures on the letter to Clinton calling for self-initiation of a 201 action, soon thereafter industry lawyers at a USTR meeting that included Esserman, Lawrence, and Klinefelter "spent most of the time saying there was no case to be made," recalls one participant. Esserman, who says she would have had to rely on steel company data to judge whether a 201 case could succeed, notes that government would not have considered self-initiating without the full support of industry. She adds, "It was disquieting to know that the industry lawyers most familiar with the facts did not think it was a good option. There was an immense interest coming from

---

28. The ITC decision provoked outrage among industry and union representatives, who claimed that in making its decision, the commission had relied on an inappropriate econometric model rather than the usual analysis of market conditions. In a letter of complaint to President Clinton, Becker and three steel executives pointed out that Commerce had already found dumping margins ranging from 16 to 80 percent, and that the volume of cold-rolled imports had doubled between 1996 and 1998 to 2.2 million tons.

the White House and from various agencies to do something that would be genuinely helpful, and not simply a political stunt."

Moreover, although Robert Rubin had left Treasury, his successor, Lawrence Summers, was equally adamant that a section 201 action, even though temporary, would be bad for the US economy and would send the wrong message to foreign trading partners, possibly spurring retaliatory trade-restricting measures. "If you looked at US economic interests overall in the eight years under the Clinton administration, it was pretty clear that regular predictable access to foreign markets was an enormous part of our economic success," explains one administration official. "As the world's largest exporter, our vulnerability to retaliation was very high in a lot of industries that employ as many or many times more workers than steel."

One final issue influenced the decision. According to many observers, Bill Clinton was acutely aware of his legacy. While he was proud of his trade record in general and such significant accomplishments as winning approval of the North American Free Trade Agreement (NAFTA), the president had been discouraged by his failure to get fast-track negotiating authority, which would have strengthened his ability to negotiate trade agreements.[29] Self-initiating a 201 case, in the eyes of some, would have further sullied Clinton's free-trade credentials. "He didn't want to add another black mark to his second term record on trade," says one insider.

Election Day arrived November 7 without a decision to self-initiate. "We were pushing them, pushing them, pushing them, trying to get Al Gore elected," says Klinefelter. "We were telling them that they had to do something very visible for Gore for us to bring back to those steel states. They wouldn't do it."

A New Administration

The results of the 2000 presidential election were mired in controversy over vote-counting irregularities in Florida. Even after it became clear that George W. Bush would be the next president, the section 201 debate lingered on. Klinefelter, who notes that Bush narrowly won normally Democratic West Virginia, believes that the results might have been different if the Clinton administration had self-initiated a 201. "It would have gone a long way if he could have walked into West Virginia saying that this administration has initiated a 201 to save the basic steel industry," he says. Although industry remained ambivalent about the trade case, union and steel caucus representatives who had Clinton's ear still hoped they might persuade the president to self-initiate. "We pushed on 201 with Clinton right up to the end," recalls Rockefeller's legislative director, Ellen Doneski.

---

29. Fast-track negotiating authority gave the president the ability to negotiate trade agreements that Congress could either vote down or approve, but not amend. The authority increased the willingness of foreign governments to negotiate with the United States.

Within the administration, there were also still a few individuals who believed Clinton should bring a 201 action. The domestic steel industry, after all, had continued to deteriorate. Wheeling-Pittsburgh filed for bankruptcy in November, followed by LTV, the nation's third-largest steel producer, at the end of December (a number of smaller companies had already filed). Moreover, some 201 supporters claimed that self-initiating would be a politically astute move—an argument that Senator Rockefeller made repeatedly. "We could easily have used the logic that we will show our friends in the steel industry that we care about them," says Robert Lawrence. "We will send this thing to the ITC and put huge pressure on the next Republican president to give them protection."

In the final analysis, however, many of Clinton's top policymakers still did not believe that a section 201 action was a legitimate response. Although the steel industry was unquestionably suffering, Lawrence says, the downturn was primarily due to the weakening US economy. "We thought it wasn't good policy, because we thought we couldn't make the case that these people merited it," he explains. "Our hearts bled for the steel industry, but we didn't think they were being damaged by imports."

The union never stopped pushing. According to Klinefelter, on January 19, six hours before the administration left office, he and Becker went to the White House to make a final pitch to Summers, Podesta, and a few others. But all the union won, Klinefelter says, was a letter from Clinton to the chairman of the ITC, urging him to look hard at the merits of a 201 case. In the letter, Clinton summarized the administration's steel initiatives, noting that it had processed more than 100 dumping and countervailing duty cases involving steel products since 1998; negotiated agreements with Russia; initiated consultations with Japan, Korea, and other significant steel exporters; and completed the global steel study, among other measures. "In spite of these efforts, however," the president concluded, "our analysis of the current and prospective import situation and recent events in the steel industry lead us to believe that Section 201 relief may be warranted in the near future. Therefore, I urge the International Trade Commission to proceed urgently, on its own motion or upon the motion of industry, union, Congressional or Executive Branch petitioners, to provide effective relief for the US steel industry."

For the union, it was too little, too late. According to one outgoing administration official, George Becker was particularly bitter, declaring, "You didn't give us any help at all."

The Case for a 201 Action

Although many Democratic members of the steelworkers union and Congressional Steel Caucus did not have established relationships with the newly inaugurated President George W. Bush or his cabinet, the change of administration did not slow their efforts to win protection from steel imports. Senator John Rockefeller, for example, wrote to President Bush within days of his inauguration urging him to self-initiate a section 201 case, and soon met with Vice President Dick Cheney, Commerce Secretary Donald Evans, and White House political staff. "The senator has made the case to those who he thought would be sensitive not just to the economic or the business or the trade argument, but the political argument," says Ellen Doneski. "They're certainly interested in winning West Virginia again."

The quickly worsening condition of the steel industry also spurred a new round of legislation. On March 1 Representatives Peter Visclosky and Jack Quinn introduced the Steel Revitalization Act of 2001, a sprawling four-pronged bill that dwarfed the quota bill they had submitted in 1999. In addition to incorporating a more restrictive quota provision, the act increased the funds available under Senator Byrd's loan guarantee program to $10 billion and upped the government-guaranteed percentage from 85 to 95 percent,[30] set a 1.5 percent surcharge on all steel to bankroll a legacy cost fund that companies could draw on for retirees' health care, and established a $500 million grant program to encourage consolidation within the domestic steel industry by funding environmental cleanups and restructuring.

Finally, in a reversal of its former position, the steel industry joined the union and Congress in calling for comprehensive relief. "One is driven by the circumstances in which one finds oneself—the factual and policy bases for getting relief in a section 201 case were now satisfied," sums up Alan Wolff, a lawyer for steel companies. In March, a broad-based coalition of steel associations called for the administration to self-initiate a 201 case or to find some other WTO-compatible way to restrict imports.[31] While mini-mills and integrated steel companies still disagreed about whether government should help with legacy costs and restructuring, they were united on the need for protection from excess global steel.

Driving industry to unify was an accelerating decline that went well beyond the bad news of 1998, as the slowing of the domestic economy dried up demand for steel. Even with imports down, capacity continued to exceed demand, and hot- and cold-rolled sheet prices fell that spring to their lowest point in 20 years. A total of 18 steel companies had filed for bankruptcy since the end of 1997, and about 23,500 workers had lost their jobs. Moreover, between November 2000 and June 2001, more than 7 million net

---

30. Only one company, Geneva Steel, had received funds under Byrd's original loan guarantee program, in part because applicants looked like such bad risks that commercial banks did not want to assume responsibility for even 15 percent of a possible loan.

31. The coalition included the American Iron and Steel Institute, the Cold Finished Steel Bar Institute, the Committee on Pipe and Tube Imports, the Specialty Steel Industry of North America, and the Steel Manufacturers Association.

tons of capacity in the United States shut down. "It's a fair assessment to say that the domestic industry was being absolutely devastated," says one insider. "You can argue about whose fault it was, but the reality is you had a quarter of the industry in bankruptcy, you had 7 million tons of it shut down as a result of actual liquidations, and you had stock valuations that had fallen through the floor."

Adding to industry's interest in a section 201 action was the reality that simply mounting cases against dumping no longer seemed adequate to stem imports. As quickly as a dumping order shut off supply from one country, another steel entrant stepped up exports of the same product to fill the gap. Despite the earlier successful hot-rolled steel dumping cases brought against Japan, Russia, and Brazil, for example, imports of hot-rolled steel crept up again in 2000; eventually, a group of companies led by Nucor filed a second round of cases against 11 countries, including India, South Africa, China, and Ukraine. "The global steel market is much more elastic than it used to be," says Klinefelter. "People know how to shop around, and these items can be made in any country in the world where there is a steel mill, so things move much more quickly than they used to."

Industry may also have felt that the ITC would be more receptive to a 201 case then than it had been in recent history. At the end of his tenure, President Clinton had decided not to renominate Commissioner Thelma Askey at the urging of the United Steelworkers of America and the Congressional Steel Caucus, whose members claimed that Askey's aggressive free trade stance had earned her the commission's worst voting record on trade relief for steel. Although President Bush had attempted to reappoint Askey, he withdrew her nomination after encountering opposition from legislators whose support was critical to moving his tax bill through the House Ways and Means and Senate Finance committees.[32] According to many observers, Askey's replacement, Dennis Devaney (a recess appointment made by Clinton), was seen as a more reliable vote for protection. "The union has changed the complexion of the commission sufficiently so that it is very difficult for them to lose," says one critic.

A Plan for Steel

The steel industry's clear sense of desperation put the steel issue "up front and center" for the new Bush administration, according to one official, who says there was also "intense pressure from the Hill"—even from legislators who had always opposed the idea of a quota. Commerce Secretary Evans, Treasury Secretary Paul O'Neill, and USTR Robert Zoellick

---

32. Bush instead nominated Askey to be director of the US Trade and Development Agency, a government agency dedicated to encouraging US exports to developing and middle-income countries.

took the lead, aided by CEA Chairman Glenn Hubbard, spending hours with Wall Street analysts to study the industry.[33] Meanwhile, the National Security Council and the National Economic Council doled out research assignments to the various agencies.

At first glance, steel's chances of getting the Bush administration to act on a 201 claim might have seemed low: Historically, the Republican Party supported free trade principles, and Bush had specifically focused on issues of free trade and noninterference in markets during his campaign. But some observers, noting that the Republican administrations of Reagan and George H. W. Bush had implemented the arguably protectionist voluntary restraint agreements, claimed that Bush might feel free to act precisely because of his free trade reputation. "After all, it took Nixon to go to China," says Peder Maarbjerg, legislative director for Representative Peter Visclosky. "It took Clinton to reform welfare. Bush already had all the business people on his side."[34] Rockefeller's aide Doneski adds, "The Republicans weren't afraid to look like they were willing to use our trade laws, because nobody is going to accuse them of being anti–free trade."

Even with industry's support, the administration's ability to make a case that imports were the primary cause of injury, as required under section 201, remained in question. Preliminary Commerce figures at the end of May showed that steel imports through March were 6.2 million metric tons, a more than 30 percent decrease from a year earlier. In order to implicate imports in the current industry slide, a 201 case would have to employ a five-year trend line encompassing the earlier 1998 import surge. But since steelmakers had never fully recovered from the 1998 crisis, 201 supporters argued that linking the two downturns was legally sound.

By May, the Bush administration—convinced that the steel industry needed some kind of intervention—was seriously grappling with the possibility of self-initiating a 201 action. To do so could bring significant political rewards. USTR Robert Zoellick believed a 201 case could serve as an olive branch to the steel union and the Congressional Steel Caucus, insiders say, improving the president's chances of winning trade promotion authority (formerly known as fast-track authority). With trade promotion authority, Bush would be in a better position to pursue two key goals: negotiating a Free Trade Area of the Americas, which would lower tariffs and encourage open borders within the Western Hemisphere, and launching a new WTO trade round. "His hope was not to get the support of the unions for either of those endeavors," says foreign steel attorney

---

33. Steel received unusual high-level attention, some insiders say, because few subcabinet-level positions had been filled.

34. Unless otherwise noted, all quotes from Peder Maarbjerg are from a September 2001 interview with the author.

William Barringer, "but to make steel a non-issue in at least launching those initiatives."[35]

White House Senior Adviser Karl Rove and other political strategists were also reportedly pushing for a 201 case, arguing that it would help Bush promote nontrade issues—such as tax cuts and education reform—as well as build support in key electoral states in preparation for the next presidential election. Klinefelter says the strategy was sound: "In 2004, Bush could go into Pennsylvania, Ohio, Indiana, Illinois, and West Virginia and say, 'I'm the president who saved your job.' Now it doesn't make any difference what the leadership of the steelworkers union says about the next Democratic presidential candidate. If Bush comes through on this 201, he's going to get our guys."

But insiders insist that political motives were taking a backseat to policy considerations. Evans, O'Neill, and Zoellick were more interested in tackling the global steel industry's chronic issues of subsidies and inefficient excess capacity than they were in blocking imports, observers say. But the members of the new administration reasoned that a 201 case could provide temporary relief, while helping to persuade steelmakers—both domestically and abroad—to address the industry's deeper problems. Officials were not sure what form such discussions should take, or whether they should be bilateral or multilateral, but they resolved to pursue some form of international steel negotiations. "People realized that if we didn't act, there was a good chance we were going to get steel quotas or something else that was going to gum up the works in terms of a broader trade agenda," one official remarks.

While still deliberating at the end of May, the White House got an unexpected prod. Rockefeller and other steel-supporting members of the Senate Finance Committee had wanted the committee to take the initiative and launch a 201 action since the beginning of the year, but Chairman Charles Grassley (R-IA) had blocked progress on the motion. After Senator James Jeffords (R-VT) defected from the Republican Party, however, giving control of the Finance Committee to the Democrats, the new chair, Montana Democrat Max Baucus, vowed to move ahead. Had the Finance Committee taken the initiative, many observers say, the Democrats would have grabbed much of the political capital to be gained from the action.

The administration, however, moved first. In a step that took industry, the union, and Congress by surprise, President Bush announced on June 5 that his administration would self-initiate a 201 investigation for 33 types of steel imports.[36] After declaring that "the US steel industry has been af-

---

35. The likely impact of a 201 self-initiation on long-held congressional stands on trade was debatable, however. As one former Clinton official notes, "The Democrats in Congress still have to work with the unions. I don't know that the unions are just going to roll over and say, 'Go ahead and get your fast track and sign your WTO agreement.'"

36. The Senate Finance Committee later filed a 201 case structured on the administration's case to demonstrate Hill support.

fected by a 50-year legacy of foreign government intervention in the market and direct financial support of their steel industries," Bush announced that his administration would conduct two sets of international steel negotiations—one to eliminate inefficient excess global capacity, and a longer-term effort to reduce market-distorting subsidies.[37] "They sat down and they actually came up with a coherent plan, not all of which we had suggested," says Alan Wolff. "The Clinton administration really never came to grips with what could be done, although, to be fair, its options were more limited. By the time the Bush administration acted, the crisis had fully arrived, and more tools were clearly available."

A Measure of Protection

President Bush's unanticipated announcement elicited an immediate and powerful response. "It is an important message that the United States will not allow its steel industry to be destroyed by illegal steel imports," declared James G. Bradley, president of Wheeling-Pittsburgh.[38] For the union and steel caucus representatives who had invested so much time and energy during both the Clinton and Bush administrations, the action was a long-awaited payoff and a welcome sign of the new president's receptiveness to steel concerns. "I was so frustrated with the Clinton people, and disappointed in the way that they dealt with this," says Klinefelter. "I've got to say, this Bush administration seems to care more about working people. They care more about jobs, and that's what working people are about."

But those opposed to trade barriers and special protection for steel reacted with anger and concern, accusing the Bush administration of caving in to union and industry pressure. "A Section 201 investigation is a very serious step," Janet Kopenhaver, executive director of the Consuming Industries Trade Action Coalition—a steel users group—asserted in a written statement. "If it results in restricting steel imports, it could severely impact US consumers and steel consuming industries, but won't solve the US industry's basic problems." Similarly, in letters sent to Zoellick, Evans, and O'Neill, the president of the American Institute for International Steel wrote, "Our firm belief is that the current difficult conditions the US steel industry finds itself in stems from living in a protected steel market for over 30 years and benefiting from subsidy programs provided by federal, state and local governments. Simply put, protectionism and subsidies do not create competitive industries."

---

37. "Statement by the President Regarding a Multilateral Initiative on Steel," White House press release, June 5, 2001, www.whitehouse.gov.

38. Bradley, quoted in Leslie Wayne, "A Significant Lift for a Long-Ailing US Industry," *The New York Times*, June 6, 2001, C4.

Foreign trading partners also expressed their strong displeasure—particularly EU representatives, who blamed US steel woes on the industry's having shirked the painful and across-the-board consolidation undertaken by European steel firms over the past two decades. Five EU steelmakers were among the world's 10 largest steel producers, EU officials noted as proof of European industry reform, while the largest American producer, U.S. Steel, came in at number 11. In a prepared statement, European Trade Commissioner Pascal Lamy declared: "The cost of restructuring in the US steel sector should not be shifted to the rest of the world. The imposition of safeguard measures would risk seriously disrupting world steel trade."[39]

On June 22 Robert Zoellick formally self-initiated the 201 action on behalf of the administration, with an ITC decision expected four months later. How the ITC would rule was debatable, particularly since many observers in mid-2001 still questioned whether the proper conditions existed to bring a 201 case. Nevertheless, in October 2001 the ITC gave a clear vote in favor of safeguards, ruling that imports were injuring US steel producers in 16—or almost half—of the 33 categories under investigation. In December, the commissioners recommended remedies ranging from moderate quotas to prohibitive tariffs of 30 to 40 percent.[40] It would be up to the president to decide on the exact remedy, if any.

During January and February, the Bush administration was flooded with appeals. These ranged from an EU proposal that, in lieu of tariffs, the United States impose a tax on both domestic and imported steel shipments, which would help to cover industry legacy costs and aid in restructuring, to a letter signed by 140 Congress members advocating across-the-board tariffs that would run a full four years. On March 6, 2002, after intense consultations with political and economic advisers, President Bush announced what many observers termed a carefully balanced compromise. The United States would impose three-year safeguards on 10 of the 12 categories of steel imports, with tariffs ranging from a low of 8 percent for stainless steel rod to a high of 30 percent for flat-rolled and 3 other categories of steel. The tariffs, which went into effect on March 20, were slated to drop each year of the three-year remedy period.

A number of exceptions softened the blow. All countries with free trade agreements with the United States—most notably Canada and Mexico—were excluded, as were developing nations with imports to the United States totaling less than 3 percent of the domestic market.[41] In certain cat-

---

39. Lamy, quoted in Alan Cowell, "Swift Condemnation of US on Steel," *The New York Times*, June 7, 2001, W1.

40. The actual recommendation covered 12 rather than 16 categories, since the ITC combined 5 into 1.

41. In addition to Canada and Mexico, Israel and Jordan had free trade agreements with the United States, and more than a dozen developing countries qualified for the exclusions.

egories of steel, these exclusions amounted to as much as 35 percent of imports. Also not covered were certain steel products that US manufacturers did not make or were not interested in making themselves. Over the next few months, the Bush administration promised to evaluate the many hundreds of further requests for exclusions it had received, both from domestic steelmakers and steel users and from foreign petitioners.

The World Reacts

The reactions of various constituencies to the tariffs were, for the most part, predictable. Though the remedies were not as extreme as most of the domestic steel industry had desired, and though the decrease in tariffs during years two and three of the 201 action would reduce the impact of the safeguard remedy, the majority of US steel producers—in particular integrated mills and mini-mills, who benefited most from the trade restraints—declared themselves satisfied. "This is protection in substance as well as appearance," said Robert Miller, chief executive of Bethlehem Steel.[42]

However, domestic steel consumers and free trade advocates—including many conservatives normally supportive of Bush and his policies—charged that the tariffs were blatantly protectionist, would damage US steel-using industries more than they would help steel producers, and were adopted for purely political reasons (notably, gaining support prior to the November midterm elections and positioning Bush for the 2004 presidential election).[43] "Sometimes politics dominates good economic decision-making in the best of administrations," said Gerald O'Driscoll, director of the Heritage Foundation's Center for International Trade and Economics. "This is purely a political decision. There is no economic justification for it."[44]

Moreover, many observers claimed that since every safeguards measure challenged in the WTO to that point had been declared illegal, the Bush administration knew full well that the 201 action eventually would be rejected by the organization. However, the almost two years likely needed for the dispute settlement process to reach any conclusion would give the tariffs ample time to block steel imports to the clear benefit of the domestic steel industry.

---

42. Miller, quoted in David E. Sanger, "Bush Puts Tariffs of As Much As 30% on Steel Imports," *The New York Times*, March 6, 2002, A1.

43. The 201 action appeared to bring quick and concrete political dividends for the administration. In July 2002 Congressional Steel Caucus support helped the administration to win trade promotion authority—perhaps its top trade goal—by a narrow margin; the law took force in August 2002.

44. O'Driscoll, quoted in Richard W. Stevenson, "Steel Tariffs Weaken Bush's Global Hand," *The New York Times*, March 6, 2002, C1.

Foreign trading partners, meanwhile, expressed outrage. The WTO Safeguards Agreement permitted a country to impose tariffs without retaliation as long as the claimed increase was documented and the tariffs were limited to three years. But according to the European Union, steel exports to the United States had fallen over the previous eight years, and it declared its intention either to get immediate compensation from the United States to account for lost trade or to begin its own retaliation against US exports. Japan and other countries also announced plans to retaliate. In early June, as predicted, the European Union requested the formation of a WTO dispute settlement panel to consider its complaint against the 201 action, and it was soon joined by seven other countries.[45]

Over the next few months, as domestic steel-using companies appealed to the administration for relief and foreign governments accused the United States of being anti–free trade, the USTR continued to consider requests for exclusions. The European Union was particularly assertive, and it backed up its requests with an ongoing threat to impose tariffs worth $335 million on a select list of US exports in advance of any WTO decision (an interim panel decision was not expected until late that year at the earliest). In part to ease cross-Atlantic tension and to make it less likely that the European Union would retaliate early, the USTR over the summer excluded a significant number of EU products from tariffs, as well as granting requests from Japan, US steel producers and users, and others. By the time a large batch of exclusions was announced in August 2002, about a quarter of the steel that could have been affected by the 201 action had been exempted, according to US officials. Largely because of the exclusions, the European Union in the fall of 2002 agreed to postpone retaliation until the WTO dispute panel issued its ruling.

A Period of Consolidation

In first announcing the section 201 action, the Bush administration had insisted that any industry protection would be accompanied by parallel efforts to pare down excess global capacity and reduce market-distorting subsidies. With the tariffs in place, serious questions remained about what the three prongs of the administration's plan might achieve and how they would interact. For example, while the ostensible purpose of the 201 case was to provide the domestic steel industry with comprehensive, short-term relief from imports, allowing it a period of recovery, Bush administration officials also hoped to use the case as a lever to encourage steel companies to take a hard look at their own operations and pursue restructuring at home. "Before they actually did this, Evans, O'Neill, and

---

45. The complainants, in addition to the European Union, were Brazil, China, Japan, New Zealand, Norway, South Korea, and Switzerland.

Zoellick sat down with the CEOs and the unions and said, 'Look, if we do this, you guys have to make good on the restructuring element of this,'" says one close observer. "We're not in this for market protection; we're in this to solve the fundamental underlying problem that has brought us here in the first place."

In June 2002, USTR Zoellick and Commerce Secretary Evans sent a letter to domestic steelmakers asking them to submit consolidation progress reports in September as well as the following March, at which point the 201 action would have been in place one year. The reports, wrote the officials, should include "measures to consolidate and rationalize operations, reduce costs, enhance efficiency, increase productivity, improve quality and service, and develop new products and markets."[46]

Meanwhile, even before the ITC ruled on section 201, the United States had brought the twin problems of global overcapacity and market-distorting practices before the steel committee of the Organization for Economic Cooperation and Development (OECD). The committee took up the issues during the fall of 2001, but some foreign participants complained that the timing of the meetings, which took place as the Bush administration was debating the extent of 201 remedies, was intended to enable the Americans to use the threat of high tariffs to force international compliance. Even so, the group produced a communiqué in mid-December 2001 declaring that governments of steel-producing countries should initiate policies supportive of restructuring and consolidation. The recommendation was purely voluntary, however, and did not hold participants to any specific course of action.

The effort to address subsidies was even less productive. Though the steel committee met several times during 2002, a US proposal at a September 2002 meeting to draw up an international agreement curbing subsidies met with widespread resistance—in part because representatives of other countries insisted that the United States' antidumping and countervailing duty laws would need to be part of that discussion, a move that the United States refused to consider.[47]

In the United States, the steel industry appeared to agree on the need for restructuring, but called for more government help to make it possible. In September 2002, steel companies began submitting reports on the impact of the 201 action on their operations and on their current and future plans for restructuring, as USTR Zoellick had requested. But companies also used the reports as an opportunity to criticize the number of tariff exclusions granted by the government, and to restate the importance of keeping

---

46. Letter quoted in "Administration Sets Mileposts for Steel Industry Restructuring," *Inside US Trade*, June 28, 2002.

47. The OECD committee kept meeting into 2004; but after members were unable to overcome key differences, participants eventually dropped the steel subsidies talks in favor of informal consultations.

the section 201 tariffs in place for a full three years, declaring that corporate consolidation efforts—while promising—had barely gotten under way.[48] Moreover, integrated steelmakers continued to request government help with legacy costs; they also stressed the need for new labor agreements with steelworkers that would aid in cost cutting and consolidation.

In fact, though, because of a number of factors, the US steel industry was restructuring, consolidating, and—for most of those companies that survived—becoming more profitable. In the year and a half following the announcement of the 201 action in March 2002, nine more US steel companies went bankrupt, taking at least some inefficient capacity off the market.[49] At the same time, steel prices were rising worldwide as the global economy recovered and as demand for steel grew, particularly in China. In the United States, overall steel imports dropped by about 30 percent during 2003 alone, both because of the section 201 tariffs and because the weak US dollar made the domestic market less attractive to foreign producers.[50] Another critical development, observers say, was the government's assumption of the legacy costs of some key companies. In March 2002 the Pension Benefit Guaranty Corporation, the federal agency that insures private pension plans, took over pension obligations for LTV Steel, and in December it assumed the obligations of the failing Bethlehem and National Steel companies (at a cost of $7.1 billion).

Higher steel prices, the federal agency's assumption of crippling legacy costs, and, in some cases, cost-cutting new labor agreements with the steelworkers union made the assets of many of these bankrupt steel companies attractive to profitable steel producers;[51] the result was a wave of consolidations. The newly formed International Steel Group bought LTV's assets as LTV's pension obligations were lifted in early 2002, and in 2003 it went on to buy the assets of Bethlehem, Weirton, and Georgetown Steel. U.S. Steel bought National Steel's assets, and Nucor bought the assets of Birmingham Steel as well as Trico Steel, which was a joint venture between LTV and two international steel companies (Hufbauer and Goodrich 2003).

---

48. There was a real chance that the Bush administration would lift the tariffs at the halfway point, particularly if the WTO panel ruled against the section 201 action and the European Union began retaliations.

49. Two companies, National Steel and Calumet Steel, were teetering on the edge and fell over even before the 201 action was formally initiated. The other seven were Birmingham Steel, Cold Metal Products, Bayou Steel, Kentucky Electric Steel, EvTac Mining, Weirton Steel, and WCI Steel (Hufbauer and Goodrich 2003).

50. Ron Scherer and Adam Parker, "Big Steel's Surprise Comeback: A Bush Decision to Lift Tariffs on Cheap Imports Could Nonetheless Have Big Political Consequences," *The Christian Science Monitor*, December 5, 2003, 1.

51. The union struck new labor agreements with the International Steel Group and U.S. Steel, for example, to aid the companies in acquiring bankrupt steel company assets and salvage jobs that might otherwise be lost.

Postconsolidation, the three newly expanded companies were expected to be more productive and better able to compete against large foreign producers in Europe and Asia. Indeed, by late 2003, the US steel industry seemed to be on its best footing in years.

Supporters of section 201 attributed much of the domestic steel industry's gains to the breathing room provided by the safeguard action, insisting that without the stability, increased investor confidence, and subsequent access to capital markets made possible by the tariffs, US companies would not have been able to make such progress in eliminating old facilities, consolidating, and reinvesting. But free trade advocates argued that there was no direct causal relationship between the 201 action and the industry's restructuring. Consolidation, they insisted, happened only in the face of bankruptcy, and the tariffs, if anything, had slowed that process by contributing to higher steel prices that might have helped some weak companies to stay afloat.

The WTO Rules

As the US steel industry underwent a recovery, the case against the section 201 action was working its way through the protracted WTO dispute settlement process. In May 2003, as many observers had predicted, the WTO dispute panel ruled that the safeguards imposed by the United States in all 10 steel categories were illegal. According to the almost 1,000-page report, the ITC in reaching its conclusions had failed to meet four main conditions required under WTO rules. For the top import category of flat-rolled steel and four other kinds, for example, the report claimed that the United States had not shown import increases since 1998; in fact, it found that there had been a general downward trend. Also inadequately documented by the ITC, according to the panel, was the claim that increased imports were the result of unforeseen developments. In every category but one, the WTO concluded that import surges were not the primary cause of the industry's malaise. Finally, the panel ruled that in reaching its injury findings, the ITC should not have included imports from countries—such as the NAFTA partners—whose products ultimately were excluded from the safeguards.

In August the United States appealed the ruling, attacking both the WTO's findings and, in some cases, the procedures the panel had used to reach them. A decision on the appeal was expected in October. Meanwhile, in September the ITC issued a midterm assessment—a requirement of the 201 process—on the impact of the measure on steelmakers. To the dismay of the steel industry, the ITC simultaneously issued a report examining how the safeguard action had affected steel users, as requested by House Ways and Means Committee Chairman Bill Thomas (R-CA).

These two assessments agreed on the difficulty of weighing the tariffs' exact impact on either steel users or producers independent of other economic factors. However, both supporters and opponents of the 201 action welcomed the reports' conclusions as validating their positions. Although steelmakers complained, USTR Zoellick indicated that the president would consider both reports in determining whether to continue the 201 case for its full three-year term or to conclude it early. Pressure was building to make such a decision soon. Although the European Union had held off on retaliation, in large part because many EU exports were covered by exclusions, it had made it clear that if the US appeal before the WTO failed and the tariffs remained in place, the European Union would retaliate in December with $2.2 billion in tariffs on US goods.[52]

In November, the WTO Appellate Body finally issued its ruling, upholding almost all of the major findings of the initial panel ruling. It was not immediately clear how President Bush would react. Though the administration was bombarded by appeals from members of Congress, foreign trade officials, steel users, steelmakers, and steel union representatives, it stayed largely silent on its plans. But on December 4, as the European Union prepared to start its retaliation, Bush announced he was terminating the 201 action at its midpoint, ending some 20 months of steel import tariffs. According to Bush's written statement, the tariffs had "now achieved their purpose, and as a result of changed economic circumstances it is time to lift them."[53]

Most observers concluded that the adverse WTO Appellate Body ruling and the prospect of punishing EU tariffs on US exports killed administration enthusiasm for the tariffs. But USTR Zoellick claimed that the decision was based instead on changed global economic circumstances, including higher steel prices in the United States brought about in part by increased demand in Russia and China, as well as by a drop in imports. In addition, Zoellick said, the September ITC report indicated that continuing the 201 action would begin to harm steel-using companies in the United States. In any event, with the tariffs lifted, the European Union and others dropped their retaliation plans.

The section 201 case remained controversial to the end. "The American steel industry and its workers were depending on President Bush for the chance to complete its restructuring and consolidation," declared Repre-

---

52. Particularly targeted on the tariff list were products from politically important states, such as textiles from the Carolinas and Florida orange juice. Although the United States claimed there could be no retaliation until an arbitration panel ruled on the timing and amount of the retaliation, the European Union claimed it could act immediately if and when the WTO ruled that the safeguards were illegal.

53. Bush's statement on steel, quoted in "U.S. Promises Self-Initiation of Trade Cases After Steel Tariff Repeal," *Inside US Trade*, December 5, 2003.

sentative Peter Visclosky, one of the most influential members of the Congressional Steel Caucus. "Unfortunately, his December 4 decision will not allow that to happen and further clouds the future of the domestic steel producing industry." But an editorial in the *Independent* of London, which credited the EU retaliation threat and criticism from US steel-using industries with having forced Bush's hand, sounded a very different note: "Mr. Bush's retrograde measure will surely be looked back on as a 20-month aberration in the long story of progress towards global free trade."[54]

---

54. "The Steel Victory Must Open Up Fair Trade As Well As Free Trade," *The Independent*, December 6, 2003.

Case Analysis

This case deals with the most basic issue in trade policy: When, if ever, should domestic industries that experience difficulties be granted protection from import competition? The answer involves economic, political, and legal considerations.

Free Trade Versus Protection

Economic theory tells us that in an economy with full employment, the nation as a whole gains by buying cheaper imports regardless of whether the low prices reflect foreign productivity or foreign subsidies. The key notion is that price signals will lead countries to specialize in the activities that bring them the highest rewards. While it may be true that domestic firms that compete with imports lose, under competitive conditions the gains to domestic consumers will outweigh those losses.

We know, however, that in the short run, there may be adjustment costs as workers lose their jobs and they, together with other resources, need to shift to alternative employment. In addition, price signals may fail to accurately capture social costs, and "market failures" may follow. For example, domestic steel production could be required to promote national defense, a consideration that a private market system will not automatically take into account. Similarly, allowing imports to enter freely could create problems if foreigners engage in predatory behavior that triggers the exit of domestic firms, thereby setting the stage for the importers to exercise monopoly power in the future. But even when these problems arise, it does not necessarily follow that trade protection is the best approach. In this instance, we could permit free trade and directly help affected workers to engage in retraining, subsidize the mills we really need for national defense, and use antitrust policies rather than protection to deal with emergent monopolies.

Although reliance on adjustment would result in superior long-term economic outcomes, domestic political realities make calls for protection difficult to resist. Political decision makers are forced to grapple with "two-level" game dynamics in dealing with trade issues—they have to simultaneously seek to advance national interests in external negotiations while balancing the competing demands of domestic winners and losers. The winners from cheaper steel imports, for example, will be consumers and those who manufacture goods that use steel as an input; the losers could be owners of steel mills, workers with steelmaking skills, and regions with steelmaking facilities.

The protection decision becomes even more charged when there are perceptions that competition is unfair, either because of the pricing behavior of foreign firms or because of subsidies and other forms of assistance given by foreign governments. Though the nation as a whole may well gain from such behavior, the perception that domestic firms are unfairly treated by foreign subsidies may make it very difficult for domestic policymakers to resist responding in kind. An international agreement or at least some defense against subsidized imports may be needed to protect a government from being compelled to undertake equally undesirable policies in order to avoid severe electoral setbacks.

Thus, offering an industry short-term protection from foreign competition can serve as a safety valve that releases domestic political pressure. The design of the dispute settlement system of the WTO makes recourse to it an attractive option, because the parties bringing suits cannot recover damages for losses incurred while the case is being processed. Powerful players in the trading system, in this case the United States, can therefore take actions to placate powerful domestic political constituencies—knowing full well that their actions will eventually be found to be noncompliant with WTO rules—at relatively little cost. In this way, the actions of the Bush administration in this case exemplify one form of "rational breach."

At its most basic level, then, the questions in this case are, why might an industry be given temporary protection? And what are the implications for the design and operation of the WTO dispute settlement system? Because of its economic and political importance, steel provides an excellent lens through which to explore the interplay of economic, political, and legal issues in the context of the two-level game.

Steel is produced in large plants, and the industry wields considerable political clout. The United Steelworkers of America is a powerful and effective union, and steel operations are an important part of the economy in many congressional districts. Steel is seen by many as being a key industry strategically, both for national defense and for the economy more generally. The industry is also a source of high-paying jobs, particularly for workers with relatively low levels of education. Proponents of steel protection frequently stress these attributes. On the other hand, opponents of protection point to the importance of steel inputs in the production of other goods and the employment that such manufacturing provides. They voice concerns that while protection may save steel jobs, it could lead to layoffs elsewhere.

The debate over steel protection is also affected by the behavior of foreign governments, many of which—for some of these same reasons—have protected, subsidized, and nationalized their steel production. American steel companies often call for a level playing field and have become skilled in the use of countervailing duties rules to provide themselves with relief. As participants in a highly capital-intensive sector, steel firms often find themselves selling below cost during cyclical downturns, and they are thus very vulnerable to the laws that regard selling below cost as dumping.

Rules

The WTO rules aim at achieving freer trade, and they require countries to bind their tariffs at agreed-on rates. But these rules do allow for protectionist responses in the face of trade that is deemed either unfair or highly disruptive.[55] Unfair trade is dealt with through provisions that allow the imposition of countervailing duties in response to foreign subsidies that "cause or threaten to cause" injury and the imposition of antidumping duties if imports cause injury as a result of being sold at "less than normal value." In addition, even without evidence of unfair trade, safeguard actions that involve temporary protection may be undertaken if imports cause injury.

In both the WTO agreements and in US law, imports that are being unfairly traded are treated more severely than those that occasion a safeguard response. While the standard for imposing antidumping or countervailing duties is "material injury," the standard for taking safeguard actions—"substantial injury"—is harder to meet. In addition, under US law, offsetting remedies must be implemented if dumping or subsidies are found; the president has no discretion. However, even if evidence of substantial injury is found by the ITC, safeguards can be implemented only if the president agrees; thus the president may choose not to act if that course is deemed to be in the national interest. It should also be noted that while safeguards must be applied irrespective of source—that is, on all imports—antidumping and countervailing duties are applied selectively, affecting only those products being unfairly traded.

A key idea in the WTO is reciprocity, and the balance of concessions between members may be disturbed when a safeguard is implemented. Accordingly, the rules state that if a country implements safeguard measures and does not offer affected countries compensatory relief, affected WTO members can suspend concessions that are substantially equivalent.

Under the original GATT agreement, this retaliation could be speedily implemented. However, Article 8 of the Safeguards Code, negotiated in the Uruguay Round, states that the right of suspension "shall not be exercised for the first three years that a safeguard measure is in effect, provided that the safeguard measure has been taken as a result of an absolute increase in imports and that such a measure conforms to the provisions of this agreement." Therefore, assuming they were legal, any US safeguard actions to protect steel could likely affect US and world markets for at least three years without any retaliation being allowed.

---

55. Responses to unfair trade are covered in GATT Article VI (Anti-dumping and Countervailing Duties) and the Agreement on Subsidies and Countervailing Measures (SCM); responses to injurious imports are covered in GATT Article XIX (Emergency Action on Imports of Particular Products) and the Agreement on Safeguards.

In this case, we see how these rules were used to provide the industry with some measure of protection; but we also see that selective application to just a few production sources may simply induce more supplies from others and not provide much relief. At the end of the day, therefore, the industry will likely seek comprehensive safeguard relief.

The case also brings out a number of interesting features of the US and WTO systems for providing trade protection. The safeguards implemented by President George W. Bush followed US law. The bipartisan ITC unanimously acceded to the president's request to find injury, and the president followed its recommendation for protection. Nevertheless, the European Union was able to challenge this action at the WTO, since the ITC had not reached its conclusions in accordance with WTO rules. First, imports in some of the steel categories given protection had not actually increased in absolute volume, as is required to avoid retaliation for three years; second, the ITC failed to make the case that the import surge reflected "unforeseen developments," another requirement in the GATT rule; and third, the ITC had excluded imports from certain countries (such as Mexico, Canada, and some developing countries) from protection even though it had used them in considering the source of injury. In response to these findings, with its appeal lost and threatened by retaliation, the United States removed the protection. Clearly, the US ITC had problems drafting a finding that would stand up to a WTO challenge.

Key Questions

What should we learn from this case? Is protection ever justified? Should the trade rules permit safeguard protection? Are the rules as currently implemented in the United States and at the WTO effective and appropriate?

The domestic political behavior in the case is unexpected. Bill Clinton, the Democrat with strong labor support, reject steelworkers' requests for help. George Bush, the Republican, was more responsive. What do their actions tell us about politics, principles, and the driving force behind trade policy?

The case also provides insights into the WTO. On the one hand, the United States resorted to protection and got away with its illegal action for several years; on the other hand, the United States was successfully challenged and induced to change its policies when they were found in violation of the rules. Does this outcome show that the international rule of law operates effectively through the WTO dispute settlement system, or does it show that the rules are too weak? There is much here to ponder and discuss.

5

Brazil's WTO Cotton Case: Negotiation Through Litigation

What we want is progress. . . . I am not worried about American interests. I am concerned with international trade interests, with Brazilian farmers, with African farmers, with developing-country farmers. I have support inside the government, in US newspapers, in talking with Americans. . . . For me, I win both ways. I win if I win, and if I lose, I still win because I'm helping to change. I add another brick. There's a lot of support for the [cotton] case. It's complete distortion.

— Pedro de Camargo Neto,
former Brazilian deputy minister of agriculture

The Change Maker

Pedro de Camargo Neto was excited. Years of persistent efforts to advance the interests of Brazilian farmers seemed to be coming to fruition. On June 18, 2004, a World Trade Organization (WTO) dispute panel sided in Brazil's favor on most of its claims against US cotton subsidies (for the findings, see appendix 5A). The West African nations of Benin and Chad, both heavily dependent on cotton for export revenue, joined Brazil's case as third-party signatories and also stood to benefit from the ruling. Two months later, in a case brought by Brazil, Thailand, and Australia, a second panel issued a preliminary ruling declaring EU sugar export subsidies illegal (for a timeline, see appendix 5B).

Brazil's WTO Cotton Case: Negotiation Through Litigation is an edited and revised version of the Harvard Business School case with the same name written by J. Katherine Milligan for Harvard Business School Professor Emeritus Ray Goldberg and John F. Kennedy School of Government Professor Robert Z. Lawrence. For copies or permission to reproduce the unabridged case please refer to www.harvard businessonline.hbsp.harvard.edu or send a written request to Harvard Business School Publishing, 60 Harvard Way, Boston, MA 02163.

Camargo could not help feeling a sense of accomplishment. As the deputy minister of agriculture in Brazil from 2000 to 2002, he had persuaded Brazilian government officials to launch the two dispute cases and even flew to the WTO headquarters in Geneva in September 2002 to file them himself. By leading the charge against the United States and European Union on cotton and sugar, Camargo positioned Brazil as an undisputed leader at the WTO and earned the respect and support of his peers in all corners of the globe.

Now he was once again returning home to Brazil from Geneva, where trade negotiators had worked day and night against their July 31, 2004, deadline to come up with a framework text for moving agriculture negotiations forward at the WTO. After the acrimonious collapse of the September 2003 world trade talks in Cancún, Mexico, some speculated that yet another failure could deal a fatal blow to the Doha Round of negotiations. But newspapers around the world praised the ambitious July agriculture framework: "Minor Miracle in Geneva" ran the headline of one *Financial Times* editorial (August 2, 2004).

News reports widely credited the challenges brought by Brazil with breathing new life into the WTO negotiations. Faced with the prospect of having to overhaul their farm programs even without a new trade agreement, the United States agreed to reductions in domestic support and the European Union offered to phase out export subsidies—concessions that were not seriously debated in Cancún. Camargo's reaction to the July framework was more subdued, however. Though he felt that the elimination of export subsidies was a real victory, he worried that trade negotiators were able to reach a compromise only because they had postponed the hard decisions for a later date.[1]

As he flew back to Brazil, Camargo reflected on this historic moment for the WTO. The cotton dispute represented the first time that a developing country had successfully challenged a developed country's agricultural subsidies. While he was impatient for reform, he recognized that nearly every country faced domestic constraints. Around the world, agriculture enjoyed significant historical and economic power, endowing farm lobbies with tremendous political influence. And, as Camargo knew from his years of experience in Brazil, the farm vote was frequently critical to providing stability. Governments were rightly concerned with food security, with providing a safety net for their agricultural producers, and

---

1. The agriculture negotiations focused on the "three pillars" of agricultural trade: market access, export subsidies, and domestic support. Countries were still far apart on market access, which the United States had designated as a top priority for reaching an agreement. The European Union, India, Japan, and South Korea in particular were reluctant to agree to tariff reductions. And some trade negotiators asserted that it remained unclear from the July framework whether the United States would actually be forced to reduce the amount of subsidies paid to domestic producers.

with managing the environment and their natural resources. He was keenly aware that for all these reasons, the road toward liberalizing world agricultural trade was loaded with political land mines.

Camargo hoped the preliminary success of the two WTO dispute cases would help break down long-standing artificial trade barriers in agricultural goods, but he was realistic about the obstacles that remained. Both the United States and the European Union had promised to appeal the panels' decisions. In addition, even though both had agreed to reforms in principle, the language in the July framework text was still quite vague. Camargo strongly believed that the United States and the European Union were not living up to past agreements and, like many of his colleagues from developing countries, he was highly suspicious that developed countries once again would attempt to avoid real reforms by creating loopholes for themselves in the current agreement.

But appeal or not, Brazil had secured two major legal victories. Would the cotton and sugar rulings give developing countries the leverage they needed to secure substantial reforms in world agricultural trade? Was this the time and opportunity, Camargo asked himself, to make a break with the past and create something positive for the future?

Pedro de Camargo Neto's Background

Camargo could not have predicted his own role in this historic turn of events. Though he was born in 1949 into a family of cattle ranchers and sugar farmers, he chose a different route from an early age. After earning a master's degree at MIT, he pursued a Ph.D. in engineering from the University of São Paulo. He had worked as an engineer for nearly two decades when, in 1990, he decided to switch careers. He ran for president of the Brazilian Rural Society (BRS), the country's oldest and most prestigious agricultural lobby group, whose membership consisted of farmers and ranchers from São Paulo state and neighboring states—and he won.

The beginning of Camargo's tenure as president of BRS coincided with the opening of the Brazilian economy. Within a very short period, the Brazilian government lowered tariffs and eliminated import controls and price interventions. Imports grew, and Camargo lobbied the Brazilian government to levy countervailing duties on subsidized imported products, such as US wheat and cotton and EU beef and dairy products. "This whole issue of trade caught my attention," he says. "We could see that it was very unequal terms, so we started advocating for stronger positions in trade negotiations."[2] At the time, the Uruguay Round of trade negotiations was

2. Unless otherwise noted, all quotes from Pedro de Camargo Neto are from a 2004 interview with the author.

under way at the General Agreement on Tariffs and Trade (GATT), the precursor to the WTO. Camargo attended many of the meetings, lobbying Brazilian trade negotiators to take a more aggressive stance. "When we went to Singapore in 1997," he says, "we pressed the minister to negotiate. We wanted more!"

The Uruguay Round Agreement on Agriculture (URAA) was the first multilateral agreement that applied international trade rules to the agricultural sector (see appendix 5C). The agreement required WTO members to implement a series of reforms over a 10-year period, beginning in 1995, and set 2000 as the deadline for launching a second round of negotiations to continue the policy reforms. The goal of the URAA was to move the agricultural sector toward more market-oriented policies. It called for tariff reductions and it put spending caps on the types of domestic support policies that distorted market signals.

For example, the amount of trade-distorting subsidies countries could give their agricultural producers, referred to as "amber box" support—more formally, the aggregate measure of support, or AMS—was capped and, over time, reduced.[3] Trade-distorting subsidies included payments coupled to prices, production levels, or to a specific commodity, because they stimulated overproduction and crowded out imports or led to low-priced exports. Because decoupled subsidies, such as direct payments, were not tied to prices or to production levels, their effects were much less distorting, and these "green box" payments were not subject to spending caps under the URAA.

Many viewed the agreement as a victory and hailed the new disciplines imposed on agricultural producers, but Camargo believed that the URAA did far too little to reduce the distortions in the world agricultural system that worked to the disadvantage of developing nations. "The Uruguay Round was such a frustration for developing countries," he says. "But I had this perception that it meant, from now on, no back steps. From now on, the next round will give me progress." He was particularly disappointed that Brazil had not assumed more of a leadership role in the negotiations. "It's our obligation to face the United States and Europe, because we have the size to do it," he declares. "We are the commercial leaders. We have to be the political leaders as well."

So when the Brazilian minister of agriculture asked Camargo to become his deputy minister in 2000, the year that new agricultural negotiations were launched, Camargo sensed an opportunity. On his first day on the job, he persuaded the minister to let him coordinate trade policy for the whole ministry. While his colleagues in the Foreign Relations Ministry continued to negotiate multilateral and regional trade agreements, he ulti-

---

3. Under the Uruguay Round agreement, the annual amount that the United States could spend on its AMS commitment was $19.1 billion.

mately prevailed in his insistence on a different strategy: litigation. "I had this idea to do dispute cases," he explains.

> I learned from the countervailing duty cases I had lobbied for as president of BRS that with the limited resources we have, cases are how you can provoke changes. . . . Cases are a communication tool. They are the best strategy to communicate what the US farm bill does to international trade. They are an important instrument to make [the United States and the European Union] sit down at the table and really negotiate seriously. . . . They are also a way to construct the Agriculture Ministry's relationship with the Foreign Relations Ministry, because our relationship with them is difficult.

On his second day as deputy minister, Camargo called together the agricultural economists at the ministry who specialized in WTO commitments. He told them to start researching commodity markets of interest to Brazil, such as soy, sugar, and cotton,[4] and to "find out where the Americans are going wrong." Camargo was determined to bring a case against US soybean producers, an endeavor he had already spent several months working on before he left BRS to join the government. He commissioned a study on US soybean programs, which "came back with what started this whole cotton case, because it came back with the peace clause," he said.

Article 13 of the URAA, commonly known as the "peace clause," effectively prohibits WTO members from challenging other members' agricultural subsidies under the Dispute Settlement Understanding (DSU), which provides the WTO's legal framework for resolving trade disagreements. The peace clause, which was included in the URAA at the insistence of the United States and the European Union, protects countries from action as long as their aggregate subsidy levels remain under their AMS commitments. If, however, countries exceed their allowable levels, they are no longer afforded protection from dispute cases under the peace clause.

Article 13 also stipulates that no specific commodity can be subsidized at a rate higher than that in force in 1992; otherwise, the peace clause does not apply. In this often-overlooked proviso, Camargo found where the Americans went wrong: "The US was not subsidizing soybeans during the Uruguay Round, and [in 2000] they were spending $2 billion. So we had a case."

But victory would not come easily. Brazil had to mount a compelling legal case to convince a WTO dispute panel that the United States had violated its commitments under the Uruguay Round agreement.

---

4. Cotton was grown on 2 million acres in Brazil, a small area in comparison to the 18 million acres devoted to soybeans. But cotton and soy are good crops to rotate with each other, and Brazil intended to expand cotton production as a strategy to enhance the efficiency and competitiveness of its growing textile industry.

Brazil Mounts a Case

From Soy to Cotton

In late 2001, Pedro de Camargo Neto hired the Chicago-based law firm Sidley Austin Brown & Woods to represent Brazil; the lead attorney was Scott Andersen, in the Geneva office. In early 2002, Andersen contacted Dan Sumner, an agricultural economist and professor at the University of California, Davis, and asked him to serve as an expert witness for Brazil. As an academic specializing in United States Department of Agriculture (USDA) support programs and econometric models, Sumner was often called on to offer expert testimony before the US International Trade Commission, a quasi-judicial federal agency that provides trade expertise to Congress and the executive branch. "We were talking about soybeans initially," Dan Sumner recalls. "They wanted to talk to someone who was very familiar with US farm programs and their operation."[5]

Sumner provided Brazil's legal team with an analysis of US farm legislation. The United States had been moving toward more market-oriented agricultural support policies for over a decade, but in 1997–98, the East Asian financial crisis knocked the bottom out of global commodity markets. The unexpected price declines put stress on agricultural producers in every country, forcing many governments to enact emergency relief programs. As the United States was reeling from depressed world demand and a severe drought in several states, Congress passed supplemental legislation that authorized additional emergency payments to farmers of $30 billion over a four-year period.

Critics charged the United States with reverting back to its old system of price supports. As a key element in what was called the "marketing loss assistance program," the emergency payments acted like a price floor, because they automatically kicked in when the world price fell below a designated target price. Renamed "countercyclical payments," the subsidies became permanent in the 2002 farm bill (for a summary of US farm policy, see appendix 5D).

The new legislation frustrated negotiators and agricultural producers abroad, and it undermined the United States' professed commitment to serious reforms in the Doha Round. "The 2002 farm bill completely undercut the credibility of the United States in WTO agricultural negotiations," says Dr. Bob Thompson, a former USDA economist under the Reagan administration and the current president of the International Food and Agricultural Trade Policy Council. "We just looked two-faced: 'do as I say, not as I do.'"[6] Joe Glauber, deputy chief economist at the USDA and

---

5. Dan Sumner, interview with the author, 2004.

6. Unless otherwise noted, all quotes from Bob Thompson are from a 2004 interview with the author.

head economist in the cotton DSU case, agrees that that was a common perception: "Brazil was the one that ultimately brought the challenge, but the criticism was coming from a lot of places."[7]

The large emergency payments and marketing loan payments caused the payments in US soybean programs to vastly exceed their negligible 1992 levels; but as Camargo and his team assembled their case, domestic politics took over and market conditions changed. Officials in the Foreign Relations Ministry requested additional soybean studies, which dragged on for months. "The Foreign Relations Ministry wouldn't approve," says Camargo. "They fought me. I think they were afraid we would lose." At the same time, soybean prices started to rise, making US soybean farmers ineligible for large payments. The soybean case disappeared.

Then an economist in Brazil's Ministry of Agriculture alerted Camargo to what was happening in the world cotton market. By most accounts, cotton is one of the most distorted commodities in the world, stemming from high levels of government subsidies (on the world cotton market, see appendix 5E). Between the 1998–99 and 2001–02 marketing years, global direct assistance to cotton producers ranged from $3.8 billion to $5.8 billion, divided among eight countries: the United States, China, Greece, Spain, Turkey, Brazil, Mexico, and Egypt.[8]

During that period, cotton prices were in precipitous decline. Between December 2000 and May 2002, the world price of cotton fell by 40 percent, shrinking the value of the global cotton market from $35 billion to $20 billion in just 18 months. The price of cotton bottomed out at 29 cents a pound, from an all-time high of 74 cents a pound in 1995. Adjusted for inflation, these were the lowest cotton prices since the Great Depression.

The reasons for this dramatic price decline were complex, but nearly everyone pointed a finger at the United States. The United States was the second-largest producer of cotton behind China, was by far the largest exporter, and spent vastly more on cotton subsidies than did any other country. The global low prices triggered US price-based support programs, causing the subsidies in US cotton programs to balloon (see table 5E.1 in appendix 5E) All told, US cotton producers received payments ranging from $1.9 billion to $3.9 billion during the 1998–2002 marketing years, far exceeding the 1992 level of $1.4 billion. "Nearly $4 billion of

---

7. Unless otherwise noted, all quotes from Joe Glauber are from a 2004 interview with the author.

8. According to the International Cotton Advisory Committee, US cotton producers received a record $3 billion in subsidies in 2001–02, accounting for more than 52 percent of global government assistance. That figure is somewhat misleading, however, because it did not include an additional $900 million US cotton producers received in direct payments and crop insurance. Also in 2001–02, China provided its cotton farmers with $1.2 billion (21 percent of the world total), the European Union paid producers in Greece and Spain a total of $980 million (17 percent), and India gave its producers $500 million (9 percent).

subsidies by one country is a lot of money in an industry where the world value of cotton at the time was $20 billion," says John Baffes, a senior economist at the World Bank. "There's no way one can claim that does not have an effect on the world market."[9]

Camargo immediately saw the possibilities. Since many of the subsidy programs used to support US cotton growers applied to other commodities as well, a victory in this case could mean the United States either would have to overhaul its domestic farm programs or would face sanctions at the WTO. "Cotton was not a routine dispute," he declares. "[It was] there for broader reasons and fought with that idea." Bob Thompson concurs that the case served to clarify the commitments made by developed countries in the Uruguay Round. "The Brazilians are absolutely right," he says. "The United States and the European Union have not been playing fair under what they agreed to in the last round. The two [dispute rulings] are going to be very strong messages about the true effects of US and EU policies."

Camargo also hoped that a legal ruling would give additional momentum to the efforts of reformers within the United States and the WTO who were seeking greater reductions in subsidies in the Doha Round of trade negotiations. "I wanted the dispute to influence the round," he declares. "It is a broad case that ... has very good, positive implications—more transparency and more clarification on what we're signing, what we've already signed, and what we will sign."

A Lucky Break

In July 2002, Brazil's cotton challenge benefited from a stroke of luck. Economists at the World Bank and the International Cotton Advisory Committee (ICAC), an international commodity organization with a membership of 42 governments, were concerned about the steep decline in cotton prices and felt that distortions in the market were not widely understood. Thus John Baffes of the World Bank and his colleagues at ICAC hosted a joint conference that July.

Pedro de Camargo was in attendance. Other participants included representatives of the US National Cotton Council, the ambassadors of Brazil and of several African countries, Oxfam's head economist, and academics. "In one room we had all the guys, and they all told their stories," says Baffes. Turkey, Brazil, Mexico, Egypt, and India had to give offsetting support totaling $600 million to keep their cotton sectors afloat. The highly indebted West African governments of Benin and Mali also were forced to divert public funds from elsewhere and give producers $40 million to prevent their domestic industries from collapsing (ICAC 2002, 2). "All the

---

9. Unless otherwise noted, all quotes from John Baffes are from a 2004 interview with the author.

West Africans were talking about cotton," says Camargo. "And I thought, 'This can't happen.' Of course it made our case much stronger."

Also at the conference, ICAC economists presented the findings of their "world textile model," an econometric simulation that found US subsidies had caused significant price suppression. In the absence of US subsidies, they claimed, US production would have declined by 900,000 tons in 1999–2000, 700,000 tons in 2000–01, and 1.4 million tons in 2001–02, raising the world cotton price for those years by 6 cents, 12 cents, and 22 cents, respectively (ICAC 2002, 8). Shortly after the ICAC conference, Scott Andersen called Dan Sumner and asked him to create a modeling framework for cotton.

Brazil's Claims Against the United States

Over the next few months, Brazil's cotton case quickly took shape. Though the arguments were highly complex and technical, they can essentially be divided into two categories: legal and economic. In legal terms, Brazil claimed that during the marketing years 1999–2002, US cotton subsidies exceeded their 1992 levels, a violation of Article 13 of the Agreement on Agriculture (the peace clause). Brazil also argued that two additional support programs, the export credit guarantee program and Step 2 payments, constituted export subsidies and as such were prohibited under the URAA.[10]

On the economic side, Brazil argued that the United States' cotton subsidies caused "serious prejudice" (i.e., substantial financial harm) to Brazilian cotton producers, a violation of the Agreement on Subsidies and Countervailing Measures (Baffes 2004a). Its basis for claiming serious prejudice to its interests was twofold. First, Brazil claimed that US cotton subsidies suppressed world cotton prices. Using hundreds of pages of USDA data and building on an econometric model developed by the Food and Agricultural Policy Research Institute (FAPRI), the econometric analysis of Dan Sumner was commissioned to bolster this argument.[11] If US cotton subsidies had been eliminated, the model predicted, US cotton production

---

10. Under the Step 2 program, the US government gives money to US companies that mill cotton into thread and cloth for export to help them buy US-grown cotton. Under the export credit guarantee program, the US government guarantees loans to foreign buyers of US cotton at below-market interest rates.

11. Ultimately, Sumner's econometric model was thrown out of the case, because FAPRI refused to divulge the parameters of its model and the USDA could not replicate the results using the same datasets. (FAPRI's refusal to cooperate irked many US officials, since the institute itself is government funded—FAPRI, jointly run by Iowa State University and the University of Missouri at Columbia, was established by Congress in 1984.) However, many people who participated in the hearings commented that Sumner's expert testimony on how US cotton support programs are administered had more influence on the panel than did his econometric model.

Figure 5.1   US area devoted to cotton production, 1990–2003

thousands of acres   price in dollars ($.01 per lb.)

Source: Paul Drazek, DTB Associates, LLP, 2004.

and cotton exports would have declined by 29 and 39 percent, respectively, causing world prices to increase by 6.5 cents per pound (12 percent of the world price). Extrapolating from that data, Brazil claimed that depressed cotton prices cost its producers $478 million in lost revenues from 1999 to 2002 (Camargo Neto 2004).

Brazil's second argument revolved around the United States' rising share of world exports. Brazil claimed that US cotton subsidies enabled US producers to capture world market share, which caused a corresponding loss in market share for Brazilian producers. While most of the world responded to declining world cotton prices by scaling back production, US cotton producers actually boosted their acreage (figure 5.1), which was increasingly planted for export. Within a span of five years, from 1998 to 2002, as US exports increased from one-third to two-third of US cotton production, its share in the world export market jumped from 24 to 48 percent. The decline of the US domestic textile industry was one of the main drivers behind the expansion of US cotton exports, as more and more mills moved overseas. Nevertheless, Brazil argued, if the United States was justified in claiming that its cotton support programs did not shelter American producers from market signals, then why in a time of declining prices were US producers planting more cotton, not less?

A Final Hurdle

Brazil's Chamber of Foreign Trade, or CAMEX (Câmara de Comércio Exterior), consisted of four of Brazil's most powerful ministers (of finance, industry and trade, agriculture, and foreign relations) and the president's chief of staff. Throughout 2002, Camargo had been briefing CAMEX about the progress he was making in preparing the cotton and sugar disputes. But he needed the ministers' formal approval to file the cases at the WTO.

Foreign relations officials were reluctant to proceed, however. "The foreign relations minister said we needed more studies," recalls Camargo. "The [diplomats] below him were not in favor. . . . It's such a pioneering case that it's natural they would get more nervous and more careful." Officials kept urging the need to take more time, citing concerns about the political implications of filing a challenge against the United States while the Doha agricultural negotiations were ongoing. "As bureaucrats, their timetables are different," Camargo observes. "I knew I was leaving government December 31, so for me it was now or never."

Camargo also wanted to see if the West Africans would join Brazil's case as co-complainants, but he could not approach them directly. As a representative of the Agriculture Ministry, he remarks, "I could not contact the African countries. That's Foreign Relations." And Foreign Relations was vehemently opposed to getting the Africans involved. "I think [they] felt that the Americans would get really irritated if Brazil started pitting Africa against the United States," he adds. Instead, he struck up a friendship with the Beninese diplomat at the WTO, Samuel Amehou, with whom he frequently crossed paths at agricultural committee meetings in Geneva, and sent him some documentation on the cotton case. While in Geneva, Camargo also met with Celine Charveriat, head of advocacy for Oxfam, to talk about trends in the world cotton market and their implications for West African smallholders. He previously had worked with Charveriat on Oxfam's fair trade campaign and was impressed with the organization's work. "I could not reach the Africans by myself, so I went through Oxfam," he says.

After three more months of internal meetings with CAMEX, Camargo once again went before the ministers: On September 19, 2002, he requested their approval to launch the cotton and sugar disputes. Most were still apprehensive, but the finance minister, Pedro Malan, urged them not to put off for the next administration what they could do themselves. "That was a crucial moment," recalls Camargo. Malan "saved it."

Camargo flew to Geneva and filed the sugar and cotton disputes at the WTO on September 27, 2002.

The West African Cotton Sectoral Initiative

Though Brazil has an economic interest in cotton, the crop is far more important to several poor countries in West Africa, where its cultivation is widely considered a success story. Initiated by the French state-owned Compagnie Française pour le Développement des Fibres Textiles (CFDT, renamed Dagris in 2001), when the countries were still colonies, production in the region grew tenfold from less than 100,000 tons in the 1960s to nearly 1 million tons by the late 1990s.[12] By 2000, the sector employed nearly 10 million people throughout Francophone Africa. The region accounted for 5 percent of world cotton production and, with 15 percent of global exports, was the third-largest exporter (after the United States and Uzbekistan). In the 1998–99 marketing year, cotton accounted for 7.1 percent, 5.1 percent, 6.7 percent, and 4.7 percent of the respective GDPs of Benin, Burkina Faso, Mali, and Chad, and between 25 percent and 50 percent of their export earnings (Sahel and West Africa Club Secretariat/OECD 2005).

Though the Francophone cotton sector was considered a success, it displayed considerable market inefficiencies. First, the national cotton companies had legal monopolies on all ginning and marketing activities, as well as on providing farmers with such inputs as seeds and pesticides. This lack of competition encouraged operating inefficiencies and rent-seeking behavior. Indeed, the high cotton prices of the mid-1990s made the national cotton companies so profitable that, according to a World Bank report, the Malian national cotton company "became a prime target for rent seekers and costs became heavily padded. When world prices started falling in 1998–99, [Mali's national cotton company] became virtually bankrupt" (Goreux and Macrae 2003, 10).

Second, farmers received only 30 to 40 percent of the world price during the 1990s, although by 2004 their percentage topped 50 percent owing to the increasing prominence of producers' organizations.[13] Third, the close

---

12. After independence, the West African countries set up their own national cotton companies, but CFDT retained about a one-third share in the companies.

13. Each spring, representatives from producers' organizations meet with government officials and representatives from ginning companies to negotiate a buying price for that year's cotton harvest. The Cotlook A index prices and ICAC price forecasts provide the starting point, and all parties bring their cost estimates to the negotiation. The national buying price is usually announced in March or April, along with input prices, so that farmers can decide if they want to plant. Because of donor pressure and the improved negotiating capacity of producers' associations, in recent years farmers have received the largest portion of the world price. The major remaining costs include transporting the cotton from the farms to the gin, ginning and packaging, overhead, and transporting the cotton from the gin to the port.

economic ties between Francophone Africa and the European Union effectively prohibited the African nations from cultivating genetically modified cotton (called Bt cotton), even though numerous studies concluded that developing countries stood to benefit the most from its adoption.[14]

Finally, attempts to replace public agents with private operators created a host of additional problems. In 1996 the World Bank pushed for reforms to enhance the competitiveness of the Francophone cotton sector, but both the French and the West Africans resisted the reforms. Recently, Benin, Côte d'Ivoire, and Burkina Faso have made progress toward liberalization, but their reforms have had extremely mixed results.[15]

The four West African countries of Benin, Burkina Faso, Mali, and Chad estimated that depressed cotton prices from 1998 to 2002 cost them a combined average of $250 million a year in lost revenues.[16] The sudden loss of export revenue triggered a balance of payments crisis for the impoverished nations and created widespread social unrest. Producers staged demonstrations on the streets of Benin's capital city, while in Mali, a produc-

---

14. EU hostility to genetically modified foodstuffs is discussed in chapter 6. Though genetically modified seed is expensive, Bt cotton requires fewer sprayings, leading to both cost savings and health benefits. Moreover, the higher yields of Bt cotton, demonstrated by many studies, would help farmers boost their profit margins. Burkina Faso therefore began testing Bt on experimental plots in 2003, and by 2005, Ghana and Nigeria were also seriously considering legalizing genetically modified seeds. In Mali and Benin, however, producer associations and nongovernmental organizations were strongly opposed to Bt cotton, citing concerns about loss of biodiversity and dependence on multinationals for seeds; Benin passed a five-year moratorium on Bt cotton in 2002.

15. In Benin, for example, some private ginners and input distributors who enjoy "political immunity" have circumvented the formal regulatory mechanisms, creating havoc in the sector. Accusations of price fixing are widespread, pesticides of dubious quality are distributed to farmers in some zones, and input costs are actually higher than before liberalization. Similarly, some private ginners in the northern areas of Benin have collected cotton from villages outside of their allocated zones, causing losses for the state-owned gins. Reforms in Burkina Faso have fared better; in 1999 the producers' association purchased a one-third share in the national cotton company, and in 2003 the state started selling off gins to private operators in the central and eastern zones. Still, some criticize Burkina Faso's reforms as merely moving from one national monopoly to three regional monopolies. Despite strong pressure from the World Bank, Mali has tabled liberalization reforms until after the 2007 presidential election.

16. This figure is somewhat controversial. In 2002 the West African ministers of agriculture commissioned an econometric study by the IMF economist Louis Goreux, who designed a partial equilibrium model to evaluate the extent of their losses due to subsidized production in the United States. Goreux estimated that US subsidies reduced the world price by 12 percent in 2001–02, which translated into $250 million in lost export earnings. (Louis Goreux, "Prejudice Caused by Industrialized Countries' Subsidies to Cotton Sectors in West Africa and Central Africa," World Bank, 2003.) As the case attracted international attention, the World Bank, the Overseas Development Institute, and the Organization for Economic Cooperation and Development also commissioned studies, which generally supported Goreux's conclusion that subsidized production did in fact reduce world prices but by varying amounts—from 2 percent to 30 percent—translating into losses of anywhere between $26 million to $350 million for West African producers.

ers' strike in 2000 slashed cotton production by one-third. The African governments clearly needed to take action. But what was the best course of action to take?

After Brazil filed the WTO case, there was still a window of opportunity for the West Africans to sign on as co-complainants, but they were reluctant to do so. WTO disputes take two to five years to resolve; what kind of relief could they expect in the meantime? What would be the political fallout of signing on to a case against the biggest member of the WTO? Most importantly, if they won the case, and the United States refused to implement the decision, what would be their recourse? Celine Charveriat, the head of advocacy for Oxfam, was heavily involved in consultations with the West Africans. She explains their dilemma: "A small country like Benin or Burkina Faso cannot really retaliate against the United States, because it would be relatively counterproductive for them to slap tariffs on US goods and it would be absolutely meaningless for the United States. So the [West Africans] thought the DSU instrument was not terribly adapted to what they wanted to achieve."[17]

Finally, after weeks of consultations with nongovernmental organizations (NGOs) such as Oxfam, only Benin and Chad decided to join Brazil's case—not as co-complainants but as third parties.[18] Third-party signatories could make presentations and submit testimony in a side venue, but they could not participate in the main panel hearings (though they were allowed to attend). Camargo was disappointed in their decision—but then again, he reasoned, other cotton-producing countries were no more willing to sign on as co-complainants. "I tried Argentina, I tried Australia, I tried South Africa," he says, but none of them "wanted to challenge the United States." He adds: "I saw all of the problems we had within Brazil to find the courage to file the case. Argentina, who was in a mess with the IMF, couldn't do it. Australia, the leader of the Cairns Group, couldn't do it because they were negotiating a free trade agreement with the United States. Why would Benin?"

An Unconventional Initiative

NGOs such as Oxfam and IDEAS Centre, a Swiss organization that helps developing countries on trade and development issues (its name stands for "international trade, development, economic governance, advisory services"), continued working with the West Africans on alternative ways

---

17. Unless otherwise noted, all quotes from Celine Charveriat are from a 2004 interview with the author.

18. Along with the Francophone nations of Benin and Chad, the third-party signatories on the Brazilian cotton case were Argentina, Australia, Canada, China, India, New Zealand, Pakistan, Paraguay, and Venezuela.

to bring forward their demands on cotton. Shortly after the African governments made the decision not to join Brazil's case, Nicolas Imboden, executive director of IDEAS Centre, traveled throughout the Francophone capitals and lobbied agricultural ministers to form a coalition. "If Brazil wins the DSU case, [the Africans] win with them," Nicolas Imboden remembers. "I told them, 'Your case is political. You need to take it directly to the negotiations.' "[19] He ultimately persuaded only four West African nations to get on board: Benin, Burkina Faso, Chad, and Mali.[20]

"There is a wider issue that the poorest members of the WTO don't know if they will get anything positive from this round," says Celine Charveriat, "so they are going with the flow, not clear about how to extract something that is actually meaningful to them." During the consultations with Oxfam and IDEAS Centre, however, it quickly became clear to the West African coalition that given the heavy dependence of their economies on cotton, the main focus of their energies should be a concession on US cotton subsidies.

They knew they would have to be creative, and so they made an unprecedented decision: they would lobby the WTO to include a separate initiative on cotton in the Cancún text. "The only way for [the West Africans] to bring an issue [to the WTO] is to do it in an unconventional way, because they are quite powerless countries with a very low profile," notes Charveriat. In fact, only two of the four nations have permanent missions at the WTO headquarters in Geneva. "Before this all happened, Benin, Burkina, and Mali—nobody even knew the names of their ambassadors," she continues. "Nobody cared about those countries at all."

The NGOs remained heavily involved with the West African efforts. Oxfam commissioned studies about the effects of low prices on West African economies and helped villagers' cooperatives to bring their stories to journalists in Europe and the United States. Oxfam also used its media contacts to facilitate press conferences and the placement of op-eds by West African officials. "We knew that 90 percent of the battle was going to be in terms of the media, and whether we could make this a moral case and win it in the public eye," says Charveriat. "From the beginning, Oxfam's strategy [was] to bring it down from something legalistic that nobody would understand to the most important story: the impact on farmers on the ground."

The *New York Times*, *Washington Post*, *Wall Street Journal*, and other newspapers picked up the story and ran articles and op-ed pieces blasting the reach of "King Cotton" and its effects on poor African farmers. Many in the media even framed the cotton case as a litmus test of whether

---

19. Unless otherwise noted, all quotes from Nicolas Imboden are from a 2004 interview with the author.

20. Senegal, Togo, and Côte d'Ivoire also produced cotton, but they decided not to join the West African coalition, possibly because cotton was of less significance to their economies.

the WTO and the international trade system could work for the poor. Meanwhile, IDEAS Centre and private donors raised funds and contributed expertise to coordinate the activities of the four Francophone countries, assist the African representatives with preparing for presentations, defray travel costs for the ministers, and create an additional post in the Benin mission at the WTO.

Four Milestones in a Landmark Case

Four major milestones marked the West Africans' campaign in the run-up to Cancún. First, on April 30, 2003, Benin, Burkina Faso, Chad, and Mali submitted a "Sectoral Initiative in Favor of Cotton" to the WTO, which demanded that developed countries phase out all domestic support and export subsidies for cotton within three years, and put in place a transitional financial mechanism to compensate cotton-exporting least-developed countries (LDCs) $250 million a year—the amount they claimed they were deprived of in lost revenues—until the subsidies were eliminated.[21]

Second, in the mini-ministerials over the summer, the West Africans secured support for their initiative from the LDC group and the African, Caribbean, and Pacific (ACP) group, critical to demonstrating the solidarity of developing countries. "It was not easy to sell our case," says one Beninese official who was present at the meetings. "For a long time, Mauritius wouldn't agree. [Mauritian sugar producers] benefit from EU subsidies, while here we are, attacking subsidies. So we had to be careful."[22]

Then, in July 2003, the president of Burkina Faso, Blaise Compaoré, became the first head of state ever to address the WTO general assembly. "That really launched the political fight to get some kind of language in the Cancún text," says Charveriat. President Compaoré spoke on behalf of the four West African countries in the coalition:

> From this platform, I am launching an appeal, in the name of several millions of women and men, who live in least developed countries and for whom cotton is the main means of subsistence. . . . I ask the WTO and its member States to prevent that these populations, who are victims of the negative impact of subsidies, be excluded from world trade. . . . The ongoing Doha Round negotiations on agriculture must imperatively address distortions in cotton trade. . . . Our countries

---

21. See "Poverty Reduction: Sectoral Initiative in Favour of Cotton," Joint Proposal by Benin, Burkina Faso, Chad, and Mali, WTO document TN/AG/GEN/416, May 16, 2003. Also see Scott Miller, "WTO Trade Talks Are Deadlocked Over Concessions—Conflict Between Rich, Poor Nations Threatens Outcome of Doha Round," *The Asian Wall Street Journal*, July 15, 2003, A1.

22. In 2000, 77 ACP countries signed the Cotonou Agreement with the European Union, which gave them preferential access to the EU market. Under the terms of the agreement, Mauritian sugar producers could sell sugar in the European Union at the internal EU price, which is kept higher than the world price to subsidize European sugarbeet producers.

are not asking for charity, neither are we requesting preferential treatment or additional aid. We solely demand that, in conformity with WTO basic principles, the free market rule be applied.[23]

President Compaoré's speech "changed everything overnight," recalls Nicolas Imboden. "Public opinion shifted and it became politically acceptable [for Europeans] to support the initiative." In short order, the Netherlands, Denmark, and Germany officially backed the West Africans' demands, IDEAS Centre received a $2 million grant from the Swiss Development Agency to coordinate the initiative, and the WTO Secretariat put cotton on the official Cancún agenda in response to tremendous pressure from WTO members. In consultation with the chairman of the General Council, the secretary scheduled the sectoral initiative for the first day of negotiations. In an extremely rare move, the WTO director-general, Supachai Panitchpakdi, chaired the session, imploring developed countries to take the West African proposal seriously.[24]

The Cancún Debacle

On September 10, 2003, thousands of trade negotiators, politicians, lawyers, representatives of NGOs, and activists descended on Cancún, Mexico. The Cancún ministerial marked the first formal negotiations since the Doha Round was launched in Doha, Qatar, shortly after the September 11, 2001, terrorist attacks. The mandate of the Doha Round—the so-called Doha Development Agenda—was to focus on the needs of developing countries, many of which, with large rural populations, viewed a good agriculture agreement as the key to achieving meaningful gains in the round.

Yet developing countries pointed to the 2002 US farm bill and the joint US-EU draft agriculture text issued just weeks before the ministerial as evidence that developed countries were not serious about reform. The US-EU draft text proposed large cuts in developing countries' agricultural tariffs, but it did not offer substantial reductions in their domestic support levels or export subsidies in return nor did it even mention the cotton issue. Indignant that they were being asked to open their markets and expose their farmers to what they commonly referred to as "competition from the US and EU treasuries," the developing countries created the G-20, a coalition led by Brazil, India, China, and South Africa. "Brazil's leadership in the dispute cases against the United States and the EU was fundamental to creating the G-20," says Camargo. The trade ministers from the 20 members of the impromptu alliance met for the first time in Cancún, one day before the start of negotiations. Over the next few days,

23. "President of Burkina Faso Denounces Rich Country Subsidies," Global Policy Forum, June 10, 2003, www.globalpolicy.org.

24. "Cotton—The 'Trips And Health' Of Cancun?" Bridges Daily Update, September 11, 2003, 1.

the G-20 proved to be a formidable force, resisting repeated attempts from the United States and European Union to splinter the coalition and pressure its members to consent to a watered-down agricultural agreement.

Outside the Cancún conference hall, protesters manipulated puppets of George W. Bush, which threw cotton. Inside, negotiations broke down. Though the Cancún talks officially collapsed in September 2003 over the contentious "Singapore issues" dealing with competition and investment policy, many who were present say the stalemate in agriculture played a more significant role. Bob Thompson recalls the breakdown in agricultural negotiations: "There's a standoff. US farm groups say they've got to have access to developing-country markets if they're going to reduce their subsidies, and the developing countries say, you've got to go first with reducing your subsidies because they artificially depress the international prices. That's the most important tension."

Some speculate that the United States' refusal to deal meaningfully with the cotton issue contributed to the acrimony of the talks. At a minimum, US negotiators underestimated the resolve of the West Africans and the widespread sympathy they enjoyed among developed and developing countries alike. The United States demanded that cotton be treated within the context of overall negotiations, not as a stand-alone issue, a position that the West Africans categorically rejected. "I think the US went through some good-faith negotiations—maybe three or four hours a day," says Joe Glauber. "That said, were we talking past one another? Yes, I think so."

Others who were present claim that the sectoral initiative was probably too unconventional to gain any real traction, since it was not part of the normal exchange of concessions that characterize WTO negotiations. The biggest stumbling block was the need to devise a compensation mechanism. "Compensation couldn't take place the way it was envisioned or designed," John Baffes points out. "If you think about it, how are you going to compensate millions of West African farmers? Is the EU Commission or the US Congress going to write them $100 or $200 checks? It's just not going to happen."

Any progress or goodwill that had been made during the first three days of negotiations evaporated when the new framework text was distributed. Not mentioning the West African cotton proposal by name, it essentially reiterated the United States' position: (1) elimination of cotton subsidies must be part of a multilateral effort, (2) broader reforms were necessary to address the distortions in the textile and synthetics sectors, and (3) multilateral donor institutions should assist the African countries with technical and development assistance.

The precise wording of that third demand was still unresolved 30 minutes before the US delegation was expected back at the conference center. "We were in our hotel going back and forth, negotiating changes in the language," said Glauber. "The phrase we worked on was innocuous. It said something like 'The multilaterals should help African countries modernize their cotton industries.'" But when the published draft was circulated on September 13, it included language he had not seen—a line instructing the WTO director-general to work with donor institutions to "effectively direct existing programs and resources *toward diversification of the economies where cotton accounts for the major share of their GDP*" (emphasis added).[25] When Glauber first saw it, "I was taken aback," he remembers. "It just seemed like a slap in the face after what had been four days of good-faith negotiations." The West Africans—and all of their supporters—were outraged at the United States' intransigence. Oxfam quickly labeled the United States' refusal to change its policies as "shockingly indifferent to poverty in Africa" (Oxfam 2004, 2).

In the wake of Cancún, progress on the cotton issue was considered a sine qua non to restarting Doha negotiations. "Everybody realized that if you want to make real progress in the Doha Round, you have to deal with this case," says Baffes. "Even the West African countries realized, since they cannot go ahead with compensation in the way they designed or thought, they've got to do something else."

To that end, the WTO and the World Bank co-hosted a conference in Benin in March 2004, to determine how the bilateral and multilateral lending institutions could best provide technical and financial assistance to the West African cotton sector. "Post-Cancún, there has been a greater realization of the importance of the cotton sector to the growth and poverty reduction efforts of these African countries," WTO Director-General Supachai said in his keynote address at the conference. "This is an African priority that deserves our support."[26]

Ripple Effects: The WTO Dispute Panel Ruling

On April 26, 2004, the WTO dispute panel issued a confidential preliminary ruling declaring the majority of US cotton programs inconsistent with

---

25. The full paragraph reads, "We recognise the importance of cotton for the development of a number of developing countries and understand the need for urgent action to address trade distortions in these markets. Accordingly, we instruct the Chairman of the Trade Negotiations Committee to consult with the Chairpersons of the Negotiating Groups on Agriculture, Non-Agricultural Market Access and Rules to address the impact of the distortions that exist in the trade of cotton, man-made fibers, textiles and clothing to ensure comprehensive consideration of the entirety of the sector. The Director-General is instructed to consult with the relevant international organizations including the Bretton Woods Institutions, the Food and Agriculture Organization and the International Trade Centre to effectively direct existing programmes and resources toward diversification of the economies where cotton accounts for the major share of their GDP" (quoted in Oxfam 2004, 7).

26. Supachai Panitchpakdi, opening remarks delivered at the WTO Africa regional workshop on cotton, March 23, 2004, www.wto.org.

the commitments the United States had agreed to during the Uruguay Round. Although only the parties involved in the dispute saw the actual report, the reaction in the press and in Congress was swift. At a press conference the following day, White House Press Secretary Scott McClellan said, "We will be defending US agricultural interests in every forum we need to, and have no intention of unilaterally taking steps to disarm."[27] United States Trade Representative (USTR) Robert Zoellick testified before the House Agriculture Committee two days later: "You can be 100 percent sure we will appeal this ruling. . . . This is a marathon, not a sprint."[28]

In sharp contrast, supporters of agricultural reform, academics, NGOs, and editorial pages around the world celebrated the decision—as did Brazilian officials. "This is a precedent; this is a war that must continue!" proclaimed Roberto Azevedo, lead counsel for Brazil and a top official in Brazil's Foreign Ministry.[29] In the words of Pedro de Camargo, "We developing countries have shown that we're prepared to do this and expose them. The panel has given us a position that's ours. It's not that we're getting it free—we paid already in the Uruguay Round. We're here to collect."

The panel issued its final ruling on June 18, 2004 (see appendix 5A); it was nearly identical to the preliminary ruling. Most significantly, the panel ruled in Brazil's favor that (1) US cotton programs were not afforded protection under the peace clause, because subsidies between 1999 and 2002 exceeded 1992 levels; (2) price-based support programs such as marketing loan payments and marketing loss assistance payments did suppress prices; (3) direct payments did not qualify as green box, because of the prohibition on fruits and vegetables; and (4) the export credit program and Step 2 program contained prohibited export subsidies.

Implications of the Panel Ruling

US Farm Programs

One of the rulings with the most far-reaching impact on US agriculture was the finding that direct payments did not qualify as green box, because of the prohibition on planting fruits and vegetables. "That is an extremely political issue, because if the appellate body confirms that, it means the whole farm bill is wrong," says Pedro de Camargo. Joe Glauber concurs: "The significance of this is substantial." If the United States had been re-

---

27. Scott McClellan, White House press secretary, "Scott McClellan Holds White House Regular News Briefing, White House Regular News Briefing," April 27, 2004.

28. Robert Zoellick, Hearing of the House Agriculture Committee, Review of Agricultural Trade Negotiations, April 28, 2004.

29. Azevedo, quoted in Elizabeth Becker, "Global Trade Body Rules Against U.S. on Cotton Subsidies," *The New York Times*, April 27, 2004, section 1, 1.

quired to classify the $6 billion in annual direct payments as amber box instead of green box, it would have been over its aggregate measurement of support (AMS) commitments for 1999, 2000, 2001, and 2002.

"This may be the first WTO-driven decision that Congress has to make about a farm program, and it won't be an easy one," says Glauber. "Congress is indignant over the idea that something we've been reporting as green . . . has now been determined by the WTO to not be green." Though many believed the prohibition on fruits and vegetables would be easy to fix, it "isn't just there by chance," he notes: "There was heavy lobbying in the 1996 farm bill by the fruit and vegetable lobby to have that in there—they didn't want producers who receive payments to quit growing those crops and follow market signals and say, 'I'm planting plum trees row to row.' . . . As far as [fruit and vegetable producers] are concerned, this [provision] is the one little thing they got out of the 2002 farm bill. So I don't think it would be easy to overturn."

A second significant aspect of the panel's ruling concerned the distinction between price-based and non-price-based forms of support. The United States had argued that its price-based programs (e.g., the marketing loan program and the countercyclical program) did not distort production, for two reasons: (1) annual outlays depended not on production levels but on what world prices were doing, because they kicked in only when world prices fell below the minimum price; and (2) the countercyclical payments were based on historical production levels, not on how many acres farmers were planting that year. Therefore, the United States claimed, the programs' effects on decisions about production were minimal. As Joe Glauber explains,

> In terms of distorting effects, you have to look at these programs on a continuum. . . . Countercyclical is somewhere [in the middle]. . . . The difference with the countercyclical program is . . . you don't have to produce a crop to receive the payments. They still allow producers to make marketing decisions and planting decisions based on market prices and not on the payment. Producers will get the payment, regardless of whether or not they plant cotton, regardless of whether they harvest 500 pounds of cotton per acre or 600 pounds per acre. From that standpoint, they're far less distorting.

But the panel disagreed, ruling that price-based support programs shielded US farmers from market signals because the countercyclical base rate and the marketing loan rate were set well above market prices at the time. In other words, the programs essentially acted as a price floor, ensuring that farmers would receive a good price for their cotton regardless of what the world market was doing—a measure of security that, the panel reasoned, clearly affected their decisions to plant cotton.

Revamping or abolishing these price-support programs, as the panel recommended, affected US commodities far beyond cotton alone. The countercyclical and marketing loan programs were designed to encourage farmers to respond to market signals in years of high prices, while at the same time incorporating a mechanism to offset rapid price declines over which farmers had no control. The United States was suddenly faced with the challenge of bringing its programs into compliance with WTO rules while still ensuring that farmers had a safety net in years of bad prices.

Yet US officials said they could hardly agree to, in McClellan's phrase, unilaterally disarm. All nations had rules and regulations that distorted market signals in the agricultural sector. The United States wanted its agricultural sector to maintain a market orientation, but US officials objected to liberalizing US commodity programs while other countries were permitted to keep their distortions. From the standpoint of the United States, the question was how all countries could deal with this problem simultaneously in a way that would resolve the issue to everyone's satisfaction.

The Doha Round

Even though experts disagreed about the precise impact that the legal rulings against cotton and sugar would have on the outcome of the Doha Round, it had clearly shifted the negotiation dynamics dramatically. For one thing, Brazil gained the leadership position that Pedro de Camargo had sought. It emerged in Cancún as a leader in the G-20 coalition of developing countries, and was one of only five entities (along with the United States, the European Union, India, and China) to be involved in behind-the-scenes consultations during the July 2004 negotiations in Geneva.

More importantly, Europe did an about-face in the weeks leading up to the July 2004 talks. The European Union offered to eliminate $3 billion in export subsidies if the United States, in turn, would eliminate the export subsidy element in its export credit and food aid programs. Many analysts speculated that the impending ruling against EU sugar export subsidies forced European trade negotiators to see the writing on the wall.

Explaining the risky move to reporters, European Trade Commissioner Pascal Lamy admitted that the dispute cases provided some impetus. "Of course I think they helped," he said. "Obviously, the US had to give ground on cotton, and we have to give ground on sugar."[30] Camargo was quick to praise the European Union in an interview with the *New York Times*. "I would not have believed it, but in agriculture it is now Europe that is for free trade, not the US," he said.[31]

---

30. Lamy, quoted in Elizabeth Becker, "Interim Trade Triumph Short on Hard Details," *The New York Times*, August 2, 2004, C1.

31. Camargo, quoted in Elizabeth Becker, "Trade Talks in Geneva Offer More Hope This Time," *The New York Times*, July 26, 2004, C1.

The European Union's concession put the United States on the defensive. Because support from farm states was considered crucial for President Bush's reelection campaign, USTR Zoellick came under intense pressure to create an agreement that US farm groups would endorse. The United States pushed hard for gains in market access and successfully lobbied to change its countercyclical program from amber to blue, despite the cotton panel's ruling that countercyclical payments had trade-distorting effects. In the end, the United States agreed to certain constraints on its export credit programs and a 20 percent reduction in allowable amber box support in exchange for substantial increases in market access. While many NGOs and think tanks initially praised the concessions on domestic support, analysts became more critical in the following weeks: Because the reductions were of subsidy ceilings, not actual subsidy levels, there would be no real short- to medium-term effect on products subsidized at less than the maximum allowable level (see appendix 5F).

Zoellick denied that the dispute cases had any effect on the outcome of the negotiations. Indeed, cotton was not maintained as a stand-alone issue, as the West Africans had wanted. Nevertheless, the July 2004 framework text created a cotton subcommittee to examine the issue and specified that subsidies and other barriers in the cotton trade would be addressed "ambitiously, expeditiously, and specifically" within the context of overall agricultural negotiations.

WTO Director-General Supachai Panitchpakdi hailed the framework agreement as a "historic achievement" and an important step toward a successful conclusion of the Doha Round in 2006. Brazil's foreign minister, Celso Amorim, declared that the framework was "a good deal for trade liberalization and for social justice."[32] Along with Amorim, who became a star of the negotiations, European Trade Commissioner Pascal Lamy and USTR Robert Zoellick were applauded for forging a consensus.

In 2006, the US farm bill would be up for renewal once again, and Congress would have to decide how to incorporate the new WTO rules into domestic farm legislation. Some Washington insiders speculated that agricultural reform would be given an additional push by the budget reconciliation process. Because of record budget deficits, US lawmakers were looking to cut government spending across the board, including farm programs. But many controversial issues remained for trade negotiators to tackle at the next ministerial, scheduled for December 2005 in Hong Kong, such as the levels of tariff cuts, the treatment of special products, and specific timetables for subsidy reductions. Some experts feared that the other regulatory policies being negotiated in the round, such as rules on food safety and sanitation, were too burdensome for some developing countries and could replace the more conventional barriers to trade.

---

32. Amorim, quoted in Elizabeth Becker, "Trade Group to Cut Farm Subsidies for Rich Nations," *The New York Times*, August 1, 2004, section 1, 8.

Other experts feared that the United States was skirting real reductions in domestic support levels, making it more likely that trade negotiators would encounter the same standoff over market access in Hong Kong. "The US has already announced [insufficient gains in market access] as the excuse not to lower their internal support subsidies," says Pedro de Camargo, who has accused the United States of "box-shifting"—changing the countercyclical program from amber to blue—to offset the 20 percent reduction in amber box support offered in the July framework text. Camargo is concerned that the United States' reluctance to decouple and trim its support programs diminished the chances for an ambitious Doha agreement:

> The US is still rejecting the idea that they have to stop dumping on the world, and that will be necessary to solve at some point in time. The panels are helping a lot, but the US and EU reactions were very different. We got a big step forward in one pillar with the EU, but the step forward the US had to do—I don't see it. . . . The US exports a lot of products, and they all have high internal support. That's what we are trying to halt. It may not solve the domestic distortions, but we have to get the subsidy component out of the international market at least. And the US is still far from that. I'm not sure we're going to be able to [resolve this] in Hong Kong.

Brazil Wins the Appeal, but Negotiations Stall

On March 3, 2005, the DSU Appellate Body upheld all of the cotton panel's main rulings from the previous summer. In order to avoid retaliation from Brazil, the United States would have to modify its price-based support programs, although the panel offered no specific guidelines or deadlines regarding the modifications. "We can either implement the ruling quickly, or drag it out," says one USTR official. "Some members of Congress say, 'Go ahead, it doesn't cost anything.' But many more do not want to implement [the ruling], albeit for different reasons. Some say even if we do comply, the panel could come back and say we didn't do enough. Others fear it will encourage countries to file cases against other commodities if it looks easy to get what they want."

In the wake of the ruling, many USTR and USDA officials spoke of feeling as if they were stuck "between a rock and a hard place." On the one hand, Brazil and other developing countries were closely watching how the United States would implement the WTO ruling; coming into compliance would increase the United States' credibility and help the agricultural negotiations move forward. On the other hand, if the United States did comply, many members of Congress, especially those from southern states who were being pressured by commodity groups, promised to vote against the Central American Free Trade Agreement (CAFTA) and the extension of the president's trade promotion authority (TPA), two priorities for the USTR.[33]

Given these political constraints, many US officials concede that the United States is likely to do as little as possible in the short term, but acknowledge that the ruling would spur major shifts in farm policy in the upcoming farm bill. "Congress will do the minimum they can get away with, and then wait for Brazil to complain," predicts one longtime Hill staffer. "Then the panel will come back with specific guidelines, and we will do more modifications. It's an iterative process. But by then we're into the 2006 farm bill. I think we'll shift out of price-related programs, but the money won't disappear."[34] Joe Glauber concurs. "I think we will see a farm bill we haven't seen to date," he says. "It will be shaped by WTO rules on domestic support."

A much more immediate problem concerned the WTO panel ruling on prohibited export subsidies. The Appellate Body gave the United States a July 1 deadline to eliminate the export subsidy element in the Step 2 and export credit guarantee programs but because such changes required congressional action, Joe Glauber was certain the United States would miss the target date. "The message from Congress was clear: don't come to us with something to implement before [the CAFTA and TPA votes in] July," says Glauber. He continues, "[Congressmen] have asked me, 'Do we have to do anything? Why not just drag our feet?' My answer is that if we appear obstinate, [Brazil] won't be flexible. They will look to retaliate in a sensitive sector, and that will get people's attention."

By June, with no movement on the Step 2 program, the Brazilian Congress evaluated proposed legislation to ease copyright rules; its effect would essentially be to suspend the intellectual property rights of American products entering Brazil. In an interview with the *Los Angeles Times*, Pedro de Camargo admitted that the strategy was an effort to get US sectors vulnerable to copyright infringement—namely, Hollywood, Silicon Valley, and the pharmaceutical industry—"to act as a counterweight to the powerful cotton lobby."[35]

---

33. TPA was extended in Congress after no member of the House or Senate succeeded in moving forward a resolution of disapproval before the deadline of July 1, 2005; CAFTA was a more hard-fought battle. After months of behind-the-scenes lobbying by Bush administration officials, it passed the Senate, 54–45, in early July, and passed the House on July 28 by an even smaller, two-vote margin, after voting was held open unusually long to allow last-minute arm-twisting.

34. The staffer offers a historical comparison: the dispute case the European Union brought against the US foreign sales corporation (FSC) legislation. "FSC is a good parallel. It took us two years to do something. The EU said it wasn't enough, so it went back to the WTO. Only now, four years later, is there new legislation."

35. Camargo, quoted in Jerry Hirsch, "White House Seeks Repeal of a Cotton Subsidy Program; Administration Aims to Avert Brazilian Retaliation That Could Hurt Other Industries," *Los Angeles Times*, July 6, 2005, C1.

On July 5 Brazil requested the right to impose sanctions on $2.9 billion worth of US imports under the Trade-Related Aspects of Intellectual Property Rights (TRIPS) agreement "as a retaliatory measure against the US delay at withdrawing prohibited subsidies." Brazil's deputy trade minister, Paulo Mesquita, stressed that Brazil had no intention of retaliating right away, adding, "We still hope the US will comply in a manner so we don't have to carry these out." That same day, the USDA announced it was sending proposed statutory changes to the Step 2 program to Congress for approval. "By implementing these proposed changes, we are being fully responsive to the WTO decision," said US Agriculture Secretary Mike Johanns. "This step is essential for the US to continue to be a leader in the WTO Doha negotiations."[36] At a special DSU session 10 days later, Brazil and the United States asked that the matter be referred to an arbitration panel, which suspended its work in accordance with the settlement agreement to give the United States time to comply.[37]

By the summer of 2005 the words "deadlocked" and "faltering" were once again being applied to the agricultural negotiations. In late July trade delegations met for a mini-ministerial in Dalian, China, where delegates reported that "no breakthrough had occurred." Days later, they met again in Geneva to continue talks. Despite intense negotiations and the last-minute presence of trade ministers, WTO members could not forge an agreement. A main sticking point remained the formula for tariff reduction. High-tariff countries such as the European Union and the G-10 of net food-importing countries disagreed with the "five tariff band formula" proposed by the G-20 at Dalian, while agricultural exporters such as the United States and Cairns Group members rejected the European Union's approach of a linear formula.

Tim Groser, the chair of the agricultural negotiations, admitted that the talks were "stalled," but tried to remain upbeat. "A set of clear political decisions—none of them easy, but at least we can now more readily identify the essential decisions—can restart this negotiation and still pave the way for a successful Ministerial meeting in December," he said. WTO Director-General Supachai offered a more pessimistic assessment, fearing that the delays caused by disagreement over tariff reductions left negotiators with little time to agree on the full modalities before the Hong Kong ministerial in December. Supachai also lamented the "reluctance on the part of key players to engage in real negotiations," pointing out that the stalemate in agriculture had postponed a resolution to the West

---

36. All quotations from "US Announces Changes to Illegal Cotton Subsidies; Brazil Reserves the Right to Retaliate," *Bridges Weekly Digest,* July 6, 2005, 3.

37. If Brazil deems that US efforts to bring its programs into compliance with the panel ruling are insufficient, it is entitled at any time to establish a new WTO arbitration panel and impose retaliatory measures.

African Sectoral Initiative and even slowed down progress in other areas of the round.[38]

"The links between agriculture and other negotiating areas appear to be posing a serious barrier to the talks," a publication of the International Centre for Trade and Sustainable Development noted. "Several developing country delegations insist that they must see some of their demands met in the agriculture negotiations before they can make concessions on NAMA [nonagricultural market access]."[39] Indeed, the chair of NAMA negotiations postponed a week of talks scheduled for late July because progress appeared unlikely in the absence of movement in the agricultural negotiations. Negotiations in trade in services were likewise on hold. "An agreement on agriculture would unlock the talks on NAMA," confirmed one trade delegate.[40]

Where to Go from Here?

Trade analysts and NGOs have cited the WTO cotton case as a wake-up call demonstrating the need to create a fair, mutually beneficial agricultural trading system that accommodates the needs of all countries. But how that trading system would evolve remains to be seen. In short, while Brazil had won the battle in the cotton case, the war is far from over. As of late 2005, the United States had hesitantly begun to deal with some of the effects of the WTO's cotton ruling, but its full impact was not yet clear. West African nations were striving to make their cotton sector more competitive, but the job was far from done. The WTO's agriculture negotiations were at a standstill. Political leaders in Brazil and other countries were continuing to ponder what they could do to build on the cotton case in order to achieve their goals.

---

38. Quotations from "Following July Stalemate, Intense Negotiations Expected in Lead-up to Hong Kong Ministerial," *Bridges Weekly Digest,* August 3, 2005, 6.

39. "Members Try to Convert Dalian Outcome into Negotiations Breakthrough," *Bridges Weekly Digest,* July 20, 2005, 2.

40. Quoted in "Members Try to Convert Dalian Outcome into Negotiations Breakthrough," 2.

Case Analysis

The Brazil cotton case raises questions about the nature of support for farmers in a market economy; the adequacy of the international trade rules for agriculture; the ability of developing countries to use the system to advance their interests, through both trade negotiations and the dispute settlement system; the impact of the trading rules on domestic farm support programs; and the role of the trading system in promoting economic development.

Do farmers deserve special support from the government in a market economy? If so, how should such support be provided? In practice, almost every country supports its farmers and gives such aid through a variety of measures, including production subsidies, import protection, export subsidies, and price supports. Payment is often tied to the production of specific crops, although sometimes it is provided to those who withdraw land from production and improve the environment. Many of these measures are justified in the name of saving the family farmer, but support is often given without income limits or through price measures that actually benefit corporate producers most.

Which approach is most desirable? From a domestic perspective, these measures raise difficult issues of equity (among family farmers, consumers, taxpayers, etc.) and efficiency. From the standpoint of the trading system as well, they are not all created equal. Their impacts on the rest of the world may vary widely. For example, food stamps and other consumption subsidies actually raise world prices, as do payments contingent on setting aside production land. By contrast, import tariffs and production subsidies reduce world prices while raising prices at home.

International Rules

Although many agricultural products are traded internationally, for much of the postwar period, agricultural trade was not fully covered in the rules of the trading system. This omission reflects the political power of farmers in many countries. As a result, the barriers in both developed and developing countries remain much higher than those for manufactured goods. This discrepancy is of particular concern for developing countries, many of which are farm commodity producers.

In the Uruguay Round of multilateral trade negotiations launched in 1986, agricultural programs were subject to extensive negotiation for the first time in the history of the GATT. The result was the URAA, which distinguished among measures according to the degree to which they distorted international trade. Export subsidies and border barriers clearly induce such distortions, and efforts were made to reduce export subsidies and to enhance market access by lowering tariffs and ensuring that minimum levels of imports be permitted through tariff-rate quotas (TRQs). In addition, domestic subsidies that distort trade because they are contingent on producing particular commodities had to be reduced by 20 percent over benchmark levels. There was more lenient treatment for less trade-distorting measures that helped farmers but were given in a general manner. Such measures included "green box" subsidies such as support for research and development, training, food aid, and disaster relief, as well as "blue box" programs such as direct payments that required farmers to limit production.

However, another part of the Uruguay Round agreement, the Agreement on Subsidies and Countervailing Measures (SCM), actually prohibited export subsidies of all types. It also indicated that actionable subsidies (e.g., government benefits to a specific enterprise or industry), even if not prohibited, could be subject to challenge if they caused "serious prejudice" to the interests of another WTO member (Article 5(c)). Potential conflicts between these agreements could therefore be anticipated. These conflicts were postponed by a "peace clause" (URAA Article 13, "Due Restraint") that forestalled any challenges to certain domestic support measures and export subsidies until 2004.[41]

While the agreement was a historic first step, large trade-distorting supports remained in place. For developing countries, particularly those like Brazil that are major exporters of farm products, these were a source of concern. Because many developing countries are net agricultural exporters and the Doha Round has been expressly focused on the needs of developing countries—indeed, it has become known as the Doha Development Agenda—agriculture was given a pivotal role in the round. At the ministerial meeting held at Cancún in 2003, a powerful coalition of developing countries united to oppose US and EU agricultural proposals, demonstrating considerable negotiating muscle; by the following year, it had forced the European Union to abandon its resistance to ending export subsidies by a certain date.

US Farm Policies

Trade rules have become increasingly important in domestic debates over farm policy. The United States provides farmers with considerable financial support. In particular, farmers are often guaranteed minimum prices for their yield through measures such as loan support programs. Whereas trade protection raises the price paid by domestic consumers, these loan support programs have the virtue of allowing consumers to pay world prices—but they also have the effect of lowering world prices.

---

41. For Brazil to challenge US agricultural subsidies under the SCM agreement, it had to (1) demonstrate that export subsidies paid to cotton producers did not conform with the URAA; and (2) to show that US domestic support to cotton producers exceeded 1992 levels.

In 1996 the United States tried to move away from closely tying the receipt of such subsidies to the production of particular crops by implementing the so-called Freedom to Farm Act, which provided subsidies to US farmers based on their past production. In the late 1990s, when falling commodity prices depressed farm incomes, the US government boosted these payments with additional emergency payments. In principle, neither of these programs was tied to current production and therefore both were considered by the United States to be green box. Many of these efforts were continued in the 2002 farm bill as "countercyclical payments." Cotton farmers in the United States benefited from marketing loan programs, direct payments, countercyclical payments, crop insurance, export credit insurance, and a Step 2 program that boosted exports and the use of domestic cotton by textile producers.[42]

WTO Rules

The WTO is a complex agreement, and members are often left in doubt as to its precise interpretation. Uncertainty sometimes occurs because the wording is ambiguous or because the agreement appears to say different things in different places. Case rulings help establish what it actually means. The peace clause to some extent postponed the need to reconcile the apparent inconsistencies between the URAA and SCM agreement, but it did not resolve them. Some members believed that as long as a country met its obligations under the URAA it did not have to conform to the SCM provisions for agricultural products, but—as the rulings in this case indicate—they were not correct. Both agreements apply.

Violations

The cotton case allows us to explore why countries violate the WTO rules and how the dispute system operates to allow others to challenge them. It shows the United States finding itself in violation of WTO rules that it had played a major role in crafting. Compliance with the WTO is not always easy, even for a developed countries. The United States believed it was in compliance with its commitments under the Uruguay Round agreement, and that therefore it would be safe from legal challenge. However, by adopting a policy of guaranteeing cotton farmers a minimum price (and payments triggered by revenue declines), it opened itself to the possibil-

---

42. By paying exporters an amount equal to the difference between the US and world market price for cotton, Step 2 guarantees that US cotton can be sold in foreign markets at a profit. It also provides a payment to textile producers who use US instead of foreign cotton in their production.

ity of exceeding the limits for subsidies when cotton prices fell.[43] In addition, because cotton farmers had been prohibited from growing vegetables in order to qualify for payments, those payments could not qualify as green box—a point overlooked by US policymakers.

Developing Countries

Does the system provide developing countries with opportunities to advance their interests? The WTO has come under considerable fire for allegedly promoting the interests of developed countries and corporations at the expense of developing countries. Many made the specific argument that the Uruguay Round agreement was unfair because it required developing countries to accept the TRIPS agreement. In addition, some have seen the developing countries as at an inherent disadvantage in the dispute settlement process, pointing out that they are less able to respond to violations with trade retaliation and claiming that they lack the capacity to bring cases.

This case study suggests that some of these concerns may have been misplaced, or at least that the situation has improved. Not only was Brazil remarkably successful in winning this case (as well as another against the European Union, on its sugar subsidies), but a group of least-developed countries used the Cancún meeting and the Doha negotiations to win a special "sectoral initiative" for cotton. We see that it is possible for a developing country to bring a case against the United States, win it, and force a shift in US policy. But we also see that it took great effort and considerable technical and political capacity. Brazil was able to mobilize support in a way that other developing countries might not. The efforts of the Brazilian government were supplemented by international experts and legal representation, and the case was funded by the private sector. By contrast, this approach seemed less attractive to the less-developed West African countries, which arguably had an even greater interest in cotton subsidies. They chose an alternative route to advance their cause and were also able to obtain some measure of success.

As in the other cases in this volume, we see here the central role that vision and organization play in the design and implementation of influence strategies. Pedro de Camargo Neto was able to parlay his position in the

---

43. The four most significant findings of the panel were that (1) Step 2 payments to users and exporters of US-grown cotton constitute prohibited subsidies; (2) export credit guarantees to exporters of cotton and other commodities constitute prohibited subsidies; (3) the peace clause is not a bar to Brazil's challenge of US domestic support to upland cotton producers; and (4) US domestic support measures caused significant price suppression in the world cotton market during the years in question and therefore caused "serious prejudice" to the interests of Brazil.

Brazilian government into a leading role for himself and his country in the Doha Round. He understood the potential for "bargaining in the shadow of the law," and he recognized that bringing a case in the WTO was a way of both influencing the agenda and leveling the playing field. He also was skilled at building coalitions, first to overcome opposition within the Brazilian government to launching the case and then to influence public and governmental opinion more broadly. At the same time, he saw that the weaker parties in the trading systems, who could not afford to directly confront the dominant players, could nonetheless play important, complementary roles in the larger campaign of influencing public opinion.

Key Questions

The case raises at least four important questions for us to reflect on. First, what precisely has Brazil achieved by winning the case? Has it simply gained a bargaining chip that it can use to obtain some concessions from the United States in the Doha Round or other negotiations? Second, what are the implications for US agricultural policies? Will the rulings really compel a fundamental change, or will the United States be able to meet its WTO obligations by making a few small modifications to its practices? If the rulings do require a major change, is this what the United States really understood and bargained for when it negotiated and signed the agreements in the first place? Third, what are the implications for agricultural producers in developing countries? What will be the impact of reductions in developed-country farm protection on poverty and economic development elsewhere? Fourth and finally, does this case provide a blueprint for how weaker players in the system can use the WTO dispute settlement mechanism to advance their interests?

Appendix 5A
WTO Dispute Panel Findings:
US Subsidies for Upland Cotton

The dispute panel ruled that US subsidy levels during the marketing years 1998–2002 exceeded the 1992 level. Therefore US cotton programs were not protected under the peace clause.

The panel found that all price-based US cotton programs caused "serious prejudice to the interests of Brazil" insofar as they suppressed prices, stating that "a causal link exists between price-contingent subsidies and significant price suppression . . . and this link is not attenuated by other factors raised by the United States."[44] The price-based support programs at issue include the marketing loss assistance payments (countercyclical payments in the 2002 farm bill), the marketing loan program, and the Step 2 program.

The panel found that US support programs not tied to price did not contribute to price suppression. Those payments included direct payments (called "production flexibility contract payments") and crop insurance payments. However, the panel ruled that because of the prohibition on planting fruits and vegetables, the direct payments did not qualify as green box support, but should have been counted as amber box instead.[45]

The panel rejected Brazil's market share argument. That is, the panel ruled Brazil had failed to show that US subsidies led to an increase in US world market share.

The panel found that the Step 2 program and the export credit guarantee (GSM) program did contain an export subsidy element. Export subsidies were prohibited for all commodities except those specific products for which countries had requested special allowances—called an "export subsidy base"—in the Uruguay Round. Since the United States did not have an export subsidy base for cotton, the panel ruled that the United States should remove the export subsidy element contained in the GSM and Step 2 programs within six months.[46]

---

44. "United States Subsidies on Upland Cotton," WTO Appellate Report, Document WT/DS267/AB/R, adopted on March 21, 2005, 291.

45. Under the program, farmers who grew fruits and vegetables on cotton base acreage were penalized (their payments were lowered). Therefore, the panel argued, the direct payments were not fully decoupled from production levels, so they did not meet the criteria of green box support. This same prohibition on fruits and vegetables existed for all program commodities that qualified for direct payments.

46. The United States had export subsidy allowances for wheat, barley, vegetable oils, butter, cheese, beef, pork, poultry, and eggs. GSM programs used for all other commodities with a zero-subsidy base, such as corn, were given the same six-month time frame for complying with this ruling.

Appendix 5B
Timeline of Key Events in Brazil's WTO Disputes

Date	Event
September 27, 2002	Brazil files two dispute cases—against US cotton subsidies and EU sugar export subsidies—under the Dispute Settlement Understanding (DSU), the legal arm of the WTO.
September 27, 2002	Oxfam publishes *Cultivating Poverty: The Impact of US Cotton Subsidies on Africa*, which focuses media attention on agricultural trade and development policies.
April 30, 2003	The Francophone nations of Benin, Burkina Faso, Chad, and Mali file the Sectoral Initiative on Cotton at the WTO.
July 22, 2003	The first WTO panel session of *Brazil v. the United States on Upland Cotton Subsidies* is held. The United States requests that the case be thrown out, claiming that US cotton programs are protected under the peace clause. The panel rejects that request and allows the case to proceed.
September 10–13, 2003	The West Africans' cotton initiative receives wide spread support in Cancún. The WTO director-general even chairs the negotiating session, but parties are unable to come to agreement. The Cancún ministerial adjourns prematurely after negotiators come to an impasse.
April 22, 2004	The European Union announces reforms of its support policies for Mediterranean products—hops, olive oil, and cotton—which include fully decoupling 65 percent of payments given to cotton growers.
April 26, 2004	The WTO dispute panel issues its confidential preliminary ruling, siding with Brazil on most of its claims.
April 28, 2004	The House Agricultural Committee of the US Congress holds hearings at which Secretary of Agriculture Ann Veneman and USTR Robert Zoellick assure lawmakers that US support programs are consistent with WTO regulations. USTR Zoellick vows to appeal the WTO ruling.

Date	Event
June 18, 2004	The WTO dispute panel issues its final ruling, siding with Brazil in finding that several US support programs—including marketing loan payments, countercyclical payments, Step 2 payments, export credits, and even direct payments—contributed to "serious prejudice" by depressing world cotton prices and recommends that the United States eliminate or modify the offending programs.
July 24–31, 2004	Trade negotiators from the 147 WTO member countries meet in Geneva to agree on a framework text for moving the Doha negotiations forward. After private negotiating sessions with the "Big Five"—the United States, European Union, Brazil, China, and India—all 147 members agree to substantial reforms in agricultural trade, including increases in market access, reductions in domestic support, and the elimination of export subsides at an undetermined date. However, most significant details are left for negotiators to resolve at the Hong Kong ministerial in December 2005.
August 4, 2004	A second WTO dispute panel issues a preliminary ruling against EU sugar export subsidies in a case brought by Brazil, Thailand, and Australia.
November 19, 2004	In accordance with the July framework, the WTO establishes a cotton subcommittee to monitor progress on the "trade track" of the West African Sectoral Initiative. In the "development track," meanwhile, donor conferences are held in Bamako, Mali, and Cotonou, Benin, to evaluate the needs of the West African cotton sector and devise technical assistance packages.
March 3, 2005	The DSU Appellate Body issues its ruling on the cotton case, upholding the panel's main findings from the previous summer. By July 1, 2005, the United States has to eliminate the export subsidy element in the Step 2 and export credit guarantee (GSM) programs. No deadlines are attached to modifications required of price-based programs.
July 5, 2005	The USDA sends legislative proposals to Congress seeking modifications of the Step 2 program

(timeline continues next page)

Timeline of Key Events *(continued)*

Date	Event
	after Brazil threatens to retaliate by refusing to recognize intellectual property rights of US products entering Brazil.
July 18, 2005	At a meeting of the WTO Subcommittee on Cotton, the West Africans announce they are "disappointed WTO members have not responded in writing" to their April proposal, which requested (1) duty-free market access for cotton and cotton by-products produced by African countries; (2) an elimination of all domestic support measures that "distort cotton trade" by September 21, 2005; and (3) an elimination of cotton export subsidies by July 1, 2005. Despite the promise of an "early harvest," most negotiators admit that any concessions to the West Africans on cotton subsidies remain highly unlikely before the December 2005 ministerial.
July 21–26, 2005	After a mini-ministerial in Dalian, China, where delegates report that "no breakthrough had occurred," trade delegations meet again in Geneva to discuss agricultural tariff and subsidy reductions and schedules. Despite intense negotiations, WTO members cannot forge an agreement. A main sticking point remains the tiered formula for market access.
July 28, 2005	After months of behind-the-scenes lobbying by USTR Robert Portman (Robert Zoellick's successor), the Central American Free Trade Agreement (CAFTA) narrowly passes in the House, 217–215. The Senate approved CAFTA weeks earlier. Citing the passage of CAFTA and the July 1, 2005, extension of President Bush's trade promotion authority for two years, USTR Portman comments that America's political leadership on trade allowed him to "come to Geneva with a little more momentum . . . to be able to knock down barriers to trade globally though the Doha Round."[47]

47. Transcript of press briefing by USTR Robert Portman, Geneva, Switzerland, July 29, 2005, available at the USTR Web site at www.ustr.gov (accessed January 6, 2006).

Appendix 5C
The Uruguay Round Agreement on Agriculture

The objective of the Uruguay Round Agreement on Agriculture (URAA) was to reform agricultural trade, encouraging more market-oriented policies for exporting and importing countries alike. After eight years of negotiations, it took effect in 1995. Developed countries had to make scheduled cuts in their subsidies and tariffs over a six-year period, while developing countries had smaller tariff reduction requirements and a 10-year time frame to implement them. Least-developed countries (LDCs) were exempt from undertaking any reforms.

The provisions in the URAA called for reforms in each of the "three pillars" of agricultural trade.

Market Access. Developed countries had to cut their tariffs by an average of 36 percent, with a minimum cut of 15 percent for any product; developing countries had to make an average cut of 24 percent, with a minimum cut of 10 percent.

Export Subsidies. Export subsidies are widely considered to be the most trade-distorting type of support because they encourage producers to export their products onto world markets at less than the cost of production, a practice also known as "dumping." The URAA prohibits export subsidies except for specific subsidies listed within members' commitments, and even then the agreement requires the countries using export subsidies to cut both the amount of money spent on them and the number of exports to which they apply.

Domestic Support. The URAA essentially said that not all subsidies are the same: Some distort trade, while others do not. Accordingly, the agreement distinguished between distorting and nondistorting types of support policies by assigning them to color-coded boxes:

- *Green box:* Green box subsidies have a negligible, or at most minimal, effect on trade. These types of subsidies are not subject to reduction commitments; in fact, countries can increase their green box spending without restraint, provided that the payments meet the green box requirements.[48] Green box subsidies include government transfers for research and environmental conservation, as well as direct income payments to farmers who do not influence production decisions (i.e., the amount of acreage planted or the type of crop grown).

---

48. The three criteria for a subsidy to be considered green box are (1) the subsidy must not distort trade, or must at most have a very minimal distorting effect; (2) it must be government-funded; and (3) it cannot involve a price-support mechanism.

- *Blue box:* Under the URAA, blue box programs are not subject to reduction commitments, on the grounds that they are not tied to current production. They include rural development programs, direct payments that require farmers to limit production, and decoupled payments given to farmers based on their historical, not current, production levels.

- *Amber box:* All domestic support programs that do not meet the criteria of one of the two categories above are considered amber box. These include price supports, coupled payments, product-specific programs, and input subsidies. Amber box subsidies are considered highly trade-distorting because they have a direct effect on production levels, and they therefore are subject to reduction commitments under the URAA.[49] Using 1986–88 as a reference period, WTO members calculated their annual spending on these types of programs, a figure that is referred to as the "total aggregate measure of support" (or AMS). Each country's AMS became the maximum allowable level it could spend on amber box programs annually; and developed countries agreed to reduce their total AMS spending by 20 percent over six years, starting in 1995. Developing countries agreed to make a 13 percent cut over 10 years.

The Peace Clause

Though countries agreed to lower tariffs and subsidy levels over a number of years, concern still remained over how the URAA would relate to other Uruguay Round agreements, such as the Agreement on Subsidies and Countervailing Measures (SCM). The SCM agreement essentially laid out the terms and conditions under which countries have recourse to impose penalties on other WTO members whose policies are inconsistent with their WTO commitments. For example, a subsidy given to producers in one country that causes "serious prejudice" (i.e., substantial financial harm) to a domestic industry in another country is actionable under the SCM agreement.[50] Both parties present their arguments before a three-person panel in the Dispute Settlement Understanding (DSU), the court system of the WTO. If after a series of panel hearings the subsidizing na-

---

49. Twenty-eight WTO members (counting the European Union as one member) had nonexempt, or amber box, domestic support programs that were subject to reduction commitments.

50. According to the SCM agreement, serious prejudice exists if the subsidies of a WTO member displace or impede imports by the subsidizing country; displace or impede the exports of another country in a third-country market; result in price undercutting, price depression, or price suppression; or lead to a loss of world market share for a competitor country (DTB Associates 2004, 2).

tion has been found to cause serious prejudice, it must remove the offending subsidy or face retaliation from the country that brought the case.

The question of which agreement took precedent—the URAA or the SCM agreement—was no small matter. Even though the URAA allowed WTO members to maintain a certain level of trade-distorting agricultural support (their AMS), they might still be open to legal challenges from other countries if serious prejudice could be proved. Some WTO members, most notably the United States and European Union, wanted extra protection against challenges of their agricultural subsidies, so they pushed to include a clause in the URAA encouraging countries to "exercise due restraint." Article 13, commonly referred to as the peace clause, effectively prohibited WTO members from bringing countervailing duty cases against other members' agricultural subsidies. Specifically, Article 13 stated that

(i) green box subsidies could not be subject to cases under the ASCM agreement, and

(ii) blue box and amber box subsidies were exempt from countervailing duty cases, as long as a country's overall AMS commitments did not exceed its 1992 levels and the amount of support given to a specific commodity did not exceed the level set in the 1992 marketing year.

The nine-year peace clause took effect in 1994 with an expiration date of December 31, 2003. Developed countries had hoped to renew the peace clause at the Cancún ministerial in September 2003, but the talks collapsed and the clause was allowed to expire at the end of the year.

Appendix 5D
US Farm Policy

The precursor to modern-day cotton programs came out of New Deal legislation, the Agricultural Adjustment Act of 1933, which set up a system of minimum prices and government stocks. The main form of government assistance was the marketing loan program, which established "loan rates," or minimum prices that farmers could enjoy, for different commodities. The objective was to allow market conditions to take over in good years, while providing a safety net for farmers when there was a sudden downturn in price.

At the time of harvest, farmers received loans that were equal to the loan rate multiplied by their actual production; these were called "nonrecourse loans" because the government had to accept the production in lieu of repayment. The loan rates of any given commodity were set to cover the costs of production, with the intention of giving farmers the choice between transferring their harvests back to the government to pay off their loans or selling their crops on the open market—whichever had the higher return. However, after World War II, many of the loan rates were set so much higher than the cost of production that the government, not the consumer, essentially became the market.

In the 1960s, Congress lowered the loan rates to "disaster levels," so that the market once again determined the crop value. The United States became more competitive in global agricultural markets as a result. Since that time, US farm bills have tried to preserve a market orientation rather than relying on government interventions, while still maintaining a safety net for farmers in stressful times of drought or low prices. With inflation running high in the late 1970s, loan rates were set at very high levels. In the 1980s, an appreciating dollar and a slump in world GDP led to a collapse in world markets, leaving loan rates at very high levels relative to market prices. Large loan forfeitures resulted in enormous government stockpiles, stimulating Congress to legislate reforms in the 1985 farm bill, which lowered loan rates considerably and ultimately set the stage for the 1996 farm bill.

Freedom to Farm: The 1996 Farm Bill

The House and Senate Agricultural Committees draft farm legislation, commonly called "farm bills," every five to six years; they must subsequently be authorized by Congress and approved by the president. When farm legislation came up for renewal in 1996, US legislators for the first time faced an international constraint on their domestic farm policy: WTO commitments to which the United States had agreed in the Uruguay Round. Price-based support programs such as loan deficiency payments, introduced in the 1985 farm bill, were considered amber box subsidies because they were tied to the production of a specific commodity.

Moreover, program outlays were impossible to determine in advance because the marketing loan payments to farmers depended on what world prices were doing. As a result, government spending often varied dramatically from year to year. Yet such volatility could lead to spending that was incompatible with the United States' WTO commitments. When the URAA was implemented in 1995, the United States' total AMS, or permissible amber box support, stood fixed at $19.1 billion a year.

But the mid-1990s were a period of record-high commodity prices. Because US farmers were doing well on the world markets, US government outlays under the marketing loan program and other price-based subsidies were minimal. "The loan rates at the time—not just for cotton, but for all the commodities—were way below market prices," comments Joe Glauber, deputy chief economist at the USDA. "In 1995 to 1996 . . . [the United States] was reporting [AMS] outlays of $7 billion to $8 billion. We were well within our limits, and everyone felt that we were looking pretty good."

Congress used the opportunity to pass the 1996 Freedom to Farm Act, which introduced a system of "decoupled" direct payments. The marketing loan program remained more or less intact, but that did not raise much concern at a time when world prices were much higher than loan rates. In general, the 1996 farm bill was applauded as a step in the right direction. Direct payments were designed to qualify as green box support, since the payments were based on historical production levels (i.e., "base acreage"), not actual production on the farm. Because farmers received direct payments regardless of whether they planted cotton, planted something else, or left their land fallow, legislators argued, they met the green box criteria of not distorting production. There was one exception, however. Farmers' direct payments would be reduced if they planted fruits and vegetables on their base acreage.

Congress Passes Supplemental Legislation

In 1997–98, the bottom fell out of commodity markets, mainly because of the East Asian financial crisis. The dollar rose, leading to a loss of US competitiveness that dampened demand for US goods across the globe.

As farmers reeled from depressed world demand and faced a severe drought in several US states, Congress passed supplemental legislation in 1998 that authorized additional "emergency" payments of $30 billion over a four-year period. Congress was criticized by supporters of the 1996 farm bill for reverting back to the old system of price supports. "At the same time the US was in Geneva saying how decoupled our programs were," remarks Joe Glauber, "Congress was passing supplemental legislation to compensate producers for low prices."

Cotton prices were still relatively high when Congress passed the supplemental legislation.[51] Nevertheless, because the emergency payments were designated for all US farmers, not just those hardest hit by drought or low prices, US cotton farmers received the extra payments as well. The emergency payments, called the "marketing loss assistance payments," were "done in an imprecise manner," says Glauber. "In 1998, corn and wheat guys were hurting, they got double payments. Cotton and rice guys were doing pretty well, but they also got double payments. It really didn't match the need."

In 2000, Congress passed the Agricultural Risk Protection Act (ARPA), which provided an additional $8 billion in subsidies to US farmers via crop insurance, a program for which cotton growers were eligible. Months later, when the world price of cotton fell below the loan rate of 52 cents, the marketing loan payments kicked in. All told, government support to US cotton growers totaled $1.9 billion in 1998–99, $3.5 billion in 1999–2000, $2.1 billion in 2000–01, and $3.9 billion in 2001–02.[52] In contrast, the amount of assistance that US cotton growers received in 1992, the baseline marketing year for the purposes of the peace clause, was $1.4 billion (see table 5D.1).

The 2002 Farm Bill

In sharp contrast to the previous three farm bills, the 2002 farm bill was passed in a time of government budget surplus. By all accounts, it was a strong reversal of the 15-year trend away from decoupling producer support to production levels. Significantly, the "emergency" marketing loss assistance payments, now termed "countercyclical payments," were made permanent. Like direct payments, countercyclical payments were based on historical, not actual, levels of production. Like marketing loan payments, they kicked in only in years of low prices, when the world price fell below the minimum price. In 2002, for example, a year of low cotton prices, countercyclical payments immediately became the largest component of government assistance to cotton growers: 36 cents of every dollar spent, for a total of $1.3 billion.

---

51. Cotton was one of the last commodity markets to be affected by the Asian financial crisis. Whereas other commodity markets bottomed out in 1998–99, cotton prices were relatively stable until 2000. Although the cotton crop in Texas was in fact affected by the drought, producers received disaster payments on top of the marketing loss assistance payments.

52. These totals include direct payments, marketing loan payments, Step 2 payments, crop insurance payments, and payments under the export credit guarantee program (Baffes 2004b, 13).

Table 5D.1   US government support to cotton producers

	1992–93[a]	1998–99	1999–2000	2000–01	2001–02	2002–03
US cotton production (thousands of tons)	3,531	3,251	3,823	3,742	4,420	3,746
A Index (US dollars per kilogram)	1.28	1.30	1.16	1.26	0.92	1.23
Total assistance (millions of US dollars)	1,443	1,947	3,432	2,149	3,937	3,075
Assistance (per kilogram)	0.41	0.60	0.90	0.57	0.89	0.82
Assistance (percent of A Index)	32	46	77	46	97	67
Breakdown of assistance (millions of US dollars)						
Coupled payments	1,303	535	1,613	563	2,507	248
Production flexibility contracts/direct payments	n.a.	637	614	575	474	914
Marketing loss assistance payments/ countercyclical payments[b]	n.a.	316	613	613	524	1,264
Crop insurance	n.a.	151	170	162	236	194
Step 2 payments	140	308	422	236	196	455
Total	1,443	1,947	3,432	2,149	3,937	3,075

n.a. = not available

a. The 1992–93 marketing year served as the threshold level that countries could not exceed to remain protected under the peace clause. Because the composition of support was different in 1992–93, all programs were considered coupled support.

b. The emergency marketing loss assistance payments, which Congress authorized in supplemental legislation in 1998, became permanent in the 2002 farm bill under the new name "countercyclical payments."

Note: "Years" refer to marketing years. The A Index is the August–July average.

Sources: US Department of Agriculture; International Cotton Advisory Committee; Baffes (2004b).

The projected outlays for the 2002 farm bill were $180 billion over a 10-year period, representing an 80 percent increase in spending from the 1996 farm bill. "All of a sudden we have a very big program again," observes Glauber. "Now we've increased the loan rate in an environment where prices are expected to be low ... the direct payment rate was increased for most commodities, and on top of that we had these countercyclical payments."

Appendix 5E
The World Cotton Market

Volatility and price declines are not new to the cotton market. Since 1990, however, both trends have become more pronounced, as a result of such factors as longer-term trends affecting supply and demand, currency fluctuations, and government policies, particularly in the United States and China.

Cotton Supply

From 1960 to 2001, global cotton production doubled from 10 million to 20 million tons. Major cotton producers include the United States and China (together comprising 40 percent of world production), as well as India (12 percent), Pakistan (8 percent), Uzbekistan (5 percent), Francophone Africa (5 percent), Brazil, Australia, Turkey, and two members of the European Union, Greece and Spain. One-third of cotton is traded internationally, with the United States by far the world's largest exporter. Behind the United States, major cotton exporters are Uzbekistan, Francophone Africa, and Australia.

In the past 40 years, cotton production has undergone dramatic technological changes. Improved seed varieties, fertilizers, pesticides, and mechanical farming have lowered costs and doubled world cotton yields. The development of a genetically modified cotton plant designed to protect itself from insects has also transformed the sector. Monsanto first introduced its genetically engineered strain, called Bollgard (Bt) cotton, in 1996; it has since been adopted in nine countries and is now grown on 13 million hectares worldwide, or 40 percent of the total acreage devoted to cotton.

Indeed, the expansion of Bt cotton—along with extremely favorable weather conditions in all major cotton-producing countries—led to record harvests in 2001–02. Countries that grow Bt cotton include the United States (where Bt accounts for 70 percent of total cotton acreage), Australia (40 percent), and China (20 percent), as well as India, Indonesia, Mexico, Argentina, Colombia, and South Africa (Cabanilla, Abdoulaye, and Sanders 2003). Although the European Union cites health and environmental reasons for not switching to Bt cotton, its adoption has significant implications for farm income, especially for developing countries.[53]

Cotton Demand

Global consumption patterns for cotton fiber are determined by several factors, the most significant of which is the size and health of the textile

---

53. Bt results in higher profit margins for farmers by both raising yields (because insect damage is reduced) and reducing input costs (because fewer insecticide sprayings are needed).

industries in cotton-importing nations. China is the largest textile producer in the world; during the 1990s, it consumed on average more than one-quarter of global cotton output. Along with those in China, the textile industries of the United States, Turkey, and India together account for three-quarters of cotton consumption.

A long-standing constraint on cotton demand is the increasing competitiveness of chemical fibers. Consumption of synthetic fibers such as polyester grew by 4.7 percent annually from 1960 to 2000 as technological innovations enabled them to be produced more cost-effectively. In contrast, cotton consumption increased only 1.8 percent annually over the same period, roughly in parallel with population growth (Baffes 2004b, 5). The United States is the only country in the world where cotton consumption has been increasing for the last 10 to 15 years; in most countries, per capita demand for cotton textiles has been declining.

Though much of the 1990s saw steady, if slow, increases in world cotton demand, cotton experienced a sharp price decline after the East Asian financial crisis in 1997. Inflation rose, demand shrank, and many mills sat idle in the textile-producing East Asian nations of Indonesia, Thailand, Taiwan, and South Korea. (By 2002, once their economies had rebounded, those four countries together absorbed 22 percent of global cotton output.)

In the ensuing global recession, the dollar appreciated against the currencies of major cotton producing countries by nearly 20 percent (Skelly and MacDonald 2003, 2). This currency fluctuation is significant because cotton, like most commodities, is traded in dollars, making cotton prices sensitive to the dollar exchange rate. The appreciation of the dollar thus exerted downward pressure on world cotton prices, as the A index (the average of the cheapest five quotations from a selection of the main upland cottons traded internationally) moved downward to keep the world cotton price in line with its value in foreign currencies.

Government Policies

The most significant distortions in the world cotton market stem from the large subsidies that countries funnel to their domestic producers (see tables 5E.1 and 5E.2). In the 2001–02 crop year, almost three-quarters of global production was government subsidized. Though US subsidies constitute the bulk of government assistance (see appendix 5D), some experts contend that policy shifts in the Chinese cotton sector during the 1990s had a greater effect on world cotton prices.

During the mid-1990s, China subsidized its cotton producers by setting the internal price above world prices, while at the same time allowing some mills to import cotton. These policies had perverse effects: China's demand for foreign cotton kept world prices high even as the government accumulated a large surplus stock. But China implemented numerous

Table 5E.1 Worldwide government assistance to the cotton sector, 1997–98 to 2000–2001

Country	1997–98			1998–99			1999–2000			2000–2001		
	Production (thousands of tons)	Average assistance per pound produced (US cents)	Assistance to production (millions of US dollars)	Production (thousands of tons)	Average assistance per pound produced (US cents)	Assistance to production (millions of US dollars)	Production (thousands of tons)	Average assistance per pound produced (US cents)	Assistance to production (millions of US dollars)	Production (thousands of tons)	Average assistance per pound produced (US cents)	Assistance to production (millions of US dollars)
United States	4,092	7	597	3,030	22	1,480	3,694	25	2,056	3,742	12	1,020
Mainland China	4,602	20	2,013	4,501	27	2,648	3,829	18	1,534	4,420	20	1,900
Greece	340	88	659	357	84	660	435	62	596	421	58	537
Spain	116	83	211	104	89	204	132	68	199	94	86	179
Turkey				871	11	220	791	16	287	880	5	106
Brazil	412	3	29	521	5	52	700	3	44	939	2	44
Egypt	342	38	290				233	4	20	210	5	23
Mexico	209	3	13	219	3	15	135	9	28	72	9	14
All countries	10,113	17	3,812	9,603	25	5,279	9,949	22	4,764	10,778	16	3,822

Source: ICAC (2002, 9).

Table 5E.2 Worldwide government assistance to the cotton sector, 2001–02 and 2002–03

Country	2001–02 Production (thousands of tons)	2001–02 Average assistance per pound produced (US cents)	2001–02 Assistance to production (millions of US dollars)	2002–03 (preliminary) Production (thousands of tons)	2002–03 (preliminary) Average assistance per pound produced (US cents)	2002–03 (preliminary) Assistance to production (millions of US dollars)
United States	4,420	31	3,001	3,747	24	1,996
Mainland China	5,320	10	1,196	4,920	7	750
Greece	435	77	735	370	88	718
Spain	107	104	245	100	108	239
Turkey	922	3	59	900	3	57
Egypt	317	3	23	291	5	33
Côte d'Ivoire	173	2	8	150	4	14
Mexico	92	9	18	41	8	7
India	2,686	8	500	n.a.	n.a.	n.a.
Benin	172	5	20	n.a.	n.a.	n.a.
Mali	240	3	14	n.a.	n.a.	n.a.
Brazil	766	1	10	n.a.	n.a.	n.a.
Colombia	26	16	9	n.a.	n.a.	n.a.
Argentina	65	5	7	n.a.	n.a.	n.a.
All countries	15,741	17	5,844	10,519	16	3,814

n.a. = not available

Source: International Cotton Advisory Committee, 2003.

reforms in the late 1990s as it prepared for accession into the WTO. In 1997–98, imports fell by half; in 1999, it floated the internal price, which required the government to dispose of 3.5 million bales of excess stocks (Skelly and MacDonald 2003, 3). Thus, in the span of four years, China changed from being the world's cotton largest importer to a net exporter and remained relatively self-sufficient until 2002–03. China continues to subsidize domestic producers, though its lack of transparency prevents analysts from knowing the exact figures (most estimates range between $1 billion and $2 billion annually).

In addition to domestic support, some cotton-exporting countries maintain a policy of taxing cotton imports in the form of tariffs or tariff-rate quotas (TRQs). Argentina, Brazil, Egypt, India, Uzbekistan, and Zimbabwe impose tariffs on cotton imports ranging from 5 to 15 percent. The United States imposes a tariff of 4.4 cents/kilogram within quota and 31.4 cents/ kilogram outside quota (with a TRQ of 73,207 tons). China has a tariff of 3 percent within quota and 90 percent outside quota (with a TRQ of 856,250 tons).

Appendix 5F
The Impact of a 20 Percent Reduction in Overall Trade-Distorting Support: The United States, the European Union, and Japan

Table 5F.1   Impact of a 20 percent "down payment" reduction in trade-distorting support

Country	Actual spending, 2000	Permitted spending under July 2004 framework	After 20 percent "down payment"
United States (billions of dollars)			
Amber box	16.8	19.1	No cut required
Blue box	0	9.5	No cut required
De minimis	7.8	19.0	No cut required
Total trade distorting	24.6	47.6	38.1
Green box	49.7		No cap
European Union (billions of euros)			
Amber box	43.6	67.2	No cut required
Blue box	22.2	12.1	12.1
De minimis	0.7	24.2	No cut required
Total trade distorting	66.5	103.5	82.8
Green box	21.8		No cap
Japan (trillions of yen)			
Amber box	0.70	4.0	No cut required
Blue box	0.09	0.5	No cut required
De minimis	0.03	1.0	No cut required
Total trade distorting	1.0	5.5	4.4
Green box	2.6		No cap

Note: Numbers are based on each country's WTO notifications in 2000, the last year for which data are available for all three countries. Amounts are in local currencies.

Source: International Food and Agricultural Trade Policy Council, 2004.

Table 5F.1 illustrates the impact on the United States, the European Union, and Japan of a 20 percent "down payment" reduction in trade-distorting support (taking 2000 as the base year for the cuts). Japan would not have been required to make any cuts in amber, blue, or de minimis support to meet the overall reduction commitment. The European Union would have had to reduce blue box spending from 22.2 billion euros to 12.1 billion euros but would have had plenty of room in its amber box, or the green box, to which blue box subsidies would be shifted.

6

Agricultural Biotechnology Meets International Trade: The US-EU GMO Dispute

Part I: Technology and Regulation

In 1996, US farm exports reached record levels: At $60.4 billion, they totaled about 10 percent of the merchandise exported by the United States.[1] "One out of every three acres of America's farms is dedicated to exports," noted US Trade Representative (USTR) Charlene Barshefsky.[2] Around the same time, US farmers undertook the first commercial plantings of genetically modified (GM) crop varieties.[3] These crops were designed to be resistant to insect pests, herbicides (weed killers), and disease. Use of GM varieties—mainly of soybeans, corn, and cotton—skyrocketed in the United States. By 2000, about 54 percent of US soybean acreage and 25 percent of US corn acreage were planted with GM varieties. By 2004 approximately

---

Agricultural Biotechnology Meets International Trade: The US-EU GMO Dispute is an edited and revised version of the two-part case with the same name originally written by Charan Devereaux for the Case Program at the John F. Kennedy School of Government. For copies or permission to reproduce the unabridged case please refer to www.ksgcase.harvard.edu or send a written request to Case Program, John F. Kennedy School of Government, Harvard University, 79 John F. Kennedy Street, Cambridge, MA 02138.

1. Figures from Economic Research Service, United States Department of Agriculture, *Foreign Agricultural Trade of the United States (FATUS) Export Aggregations,* www.ers.usda.gov.

2. Testimony of Ambassador Charlene Barshefsky, United States Trade Representative, before the Senate Committee on Agriculture, Nutrition and Forestry, 105th Cong., 1st sess., June 18, 1997. Barshefsky also noted that the US agricultural trade surplus was $27 billion in 1996—the largest in history—making the agricultural sector the largest positive contributor to the US balance of trade.

3. The term *genetically modified* is not an entirely accurate descriptor. The process of genetic modification has taken place for thousands of years, via controlled breeding.

Table 6.1 Total US crop acreage in biotechnology varieties, 1996–2004
(percent)

Crop	1996	1997	1998[a]	1999	2000	2001	2002	2003	2004
Soy	7.4	17.0	44.2	55.8	54	68	75	81	85
Corn	n.a.	n.a.	n.a.	n.a.	25	26	34	40	45
Bt	1.4	7.6	19.1	25.9	18	18	22	25	27
Ht	3.0	4.3	18.4	n.a.	6	7	9	11	13
Stacked	n.a.	n.a.	n.a.	n.a.	1	1	2	4	5
Cotton	n.a.	n.a.	n.a.	n.a.	61	69	71	73	76
Bt	14.6	15.0	16.8	32.3	15	13	13	14	16
Ht	2.2	10.5	26.2	42.1	26	32	36	32	30
Stacked	n.a.	n.a.	n.a.	n.a.	20	24	22	27	30

n.a. = not available

a. 1998 estimates for corn and cotton include acreage and production with stacked varieties (with both Bt and Ht genes).

Note: Bt = insect-resistant. Ht = herbicide-tolerant. Stacked gene varieties include those containing biotechnology traits for both herbicide and insect resistance.

Sources: For 1996–99: Fernandez-Cornejo and McBride (2000, 13; 2002, iv, 10). For 2000–2004: National Agricultural Statistics Service (NASS), US Department of Agriculture, *Acreage,* June 30, 2000; June 29, 2001; June 28, 2002; June 30, 2003; June 30, 2004.

85 percent of US soybean acreage and 45 percent of US corn acreage were planted with genetically engineered varieties (see table 6.1). In addition, about 75 percent of the processed food sold in the United States contained ingredients derived from GM crops.[4] Canada and Argentina also adopted GM crops.[5]

After some public debate, GM foods were generally treated the same as non-GM foods by the US regulatory system. But not all countries were as quick to embrace agricultural biotechnology. The European Union developed a separate regulatory approach for GM products, including a different approach toward risk. Resistance to the technology grew in Europe, and many consumer groups, environmentalists, nongovernmental organizations (NGOs), and politicians rejected genetically modified organisms (GMOs). In the end, the European Union placed a de facto moratorium on the approval of new GM products, frustrating US exporters. As the use of GM technology increased in the United States, US corn sales to the European Union declined from 4 percent of total US corn exports before 1997 (generating about $300 million) to less than 0.1 percent in 2004.[6]

4. Pew Initiative on Food and Biotechnology, "US vs. EU: An Examination of the Trade Issues Surrounding Genetically Modified Food," December 2005, 1.

5. Of the 120 million acres of GM crops planted worldwide in 2002, the United States grew 68 percent; Argentina, 22 percent; Canada, 6 percent; and China, 3 percent (see Pringle 2003, 2).

6. Pew Initiative on Food and Biotechnology (2005, 4).

Some US government officials and agribusiness industry representatives argued that the European Union's approach to agricultural biotechnology amounted to protectionism—that Europe had erected barriers to impede trade. Without scientific proof that GM crops caused harm to human health or the environment, how could Europe reject these products? Others noted that though European GM policies restricted trade, they did not amount to a simple case of protectionism. Instead, the European Union's de facto moratorium and more recent strict GM legislation resulted from consumers' lack of confidence in regulators, demands for choice, and suspicion of big business, as well as ethical and environmental considerations, growth of the green and consumer movements, and tensions related to internal EU politics.

The US government continued to pressure Europe to enact reliable regulations based on science and to resume the approval and import of GM crop varieties. US frustration culminated in a complaint against the European Union at the World Trade Organization (WTO), launched in May 2003. But in anticipation of such a complaint, both the European Union and the United States had worked to enshrine their approaches to GMOs in relevant international institutions. Debate had been ongoing for years at the Codex Alimentarius Commission (the international food standards body), at the WTO, and in negotiations for a Biosafety Protocol.

As these debates continued, some observers noted that the US-EU dispute had distracted the international community from a more important goal. It was poorer tropical countries that had the most to gain from engineered seeds, they argued. Resources should be directed not to transatlantic debate but to funding public agricultural research to develop GM crop varieties for the nations that needed them the most.

A History of Innovation

Genetic modification was not the first new technology to transform the practice of agriculture. In the early part of the 20th century the important developments were mechanical. US farmers started adopting gasoline-powered tractors in 1910, replacing horses and mules. Later came other farm machinery such as self-propelled harvesters. The manufacture and use of farm machinery increased steadily in the United States until the 1960s, when they leveled off.[7]

Mechanical advances in agriculture were followed by chemical and biological innovations. Chemical engineering brought synthetic fertilizers, herbicides, and pesticides. For example, in 1974, Monsanto Company introduced Roundup, a broad-spectrum herbicide sprayed on fields before

---

7. See National Agricultural Statistics Service (NASS), USDA, *Trends in US Agriculture,* at www.usda.gov.

or after harvest to kill weeds, which would become the world's best-selling agricultural chemical of all time.[8] Meanwhile, plant-breeding techniques such as hybridization (breeding between two varieties of plants) were used to create heartier or healthier crops, making food production more efficient. Double-cross hybrid corn varieties designed to increase yields were introduced in the 1930s.[9] By 1960, hybrid corn accounted for 96 percent of US corn acreage.[10]

As a result of these mechanical, chemical, and plant-breeding technologies, agricultural output per acre and per worker increased dramatically in the developed world, and the real price of food dropped. Many countries achieved a 30-fold increase in crop production between the 1930s and 1960s (Bernauer 2003, 28). A number of the plant-breeding breakthroughs of the 1960s and 1970s also spread to some developing nations. The increase in food production caused by the introduction and diffusion of new wheat and rice varieties in Asia became known as the "green revolution."[11]

In addition to its impact on agriculture, plant hybridization also provided the foundation for modern genetics. In the mid-1800s, an Augustinian monk named Gregor Mendel traced the characteristics of successive generations of pea plants in his monastery's garden. By crossbreeding plants over seven years, Mendel proved the existence of paired units of heredity—now called genes—and established the statistical laws governing them, leading to his 1865 paper "Experiments in Plant Hybridization."

Scientists' understanding of genetics continued to grow at an increasing rate. In 1944, Oswald Avery identified deoxyribonucleic acid, or DNA, as the substance associated with the storage and transfer of genetic information. In 1953, James Watson and Francis Crick described the structure of a DNA molecule. By 1973, scientists had successfully transferred DNA from one organism to another. Out of this event grew a new technique—recombinant DNA technology—that would become the most important tool of genetic engineering. To create a recombinant DNA molecule, one gene or, most commonly, a set of a few genes is taken out of the DNA of one organism and inserted into the DNA of another.[12] The new genes,

---

8. David Barboza, "Monsanto Struggles Even as It Dominates," *The New York Times*, May 31, 2003, C1.

9. In addition, Congress passed the Plant Patent Act in 1930, enabling the products of plant breeding to be patented.

10. National Agricultural Statistics Service, USDA, *Trends in US Agriculture*.

11. This "revolution" largely missed Africa. For example, between 1970 and 1983, new high-yield rice varieties spread to about 50 percent of Asia's rice lands but only 15 percent of sub-Saharan Africa (Paarlberg 2000, 24).

12. Enzymes are used to break the DNA strand, a vector is used to carry the new genes to the strand, and after the new segments are inserted, the strand is "stitched" back together.

which code for specific proteins, allow the expression of a desired trait in the recipient organism.

With the discovery of recombinant DNA techniques came new questions. Were there hazards associated with such research? Should recombinant DNA research be restricted or regulated? At first, some scientists were cautious. In 1974, the biologist Paul Berg along with 10 other genetic researchers published a letter in the journals *Science* and *Nature* asking scientists throughout the world to join them in "voluntarily deferring" certain types of experiments "until the potential hazards of such recombinant DNA molecules have been better evaluated or until adequate methods are developed for preventing their spread" (Berg et al. 1995, 512). In 1975 scientists from all over the world came together at a conference in Asimolar, California, to discuss the possible risks associated with recombinant DNA. Members of the public worried that use of this new technology could create dangerous "mutant" organisms that might escape the laboratory or harm researchers. For example, in 1976, the mayor of Cambridge, Massachusetts, urged Harvard University to halt the construction of a genetics lab out of fear that strains created by biologists might spread incurable disease. Lawmakers "better hurry up and pass laws to control what goes on—and what crawls out of—these laboratories," Mayor Alfred Vellucci said.[13] Critics also wondered if researchers should be "tampering" with nature.

Regulating Agricultural Biotechnology in the United States

Government oversight of biotechnology in the United States began in the mid-1970s when scientists asked the National Institutes of Health (NIH) to create a set of laboratory safety guidelines for biomedical research using recombinant organisms. In 1976 the NIH published guidelines for laboratories conducting federally funded experiments (the guidelines did not cover private industry, an omission that some observers protested). In the years that followed, the guidelines were revised and relaxed as more experiments and organisms were shifted to lower-risk categories (Office of Technology Assessment 1991, 173). As safety problems with recombinant DNA research in the lab failed to materialize, public concern declined. By the early 1990s, most recombinant DNA research in the United States was exempt from review and subject to minimal restrictions.

While the controversy over the hazards of recombinant DNA research waned, a debate began over how to regulate the uses of that research. By

---

13. Velluci, quoted in "Scientists Say Law Is Needed to Regulate Genetic Research," *The Washington Post*, March 8, 1977, A6. The mayor was unsuccessful in persuading the Cambridge city council to pass an ordinance outlawing all research that combined genetic material of different species.

the early 1980s, it was becoming clear that genetic engineering would play a major role in agriculture. In 1982, scientists at Monsanto pioneered the modification of a plant cell's genetic structure.[14] New genetic information could be added to plant DNA to form new proteins, creating new traits. Genetically engineered crop plants designed to resist insects and herbicides were soon ready to be field-tested. The first such test, of genetically engineered tobacco, took place on a Wisconsin farm in 1986. Agracetus, the company conducting this first test, would not disclose the site's location because it feared protesters might sabotage the experiment.[15]

Some observers believe that early objections raised in the United States to genetic engineering were significant in the history of the US-EU GM dispute. According to Robert Paarlberg, a professor of political science at Wellesley College and an associate at the Weatherhead Center for International Affairs at Harvard University,

> In the United States, we went though a period of public and open debate about genetic modification in the 1970s and the 1980s. Even here at Harvard, I remember when Harvard genetically engineered its own mouse for laboratory experiments; there were enormous anxieties about the consequences of doing this. Anti-GM activist groups were trying to stop the planting of test plots of genetically modified strawberries. The European Union didn't have the same type of early public debates about these technologies as the United States.[16]

At the same time, researchers and industry were looking to the government for guidance on the use of agricultural biotechnology. Some industry executives believed that government regulation was a key part of a strategy to gain public acceptance of GM technology. "We recognized early on that while developing lifesaving drugs might be greeted with fanfare, monkeying around with plants and food would be greeted with skepticism," said Earle Harbison Jr., Monsanto's president and chief operating officer from 1986 to 1993.[17] Two industry associations were created, the Industrial Biotechnology Association (in 1981) and the Association of Biotechnology Companies (in 1983), which by the end of the 1980s had hundreds of members; these groups would merge in 1994 to form the Biotechnology Industry Organization (Cantley 1995, 535). Congress also showed some initial interest in legislating restrictions on biotechnology.

---

14. Monsanto's scientists genetically modified both petunia and tobacco cells to make the host plants and their offspring resistant to an antibiotic.

15. Keith Schneider, "Gene-Altered Tobacco Is Planted in Wisconsin," *The New York Times*, May 31, 1986, 9. Agracetus was jointly owned by the Cetus Corporation and W. R. Grace & Company.

16. Unless otherwise noted, all quotes from Robert Paarlberg come from a 2004 interview with the author.

17. Harbison, quoted in Kurt Eichenwald, "Redesigning Nature: Hard Lessons Learned; Biotechnology Food: From the Lab to a Debacle," *The New York Times*, January 25, 2001, A1.

In response to the growing calls for policy coordination, the Reagan administration established an interagency working group under the cabinet council of economic affairs and charged it with drafting an overall federal framework for regulating biotechnology. Some suggest that by convening a group under White House auspices, thereby ensuring that meetings would not be open to the public, the administration was able to avoid public oversight (Vogel 2001, 4). The working group first circulated a set of guidelines for comment in December 1984. In June 1986, with the approval of President Reagan, the *Coordinated Framework for Regulation of Biotechnology* was published in the *Federal Register*.[18] The Coordinated Framework remains the key US government document on biotechnology.

Under the Coordinated Framework, the administration decided that products of biotechnology would generally be regulated in the same way as products of other technologies, using existing health and safety laws; no new legislation was required.[19] "No new legislation was needed, because experts agreed with the National Academy of Sciences' recommendations that there were enough provisions in existing laws to deal with agricultural biotechnology," says Dr. Isi Siddiqui, former senior trade advisor to US Department of Agriculture (USDA) Secretary Dan Glickman. "So US agencies would adopt regulations pursuant to existing acts. These laws were the backbone of the Coordinated Framework."[20]

Agencies that were responsible for regulatory oversight of certain products were now also responsible for evaluating the same kinds of products that were developed using genetic engineering. Thus, for agricultural biotechnology, the Environmental Protection Agency (EPA), the USDA's Animal and Plant Health Inspection Service (APHIS), and the Food and Drug Administration (FDA) would have authority over different aspects of GM product regulation. The USDA would check that GM plant varieties were safe to grow; the FDA would check that GM food and plants were safe to eat (for both humans and animals); and the EPA would monitor GM crops that produced their own pesticides. The USDA was also tasked with issuing licenses for the field-testing of food crops before their

---

18. "1986 Coordinated Framework for Regulation of Biotechnology," *United States Federal Register* 51 (June 26, 1986): 23302–93.

19. The framework noted "upon examination of the existing laws available for the regulation of products developed by traditional genetic manipulation techniques, the working group concluded that, for the most part, these laws as currently implemented would address regulatory needs adequately" ("1986 Coordinated Framework for Regulation of Biotechnology," 23302).

20. Unless otherwise noted, all quotes from Isi Siddiqui come from a 2005 interview with the author. Siddiqui is now a vice president of science and regulatory affairs at CropLife America, which represents companies that produce, sell, and distribute almost all the crop protection and biotechnology products used by US farmers. In this interview, he was speaking in a personal capacity and not on behalf of CropLife America or its member companies.

commercial release.[21] Moreover, the framework established the Biotechnology Science Coordinating Committee, an interagency committee chaired by the National Science Foundation that was responsible for continuing policy coordination.

The Business of Agricultural Biotechnology

The potential benefits of GM technology for agriculture created much excitement in industry, and interest increased when the Supreme Court extended patent protection to new types of plants in 1980. "Only after the Court guaranteed the protection of intellectual property rights did private corporations make the substantial investments necessary to develop commercially attractive transgenic crops," notes Robert Paarlberg (2000, 24).

While traditional crossbreeding could be time-consuming—sometimes several generations of breeding were required before the desired plant emerged—genetic engineering techniques made possible faster and more precise development of new crop varieties. Genetic engineering also increased the range of available traits: Because genes could be introduced from unrelated species, new varieties might be created that traditional breeding methods never could have produced. For example, one popular strain of GM corn (Bt) includes genes from the soil bacteria *Bacillus thuringiensis*. Like the bacteria, Bt corn produces a toxin that kills some insects—notably the corn borer, which annually destroyed about 7 percent of the world's corn crop.[22] Supporters of agricultural biotechnology saw many possibilities for higher crop yields, lower pesticide use, greater food security in the developing world, increased profits for farmers, and more nutritional food.

In the end, the GM plants that entered mass production in the United States were those whose traits led to commercial or production advantages that appealed to farmers (such as cheaper weed and insect control), as opposed to those whose traits directly benefited consumers (such as increased nutritional value). There were thus two main categories of genetically engineered crops: herbicide-tolerant (i.e., crops modified to resist the effects of common weed killers) and insect-resistant.

The companies involved in agricultural biotechnology included DuPont, W. R. Grace, Pioneer Hi-Bred, Ciba (which later became part of Novartis), and Dow/AgroSciences. For example, Ciba became the first

---

21. The relevant laws were the Plant Pest Act, which regulates crops and microbes that might be plant pests; the Federal Insecticide, Fungicide, and Rodenticide Act, which requires EPA to regulate the sale and use of pesticides in the United States; the Toxic Substances Control Act; and the Food, Drug, and Cosmetic Act.

22. Jenny Luesby, "Patents Wars over High-Tech Seeds," *The Financial Times*, March 22, 1996, 3. In 1995, the corn borer knocked out almost 30 percent of Canada's corn harvest.

company to market and sell GM corn in the United States when it introduced its Bt corn—the Maximizer hybrid with Knockout corn borer control—in 1995.[23] In 1996, Pioneer Hi-Bred, the largest US seed company, was forecasting that transgenic products would account for one-third to one-half of its seed lines by 2000[24] (Pioneer Hi-Bred was acquired by DuPont in 1999). US companies were not alone in engaging with agricultural biotechnology: Switzerland's Novartis and Britain's Zeneca (which merged in 2000 to become Syngenta) sold seeds resistant to herbicides, as did Germany's AgrEvo and France's Rhône-Poulenc (which merged in 1999 to form Aventis).

But the company that became most identified with GM crops was American: St. Louis–based Monsanto. Founded by a chemist in 1901 to manufacture the artificial sweetener saccharin, Monsanto would become a big supplier of plastics, chemicals, and synthetic fabrics before developing the two herbicides, Lasso and Roundup, that turned it into the most profitable agricultural company in the world. Monsanto first became active in biotechnology in the early 1980s. Starting in 1992, Monsanto began to reinvent itself as a life sciences company. In 1996, it announced plans to spin off its chemical operations and dedicate itself fully to biotechnology. By 1999, Monsanto had invested more than $8 billion to buy seed companies and close marketing agreements with some of its largest competitors, making a greater commitment to producing genetically modified crops than any other organization in the world (Specter 2000, 60).

In 1985, company scientists developed Monsanto's first product that relied on genetic modification—a hormone called recombinant bovine somatotropin (rbST), which was designed to increase milk production in cows by 10 to 25 percent. Produced by genetically engineered bacteria, it was marketed under the name Posilac. The FDA approved its use in 1993, noting that there was no significant difference in milk from cows treated with the hormone and milk from untreated cows. The hormone bovine somatotropin (bST) occurs naturally in milk because cows produce it. Recombinant bST was "a safe and effective product when used as indicated on its approved label," an FDA spokesman said.[25]

But rbST became the focus of what many describe as the first battle over biotech foods. Its introduction was accompanied by controversy as protests were voiced by consumers who were wary of potential health risks both to humans and cows. Concerns about cows ranged from increased udder in-

<hr/>

23. Timeline at www.syngenta.com (accessed in November 2004). Ciba and Sandoz merged in 1996 to become Novartis (one of the largest corporate mergers in history), and Novartis Agribusiness and Zeneca Agrochemicals merged in 2000 to become Syngenta.

24. Barnaby J. Feder, "Out of the Lab, a Revolution on the Farm," *The New York Times*, March 3, 1996, section 3, 3.

25. Sharon Schmickle, "FDA Stands Behind BST After Canada Bans Growth Hormone," *The Star Tribune* (Minneapolis), January 16, 1999, 14A.

fections to infertility. Mothers wrote op-ed pieces worrying about the safety of the milk they gave their children.[26] As a result, some questioned the wisdom of introducing rbST as the first major agricultural biotechnology product. "From the point of view of the many advances of the biotechnology industry, this was an unfortunate product to lead with, in the sense that the public doesn't perceive a benefit from it or feel it has control over whether it uses it," said Dr. C. Wayne Callaway, a spokesman for the Dairy Coalition, which represented milk producers and processors.[27]

Yet efforts by US consumer groups had little success in insisting that milk produced from cows treated with rbST should be so labeled. While companies could voluntarily label products as produced from cows that had not been treated with the hormone, they could not tout their milk as "bST free." Much of the consumer protest had subsided by 1996, though debate continued in California, Maine, Vermont, and some other dairy states. By the beginning of 1999, according to Monsanto, about 30 percent of US dairy cows, or around 2.7 million animals, were in herds supplemented with Posilac.[28] The product was not sold in Europe, however, where a moratorium was declared on rbST in 1990. Canada banned rbST in 1999 because of concerns about animal health.

Monsanto also developed GM crop varieties, including corn and soybeans that were engineered to tolerate the use of its Roundup herbicide. Farmers purchasing Monsanto's GM seeds agreed not to resell the seeds, not to retain them without planting them, and not to collect seeds from the plants they grew. They also agreed to crop inspections by company representatives. Farmers who bought Roundup Ready seeds also paid a per-acre licensing fee and committed to using Roundup pesticide. In explaining the need for its fees and restrictions, Monsanto representatives told farmers that Monsanto had spent $500 million over the past 10 years just to develop Roundup-resistant crops.[29] Nor was Monsanto alone in the use of these technology fees; other companies followed the same practice. The adoption of Monsanto's pesticide- and herbicide-resistant corn, cotton, and soybeans in the United States increased from 14.5 million acres in 1997 to 46.5 million acres in 1998 to 68 million acres in 1999 (Leamon 2003, 14, exhibit 1).

Observers say that the quick embrace of GM crops was not hard to understand, given that they decreased the need for tillage and chemical

---

26. See Trisha Flynn, "Mother Knows Best: Leave Milk to the Cows and the Consumer, Please," *Rocky Mountain News* (Denver), April 17, 1994, 4M.

27. Callaway, quoted in Kathleen Day, "Hormone Hubbub Hinders Program; Genetic Drugs Dealt Setback in Foods," *The Washington Post*, March 15, 1994, D1.

28. George Gunset, "Growth Hormone Controversy Shrinks Higher Milk Production; Hasn't Hurt Profits," *The Chicago Tribune*, January 2, 1999, 1.

29. Feder, "Out of the Lab, a Revolution on the Farm."

sprays. Because most US farmers growing Roundup Ready soybeans cut their chemical costs by 10 to 40 percent, they profited. "While the seed companies made money, American farmers were the biggest winners, capturing roughly half of the total economic benefit from the new technology," notes Robert Paarlberg. "Patent-holders and seed companies gained only about a third of the added profits, while consumers got less than that" (2000, 24). Many farmers also believed that reducing their use of chemicals allowed them to deliver healthier crops. "Personally, I'd rather eat a bowl of cornflakes made from Bt corn than from regular corn," said Nebraska corn farmer Rick Gruber.[30]

Regulating Agricultural Biotechnology in Europe

As GM products were taking hold in the United States, Europe's approach to regulating agricultural biotechnology was evolving. In 1983, the European Commission became concerned that Europe was falling behind the United States and Japan in biotechnology development. That year, the Commission submitted a report to the European Council making clear its objective to increase the competitiveness of Europe's biotechnology industry (Patterson 2000, 320). In 1984, the Commission created a senior policy discussion group at the director-general (DG) level called the Biotechnology Steering Committee (BSC), chaired by DG XII (Science, Research, and Development). When it became clear that more technical discussions were needed, the committee established the Biotechnology Regulations Interservice Committee (BRIC) a year later.

The importance of the BSC faded and the BRIC became the main forum in the Commission for developing biotechnology regulation. The chair alternated between DG III (Industry) and XI (Environment).[31] The participating Commission directorates had different perspectives on GMOs. For example, DG XII (Science) argued that any regulation should be based on accumulated information about risks, not on unproven concerns. DG VI (Agriculture) and DG III (Industry) argued that existing regulations were adequate or could be adapted to address biotechnology products.[32]

In contrast, DG Environment viewed biotechnology more skeptically. It urged that Community-wide regulatory directives specifically for GMOs

---

30. Gruber, quoted in Scott Kilman, "Seeds of Doubt: Once Quick Converts, Farmers Begin to Lose Faith in Biotech Crops—DuPont and Others, Mindful Of Their R&D Billions, Struggle to Hold Ground—Prospects for Labeling Law?" *The Wall Street Journal*, November 19, 1999, A1.

31. The secretariat for the committee was DG XII's Concentration Unit for Biotechnology in Europe (CUBE) (Cantley 1995, 544).

32. This discussion of the positions of DG X11, DG IV, DG III, and DG XI on biotechnology is based on Patterson (2000, 327–28).

were necessary because "Microorganisms with novel properties could cause adverse effects in the environment if they survive and establish themselves, out-competing existing species or transferring their novel traits to other organisms."[33] In taking this stand, it dissented from a 1986 Organization for Economic Cooperation and Development (OECD) report, which noted that "there is no scientific basis for specific legislation to regulate the use of recombinant organisms."[34]

Up until this point, Commission communications on biotechnology were largely drafted by DG Science—the other DGs had seen "the mysteries of biotechnology as still playthings of DG XII and their scientific community," according to one former DG Science employee (Cantley 1995, 535, 543). But it was DG Environment that took the lead in drafting the November 1986 Commission report, "A Community Framework for the Regulation of Biotechnology," which laid out plans to introduce EC-wide regulatory proposals.[35] The report noted that some member states (including Denmark and Germany) had already moved to adopt national measures on biotechnology, thereby threatening the EC's single market.[36]

In May 1988, the Commission released drafts for two new directives on GMOs, one on safety procedures for laboratories and the other on the planned release of GMOs into the environment.[37] DG Environment was the *chef de file* for the directive on planned release, which would also deal with the marketing of GM foods and crops. In fact, DG Environment drafted most of the language with very little input from the other directorates general (Patterson and Josling 2002, 9). "Unlike in the US, where EPA's role had been limited, DG XI became the . . . responsible authority," note University of California at Berkeley's David Vogel and Diahanna

---

33. European Commission, DG XI/A/2 Biotechnology, *The European Community and the Contained Use of Genetically Modified Micro-organisms* (Brussels, 1988); quoted in Patterson (2000, 327).

34. OECD, "Recombinant DNA Safety Considerations" (1986); quoted in Cantley (1995, 550).

35. According to the report, the Commission's intention was to introduce proposals for Community regulation of biotechnology "with a view to providing a high and common level of human and environmental protection throughout the Community, and so as to prevent market fragmentation by separate unilateral actions by Member States." The report added, "microorganisms are no respecters of national frontiers, and nothing short of Community-wide regulation can offer the necessary consumer and environmental protection." European Commission, "A Community Framework for the Regulation of Biotechnology," November 4, 1986, vii, viii, quoted in Cantley (1995, 553).

36. In June 1986, Denmark adopted the Gene Technology Act.

37. Two directives would emerge from this effort—Directive 90/219, on the contained use of GMOs (which focused on safety procedures for the laboratory), and Directive 90/220, on the deliberate release of GMOs into the environment, which also dealt with the marketing of GM foods. This case will focus on Directive 90/220.

Lynch (2001). As *chef de file*, DG Environment was also able to determine how the proposed directive was presented to the Council of Ministers. It was the Council of Environmental Ministers that received the proposal.

The Commission's draft directive on deliberate release followed the approaches of Germany and Denmark in creating special and distinct regulations for the approval and marketing of GMOs (Shaffer and Pollack 2004, 17). The United States did not support this approach. "By basing the Directive on the technique by which the organism is modified, the EC is regulating organisms produced by a given process," noted one government statement.

> As expressed in the US Coordinated Framework for the regulation of biotechnology, the US generally regulates products rather than the process by which they are obtained. We are concerned whether differences in approaches and their implementation may lead to difficulties in our attempts to achieve international harmonization. It is important to understand that whether an organism is "unmodified" or "genetically modified" is, in itself, not a useful determinant of safety or risk.[38]

In August 1989, a number of companies involved in biotechnology expressed their concerns about the lack of overall coordination in the proposals to regulate biotechnology and argued the need for science-based regulations based on the safety of the product, not the process by which it was made, in a letter sent to EC President Delors and the commissioners. But the group—the Senior Advisory Group for Biotechnology (SAGB)—was not organized in time to affect the passage of the directives (see Patterson 2000, 334).[39]

In April 1990, the European Council adopted the Deliberate Release Directive (90/220) creating a complicated approval procedure for GM crops. The directive required an environmental risk assessment to be carried out before any GM crop or food could be cultivated or placed on the market. Individual member states were given a significant role in the process. Any individual or firm seeking to market or cultivate a GM product was required to submit a request (with the completed risk assessment) to the member state in which it would first be marketed. That country would approve or reject the application. If it was approved, and if no objections were raised by the European Commission or other member states, then the product could be marketed throughout the European Community.

However, if the request was rejected or faced any objections, then the application would be forwarded to the European Commission. The Commission's decision would be voted on by a regulatory committee of

---

38. US Ambassador to the European Communities, "International Harmonization in the Biotechnology Field," July 7, 1989; quoted in Cantley (1995, 559).

39. The founding members of SAGB were Monsanto Europe, Hoechst AG, ICI PLC, the Ferruzzi Group, Rhône-Poulenc, Sandoz, and Unilever (Patterson 2000, 334).

member-state representatives. If a qualified majority of the committee supported the Commission's decision, it was approved.[40] If not, the decision would be forwarded to the Council of Ministers, where it could only be rejected by a unanimous vote. Failure to act by the Council in three months would result in the adoption of the Commission's decision. Finally, in a move that would become important later, Article 16 of the directive also allowed individual member-states to "provisionally restrict or prohibit the use and/or sale" of a GM product as a safeguard measure (on the approval process, see Shaffer and Pollack 2004, 19–20).

European Food Scares and the Introduction of GM Crops

In 1996, the year GM crops went into commercial production in the United States, food safety became a burning issue in Europe. The European Commission banned all exports of British beef in response to the appearance of bovine spongiform encephalopathy (BSE), popularly known as mad cow disease. The deadly brain disease had spread through British herds from processed cattle feed containing the ground-up remains of already-infected animals (using animal parts in feed was outlawed in 1996). The condition was transmissible as new variant Creutzfeldt-Jakob disease (nvCJD) to humans who ate brain or spinal material from afflicted animals. After a long incubation period that could extend decades, the disease induced dementia and death. Britain was forced to slaughter hundreds of thousands of cattle, and most countries banned imports of British beef. And because UK government officials had initially assured consumers that eating beef from diseased animals posed no danger, the mad cow outbreak also magnified Europeans' distrust in governments' abilities to monitor food safety. Robert Paarlberg sums up the result: "The believabilities and credibility of the European regulatory system was undercut." Similarly thrown into doubt were modern methods of industrial farming and food processing. In the end, the BSE crisis was a multibillion-dollar catastrophe for Europe.

Other questions about food safety and industrial farming methods were raised in 1996 when the United States brought a WTO case against the European Union over its ban on hormone-treated beef. In the United States, hormones were widely used to speed growth and lean-meat production in beef cattle. In 1989, Europe had banned the use of such hormones, effectively closing its market to US beef. To justify their position, some European officials invoked the "precautionary principle," claiming that it entitled the European Union to prohibit or restrict products that were suspected, but

---

40. A qualified majority is not a simple majority. Each member state is given a certain number of votes based on its population. As of November 2004, a qualified majority in the European Council is 232 votes out of a total of 321. A majority of the countries must also be in favor (see http://europa.eu.int).

not proved, to be hazardous. In addition, officials argued that European consumers had made clear their desire not to eat beef from cows raised with hormones. For its part, the United States argued that the European Union was protecting its beef market from foreign competition by invoking scientifically unsupported claims about the harmful effects of hormones. The case would be decided under the WTO's Agreement on Sanitary and Phytosanitary Standards (SPS), which mandated that measures taken by member countries to protect human, animal, or plant health or life must follow international standards or be based on science.

Interestingly, not every GM food introduced to Europe met resistance. In 1996, GM tomato puree was sold in the United Kingdom by Safeway and Sainsbury's supermarkets. Marketed by the UK-based Zeneca Group,[41] the puree was made with GM tomatoes designed to produce more pectin and less water, thereby reducing the need for heat treatment and concentration before canning. The production advantages were transferred to consumers in the form of cost savings (Bernauer 2003, 24).[42] Safeway and Sainsbury's did not try to hide the technology—in fact, a prominent label on each can informed shoppers that the puree was made from "genetically modified" tomatoes. The Safeway label explained, "This modification helps the farmer to harvest the crop at the best time, which in turn leads to a more usable, ripe fruit. Less energy is used in processing these tomatoes when compared to non-modified types." Initial sales were brisk; by early 1998, more than 1.6 million cans of the puree had been sold.[43]

The European Union first approved a GM crop in May 1996: Roundup Ready soybeans, soon followed by Novartis's Bt corn. Using a gene that conferred resistance to its Roundup herbicide, Monsanto had developed the soybeans to yield larger harvests at lower costs. One of the first projects of Peter Scher, the new chief of staff at the Office of the USTR and later the special trade ambassador for agriculture, was to monitor the European approval process. "I stayed up all night trying to get a Portuguese minister to vote 'yes,'" he remembers.[44] The Advisory Committee on Novel Foods and Processes within the British Ministry of Agriculture, Fisheries,

---

41. Zeneca Group would later merge with the Swedish drug company Astra to become AstraZeneca.

42. Zeneca officials announced that the product would be 10 percent cheaper than conventional tomato puree. According to British news reports, a 170-gram can of the GM puree cost 29p, which would buy only 140 grams of the traditional product ("On Sale Now, the Puree Taste of the Future," *Daily Mail*, February 5, 1996, 7).

43. Paul Durman, "Sales of Modified Tomato Puree a Success," *The Times* (London), February 18, 1999. See also Alison Goddard, "A Puree Genius at His Work; Interview with Don Grierson," *The Times Higher Education Supplement*, July 17, 1998, 16.

44. Unless otherwise noted, all quotes from Peter Scher are from a 2005 interview with the author. Scher served as USTR chief of staff from 1995 to 1996 and USTR special trade ambassador for agriculture from 1997 to 2000.

and Food noted that the flour and oil made from the soybeans contained no trace of the gene or the enzyme it produced and could be sold without special labeling. "The flours produced by ordinary soya and the genetically modified form are indistinguishable," said Professor Derek Burke, the committee's chairman.[45]

Within months, however, European consumer and environmental groups had taken a stand against Roundup Ready soybeans as "their main line of resistance against a coming wave of bioengineered crops," according to the *New York Times*.[46] In the end, Greenpeace and Friends of the Earth—the two largest environmental interest groups in Europe—would make campaigning against GM foods one of their top priorities. Groups like Greenpeace believed that scientific understanding of the impact of GMOs on the environment and human health was inadequate. Once these organisms were released into the environment and the food chain, the organization argued, there was no way of recalling them. Critics also voiced continuing ethical concerns about the transfer of genetic material across different species and worried about decreasing biodiversity.

In November 1996 Greenpeace sent out a barge in an attempt to block the freighter *Ideal Progress*, which contained the first shipment of Roundup Ready soybeans, but the freighter successfully docked in Hamburg, Germany. In Germany, Unilever, Nestlé Deutschland A.G., and other packaged-food companies pledged not to use the Monsanto soybeans. While many companies, including Swiss-based Nestlé S.A.—the parent of Nestlé Deutschland—stressed their commitment to the new products and saw their acceptance as inevitable, they were worried about consumer response. "The soya bean has wide-ranging approval and in our assessment it is safe," said Frank Vanooyen, a spokesman for Unilever in the Netherlands. "But the fact remains we are a consumer-driven company, and therefore we leave the decision up to our operating companies on a country-by-country basis."[47]

Controversy also grew over the approval of Novartis's Bt corn. In April 1997, the European Parliament challenged the Commission's decision to approve the corn, and called on the Commission not to implement that approval pending further investigation. "Most disturbingly for the European Union, whose internal market provides for the free movement of goods (including agricultural goods)," notes the European academic Thomas Bernauer, "some EU countries imposed unilateral restrictions or bans on GM products that had been cleared by the European Union" (2003, 45). In-

---

45. Burke, quoted in Nigel Hawkes, "Superbean Leads Shops into Battle with Gene Scientists," *The Times* (London) August 21 1996.

46. Youssef M. Ibrahim, "Genetic Soybeans Alarm Europeans," *The New York Times*, November 7, 1996, D1.

47. Information about Nestlé and Vanooyen, quoted in Ibrahim, "Genetic Soybeans Alarm Europeans," D1.

deed, Austria, Italy, and Luxembourg banned the importation of the corn under the 90/220 safeguard clause.

It was in this environment that the European Parliament and Council turned to making rules for foods containing or produced from GM crops. On May 15, 1997, these rules came into force under the Novel Foods and Novel Food Ingredients Regulation 258/97, which supplemented but did not replace Directive 90/220. A "novel food" was defined as one that was hitherto unknown in Europe. The regulation created an approval process for such foods that was similar to the approval process of Directive 90/220.[48] It also mandated that foods containing or derived from GMOs be so labeled, but it failed to define a threshold percentage of GM ingredients a product could contain before triggering this requirement. In addition, the regulation did not apply to granted or pending approvals such as Bt corn or Roundup Ready soybeans (Bernauer 2003, 47). Dissatisfied, some countries started to introduce their own labeling regulations. In response, fearing that such unilateral actions could confuse consumers and distort the European Union's single market, in September 1997 food safety representatives from the 15 member states unanimously passed additional regulations requiring labels for foods produced from the Bt corn and GM soybeans that were already on the market.[49]

Clearly, one of the challenges of introducing GM products in Europe was the mixed response to the technology. Some Europeans took note of the "astonishing multitude of reactions [among EU member states] to the challenges that biotechnology presented in terms both of public debates as well as regulation" (Torersen et al. 2002, 24). As the debates and regulations continued to evolve, US officials became increasingly concerned about their trade implications for US producers of GM crops. "During the Clinton administration there was a lot of White House interest in this," remembers Peter Scher.

> It was very serious when you looked at how much was being grown within the United States. The failure to approve these [GM] products could have a significant impact on US farm exports. Moreover, one of the most important accomplishments of the Uruguay Round Agreement, which established the WTO, was the adoption of the SPS agreement, the Agreement on Sanitary and Phytosanitary Standards, which required countries to adhere to sound scientific principles in making these types of regulatory determinations. Prior to this, there were few tools available to address these types of issues. We felt that if the EU could ignore

---

48. Like Directive 90/220, the Novel Foods Regulation contained a safeguard clause that allowed member states to restrict or suspend the trade or use of a GM food. The regulation also established a simplified approval process for foods derived from, but not containing, GMOs, such as refined oils. These products could be placed on the market provided they were found "substantially equivalent" to existing conventional foods by the competent authority of a member state.

49. Neil Buckley, "EU Wants Labels for Genetically Modified Foodstuffs," *The Financial Times*, August 4, 1997, 1.

sound science in their regulatory process, it would be a signal to other countries that it was OK to do the same.

US industry was not happy about the European regulatory process. In September 1997, 48 US food industry companies and trade associations wrote to Scher, expressing frustration at the slow pace of EU approval of each new GM variety. "The length of the process was one concern, but the politicization was the bigger problem," says Scher.

> Companies that wanted to get approval for a new product had to go through a fairly lengthy process to provide data and other scientific information about these products. They played by the rules and they would meet the standards, but then you'd have European politicians saying, "No, we won't approve that." We weren't suggesting that the EU had to adopt the US regulatory regime. We just wanted a transparent and science-based regime that made sense.

Discussions with European officials about the GM approval process were sometimes challenging. "The problem when dealing with Europe is that there is not one person you can go to and bring your complaints," Scher observes.

> Many in the Commission agreed with us, but then you had the member states. The frustrating response I would get from some of the agriculture ministers and trade ministers was, "Our consumers don't want these products," which I always found to be a fairly bogus argument. The issue wasn't whether consumers would buy them, it was whether we had the right to try and sell them. From a trade policy perspective, if we are going to get into a situation where politicians can use what they believe is consumer acceptance or lack of acceptance as a basis for stopping trade, how do you control that? Think if we said, "US consumers don't like German cars. Sorry. We are not going to let you sell them." You can't have a trading system based on that principle.

The De Facto Moratorium

In the end, no food containing GMOs would be approved under the terms of Europe's 1997 Novel Foods Regulation.[50] Instead, the process ground to a halt in October 1998 when a number of member states led by France said they would block GM product approvals until safety and labeling rules were further tightened.[51] (Before 1998, 11 GM agricultural crops had been approved in the European Union.) In other words, the European Union effectively placed a moratorium on the approval of additional GM prod-

---

50. Though no food containing GMOs was approved under the regulation, some foods that were derived from but no longer contained GMOs themselves were approved after being found "substantially equivalent" to existing foods in "their composition, nutritional value, metabolism, intended use and the level of undesirable substances contained therein" (Article 3; quoted in Shaffer and Pollack 2004, 21).

51. Pew Initiative on Food and Biotechnology 2005, 10.

ucts. US trade officials were not completely surprised. "I think the moratorium had been building for years," Scher says. "Frankly, there was really an informal moratorium before the moratorium started." Though European Commission officials initially indicated that product approvals would resume, the process remained stalled.

In 1999, high-level discussions began between US government officials and the European Commission in an effort to resolve the growing trade dispute. "On one level it was helpful in terms of developing a dialogue between the US and the European Commission," remembers Scher. "But ultimately, the problem wasn't really the Commission. It was mostly the member states."

As negotiations continued, food scares featured prominently in the European media. In May 1999, following a TV report on contaminated animal feed in Belgium, European retailers began yanking from their shelves foods feared to have been tainted with dioxin. At the order of the Commission, Belgium destroyed huge quantities of chicken, dairy products, eggs, baked goods, and some beef products. Because Belgian government officials had reportedly known about the tainted feed, the dioxin crisis led to the resignations of Belgium's farm and health ministers, and ultimately toppled the incumbent Belgian government. The US response was to halt all EU poultry and pork imports, an action that some observers criticized as based more on fear than on fact. A *Journal of Commerce* editorial described the move as "ironic" in light of US diplomats' concurrent efforts to convince Europe that its fears about GM crops and growth hormones were rooted in emotion rather than science.[52]

In another incident, hundreds of people in Belgium and France, including children, reported feeling ill in June 1999 after drinking Coca-Cola products. In the company's largest-ever product recall, 17 million cases of Coke, Fanta, and Sprite were pulled off the shelves. Later, in 2001, English farms were hit by foot-and-mouth disease. The severe measures taken to quickly bring the outbreak under control included the slaughter of more than 4 million cattle, sheep, and pigs. Seventy countries imposed bans on importing UK animal products (Josling, Roberts, and Orden 2004, 89). These events also shaped opinions in Europe about the food regulatory system.

The European movement against GM food moved into full swing. In May 1999, Greenpeace launched its True Food campaign, which took aim at the release of GMOs into the environment. In a nationally publicized event in England, Greenpeace volunteers dressed in white decontamination suits entered a GM cornfield and attempted to cut down the crop and seal it in bags. In June, Prince Charles announced that he was barring new tenant farmers on his land from using GM products, pending further testing. "I happen to believe that this kind of genetic modification takes

---

52. "Global Food Panic," editorial, *Journal of Commerce*, June 9, 1999, 7.

mankind into realms that belong to God, and to God alone," the Prince of Wales said (quoted in Specter 2000, 58). Green Party representatives in member-state parliaments also rejected GMOs. However, some observers argued that GM products could actually help the environment, pointing out that farmers who planted insect-resistant crops would reduce their pesticide use.

In Europe, the primary target for concerns about biotechnology was the Monsanto Company. For one thing, Monsanto chose to be aggressive in pushing GM foods in Europe. Convinced of the merits of its products and faced with competition from other companies, the company used what some called a "legal approach" in its efforts to win product approvals. Observers also noted that Monsanto's enormous investment in GM crops made it a target. Lord Peter Melchett, who led Greenpeace's efforts to stop the use of GMOs, declared, "Of all the companies in this business, Monsanto is the most committed to agricultural biotechnology. They are no worse than DuPont. But DuPont can survive without genetically modified organisms, and I don't think Monsanto can. So we have had an opportunity with them that we did not have with anyone else" (quoted in Specter 2000, 63).

To improve public perceptions of GM foods, Monsanto began a $1.6 million advertising campaign in the United Kingdom and France (Vogel 2001, 9).[53] Monsanto invited European companies to participate in the campaign, but Zeneca, Novartis, and others declined. "Corporate-backed issue campaigns aren't the European way," noted the *Wall Street Journal*. In June 1998, a series of advertisements debuted in British newspapers. One ad featured hungry children in developing countries and stated, "While we'd never claim to have solved world hunger at a stroke, biotechnology provides one means to feed the world more effectively."[54] The company's public relations campaign did not have the desired effect; Monsanto continued to be a lightening rod in the biotechnology debate, and it admitted that it had acquired "bogeyman" status. "Greenpeace and so on are doing a much better job than we are," conceded Monsanto president Hendrik Verfaillie.[55]

More companies backed away from marketing GM foods. By July 1999, Sainsbury's had eliminated GM ingredients from its own store brands and both Sainsbury's and Safeway had withdrawn the GM tomato puree

---

53. By March 1999, Monsanto had spent an estimated $5 million on advertising and public relations activities related to GM foods in Europe (Nikki Tait and Vanessa Houlder, "Monsanto Admits Promotion of Modified Foods in Europe Has Backfired," *The Financial Times*, March 15, 1999, 18).

54. Scott Kilman and Helene Cooper, "Crop Blight: Monsanto Falls Flat Trying to Sell Europe on Bioengineered Food," *The Wall Street Journal*, May 11, 1999, A1.

55. Tait and Houlder, "Monsanto Admits Promotion of Modified Foods in Europe Has Backfired," 18.

that had initially sold so well (see Bernauer 2003, 24). Switzerland's Novartis also confirmed that it would stop using GM soy and corn in its Gerber brand baby food, not because it had any doubt about the safety of the genetically engineered crops but because buyers seemed to be wary of them (the company continued to sell GM seeds).

Concern about GM food was spreading to nations outside of Europe. Japan, South Korea, Australia, and New Zealand made plans to begin labeling some GM foods, including heavily imported products such as GM soybeans and GM corn, if intended for human consumption (Paarlberg 2000, 24). Many of these countries did not accept all of the GM varieties approved in the United States. In addition, some observers noted, the US approach to GMOs, in both government and industry, was evolving. In 1999, the EPA requested that farmers plant conventional crops around GM crops to act as a "buffer." And the USDA announced it was setting up an independent scientific review of its GM crop approval process in order to bolster public confidence and ensure consumer safety.[56] Also in 1999, Archer Daniels Midland Company, a major US grain processor, told farmers to begin efforts to segregate GM crops from conventional crops. Though "supportive of the science and safety" of GM crops, the company wanted to supply the growing number of overseas customers who were skeptical of such claims.[57]

Meanwhile, the EU Council began debating a new directive on the release of GMOs into the environment; it would replace Directive 90/220. In June 1999, the Environmental Council reached a political agreement, but some member states balked and demanded additional legislation. The Danish, Greek, French, Italian, and Luxembourgian delegations called for the labeling and traceability of GMOs and all GMO-derived products, declaring that "pending the adoption of such rules, in accordance with preventive and precautionary principles, they will take steps to have any new authorisations for growing and placing [GMOs] on the market suspended."[58]

During this time, the United States seriously considered bringing a case against Europe at the WTO. "We talked about it for a long time," says Scher, "but it didn't seem to make sense in 1999 and 2000." One issue was competing priorities. In 1999 the USTR was both negotiating a major market access agreement with China and preparing for the Seattle WTO ministerial. US officials were also concerned that filing a complaint at the WTO

---

56. David Barboza, "Monsanto Faces Growing Skepticism on Two Fronts," *The New York Times*, August 5, 1999, C1.

57. Scott Kilman, "ADM Warns Grain Suppliers to Start Segregating Genetically Altered Crops," *The Wall Street Journal*, September 2, 1999, A2.

58. "Declaration by the Danish, Greek, French, Italian and Luxembourg Delegations Concerning the suspension of new GMO authorizations," 2194th Council Meeting, Environment, Luxembourg, June 24/25, 1999.

could have the unintended consequence of extending the existing European moratorium. "The dilemma was that if you go to the WTO, you could just end up stopping the clock," Scher points out. "Going to the WTO takes a long time and the fear many officials had was that once we launched a complaint, it would just become an excuse for European officials to say, 'Well let's just hold off on everything until we hear what the WTO says.'"

Some also wondered what would be gained by bringing a case to the WTO. In its WTO case against Europe's ban on beef raised with growth-promoting hormones, the United States had emerged the winner. But the beef ban remained in place, even after the United States imposed punitive tariffs on $117 million of European food imports beginning in 1999. (WTO rules allow the unilateral imposition of trade sanctions only if the defendant refuses to comply after "losing" a case.) As former US ambassador to the European Union Richard Morningstar puts it,

> As I saw it at the time, the biggest problem with a WTO GMO case was: What happens if we were to win the case? It could be very similar to the beef hormone case where we won, some form of sanctions was awarded, but then the ban continued. If we won this case, would the EU be willing to try and force member states to allow GMOs, or would they just simply take the political decision to accept sanctions? So there was a reluctance to bring the GMO case and a hope that maybe the issue could be resolved.[59]

Yet, as some analysts note, the United States significantly benefited from the beef hormone case. Though Europe did not lift its ban, the US victory sent a strong signal to other countries, discouraging them from following the EU policy.

Observers perceived no unified push within industry to bring a WTO GMO case at the time. Interested groups ranged from the processed-food industry to seed companies to agricultural companies. "There were different stakeholders in the US who had differing views as to what to do," remembers Morningstar. "There were even different views within certain companies. For example, a government relations person in Washington would always take a maximalist view on the issue and would push the government to take action. A person at corporate headquarters might take a different view. And their representative in Europe might take a third view. I saw that in any number of instances."

US-EU efforts to solve the conflict continued. In May 2000, European Commission President Prodi and President Clinton agreed to launch another bilateral effort to solve the GM trade dispute—the EU-US Biotechnology Consultative Forum. The forum, composed of 10 US experts and 10 EU experts, was charged to "consider the full range of issues of concern in biotechnology in the United States and the European Union, most of which

---

59. Unless otherwise noted, all quotes from Richard Morningstar are from a 2004 interview with the author. Morningstar was US ambassador to the European Union from 1999 to September 2001.

relate to the use of modern biotechnology in food and agriculture" (EU-US Biotechnology Consultative Forum 2000, 4). Members included a Nobel Prize–winning agriculture scientist and representatives from biotech companies, environmental groups, agriculture associations, and academia.

In December, the forum issued its final report at the EU-US summit meeting. The report called for GM foods to be labeled and traced and urged a precautionary approach to protecting the environment and health. One of the recommendations read: "Consumers should have the right of informed choice regarding the selection of what they want to consume. Therefore, at the very least, the EU and US should establish content-based mandatory labeling requirements for finished products containing novel genetic material" (EU-US Biotechnology Consultative Forum 2000, 16). Some argued that this recommendation differed from FDA regulations, which required labeling of a GM product only if its nutritional value or other characteristics made it different from its conventional counterpart, but others disagreed, pointing to the term *content-based* (as opposed to *process-based*). In any case, according to many observers, the report would provide new ammunition to critics of biotechnology. One industry source noted that its "practical effect is to give license to those who want no risk at all."[60] Critics of labeling all foods produced from GM crops objected to the expense of such a requirement. US officials estimated that the need to separate GM and conventional foods at every step of production could increase costs by 10 to 30 percent (Paarlberg 2000, 24).

The Science

As debates over GM food gathered steam, scientists tended to agree that new risks to human health from currently marketed GM foods had not been found.[61] Some GM crops had been on the market for a number of years, and scientific evidence for any human health risks was negligible. As one historical overview noted, "Twenty-five years have elapsed without a single major accident caused by biotechnology" (Torersen et al. 2002, 22). While there were concerns about the potential for health problems in the future, such as the introduction of GM products that contained a human allergen, many NGOs chose not to make the human health risks of agricultural biotechnology the central component of their campaigns.[62]

---

60. "Expert Panel Recommends Strict Regime for Biotechnology," *Inside US Trade*, December 22, 2000.

61. These researchers included European scientists whose studies were published by the EU Directorate of Research, the Royal Society of London, and the French Academy of Sciences.

62. However, a new debate was growing about plants that were genetically modified to produce pharmaceuticals—some feared that traits from these plants could contaminate the food supply.

Some disagreement existed as to the long-term environmental risks of GM crops (Bernauer 2003, 27). In May 1999 John Losey, an entomologist at Cornell University, fed monarch butterflies milkweed dusted with pollen from Bt corn. Forty-four percent of the monarch larvae died, while the entire control group survived. The British journal *Nature* rejected the article documenting these results but carried a letter from the researchers (Losey, Raynor, and Carter 1999, 214). Some media reports of the findings were dramatic—a *Washington Post* headline read "Biotech vs. 'Bambi' of Insects? Gene-Altered Corn May Kill Monarchs."[63] But Losey himself noted that his study was not conclusive. "We need to look at the big picture here," he said. "Pollen from Bt corn could represent a serious risk to populations of monarchs and other butterflies, but we can't predict how serious until we have a lot more data. And we can't forget that Bt corn and other transgenic crops have a huge potential for reducing pesticide use [because farmers no longer have to spray in the old-fashioned way] and increasing yields."[64] Subsequent studies conducted by independent research teams under field conditions (not in the laboratory) found that Bt corn pollen posed a "negligible" risk to monarch butterfly populations.[65]

Critics of GMOs also underscored the potential for GM crop traits to be inadvertently introduced to other plants, such as weeds. Others worried about GM crop traits mixing with conventional crops, a process that some called "biotech pollution."[66] For example, in a front-page story in the *Wall Street Journal*, organic farmers in Europe and the US complained that their crops were being contaminated by GM varieties.[67]

---

63. Rick Weiss, "Biotech vs. 'Bambi' of Insects? Gene-Altered Corn May Kill Monarchs," *The Washington Post,* May 20, 1999, A3.

64. Clive Cookson, "Comment and Analysis—The Juggernaut and the Butterfly," *The Financial Times,* May 22, 1999, 13.

65. For example, see Mark K. Sears, Richard L. Hellmich, Diane E. Stanley-Horn, Karen S. Oberhauser, John M. Pleasants, Heather R. Mattila, Blair D. Siegfried, and Galen P. Dively, "Impact of Bt Corn Pollen on Monarch Butterfly Populations: A Risk Assessment," *Proceedings of the National Academy of Sciences,* 98, no. 21, Washington, DC, October 9, 2001, 11937-942. This 2-year study suggests that the impact of Bt corn pollen from current commercial hybrids on monarch butterfly populations is negligible.

66. Studies noted that the environmental effects of GM crops, such as gene transfer, were similar to those that existed for traditional agricultural crops. See G. J. Persley, The Doyle Foundation for The International Council for Science, "New Genetics, Food and Agriculture: Scientific Discoveries—Societal Dilemmas," The International Council for Science, June 2003, 29, www.icsu.org.

67. Scott Miller and Scott Kilman, "Out of the Lab: Biotech-Crop Battle Heats Up as Strains Mix with Others—Nations Seek Rules to Attempt to Keep Varieties Separate; Fears Hurt US Farmers—Mr. Ballarin's Tainted Corn," *The Wall Street Journal,* November 8, 2005, A1.

Agricultural Biotechnology and International Institutions

Codex Alimentarius Commission

Concerns about trade and GM foods spurred efforts to address agricultural biotechnology on the multilateral level. One organization that turned to the issue of GM foods was the Codex Alimentarius Commission. An international food standards body, Codex was established in 1962 by the UN Food and Agriculture Organization (FAO) and the World Health Organization (WHO). Its main goals were to protect the health of consumers, ensure fair practices in food trade, and coordinate food standards.

Codex moved into the spotlight when its standards and guidelines were recognized under the WTO's SPS agreement in 1994. Under the SPS agreement, WTO members had the right to take measures that protected health and life within their territories, but such measures could not be used to restrict international trade in arbitrary or unjustifiably discriminatory ways. The benchmarks for food safety standards, guidelines, and recommendations would be those established by Codex (see the SPS agreement in appendix 1C in chapter 1 and appendix 6B). While WTO members could set standards higher than the international Codex standard, they needed scientific evidence in order to do so. Codex's new role in world trade arguably made its deliberations subject to more political pressure.

Codex played an important role in the US-EU dispute over beef hormones. A scientific committee commissioned by Codex, the Joint FAO/WHO Expert Committee on Food Additives (JECFA),[68] concluded that residues of the growth-promoting hormones in meat did not create a safety hazard to humans as long as their use followed proper veterinary practice. In 1995, Codex representatives voted 33–29 to adopt standards on the hormones that were supported by the United States—though Europe lobbied hard to defeat them.[69] According to Lester Crawford, the former head of the FDA's Center for Veterinary Medicine and a US representative to Codex, the Codex vote "marginalized the Europeans for sure. They had staked a lot of political and Codex capital in their position. And once they lost that, then their side went into retreat and [the hormone case] was immediately referred to the WTO."[70] In 1997, as noted above, the WTO ruled against Europe in the beef hormones case, declaring that

---

68. JECFA is made up of independent scientists serving as individuals, not as representatives of their governments or other organizations.

69. The vote established maximum residue limits (MRLs) for the hormones in meat.

70. Crawford quoted in Chapter 1.

the European Union had not provided the scientific evidence necessary to impose rules stricter than the Codex standards.

Also in 1997, Codex failed to adopt a draft standard on rbST, the hormone produced by GM bacteria to increase milk production in cows. Setting a Codex standard for rbST was strongly opposed by Europe, and the issue was sent back to JECFA. After reevaluating the scientific data, JECFA concluded that milk produced by cows treated with rbST was safe for human consumption, but Codex remained divided over the hormone.[71] In 1999 and again in 2003, the EU perspective prevailed—unlike in the beef hormones case, where the US position won out—and the standard failed to be adopted; it remained parked at Step 8 of the eight-step Codex approval process. The United States reaffirmed its position that the establishment of a standard for veterinary drugs was a food safety issue and that maximum residue limits (MRLs) for rbST should be adopted.[72]

In 1999, Codex set up a task force to spend four years looking at GM foods. The stated goal of the Ad Hoc Task Force on Foods Derived from Biotechnology was to "develop standards, guidelines or recommendations, as appropriate, for foods derived from biotechnology or traits introduced in foods by biotechnology, on the basis of scientific evidence, risk analysis and having regard, where appropriate, to other legitimate factors relevant to the health of consumers and the promotion of fair trade practices."[73] European pressure led to the inclusion of "other legitimate factors" in addition to scientific evidence and risk analysis. The Codex task force, which was chaired by Japan, included not only scientists but also representatives from governments of Codex member countries, consumer and industry organizations, and international NGOs.

The group's first meeting was contentious. While US members argued that the task force should consider only science when evaluating the safety of foods derived from biotechnology, European members believed that additional issues should be taken into account. "Essentially the entire meeting was spent discussing what the task force should look at and what it should not look at," says a US Codex representative.

> The task force acknowledged that there was a raft of other issues such as labeling, ethics, animal welfare, consumer right to know, environmental concerns—all of these things that we agreed are important. But [the United States] said those issues are not within the mandate of Codex and therefore Codex should stick strictly to

---

71. JECFA also concluded that bST residue levels in milk were very low and that bST naturally found in milk is nontoxic. According to JECFA, no MRL was necessary when rbST was administered properly.

72. "Codex Holds Draft Maximum Residue Levels for BST at Step 8," *Food Chemical News* 41, no. 21, July 12, 1999.

73. FAO press release 00/16, "Codex Alimentarius Commission Task Force Opens Session to Develop Standards and Guidelines on Biotech Foods," March 14, 2000.

food safety. Everyone agrees what the safety questions are; it is all of these other issues that are much, much more difficult. In the end, the task force decided it would simply look at the science of evaluating the safety of foods derived through biotechnology.

It focused first on GM foods of plant origin (rather than animals or microorganisms). The scientific data were provided by the FAO and WHO, which set up independent expert consultations to offer advice on the safety and nutritional features of foods derived from biotechnology.

The Biosafety Protocol

Meanwhile, trade and GMOs were also being debated in negotiations under the auspices of the United Nations. Europe and some developing countries worked to include provisions on trade and biotechnology in the 1992 United Nations Convention on Biological Diversity. While these efforts were unsuccessful, language in the convention allowed participating governments to explore the need for a supplementary agreement on trade and GMOs that might harm biological diversity.

In the mid-1990s, European and other countries pushed to begin negotiations for such an agreement, later called the Biosafety Protocol (also known as the Cartagena Protocol).[74] Because the Senate had failed to ratify the Convention on Biological Diversity due to objections from a blocking minority, the United States could not formally participate in these talks. However, along with Canada, Australia, Uruguay, Argentina, and Chile—grain-producing nations known as the Miami Group—it blocked the first attempt to negotiate the Biosafety Protocol. In early 1999, the talks recommenced. The United States fought for language that would place the protocol under WTO authority, but the European Union joined many developing countries in thwarting this move. "When the protocol was negotiated, the United States and other members of the Miami Group worked hard to insert something called a savings clause into the protocol, which would have left the authority of the World Trade Organization unchallenged and intact," says Robert Paarlberg. "There would have been reference to the continued authority of the WTO, but the US could not get that savings clause inserted." As recalled by Calestous Juma, the former executive secretary of the Convention on Biological Diversity and now profes-

---

74. See the Cartagena Protocol on Biosafety to the Convention on Biological Diversity, Article I: "In accordance with the precautionary approach contained in Principle 15 of the Rio Declaration on Environment and Development, the objective of this Protocol is to contribute to ensuring an adequate level of protection in the field of the safe transfer, handling, and use of living modified organisms resulting from modern biotechnology that may have adverse effects on the conservation and sustainable use of biological diversity, taking also in account risks to human health, and specifically focusing on transboundary movements."

sor of the practice of international development at the John F. Kennedy School of Government, "Those countries that already had some biotechnology capacity lined up with the US but those that didn't defined it as a threat and lined with the Europeans."[75]

In the end, the United States came to support the Biosafety Protocol after ensuring that it would apply only to living modified organisms (LMOs), such as GM seeds for planting, and not GMO commodities used for processing and feed. In January 2000, more than 130 countries adopted the Biosafety Protocol, which would enter into force in September 2003. The European Union ratified it in 2002.

Unlike the WTO's SPS agreement, the Biosafety Protocol explicitly addressed the precautionary principle, stating in Article 10 that a "lack of scientific certainty" could justify a country's rejecting imports of LMOs.[76] "That is very different from the WTO standard," explains Paarlberg. "The SPS agreement says that you need to have a science-based risk assessment to back up any restrictions on imports. You can block imports on a provisional basis while you are gathering more information, but you can't block imports on a precautionary basis."[77]

Some observers believe that by enshrining such language in the Biosafety Protocol, Europe was building an international case for its approach to GM foods. Codex debated the significance of the Biosafety Protocol, and some members suggested that it should adopt similar language. "It has definitely been a point of contention," says a US Codex representative. For example, in 2001, the Codex Executive Committee issued a recommendation that Codex should ensure "coherence between Codex and texts arising from the Cartagena Protocol dealing with such matters as traceability, labeling and identification of Living Modified Organisms used as food."[78]

---

75. Unless otherwise noted, all quotes from Calestous Juma are from a 2005 interview with the author.

76. "Lack of scientific certainty due to insufficient relevant scientific information and knowledge regarding the extent of the potential adverse effects of a living modified organism on the conservation and sustainable use of biological diversity in the Party of import, taking also into account risks to human health, shall not prevent that Party from taking a decision, as appropriate, with regard to the import of the living modified organism in question as referred to in paragraph 3 above, in order to avoid or minimize such potential adverse effects" (Biosafety Protocol, Article 10.6; similar language appears in Article 11.4). See also Annex III, which deals with risk assessment: "Lack of scientific knowledge or scientific consensus should not necessarily be interpreted as indicating a particular level of risk, an absence of risk, or an acceptable risk."

77. Many in Europe claimed that Article 5.7 of the SPS agreement indirectly sanctioned the use of the precautionary principle by allowing members to take provisional measures to protect plant and animal health while they are conducting further scientific research.

78. "Codex Rejects EU Effort to Endorse Biotech Traceability, Labeling," *Inside US Trade*, July 27, 2001. See also "EU to Seek International Backing for Biotech Regulations," *Inside US Trade*, February 16, 2001.

The United States, with support from Argentina, Malaysia, and other countries, rejected the recommendation.

The World Trade Organization

Efforts to bring discussions about trade and biotechnology directly into the WTO were also under way. At the November 1999 WTO ministerial in Seattle, the United States and Canada sought to establish a biotechnology working party. Canadian officials noted that such a group was necessary to move the GMO debate out of nontrade arenas, such as the proposed Biosafety Protocol.[79] In a controversial move, EU Trade Commissioner Pascal Lamy initially agreed to the plan. European environmental groups and many member states were incredulous. "You didn't just shoot yourself in the foot. You machine-gunned yourself in the foot," Denmark's trade minister told Lamy. The environment ministers of France, the United Kingdom, Italy, Denmark, and Belgium issued a joint statement calling the Biosafety Protocol negotiations the only "proper forum for deciding a multilateral approach to biotechnology issues" and claiming that the talks would be undermined by the creation of the WTO working group. Greenpeace also criticized Agriculture Commissioner Franz Fischler for the move, declaring, "He will have a lot of explaining [to do] to the millions of citizens across Europe and the rest of the world who demand the right to choose not to swallow genetically-modified food." In response, the Commission released a statement noting that its priority remained the timely completion of the Biosafety Protocol and that no WTO working group would interfere with Europe's power to reject GM seeds on safety grounds. Lamy admitted, "We have taken flak from all sides . . . the Member States, parliamentarians, unions, businessmen. But that is my job."[80]

In the end, the Seattle ministerial collapsed and efforts to launch the working party did not move forward. According to sources speaking to *Inside US Trade*, Assistant USTR for Agricultural Affairs Jim Murphy told US agricultural and biotechnology groups that the United States had secured support for a WTO working group and had moved on to the question of how to formally propose this approach when the ministerial broke down.[81]

Around the same time, in September 1999, the European Commission formed a new directorate for health and consumer protection, which had

---

79. "US, Ag Interests Split on How to Tackle Biotech in WTO Round," *Inside US Trade*, September 24, 1999.

80. All quotations in the paragraph are from "EU/WTO: Seattle Delegates Grind Through Painful Agenda," *European Report*, no. 2456, December 4, 1999.

81. "US Seeks Biotech Deal in WTO, to Announce Group at Summit with EU," *Inside US Trade*, December 10, 1999.

a special responsibility for food safety. The directorate's first commissioner, David Byrne, had served as Ireland's attorney general and as one of the negotiators for the 1998 Good Friday Agreement that provided a framework for resolving hostilities in Northern Ireland. In his new role, Byrne attended the WTO ministerial in Seattle. During his time there, Byrne spoke to many US officials and left the ministerial with strong feelings about the need to clarify the European Union's position on the precautionary principle. As he remembers,

> Seattle was a very valuable few days for me because it was the very beginning of my time in the Commission. What struck me when talking to US government officials was the major concern about the application of the precautionary principle. I came back to Europe and spoke to my colleague [Environment] Commissioner Margot Wallström. I told her there was an enormous amount of confusion and distrust in the United States related to the precautionary principle and we should do something about it. And we did.[82]

Returning to Europe, Byrne and Wallström coauthored a communication on the precautionary principle in February 2000, setting out the circumstances under which it should be applied. The paper was welcomed by some in the United States, where the Commission's interpretation of the precautionary principle was viewed as more acceptable than that of some of the member states. As Richard Morningstar puts it,

> At the Commission, it was pretty clear that the precautionary principle could only be invoked when a specific risk was identified, that the action taken had to be proportional, time sensitive, and could only be invoked if there was some reasonable scientific evidence to support taking action—even if it was in the minority. Many member states believed the precautionary principle created an absolute right to ban a product just if there was concern.

Byrne also believed that the precautionary principle needed to be discussed at Codex. "It was my ambition to commence a debate in Codex about the precautionary principle and when it should be applied," he says. "That would feed into the SPS agreement and in turn would affect the operation of the WTO. And I have to say that I found it very much an uphill battle to get any discussion in relation to this issue. . . . I couldn't get the US to agree." In the Committee on General Principles, Codex members debated the role of the precautionary principle in risk analysis. For example, European countries hoped to insert a footnote to language outlining a country's ability to take interim health measures that referred directly to the precautionary principle, but the United States and Latin American

---

82. Unless otherwise noted, all quotes from David Byrne are from a 2005 interview with the author.

83. "Codex Rejects EU Effort to Endorse Biotech Traceability, Labeling," *Inside US Trade*, July 27, 2001.

countries objected.[83] (At Codex, Europe was represented by the member states.) Industry groups resisted the inclusion of any language referring to the precautionary principle, arguing that such a move by Codex could ultimately erode the protections offered by the SPS agreement at the WTO. These debates would continue for years to come.

StarLink

In the fall of 2000 GM corn hit the front pages in the United States and disrupted agricultural markets when a type of GM corn called StarLink turned up in laboratory tests of taco shells bought at grocery stores. StarLink was developed by Aventis CropScience of France to resist corn borer insects by producing a protein that acted as an insecticide. In 1998 the EPA had approved the corn for animal feed and industrial use but not for human consumption, concerned that the protein resembled some that were known human allergens. After environmentalists led by Greenpeace and Friends of the Earth demonstrated that segregation had broken down—the corn was found in more than 300 products—Aventis, working with the USDA, took aggressive steps to track down the StarLink corn and compensate its owners for any loss in value. Estimates of the damages to Aventis ran to half a billion dollars. The Centers for Disease Control was unable to confirm a single allergic reaction to the StarLink protein.

This incident highlighted two growing concerns about the challenge of keeping GM crops separate from conventional crops. First, there was the risk that bioengineered plants might accidentally pass on their modified traits through cross-pollination. Experts said that StarLink—which was planted on less than 0.02 percent of corn cropland in 2000—was most likely bred inadvertently into seed corn through the drift of pollen from other cornfields. Second, the grain-processing infrastructure was not designed to keep grains segregated. "The US system developed over 100 years to handle massive quantities of grain which are basically interchangeable in their suitability for all end uses," said James Bair of the North American Millers Association, a trade group then representing 45 US milling companies. "That system is fantastic in its ability to do that. But it's not very nimble when it comes to satisfying special needs."[84] As a result, some observers say, a key lesson of the StarLink incident was to not grant "split approvals"—allowing GM products to be used in animal feed but not in food market channels.

The StarLink corn debacle also intensified negative attitudes toward GM foods in major foreign markets. US corn exports to Japan, the United

---

84. Bair, quoted in Anthony Shadid, "Biotechnology: Against the Altered Grain—Some North American Crops Grown from Bioengineered Seeds Face Bans in Certain Lucrative Export Markets," *The Boston Globe*, May 2, 2001, C4.

States' biggest corn export market, declined by 11 percent in the months after Japanese tests found traces of StarLink in US shipments.[85] As it stood, while 16 GM corn varieties were approved in the United States, only 10 were allowed in Japan (and just 4 in the European Union). Because Japan imported billions of dollars worth of farm goods, exporters were concerned. Monsanto announced the recall of hundreds of tons of GM canola seed from Canadian farmers because the shipments might have contained genetic material not approved for consumption in Japan.[86] Some US grain processors began discouraging US farmers from growing GM crops. In a radio advertisement aired in Iowa and Illinois, Archer-Daniels-Midland warned farmers they would buy only crops "that have full feed and food approval world-wide."[87] US-based companies as well began to back away from using GM ingredients. Frito-Lay and McDonald's made moves to offer GM-free foods, and H. J. Heinz announced it would eliminate GM ingredients from its baby food products.

Around the same time, Monsanto developed the first genetically engineered variety of wheat designed for sale to farmers, expecting to bring it to market a few years later. Half of all American wheat was exported, accounting for $3.7 billion in sales in 1999. As news about the Roundup Ready wheat spread, buyers in Japan, Europe, and Egypt said that their consumers would not accept it. A letter from a spokesman for the Japan Flour Millers Association noted that "Japanese consumers are highly suspicious and skeptical about safety of 'genetically modified' farm products. . . . I strongly doubt that any bakery and noodle products made of 'modified' wheat or even conventional wheat that may contain 'modified' wheat will be accepted in the Japanese market." The US wheat industry was responsive to these concerns. "We may in the future have a biotech wheat that the world does want," said Darrell Hanavan, chairman of a joint wheat industry committee on biotechnology. "But we need to proceed now under the assumption that some markets won't want it anytime soon. And the challenge will be to make sure that buyers and their customers get exactly what they want." Phil Isaak, a board member of US Wheat Associates, which promoted American wheat exports for growers, added: "Unless we get worldwide public approval of it, we have to take the position of resisting release for commercialization."[88] Monsanto agreed to hold its plans to release the GM wheat commercially.

---

85. Satoko Adachi and Edmond Lococo, "Japan Likely to Return to US Corn; Exports Dropped 11% after Traces of StarLink Found," Bloomberg News, April 22, 2001.

86. Shadid, "Biotechnology." C4.

87. Quoted in Scott Kilman, "Some Grain Companies Dissuade Farmers from Using Biotech Seed," *The Wall Street Journal*, November 20, 2000, B4.

88. All quotations in the paragraph are from Marc Kaufman, "Gene-Spliced Wheat Stirs Global Fears; Buyers Spurn Grain Before It's Planted," *The Washington Post*, February 27, 2001, A1.

Canada, which then exported about 85 percent of its wheat, was also concerned; Algeria, which purchased more than 40 percent of Canada's durum wheat, had recently banned all GM foods. The Canadian Wheat Board, the marketing organization that controlled about 95 percent of Canada's wheat production, lobbied the Canadian government to make market acceptance a factor when deciding whether a GM product should receive regulatory approval. Monsanto opposed the idea—"That would give everyone outside Canada a say in how Canada runs its business," said spokeswoman Trish Jordan.[89]

New Developments in Europe

In Europe, Commissioner Byrne was working to find a solution to the biotech food challenge. Observers spoke highly of his efforts to manage the US-EU GM dispute and the debates within Europe over food safety. As Ray Goldberg, professor emeritus of agriculture and business at Harvard Business School, reflects,

> The globalization of the food system requires a common understanding of standards, a common definition of terms, and common understanding of science. For the long-run mutual benefit of all nations, we have to find that common ground. Commissioner Byrne was a unique person in his ability to create consensus with his background in Ireland and his work to bring different religious groups together. He was the right kind of person for the job.[90]

Richard Morningstar, the former US ambassador to the European Union, agrees that the Commission and David Byrne were trying to find workable answers: "I do think that the Commission was doing their best to try and come to a solution. I think that David Byrne definitely tried his best. He had his own politics to deal with."

In March 2001, the European Parliament and the Council adopted a new directive on the deliberate release of GMOs into the environment—Directive 2001/18/EC—that would supersede Directive 220/90. Under the new legislation, approvals for GM crops would be limited to 10 years (with the possibility for renewal) and environmental monitoring for field trials and commercial cultivation would increase. Approvals and field trials would also be subject to increased transparency, such as public registration of trial sites (Bernauer 2003, 47). For its implementation, all 15

---

89. Information about Canadian wheat trade and Jordan quoted in Scott Morrison and Nikki Tait, "Commodities and Agriculture: Concern in Canada over Biotech Wheat: Growers Fear Loss of Exports to Countries That Have Banned GM Food," *The Financial Times*, April 27, 2001, 42.

90. Unless otherwise noted, all quotes from Ray Goldberg come from a 2004 interview with the author.

member states had to create national legislation adopting the directive by October 17, 2002. Twelve of the 15 states would fail to meet this deadline.

Directive 2001/18/EC contained calls for new legislation on labeling and traceability as well. Labeling rules would set a threshold above which consumers would have to be informed of the presence of GM products in food. Traceability rules would require shippers of bulk products to detail what GMO materials could be present and to track and document these materials through any processing and manufacturing steps from farm to fork," as some advocates put it. The European Commission proposed the new rules in July 2001, and debate over the details ensued.

One issue to be determined was what percentage of GM material could be present in a product before it had to be labeled "produced from GMOs." Environmental campaigners hoped to set the threshold at 0.1 percent, while some agricultural ministers were demanding 0.5 percent. A low threshold was particularly important to Germany, where elections were approaching and fears about GM food ran high. "I wanted 1 percent—that was my proposal," remembers David Byrne. "I was advised that 0.5 percent would be difficult to achieve and was impractical." After negotiations with Byrne, EU farm ministers agreed on a level of 0.9 percent for labeling of all food and animal feed containing EU-approved GM material in November 2002. Below this threshold, no label would be required. "I was asked later, 'What is the difference between 1 percent and 0.9 percent?'" Byrne recalls. "I said, 'Mathematically, 0.1; scientifically, none; but politically, all the difference in the world.'"

Many in the United States worried that the labeling and traceability proposals would prove costly, unworkably bureaucratic, and restrictive—and thus harmful to trade. "Potentially, these new regulations would be more disruptive to international trade than the moratorium on new approvals or the Cartagena Biosafety Protocol, because they set in place requirements that would be very difficult for exporters to satisfy," says Robert Paarlberg. And a more fundamental objection was raised to the very idea of labeling GM products. As one senior House Republican aide explains, "The Europeans say consumers need to know what they are buying. But if there is no substantive difference in a product from conventional products and you put a label on it that says 'This contains X,' you are basically saying something could be wrong with it. It is tantamount to putting a skull and crossbones on it, especially in Europe."

Codex also debated the labeling of biotech foods, but was unable to come to any agreement. The United States argued that labeling was appropriate only if there was a significant difference between a GM food and its conventional counterpart; the European Union argued that all foods derived from biotechnology should be labeled. "There is just no compromise between those two positions," says a US Codex representative. "We've been beating our heads on that for years with very little progress." In fact, discussions on biotech labeling had been under way since 1992. "Codex has been criticized in the past for being too slow in the new trade environment—that we have to develop standards more quickly," the Codex representative adds. "The poster child for that criticism is biotech labeling." And the lack of progress could have serious consequences: "Frankly, part of our concern is that if Codex can't find a way to get over these impasses, it will lose its credibility in the WTO sense. That would be a real tragedy. Codex should be able to develop standards that everyone agrees on, but if we've been arguing biotech labeling for 12 years, we are just not doing our job."

Despite the US lack of enthusiasm for the European legislative proposals, former commissioner Byrne notes the growing recognition that the European approach toward GM food was not motivated by protectionism. US officials "might not agree with [the imposition of labeling and traceability rules], but they understand it was not motivated by trade protectionism," he says. "They accept that now—they didn't in 1999 when I was in Seattle. . . . I worked hard on that." Trade requires consumer confidence, he argues.

A number of US participants agree that protectionism was not the central motivation for the European Union's de facto moratorium. "When I first got involved in the summer of 1999, [the EU moratorium] was really looked at principally as a trade protectionist issue," says Richard Morningstar. "Most of those involved in the US, including myself, didn't appreciate at the time that the issue went far beyond protection and was in fact much more of a political/consumer issue." Some, including Peter Scher, say that this element distinguished the GM dispute from the beef hormone case: "I think there is some protectionist element to the beef hormone dispute," he declares. "I don't believe there is a protectionist element to the GM dispute. I really don't. I don't believe it has to do with Europe trying to protect its industry. I think it had to do with the inability or unwillingness of European officials to take politics out of their regulatory decisions."

As the debate continued, David Byrne was working to create a coordinated food safety system in Europe. The new agency would be known as the European Food Safety Authority (EFSA), and its primary function would be to conduct risk assessments of new food products. While the development of EFSA drew much interest, some noted that its approach to risk would be fundamentally different than that of the US FDA. At the FDA, regulators both assessed the risks of a given product and created the regulations to manage that risk, as guided by applicable statutes. Proponents of this arrangement argued that it ensured a regulatory body that would make rules based on sound science, independent of politics.

EFSA, in contrast, would leave risk management to the Commission and the ministers. Europeans generally argued that a functional separation between risk assessment and risk management was necessary. Byrne describes that position:

> Some people say we must rely on good science and that scientists take decisions that are purported to be purely scientific. But how often is this the case? If they are independent and are also effectively the lawmakers because they are regulating what will happen in relation to all citizens, they are not answerable to anybody. As a lawyer, I have a problem with that. And from a political science point of view, and a democratic accountability point of view, I have a problem with that. I believe that if you have a function in lawmaking, you must be answerable and accountable to the people.

EFSA was established in 2002; as planned, it came into operation in 2003.

Expanding Resistance

In October 2002 Zambia turned away 26,000 tons of US food aid, invoking the precautionary principle and claiming that the shipments contained potentially unsafe GM corn. Though the country was facing a famine, Zambia's agriculture minister argued that the corn could pollute the country's seed stock and hurt its export markets.[91] According to observers, while food safety and environmental issues related to GM foods dominated discussions in Europe, many developing countries were more worried about exports. In particular, Robert Paarlberg emphasizes, EU export markets were crucial to many African countries. "The European Union imports more agricultural commodities from developing countries than the United States, Canada, Argentina, Japan, and Australia combined," he points out. "So whatever Europe does, Africa likes to follow because African exports are frequently targeted to the European market."

As a result of Zambia's rejection of US food aid, transatlantic tensions increased. "Fairly or unfairly, there was a lot of bad publicity for the EU when the famous Zambia situation happened," says Richard Morningstar. "That [incident] really rubbed people the wrong way in the United States. I think that contributed to the frustration." While some in the United States believed that European officials had encouraged African countries to reject GM foods, others blamed European NGOs.

China also imposed restrictions on varieties of GM crops and required lengthy safety tests and labeling rules before such foods could be imported. Though some hoped that China's entry into the WTO would increase imports of US agricultural products, the sale of US soybeans to

---

91. Neil King Jr., "US Ponders Next Course in EU Food Fight—Trade Suit Is Possible in Biotech-Crop Battle for Big Markets in Asia and Elsewhere," *The Wall Street Journal*, December 2, 2002, A4. The leaders of Lesotho, Swaziland, Zimbabwe, Mozambique, and Malawi also initially rejected GM US food aid; but later, after consultations with the WHO, they retracted their bans or accepted milled GM maize (a form that could not be planted).

China dropped by 23 percent from January to September 2002 compared to the same period in 2001.[92] Beijing also prohibited biotechnology companies such as Monsanto and Syngenta from investing in China to develop GM corn, soybeans, and rice seeds. While China justified such moves by stressing its concerns about access to EU agricultural markets, some in the US biotech industry believed that the real motivations were protectionist—China wanted to shield its domestic soybean producers, and also to build its own GM capacity.

At the same time, other countries—including India, Colombia, Honduras, and the Philippines—were adopting GM crops. In Brazil, one of the world's largest growers of soybeans, many farmers were planting them illegally, a development that took on added significance in light of Brazil's role as the main source of non-GM produce for Europe.[93] To further increase acceptance of agricultural biotechnology in developing countries, GM crops would have to be developed that directly benefited them. Some research was being undertaken at the international level through the Consultative Group on International Agricultural Research (CGIAR), an alliance of international agricultural centers whose aim is to mobilize science to benefit the poor. Emmy Simmons, who formerly was assistant administrator for economic growth, agriculture, and trade at the US Agency for International Development (USAID), explains: "Within that system, there is research going on to engineer new varieties of crops that are drought resistant or drought tolerant, can overcome aluminum toxicity, or have specific characteristics in terms of nutrient content, for example"[94]—all traits highly important to developing countries.

But funding for such research was limited, especially in comparison with the billions of dollars invested each year by private industry. In 2004, CGIAR spent $425 million on its research agenda (CGIAR 2004). About 7 percent of that research was dedicated to exploring the solutions that new technologies had to offer, and only about 3 percent of that fraction was dedicated to exploring GMOs (CGIAR 2004–05). USAID had an earmark from Congress to support agricultural biotechnology research, but it amounted to just $25 million annually. Some have argued that research on behalf of farmers in poor countries should be undertaken by biotechnology companies, but a source in academia strongly disagrees: "That is not a job that should be left to private companies. They would have to invest

---

92. Joseph Kahn, "The Science and Politics of Super Rice," *The New York Times*, October 22, 2002, C1.

93. Edward Alden, Tobias Buck, and Guy de Jonquières, "The Washington-Led Challenge to the European Union Moratorium Will Take Trade Disputes into Untested Areas, Further Straining the Legitimacy of the World Trade Organisation," *The Financial Times*, May 14, 2003, 21.

94. Unless otherwise noted, all quotes from Emmy Simmons are from a 2005 interview with the author.

millions of dollars in a trait that won't provide adequate return on that investment. That is what the publicly funded international agricultural research centers should be doing."

Part II: A Case at the WTO

The key question became: Would the Bush administration file a case against the European Union at the WTO over the GM moratorium? Pressure was growing from US farm organizations, the food industry, and biotechnology companies to take the issue to the WTO. A senior House Republican aide notes, "We were continuing to see numbers such as $300 million in annual losses for corn exports because of a lack of approvals. The problem had been brewing for a couple of years and people were urging the administration to finally bring a case."

In a November 2002 letter, 25 US farm organizations urged USTR Robert Zoellick to "end US patience" and bring the case.[95] "We've been very patient with the Europeans, but their use of this ban as a trade barrier sets a precedent for countries around the world," said Mary Kay Thatcher, director of public policy at the American Farm Bureau Federation. "We rely on export markets for one-third of our crops; this is a nightmare."[96] Key groups that advocated taking action included the National Corn Growers Association, American Soybean Association, the American Farm Bureau, the US Biotechnology Industry Organization, and the National Grain and Feed Association.

The Senate was also exerting more pressure. In a December 19 letter, seven farm-state senators—including Max Baucus (D-MT), the outgoing Senate Finance chairman; his replacement, Chuck Grassley (R-IA); and Tom Harkin (D-IA)—urged President Bush to file a case "without delay." "Despite repeated assurance from European officials that the moratorium would be lifted," they argued, "there is no indication that this will happen in the foreseeable future. Indeed, the situation continues to worsen." The writers also criticized Europe's proposed traceability and labeling rules.[97] House Speaker Dennis Hastert (R-IL), who represented a major corn and soybean producing area, also pressed the Bush administration to challenge the European Union at the WTO, as did Representative Frank Wolf (R-VA), the chairman of the House Agriculture Committee, and Majority Whip Roy Blunt (R-MO).

---

95. The letter is quoted in King, "US Ponders Next Course in EU Food Fight," A4.

96. Thatcher, quoted in Elizabeth Becker with David Barboza, "Battle over Biotechnology Intensifies Trade War," *The New York Times*, May 29, 2003, C1.

97. The letter is reprinted in a State Department press release, "Senators Urge WTO Dispute Case Against EU Biotech Policy," December 20, 2002; the other senators who signed it were Kit Bond (R-MO), Pat Roberts (R-KS), Chuck Hagel (R-NE), and Thad Cochran (R-MS).

In December, participants in interagency meetings debated whether to bring a case but reached no consensus. Discussion apparently centered on the possible benefits of bringing a case even if officials believed it would not lead to an earlier lifting of the moratorium. The State Department advocated giving European member-states one more chance to move forward on approvals. In response, the European Commission decided to allow sales of cottonseed oil derived from GM seeds, but not containing GM material. US officials said the decision was a positive signal, but fell short of addressing the issue of the moratorium.[98] The European Commission also wrote a letter assuring almost 200 members of Congress that approvals could start as early as the middle of 2003.[99]

USTR Robert Zoellick was in favor of moving forward with a case, as was US Agriculture Secretary Ann Veneman, but not all Bush administration officials were persuaded. Some worried that a backlash in Europe over the case would complicate US diplomacy on Iraq. In addition, other US-EU trade tensions were on the rise. The WTO had ruled against the United States in the foreign sales corporation/extraterritorial income (FSC/ETI) dispute concerning tax provisions seen as benefiting US companies. In March 2003, EU Trade Commissioner Pascal Lamy announced a draft list of more than 1,800 US products whose export value exceeded $4 billion that could be subject to retaliatory tariffs unless the United States complied with the WTO ruling.

The GMO issue went up to the cabinet level several times before a decision was made. In the end, the administration decided to bring the case. On May 13, 2003, Zoellick and Veneman announced that the United States was moving forward in requesting WTO consultations with the European Union, backed by Argentina, Canada, and Egypt as co-complainants.[100] "Biotech food helps nourish the world's hungry population, offers tremendous opportunities for better health and nutrition and protects the environment by reducing soil erosion and pesticide use," said Zoellick. "We've waited patiently for five years for the EU to follow the WTO rules and the recommendations of the European Commission, so as to respect safety findings based on careful science."[101] If Europe did not lift its moratorium on the approval of GM commodities by the time the consultation

---

98. "Administration Mulls WTO Biotech Case Against EU, Reaches No Decision," *Inside US Trade*, January 3, 2003. Approval of the cottonseed oil was allowed under the EU's 1997 Novel Food Law.

99. "EC Moves to Defuse Possible US WTO Biotech Challenge," *Inside US Trade*, April 18, 2003.

100. Australia, Chile, Colombia, El Salvador, Honduras, Mexico, New Zealand, Peru, and Uruguay expressed support for the US case by joining it as third parties.

101. USTR and USDA press release, "US and Cooperating Countries File WTO Case Against EU Moratorium on Biotech Foods and Crops EU's Illegal, Non-Science Based Moratorium Harmful to Agriculture and the Developing World," May 13, 2003.

period expired, Zoellick said, the United States would request the formation of a WTO panel.[102]

In a speech delivered at the Coast Guard Academy, President Bush added that the EU moratorium impeded the fight against famine. Genetic engineering of crops provided a way to feed more people, especially in Africa, Bush said. "Yet, our partners in Europe are impeding this effort. They have blocked all new bio-crops because of unfounded, unscientific fears. This has caused many African nations to avoid investing in biotechnologies, for fear their products will be shut out of European markets. European governments should join—not hinder—the great cause of ending hunger in Africa."[103] Lamy responded that such accusations were "unacceptable" and "should not be used in this kind of debate" (quoted in Pew Initiative on Food and Biotechnology 2005, 31).

Some observers were surprised at the US move. By May 2003 the EFSA was close to being operational, and EU Health and Safety Commissioner David Byrne expected the moratorium against approving new GMOs to be lifted sometime in the autumn (Goldberg and Hogan 2003, 2). In addition, the new European labeling and traceability rules were close to being adopted. At a time when new laws and institutions were being developed to try to solve the problem, bringing a WTO case appeared to make little sense.

Another argument—that bringing such a contentious case to the WTO would open the organization to further attacks, potentially undermining its authority—fell on skeptical ears. "Trade policy can be funny," says Peter Scher. "Every time a case is brought that someone doesn't like, whoever is on the defending end of it says, 'This is going to bring down the WTO!' The fact is that the WTO was able to handle the beef hormones case and they are handling the GMO case."

Others saw significance in the timing of the US action, pointing out that the Cartagena Biosafety Protocol was scheduled to come into force in September 2003. "The filing of the case was just before the protocol came into force," says Calestous Juma, former executive secretary of the Convention on Biological Diversity. "The US was saying, 'We really want this settled legally as opposed to sorted out politically by the influence of the protocol.'"

Europe warned that taking the dispute to a higher level could create an even stronger backlash against GM foods and thereby frustrate the US objective of opening EU markets. A 2002 European public opinion study had shown that majorities in most EU countries rejected GM foods as

---

102. "US To Push WTO Case Unless EU Biotech Moratorium Lifted," *Inside US Trade*, May 16, 2003.

103. President George W. Bush's commencement address at the Coast Guard Academy, May 21, 2003, www.whitehouse.gov.

"risky" and "not useful" for society.[104] But some, including Robert Paarl-berg, suspect that the European Commission may not have been com-pletely against the idea of a WTO case. He explains:

> The European Commission doesn't like encountering defiance from member gov-ernments—they want their authority established and they want to get beyond the dysfunctional approval process. One way to do that is to sponsor a new set of reg-ulations on tracing and labeling, which they've done, and to create a higher bar for regulatory approvals, which they've done. But still there is resistance from member governments. So the Commission might not have been altogether op-posed to some external pressure from the United States in the form of a WTO case. Indeed, when the WTO case was brought, it didn't take more than about a year for some approvals to be granted.

In addition, a ruling against the European Union might benefit Euro-pean officials by enabling them to blame unpopular policies on outside pressures.

Initially, it was announced that the United States would be joined by Ar-gentina, Canada, and Egypt as co-complainants in the case. Egypt was in a difficult position, however, since the European Union was its largest ex-port market (and one of its biggest markets for fresh fruits and vegetables). Senate Finance Chairman Grassley sent a letter to Foreign Minister Ahmed Maher, warning that Egypt's failure to join the United States in the WTO case could hurt its chances of reaching a free trade agreement (FTA) with the United States. Grassley said that while he was supportive of a possible US-Egypt FTA, "one of the criteria that ought to be used to determine with whom the United States negotiates future FTAs is whether a country shares the same vision of the global trading system as does the United States. I certainly would like to be able to include Egypt in that camp."[105] In the end, Egypt decided that it would not support the US complaint at the WTO. Following that withdrawal, US interest in negotiating an FTA with Egypt cooled dramatically. According to one US trade official, Egypt's decision raised doubts about its willingness to live up to other commit-ments. "Negotiations require being able to follow through on what you said you would do," he said.[106]

In July 2003, Codex adopted the first-ever international guidelines for evaluating the consumer safety of biotech foods, guidelines developed by its task force.[107] Codex Commission Secretary Alan Randall noted,

---

104. Pew Initiative on Food and Biotechnology 2005, 6.

105. Grassley, quoted in "US Announces Panel on EU GMO Moratorium, as Grassley Warns Egypt," *Inside US Trade*, June 20, 2003.

106. "US Interest in FTA Cools After Egypt Fails to Join GMO Complaint," *Inside US Trade*, July 4, 2003.

107. The Codex Commission published the guidelines in three documents: *Principles for the Risk Analysis of Foods Derived from Modern Biotechnology*, *Guideline for the Conduct of Food Safety Assessment of Foods Derived from Recombinant-DNA Plants*, and *Guideline for the Conduct of Food Safety Assessment of Foods Produced Using Recombinant DNA Microorganisms*.

"Consumers can be assured that foods assessed by these methods are fit to eat."[108] Some analysts pointed out that the adoption of the guidelines strengthened the US position. "If a country was applying more rigorous requirements than the Codex guidelines, the United States would be in a fairly good position to take a trade case against them at the WTO," says a US Codex representative.

Arguments at the WTO

After the US-EU WTO consultations on the GM case failed to resolve the dispute, the United States, Canada, and Argentina requested a panel in August 2003. Before the end of the month, the WTO Dispute Settlement Body established a panel on the European Union's "Measures Affecting the Approval and Marketing of Biotech Products"; its members were named in March 2004.[109] The panel heard arguments from the parties and also met with a group of experts to answer scientific and technical questions on GMOs.

In its arguments to the panel, the United States held that the European Union was in violation of the SPS agreement. As noted above, this agreement applies to measures taken by WTO members for the protection of human, animal, or plant life or health that affect international trade (for a definition of SPS measures, see Annex A.1 in appendix 1C in chapter 1). Members are obligated either to follow international standards or to ensure that any SPS measures designed to result in higher levels of protection are supported by risk assessments based on available scientific evidence.

First, the United States argued that Europe's biotech approval regime was "unquestionably" an SPS measure because both Directive 2001/18 and Directive 90/220 state that one of their objectives is "to protect human health and the environment" when placing GMO products on the market or deliberately releasing them into the environment, and Regulation 258/97 states that foods "must not present a danger for the consumer." The United States alleged that the European Union's failure to approve any new GM products since 1998 constituted a general moratorium. Though adopted "in a nontransparent way, without official publication," this moratorium clearly existed, affected international trade, and was an SPS mea-

---

108. FAO/WHO press release, "Codex Alimentarius Commission Adopts More Than 50 New Food Standards; New Guidelines on Genetically Modified and Irradiated Food," July 9, 2003.

109. WTO Director-General Supachai Panitchpakdi selected the panelists. The chair was Christian Haeberli, deputy head of the GATT/WTO division in the Swiss Federal Office for Foreign and Economic Affairs, and he was joined by Mohan Kumar, India's deputy high commissioner in the Diplomatic Mission in Sri Lanka, and Akio Shimizu, a law professor at Waseda University in Tokyo, Japan. (See "ASA Takes Lead in Pushing for New WTO GMO Case Against EU," *Inside US Trade*, March 12, 2004).

sure. Similarly, the United States argued that the SPS agreement also covered the European Communities' "product-specific moratoria"—namely, its failure to consider 27 pending applications of biotech products for approval.[110]

Undue Delay

The United States made clear that it was not asking the panel to judge whether Europe's legislation on novel foods and their deliberate release was WTO-consistent—it had no objection to Europe's maintaining a biotech approval system. Instead, the United States' central argument was that the European Communities' general and product-specific moratoria violated WTO rules because the SPS agreement required regulatory authorities to follow their procedures without "undue delay." As the USTR observed in its submission, "It is hard to think of a situation that involves 'undue delay' more than a complete moratorium on approvals."[111]

More specifically, the United States contended that the EC approval process for biotech products was subject to the requirements of SPS Article 8 and Annex C. Article 8 obligates members to "observe the provisions of Annex C in the operation of control, inspection, and approval procedures," and Annex C, paragraph 1(a) obliges WTO members to ensure "with respect to any procedure to check and ensure the fulfillment of sanitary or phytosanitary measures, that such procedures are undertaken and completed without undue delay."

The United States also argued that in adopting a moratorium, the European Union had failed to notify other WTO members of changes to its biotech approval process, as called for in Article 7 and Annex B.1 (see appendix 1C in chapter 1 and appendix 6B). In addition, the United States noted that the general moratorium was inconsistent with certain procedural obligations for SPS measures, such as communicating the processing period of an application, promptly examining the documentation to check for its completeness, and explaining any delays, as described in Annex C.1(b). In short, the United States maintained that having established a biotech approval regime, the European Communities were "obligated to apply those procedures fairly and transparently, and without undue delay."[112]

---

110. "European Communities—Measures Affecting the Approval and Marketing of Biotech Products (WT/DS291, 292, and 293), First Submission of the United States," April 21, 2004, 31, 33, 49.

111. "European Communities—Measures Affecting the Approval and Marketing of Biotech Products," first US submission, 1.

112. "European Communities—Measures Affecting the Approval and Marketing of Biotech Products," first US submission, 1.

Unscientific Criteria

In addition, the United States argued that there was no scientific basis for the moratorium on biotech approvals. "In fact, many of the products caught up in the EC moratorium have been positively assessed by the EC's own scientific committees," its submission noted.[113] The United States claimed that the European Union's general moratorium was not based on sufficient scientific principles, as required by Article 2.2, or a scientific risk assessment, as required by Article 5.1 and defined by Annex A.4. As a result, in setting its level of protection against risk, Europe had applied arbitrary or unjustifiable distinctions that led to discrimination or disguised restriction in international trade, violating Article 5.5.

The United States made the same arguments regarding product-specific moratoria, contending that the European Union had violated the SPS by imposing "undue delay," by failing to publish the moratoria, by applying its approval procedures in a nontransparent manner, by failing to base the product-specific moratoria on risk assessments and scientific principles, and by applying arbitrary or unjustifiable distinctions in its levels of protection that resulted in trade discrimination.[114]

The United States also challenged nine measures enacted by six EC member states (Austria, Italy, France, Germany, Greece, and Luxembourg) that prohibited the importation or marketing of certain biotech products that had been approved under Directive 90/220 and Regulation 258/97, claiming that the measures were not based on risk assessments and scientific principles and that the arbitrary or unjustifiable distinctions in their levels of protection against risk resulted in trade discrimination.[115]

The EU Response

The European Union rejected the US assertion that a moratorium on approvals existed, either as a general practice or in a product-specific form. Its first written submission declared that "the European Communities has not adopted any 'moratorium' on the approval of GMOs and nor has it suspended the application of its GMO legislation. . . . The Complainants' assertions about a 'moratorium,' or a 'suspension of procedures' or any 'failure to consider applications' are all in reality complaints about delay." The European Union also maintained that applications for specific products

---

113. "European Communities—Measures Affecting the Approval and Marketing of Biotech Products," first US submission, 1.

114. "European Communities—Measures Affecting the Approval and Marketing of Biotech Products," first US submission, 49.

115. "European Communities—Measures Affecting the Approval and Marketing of Biotech Products," first US submission, 56.

had reached various stages depending on when additional information was required. Even if a repeated pattern in the treatment of applications was found, the European Union argued that such a pattern constituted not a challengeable measure under the WTO but a "practice"—and according to prior case law, a practice is not actionable under the WTO.[116]

The United States argued that it had provided overwhelming evidence that the European Communities had adopted and maintained a general moratorium. Among that evidence were comments from European officials that acknowledged its existence. For example, in a June 2000 speech Commissioner Byrne said the reluctance of member states to approve new biotech products "has resulted in a complete standstill in the current authorisations and a de facto moratorium on the commercial release of GMOs." The United States also highlighted the July 2000 remarks, made by Environment Commissioner Margot Wallström, that the moratorium was "illegal and not justified."[117] But the European Union argued that none of these statements proved the existence of a moratorium. Prior cases had shown that "casual statement of any of the numerous representatives" of a sovereign state did not demonstrate that state's legal position.[118]

The European Union also rejected the charge that the import bans maintained by six of its member states on GMO products approved by the European Union violated the SPS agreement, pointing out that Article 5.7 permits "provisional" measures while more information is gathered. ("In cases where relevant scientific evidence is insufficient, a Member may provisionally adopt sanitary or phytosanitary measures on the basis of available pertinent information.") The article also obligates members to obtain "additional information necessary for a more objective assessment of risk . . . within a reasonable period of time"—a requirement that member states failed to meet, according to the United States.

Perhaps most importantly, the European Union argued that most of the objectives of its GMO approval system addressed risks that fell outside the scope of the SPS agreement. Basing its arguments on Article I and the definition of an SPS measure in Annex A.1, the European Union declared that the "SPS Agreement was not intended by its drafters to apply to all products and all risks in all circumstances—it has a limited and defined

---

116. European Communities—Measures Affecting the Approval and Marketing of Biotech Products (DS/291, DS/292, DS/293): First Written Submission by the European Communities," May 17, 2004, 118, 168.

117. "Biotechnology: Building Consumer Acceptance," speech by David Byrne, European Commissioner for Health and Consumer Protection, European Business Summit, June 10, 2000, and "EU Moves to Break Gene Crop Deadlock," Reuters, July 13, 2000; both quoted in "European Communities—Measures Affecting the Approval and Marketing of Biotech Products," first US submission, 18.

118. "European Communities—Measures Affecting the Approval and Marketing of Biotech Products," first EC submission, 165.

scope of application," adding, "It is clear that the SPS Agreement was not drafted with products having the particular characteristics of GMOs in mind."[119] It argued that the three main characteristics of the GM products that were the subject of the proceedings—herbicide tolerance, insecticidal properties, and antibiotic resistance—entailed a total of 13 related risks and that only 3 of these were completely covered by the SPS agreement, which addressed measures intended to protect human, animal, or plant life or health. For example, the European Union claimed that the agreement does not cover certain measures taken to protect the environment, such as those that address the risks that handling GMOs might pose to soil biogeochemistry.[120] The United States countered that environmental protection fell within the SPS agreement.

Another EU argument was that the other elements of its regulatory regime could be reviewed under the Agreement on Technical Barriers to Trade (TBT).[121] The United States did not make any claims that the European Union's system violated the TBT rules, though it "reserved the right to do so."[122] The European Union also argued that GATT Article XX could also be used to justify its regulatory procedures.[123]

The European Union asserted that the issues raised by GMOs went far beyond the risks envisaged and regulated by the SPS agreement: "Indeed they deserve their own agreement, and so a specific agreement has been negotiated outside the WTO context and subsequent to the conclusion of the WTO Agreement. It is the Biosafety Protocol which lays down the most pertinent provisions to any consideration of problems related to

---

119. "European Communities—Measures Affecting the Approval and Marketing of Biotech Products," first EC submission, 122, 120.

120. "WTO Panel Close to Completing Fact Finding in GMO Case," *Inside US Trade*, March 4, 2005.

121. The WTO's TBT agreement sets out rules for regulations, standards, and testing and certification procedures not covered in the SPS agreement. Josling, Roberts, and Orden note, "In the implementation of the TBT agreement, the appropriate use of labels for agricultural and food products to signal quality attributes has been one of the most contentious issues" (2004, 54).

122. "EU GMO Defense Seeks to Circumvent Possible WTO Negative Ruling," *Inside US Trade*, May 28, 2004. In its submission to the WTO, the United States noted, "The United States submits that the measures subject to this dispute are within the scope of the SPS Agreement. Should the EC in its First Submission argue otherwise, the United States reserves the right to explain, in the alternative, the manner in which the EC measures are inconsistent with the Agreement on Technical Barriers to Trade" (see "European Communities—Measures Affecting the Approval and Marketing of Biotech Products," first US submission, note 156 at 29).

123. Article XX of the GATT allows members to take measures "necessary to protect human, animal or plant life or health" so long as those measures are not applied in a way that creates "arbitrary or unjustifiable discrimination between countries."

GMOs."[124] In its very first decision, the WTO's Appellate Body concluded that "the General Agreement is not to be read in clinical isolation from public international law," and the European Union submitted that as a result, the norms reflected in the Biosafety Protocol on the precautionary principle and on risk assessment must be taken into account when interpreting and applying WTO rules.[125] It was thus not the role of the WTO agreement to trump the other relevant rules of international law that permitted—or even required—a prudent and precautionary approach.[126]

But the United States argued that other sources of international law could be pertinent to the dispute only if those sources would assist the panel in "clarifying the existing provisions of the [covered] agreements in accordance with customary rules of interpretation of public international law," as Article 3.2 of the Dispute Settlement Understanding stipulates. And according to the United States, the European Union had not identified how the Biosafety Protocol or a precautionary principle would be relevant to interpreting any particular provision of the WTO agreement.[127]

The European Union's Labeling and Traceability Regulations

Meanwhile, the European Union was still working on regulations for labeling and tracking biotech crops. In September 2003, the European Council of Ministers and the Parliament passed Regulations 1830/2003 and 1829/2003. As described above, under the new regulations, which were to take effect in April 2004, products with more than 0.9 percent EU-approved GM content would have to be labeled "This product is produced from GMOs." Animal feed would also have to be labeled. In addition, a paper trail would track the history and content of GM foods at all stages of production. The regulations also streamlined the approval process for GM products. Industry continued to argue that the new labeling and traceability regulations would be extremely difficult and expensive to implement, further impeding trade, but a number of NGOs showed support. "This vote is a slap in the face of the US administration, which

---

124. "European Communities—Measures Affecting the Approval and Marketing of Biotech Products," first EC submission, 121.

125. Appellate Body Report, US—Gasoline, p. 621. See generally Cameron and Gray (2001), as cited in "European Communities—Measures Affecting the Approval and Marketing of Biotech Products," first EC submission, 139.

126. "European Communities—Measures Affecting the Approval and Marketing of Biotech Products," first EC submission, 4.

127. "European Communities—Measures Affecting the Approval and Marketing of Biotech Products (WT/DS291, 292, and 293): Executive Summary of the Rebuttal Submission of the United States," July 29, 2004, 3.

thought that by bullying, . . . Europe, and eventually others, would swallow its GMO policy," declared Greenpeace's Eric Gall[128] The European Commission also referred Austria, Belgium, Finland, France, Germany, Greece, Ireland, Italy, Luxembourg, Netherlands, and Spain to the European Court of Justice for failing to adopt and promulgate national legislation implementing Directive 2001/18/EC.

Former commissioner David Byrne notes that the adoption of the new labeling and traceability framework—pending even as the WTO case on the moratorium was brought—made the US action even more puzzling. "Yes," he says, "the United States may at last get a technical win at the WTO, but we brought the legislation within a very short time of that. So even if they do succeed in getting a positive outcome, I can't see it is going to be of any great advantage. What will the panel say? [Perhaps it will say to Europe,] yes, you should have harmonized, you should have authorized these applications, you were still bringing through legislation—you should have done it more quickly." But what is going to be the practical outcome of that?

The United States did not accept Europe's new legislation as "lifting the moratorium" and pushed on with its case. Groups like the American Soybean Association (ASA) hoped that the United States would challenge the European Union's labeling and traceability regulations in a separate case at the WTO. In November 2003, ASA and 21 other agriculture-based organizations sent a letter to the USTR requesting that such a case be brought.[129] These groups were particularly concerned that the EU regulations on biotechnology imports would become a model for other countries. Commissioner Byrne countered that the United States should allow the legislation time to work instead of immediately challenging it as a WTO violation.[130] But US industry representatives were not optimistic as the signatories to the Biosafety Protocol worked out the details of the agreement's implementation in February 2004. "Although the treaty underlying the Biosafety Protocol has a noble goal of protecting the world's biodiversity, the European Union and anti-biotech activists hijacked the process to serve their own political ends of further restricting trade in biotech products," lamented ASA President Ron Heck.[131]

---

128. Gall, quoted in Peter Ford, "Europe to Allow GM foods, with 'Farm-to-Fork' Labels," *The Christian Science Monitor*, July 3, 2003, 7.

129. The letter is available at the Web site of ASA, www.soygrowers.com, and reprinted in *Inside US Trade*. Also see "Agriculture Groups Seek New WTO Action Against EU on GMO Rules," *Inside US Trade*, November 28, 2003.

130. "Byrne Expresses Confidence EU Will Soon Approve Two GMOs," *Inside US Trade*, March 26, 2004.

131. Farm Press Editorial Staff, "Soybean Group Disappointed in Trade Restrictions," *Insight*, March 2, 2004.

Observers noted that a US challenge against the new EU labeling and traceability regulations at the WTO would be difficult to mount. Georgetown University's John Jackson argued that to mount an effective case, the United States would need to show that GM foods are "like products," comparable with other conventional foods. (Article III:4 of the GATT 1994 states that imported products are due "treatment no less favourable than that accorded to like products of national origin.")[132] According to the *Financial Times*, the argument before the WTO would involve "almost theological complexity."[133] In the ongoing WTO case, the European Union had argued that the only product "like" a given imported GM product was the same GM product cultivated or processed domestically.[134] Indeed, some have contended that the fundamental difference between the US and EU perspectives is that the United States treats GM products as substantially equivalent to or "like" conventional products, while the European Union does not.[135]

In May 2004, the European Commission gave the green light for the Swiss company Syngenta to sell its canned GM sweet corn in supermarkets across the European Union—the first approval of a new GM food for sale since 1998.[136] The sweet corn, from the maize line Bt-11, would be clearly labeled as a GM product, in line with the new EU legislation.[137] Commissioner Byrne said the corn had been "subject to the most rigorous pre-marketing assessment in the world. It has been scientifically assessed

---

132. See GATT Article III:4: "The products of the territory of any contracting party imported into the territory of any other contracting party shall be accorded treatment no less favourable than that accorded to like products of national origin in respect of all laws, regulations and requirements affecting their internal sale, offering for sale, purchase, transportation, distribution or use. The provisions of this paragraph shall not prevent the application of differential internal transportation charges which are based exclusively on the economic operation of the means of transport and not on the nationality of the product."

133. Quote and Jackson's argument described in Alden, Buck, and de Jonquières, "The Washington-Led Challenge to the European Union Moratorium," 21.

134. "European Communities—Measures Affecting the Approval and Marketing of Biotech Products," first EC submission, 160.

135. The WTO generally prohibits discrimination among products based on production processes—how the product is made. In some cases, such as edible oil made from soybeans, GM-derived and non-GM-derived products cannot be distinguished because the oil contains no genetically modified DNA or protein; therefore, some say, there seem little grounds for arguing that the two oils are not like products.

136. "EU Commission Authorizes Import of Canned GM Sweet Corn under New Strict Labelling Conditions: Consumers Can Choose," press release 82/04, European Union—Delegation of the European Commission to the United States, Washington, DC, May 19, 2004, www.eurunion.org.

137. The Commission's decision came after agriculture ministers failed to agree on how to proceed with the authorization in April.

as being as safe as any conventional maize. Food safety is therefore not an issue, it is a question of consumer choice."[138]

In light of the corn approval, EU Trade Commissioner Pascal Lamy argued that the current WTO case was unnecessary and that the United States was "trying to dynamite the door that is already open." But a US spokesman in Brussels maintained that this approval did not mark "an end of the biotech moratorium."[139] "We are not seeing this as a major move," said a US official. "The approval of a single product will not affect our WTO challenge. . . . [It] is not evidence that applications are moving routinely through the approval process in an objective, predictable manner based on science and EU law, rather than political factors."[140] The US Biotechnology Industry Organization agreed: "In our view, the moratorium is not over until a decision is reached on the more than 30 applications that have been pending for six years, and until a new application is acted on in a timely manner, meaning 12 months or less."[141] But Commissioner Byrne said that since the European Union was no longer delaying the application of its own laws, "that part of the [WTO] complaint seems to me to be very difficult to make."[142]

However, some frustration was building within Europe over the new process for approving GMOs. Once EFSA ruled that a GM product was safe, the Commission would make a decision and then ask a regulatory committee, composed of member states' authorities, to approve it. But disagreement among member states prevented the committee from reaching a qualified majority. As a result, the Commission had to forward proposals to the Council of Ministers, where discussions consistently ended in stalemate, forcing the Commission to make the final decision.[143] Markos Kyprianou, who became commissioner for health and consumer protection in November 2004, was reportedly "chafing" over ongoing logjams in the committees and concerned that the approval process pushed all the responsibility onto the Commission, making it appear unbalanced.[144]

---

138. "EU Commission Authorizes Import of Canned GM Sweet Corn," EU press release.

139. Lamy and US spokesman, quoted in Tobias Buck and Raphael Minder, "US Keeps Pressure up on Biofoods," *The Financial Times*, May 20, 2004, 10.

140. US official quoted in Anthony Brown, "Protests After Europe Ends GM Food Freeze," *The Times* (London), May 20, 2004, 18.

141. US Biotechnology Industry Organization, quoted in Kara Sissell, "EU Approves Syngenta's GM Corn," *Chemical Week*, May 26, 2004–June 2, 2004, 36.

142. Byrne, quoted in Paul Geitner, "EU Ends Six-Year Biotech Moratorium with Approval of Sweet Corn Imports," Associated Press, May 19, 2004.

143. "Trying to Sow the Seeds of Certainty over GM Crops," *European Voice*, March 10, 2005.

144. "GMO Issue Moving Back Up Commission Agenda," *Agra Europe*, February 25, 2005; "Trying to Sow the Seeds of Certainty over GM Crops."

New Initiatives

As the case at the WTO continued, new agricultural biotechnology policy initiatives were developing in Europe. One of the European Union's objectives was to become the most competitive and sustainable knowledge-based economy by 2010, and some European leaders worried that it was lagging behind the United States in agricultural biotechnology research. In March 2003, the European Council called for a forum of stakeholders to develop a strategic agenda for plant genomics research. In June 2004, European Research Commissioner Philippe Busquin released the first results of the effort, a document titled *Plants for the Future: A 2025 Vision for European Plant Biotechnology*; it was prepared by a variety of interested parties, including researchers, industry, farmers, regulatory bodies, consumer and environmental groups, and policymakers.

The vision paper noted that the agro-food industry was the European Union's leading industrial sector, with more than €600 billion in annual turnover. "The future competitiveness of Europe's agricultural and food processing industries will depend on plant genomics, biotechnology and their smart application," its executive summary concluded. "These areas are developing rapidly around the world, and Europe risks losing the competitive edge it once possessed as the mantle of innovation passes to the United States. . . . If Europe is not to fall behind its major global competitors in this crucial area of innovation and future prosperity, the legitimate concerns of both critics and advocates need to be addressed" (European Communities 2004, 2, 8). As the European strategic research agenda continued to develop, some believed that the collaborative effort would provide a foundation for new attitudes in Europe about GMOs.

New public initiatives were also in the works to bring the benefits of GM technology to poorer countries. In 2005, scientists from the publicly funded International Rice Genome Sequencing Project (IRGSP) announced that they had completed a genetic map of the rice plant; their paper describing the genome was published in the journal *Nature* in August.[145] The data, available anywhere in the world at no cost, would be a key tool for researchers working on improved strains of rice, the researchers said. Across the developing world, 3 billion people relied on rice as the staple of their daily diet, but many went hungry. "This is really a project that can lead to important discoveries and findings that can help the condition of the poor. The poorest of the poor are the ones that depend on rice the most," said project participant Rod Wing, a scientist at the University of Arizona. Supported by the Rockefeller Foundation, the IRGSP was a collaborative undertaking, led by scientists in Japan and involving others in China, Taiwan, Thailand, Korea, the United States, Canada, France, India, Brazil, the Philippines, and the United Kingdom. Monsanto and Syngenta

---

145. International Rice Genome Sequencing Project, "The Map-Based Sequence of the Rice Genome," *Nature* 436, August 11, 2005, 793–800.

contributed genetic information to the project that sped up its completion by at least a year.[146]

The Preliminary WTO Decision

The WTO panel's decision on the GM case was scheduled to be circulated in March 2005, but the report's release was delayed until June, then October, and then until December.[147] Some believed that the postponement was intended to prevent a controversial decision from disrupting the lead-up to the December 2005 WTO ministerial in Hong Kong. At the ministerial, a petition calling on the WTO to honor the right of governments to "protect their citizens and the environment from GMO food and farming" was presented to WTO Deputy Director-General Alejandro Jara; it was signed by more than 740 organizations in 100 countries.[148] Analysts saw little progress in Hong Kong toward the successful completion of the Doha Round of trade talks, and they mainly blamed ongoing disagreements over agriculture. Europe—and especially France—needed to make further concessions to open its agriculture markets in order to save the Doha Round, some argued.

After the ministerial, the WTO announced that it needed yet more time to complete the panel report because of the "large number of issues to be addressed" in the case. The panel chairman also cited human resource issues, noting that "since much more time and effort was required for this case than originally planned for, some of the Secretariat staff is no longer available to the panel."[149] The final report's release was rescheduled for March 2006, making the GM case the longest panel process in WTO history.

In the lead-up to the report's release, the *Financial Times'* Raphael Minder noted the WTO decision was "likely to have more political resonance than actual impact on European food and agriculture sectors."[150] Some

---

146. Justin Gillis, "Secrets of Rice for All to Read; First Genetic Map of Major Food Crop Is Major Step Toward Reducing Hunger," *The Washington Post*, August 11, 2005, A1.

147. See WTO, "European Communities—Measures Affecting the Approval and Marketing of Biotech Products, Communication from the Chairman of the Panel," WT/DS291/27, November 2, 2004, and WTO, "European Communities—Measures Affecting the Approval and Marketing of Biotech Products, Communication from the Chairman of the Panel," WT/DS291/28, June 15, 2005.

148. Petition, quoted in "Civil Disobedience Called to Oppose GMOs At WTO," *All Africa*, December 21, 2005.

149. WTO, "European Communities—Measures Affecting the Approval and Marketing of Biotech Products, Communication from the Chairman of the Panel," WT/DS291/30, December 21, 2005.

150. Raphael Minder, "GM Foods Verdict Unlikely to Alter EU Rules," *The Financial Times*, January 5, 2006, 7.

observers agreed. "If the United States wins the case, it will be a win in terms of trade law, but not necessarily in terms of trade itself," says Robert Paarlberg.[151] The ruling would not change the wariness of European consumers toward GM foods, many argued. As Michael Taylor (2003) put it, "The United States cannot successfully litigate its way to public acceptance of biotechnology." The European Commission announced that the ruling would not force changes to EU approval procedures. "Only products recognized as safe will be allowed and the WTO report will not influence the decision-making process in the EU," the Commission noted. "Any idea that there is going to be a flood of GMOs is simply not the case."[152]

In February 2006, the WTO released its confidential preliminary decision to the parties—at 1,050 pages, the panel report was the longest in the WTO's history. Many interpreted the preliminary decision as a win for the United States and the agricultural biotechnology industry. Some NGOs criticized the "secretive" nature of the decision, and posted parts of the panel's confidential report on the Internet.

The WTO panel found that between June 1999 and August 2003, the European Commission had indeed "applied a general de facto moratorium on approvals of biotech products," which "resulted in a failure to complete individual approval procedures without undue delay"—and was therefore in violation of Article 8 and Annex C(1)(a) of the SPS agreement. In terms of product-specific approvals, the panel found "undue delay in the completion of the approval procedure with respect to 24 of the 27 relevant products." Finally, the safeguard measures taken by Austria, Belgium, France, Germany, Italy, and Luxembourg were found to be inconsistent with Articles 5.1 and 5.7 of the SPS agreement. However, the panel noted that it did not examine "whether biotech products in general are safe or not" or "whether the biotech products at issue in this dispute are 'like' their conventional counterparts." It also did not express a view as to whether "an amended de facto moratorium continues to exist or whether a new general de facto moratorium has since been imposed." The panel offered no findings under GATT Article XI or the TBT agreement. Finally, the panel did not find that the European Commission had violated all of the SPS articles that it was accused of violating.[153]

---

151. Comments from Robert Paarlberg from a January 2006 interview.

152. European Commission, quoted in Minder, "GM Foods Verdict Unlikely to Alter EU rules," 7.

153. For example, the panel said the United States had not established that the European Commission acted inconsistently with its obligations under SPS Annex C(1)(b), Annex B(1) and Article 7, Article 5.5, Article 2.2 or Article 2.3 by applying a general de facto moratorium between June 1999 and August 2003 (see paragraph 8.14). The "Conclusions and Recommendations" section of the panel's interim report (pg. 1029–50) were posted on the Web site of the Institute for Agriculture and Trade Policy, www.iatp.org. See paragraphs 8.3, 8.6, 8.7, 8.9, 8.10, 8.16.

Response to the WTO's preliminary decision was mixed. Some US officials celebrated the decision, saying it would speed approvals of GM products in the European Union and discourage other countries from adopting measures blocking GM imports. The panel's findings "will encourage the process of approvals and adoption within the European Union," summarized US agriculture negotiator Richard Crowder.[154] "This is a good, clear signal to the world that Europe was wrong," said Leon Corzine, chairman of the National Corn Grower's Association.[155] Observers also noted that the decision highlighted the importance of honoring global trade agreements. But a spokesperson for the European Union said the WTO report "is largely of historical interest" since the European Union had changed its approval process in 2004 and cleared nine products for import.[156] US trade officials countered that some applications filed in the 1990s still had not been approved.

NGOs sharply criticized the decision. "The WTO has bluntly ruled that European safeguards should be sacrificed to benefit biotech corporations," said Friends of the Earth Europe's Adrian Bebb.[157] The Institute for Agriculture and Trade Policy, a US nonprofit, called the decision "a major step back for the democratic rights of national and local governments to set their own environmental and human health regulations when there is scientific uncertainty."[158] NGOs also accused the WTO of challenging the authority of the Cartagena Protocol on Biosafety. Some observers said that the decision could harden European opposition to GMOs—and be bad publicity for the WTO. Robert Paarlberg notes that resentment over the case "could weaken the authority of the WTO across the board in Europe and further reduce the chances for a satisfying outcome in the Doha Round."

Observers also wondered if the WTO decision would exacerbate continuing internal conflicts between the European Commission and the member states. Though the European Union had passed new labeling and traceability directives, many member states continued to impose their own moratoria on the approval of new GMOs. But the Council of Envi-

---

154. "US, EU Split on Significance of WTO Panel on EU GMO Ban," *Inside US Trade*, February 10, 2006.

155. Andrew Pollack, "World Trade Agency Rules for US in Biotech Dispute," *The New York Times*, February 8, 2006.

156. Paul Meller, "Europe Defends Stance on Genetically Altered Foods," *The New York Times*, February 8, 2006.

157. Paul Geitner and Andrew Pollack, "A Line in the Sand Over WTO's Modified-Food Ruling," *The International Herald Tribune*, February 9, 2006.

158. Institute for Agriculture and Trade Policy, press release, "WTO Ruling on Genetically Engineered Crops Would Override International, National and Local Protections: Preliminary Ruling Favors US Biotech Companies Over Precautionary Regulation," February 7, 2006, 1.

ronmental Ministers rejected proposals from the Commission calling on Germany, Austria, Luxembourg, France, and Greece to lift their bans on approved GM products.[159] In addition, as noted above, the European Commission brought a case against some member countries at the European Court of Justice for failing to implement the new directives.[160] These moves were taking place after the defeat of the proposed EU constitution in the 2005 Dutch and French referendums, at a time when the authority of the Commission in Europe was weakened and thus more easily questioned.

Finally, some argued that the dispute had slowed the development of GM technology in Europe and the United States, risking economic competitiveness. Without better management and increased access to biotechnology, leadership would move to other players. "Europe and the United States should learn to manage new technologies collectively, not to suppress them," noted Calestous Juma. "Failure to do so will shift technological leadership to other regions, such as China, that have made significant strides in using new technologies for economic growth."[161]

---

159. "EU Member States Clash with Commission over GMOs, Could Signal Changes," *Inside US Trade*, July 8, 2005.

160. "US, EU to Face Off at WTO Early This Year over GMOs, Aircraft," *Inside US Trade*, January 6, 2006.

161. Calestous Juma, "'Satan's Drink' and a Sorry History of Global Food Fights," *The Financial Times*, February 9, 2006.

Case Analysis

A central issue in the trading system is how to deal with divergent regulatory approaches and rules. On the one hand, regulatory uniformity facilitates free trade; on the other hand, regulatory diversity accommodates different national preferences, conditions and beliefs. In this case, we see that the very different approaches to GMOs adopted by the United States and the European Union have resulted in conflicts at the WTO, the Codex Alimentarius Commission and in negotiations for a UN Protocol on Biosafety. The case allows us to explore the origins of these differences and to consider whether they can be reconciled through the WTO dispute settlement system; in particular, it sheds light on the question of whether litigation is likely to help or hinder negotiation.

The case outlines the very different treatment accorded to GMOs in the two systems, the disputes generated by the dissimilarity, and the nature of the institutional barriers to achieving negotiated agreements to resolve these disputes. In the United States, initially there was no special legislative treatment of GM products, which were thus subject to the same health and safety procedures as other goods. At its essence, the US view, like that expressed in the WTO's SPS agreement, is that regulations should be based on science and on risk analysis. The net result is that the US system has allowed many GM products to be introduced into the market.

In the European Union, by contrast, these products were subject to special rules and directives influenced by the Environmental Directorate-General of the European Commission. By seeking compelling evidence that a GM product is safe before it is introduced, the European approach puts far more emphasis on taking precautions. The net result is that for long periods of time, few or no GM products have been approved for sale in the European Union. In addition, the European Union has insisted that if they are introduced, products must meet very strict labeling and traceability requirements.

What explains these different approaches? Why is it that in the United States GMOs are presumed innocent until science proves them guilty, while in the European Union they seem to be guilty until science proves them innocent? Is it that Americans are by nature more willing to accept new products and technologies? Do the two political and regulatory systems weight the different actors differently? Producers and biotech firms seem to be more powerful in the United States; consumer and environmental groups play a major role in the European Union. Have different national experiences with food regulation shaped these stances? Mad cow disease and other food scares have certainly reduced public confidence in food regulation in the European Union; Americans, who have had fewer scares, appear to be more trusting. Many observers add that culturally, Europeans have a different attitude toward food than do Americans.

Article 3.7 of the WTO Dispute Settlement Understanding (DSU) states, "Before bringing a case, a Member shall exercise its judgment as to whether action under these procedures would be fruitful." Whatever the reasons for these differences in regulatory systems, are they likely to be reconciled through litigation in the WTO dispute settlement system? American farmers and biotech producers have clearly been very frustrated with the European approach, and bringing a case allows the Office of the USTR to voice their concerns—but would a US victory be effective in changing EU policies, or is it likely to simply harden attitudes on both sides of the Atlantic and make compromise more difficult? On the one hand, Americans favoring a case suggest that victory could strengthen the hand of those Europeans who argue in favor of more liberal treatment. They also feel that the United States must insist on enforcing its WTO rights and discourage other countries from following the EU policy example. On the other hand, Europeans against such a case see it as unnecessary, since approvals are being granted again, even if not as quickly as Americans might like; potentially counterproductive, since it could appear that US pressure rather than credible evidence that the products are safe is the reason for their approval; or ineffective and likely to result in more trade friction if the United States feels compelled to retaliate.

The arguments introduced by each side in the WTO dispute reflect their fundamental differences. The United States stresses in particular the role given to science in the SPS agreement. Specifically, Article 2.2 makes clear that such measures must be based on scientific principles and may not be maintained without sufficient scientific evidence. The Europeans, however, find support for a precautionary principle in Article 5.7, which says that if members have insufficient relevant scientific evidence, they may provisionally adopt protective measures "on the basis of available pertinent information."

The conflict between these two trade superpowers has important implications for other nations. As the old saying goes, "When the elephants fight, the grass gets trampled." What approach should other nations adopt? Many developing countries are attracted to the promise that biotechnology offers for improving farm productivity, saving on pesticides, and providing healthier foods. At the same time, many are wary about its possible impact on health and the environment and, as the Zambian example in the case makes clear, they are concerned that the use of GM products could prevent their exports from being accepted in the European Union. Egypt's experience in being forced to withdraw its support for the US case at the WTO exemplifies the tensions this issue introduces not only in the WTO but also in the international forums concerned with food safety.

Are the two systems ultimately reconcilable? One approach might envisage GM and non-GM products coexisting, distinguished by agreed-on labels, and consumers ultimately being allowed to choose between them.

But there are problems with such an approach. First, as the case brings out, informed choice requires both labeling and traceability, and the devil lies in the details. Such requirements could be so demanding, and meeting them so costly, that in practice they could operate as a ban. Second, there are technical problems in actually segregating GM and non-GM crops and distribution systems, as the example of Starlink in the case demonstrates. And third, what if in some countries, regulators still believe it necessary to maintain bans on GM products until there is scientific evidence that the products are safe? Should the trading rules be used to try to force countries to import such products? If so, what would such pressure mean for the long-run legitimacy of the rules?

Appendix 6A
Timeline of Key Events in the GM Crop Dispute

Date	Event
1973	Scientists transfer DNA from one cell to another.
1975	Asilomar conference on recombinant DNA is held.
1976	US National Institutes of Health (NIH) publishes guidelines for biomedical research using recombinant organisms for labs conducting federally funded experiments.
1980	The US Supreme Court extends patent protection to new types of plants including seeds, tissue cultures, and genes.
1981	Industrial Biotechnology Association created (United States).
1982	Scientists at Monsanto pioneer the modification of a plant cell's genetic structure.
1983	Association of Biotechnology Companies created (United States). The organization later merged with the Industrial Biotechnology Association in 1994 to form the Biotechnology Industry Organization.
1984	European Commission forms the Biotechnology Steering Committee, which establishes the Biotechnology Regulations Interservice Committee a year later.
1986	DG XI (Environment) takes the lead in drafting the European Commission report "A Community Framework for the Regulation of Biotechnology."
	United States publishes the Coordinated Framework for Regulation of Biotechnology.
	First US outdoor field test of a GM crop plant.
1988	European Commission proposes directives on GMOs with leadership from DG XI (Environment).

(timeline continues next page)

Timeline of Key Events *(continued)*

Date	Event
1990	European Council adopts Directives 90/219 and 90/220 on the contained use and deliberate release of GMOs.
1993	The FDA approves rbST.
1996	GM crop varieties are introduced for commercial production in the United States.
	British BSE ("mad cow") crisis leads to slaughter of cattle and public distrust of food safety.
1996–97	The European Commission approves Monsanto's Roundup-Ready soybeans and Novartis's GM corn; Austria, Italy, and Luxembourg invoke safeguard clause and ban the corn.
1997	The European Council and Parliament adopt the Novel Foods regulation that provides for labeling of some foods with GM ingredients.
October 1998	De facto moratorium on approval of new GM varieties starts.
1999	By 1999, Monsanto had invested more than $8 billion to buy seed companies and close marketing agreements in its commitment to produce GM crops.
	Denmark, France, Greece, Italy, and Luxembourg say they will refuse to approve new GM products until rules on traceability and labeling are in place.
	Prince Charles bans new tenant farmers on his land from using GM products.
	Codex establishes Ad Hoc Task Force on Foods Derived from Biotechnology.
	Some companies begin to back away from GM ingredients.
January 2000	One hundred thirty countries adopt the Cartagena Protocol on Biosafety.

Date	Event
April 2000	European Food Safety Authority (EFSA) is created.
September 2000	StarLink corn—a GM variety approved only for animal consumption in the United States—is found in taco shells.
March 2001	European Council and Parliament adopt Directive 2001/18 on deliberate release of GMOs, replacing Directive 90/220, to be implemented in October 2002.
January 2002	EFSA becomes operational.
June 2002	European Union ratifies the Biosafety Protocol.
October 2002	Directive 2001/18 enters into force.
May 2003	United States launches a WTO complaint over EU regulation of GMOs.
July 2003	The European Commission refers 11 member states to the European Court of Justice for failing to adopt national legislation implementing Directive 2001/18.
September 2003	Council and European Parliament adopt Regulation 1830/2003 on Traceability and Labeling of GMOs and Regulation 1829/2003 on Genetically Modified Food and Feed.
April 2004	Regulations 1829/2003 and 1830/2003 enter into force.
May 2004	European Commission approves the marketing of canned Bt-11 sweet corn for 10 years, the first GM approval since October 1998.
July 2005	The European Council of Environment Ministers rejects the Commission's proposal to lift Austria, France, Germany, Greece, and Luxembourg's bans on authorized GMOs.
February 2006	The WTO panel announces its preliminary decision.

Appendix 6B
Excerpts from Annexes B and C of the Agreement on the Application of Sanitary and Phytosanitary Measures

For the body of the agreement and Annex A, see appendix 1C in chapter 1.

Annex B
Transparency of Sanitary and Phytosanitary Regulations
Publication of Regulations

1. Members shall ensure that all sanitary and phytosanitary regulations[1] which have been adopted are published promptly in such a manner as to enable interested Members to become acquainted with them.

Annex C
Control, Inspection and Approval Procedures[2]

1. Members shall ensure, with respect to any procedure to check and ensure the fulfilment of sanitary or phytosanitary measures, that:
   (a) such procedures are undertaken and completed without undue delay and in no less favourable manner for imported products than for like domestic products;
   (b) the standard processing period of each procedure is published or that the anticipated processing period is communicated to the applicant upon request; when receiving an application, the competent body promptly examines the completeness of the documentation and informs the applicant in a precise and complete manner of all deficiencies; the competent body transmits as soon as possible the results of the procedure in a precise and complete manner to the applicant so that corrective action may be taken if necessary; even when the application has deficiencies, the competent body proceeds as far as practicable with the procedure if the applicant so requests; and that upon request, the applicant is informed of the stage of the procedure, with any delay being explained[.]

---

1. Sanitary and phytosanitary measures such as laws, decrees or ordinances which are applicable generally.

2. Control, inspection and approval procedures include, inter alia, procedures for sampling, testing and certification.

References

Allen, G. C. 1981. *The Japanese Economy.* New York: St. Martin's.

Allison, Graham T. 1971. *Essence of Decision: Explaining the Cuban Missile Crisis.* Boston: Little, Brown.

Arrow, Kenneth, Robert Mnookin, Lee Ross, Amos Tversky, and Robert Wilson, eds. 1995. *Barriers to Conflict Resolution.* New York: Norton.

Asanuma. 1971. *Asanuma: A Commemorative History of the First Hundred Years.* Tokyo, Japan (privately published).

Baffes, John. 2004a. *Brazil vs. US: Cotton Subsidies and Implications for Development.* Trade Note 16. Washington: World Bank Group.

Baffes, John. 2004b. *Cotton: Market Setting, Trade Policies, and Issues.* Policy Research Working Paper 3218. Washington: World Bank.

Berg, Paul A., D. Baltimore, H. W. Boyer, S. N. Cohen, R. W. Davis, D. S. Hogness, D. Nathans, R. Roblin, J. D. Watson, S. Weissman, and N. D. Zinder. 1995 [1974]. Letter: Potential Biohazards of Recombinant DNA Molecules. *Science* 185, no. 148:303 (July 26, 1974). Reprinted in Cantley (1995).

Bernauer, Thomas. 2003. *Genes, Trade, and Regulation: The Seeds of Conflict in Food Biotechnology.* Princeton, NJ: Princeton University Press.

Bhagwati, Jagdish. 2002. *Free Trade Today.* Princeton, NJ: Princeton University Press.

Bhagwati, Jagdish, and Hugh T. Patrick, eds. 1991. *Aggressive Unilateralism: America's 301 Trade Policy and the World Trading System.* Ann Arbor: Michigan University Press.

Borrell, Brent. 1994. *EU Bananarama III.* Policy Research Working Paper 13/86. Washington: World Bank.

Bradford, Scott C., Paul L. E. Grieco, and Gary Clyde Hufbauer. 2005. The Payoff to America from Global Integration. In *The United States and the World Economy: Foreign Economic Policy for the Next Decade,* by C. Fred Bergsten and the Institute for International Economics. Washington: Institute for International Economics.

Cabanilla, Liborio, Tahirou Abdoulaye, and John Sanders. 2003. Public Goods and Public Policy for Agricultural Biotechnology. Paper presented at the 7th International Consortium on Agricultural Biotechnology Research (ICABR) International Conference, Ravello, Italy, June 29–August 3.

Camargo Neto, Pedro de. 2004. The WTO Cotton Dispute. Presentation at the Cordell Hull Institute, May 28, Washington.

Cameron, J., and K. R. Gray. 2001. Principles of International Law in the WTO Dispute Settlement Body. *International and Comparative Law Quarterly* 50: 248–98.

Cantley, Mark. 1995. The Regulation of Modern Biotechnology: A Historical and European Perspective. In *Legal, Economic and Ethical Dimensions*, ed. D. Brauer, vol. 12 of *Biotechnology*, ed. H.-J. Rehm and G. Reed with A. Pühler and P. Stadler, 2d ed. Weinheim: VCH.

CGIAR (Consultative Group on International Agricultural Research). 2004. *Annual Report 2004—Innovations in Agricultural Research*. Washington: CGIAR Secretariat. Available at www.cgiar.org.

CGIAR (Consultative Group on International Agricultural Research). 2004–05. Research and Impact: CGIAR and Agricultural Biotechnology. Available at www.cgiar.org.

Cialdini, Robert B. 1993. *Influence: The Psychology of Persuasion*. Rev. ed. New York: William Morrow.

Codex Alimentarius Commission. 1985. *Report of the Sixteenth Session of the Joint FAO/WHO Codex Alimentarius Commission*. ALINORM 85/47. Rome: FAO.

Codex Alimentarius Commission. 1991. *Report of the Nineteenth Session of the Joint FAO/WHO Codex Alimentarius Commission*. ALINORM 91/40. Rome: FAO.

Codex Alimentarius Commission. 1993. *Report of the Twentieth Session of the Joint FAO/WHO Codex Alimentarius Commission*. ALINORM 93/40. Rome: FAO.

Codex Alimentarius Commission. 1995. *Report of the Twenty-first Session of the Joint FAO/WHO Codex Alimentarius Commission*. ALINORM 93/40. Rome: FAO.

Cooter, Robert D., Stephen Marks, and Robert Mnookin. 1982. Bargaining in the Shadow of the Law: A Testable Model of Strategic Behavior. *Journal of Legal Studies* 11: 225–51.

Davis, Christina L. 2003. *Food Fights over Free Trade: How International Institutions Promote Agricultural Trade Liberalization*. Princeton, NJ: Princeton University Press.

de Gorter, Harry, Merlinda Ingco, and Laura Ignacio. 2003. *Domestic Support for Agriculture: Agricultural Policy Reform and Developing Countries*. World Bank Group Trade Note 7. Washington: World Bank. Available at www.worldbank.org.

Devereaux, Charan. 2006. International Trade Meets Intellectual Property: The Making of the TRIPS Agreement (TRIPS, Case 1). In *Case Studies on US Trade Negotiation: Making the Rules, vol. 1*, by Charan Devereaux, Robert Lawrence, and Michael Watkins. Washington: Institute for International Economics.

Dewey Ballantine. 1995. *Privatizing Protection: Japanese Market Barriers in Consumer Photographic Film and Paper*. Report prepared for Kodak. Washington: Dewey Ballantine.

DTB Associates. 2004. Fact Sheet on the Peace Clause and the WTO Subsidies Agreement. Washington.

European Commission. 2000. *2000 Report on United States Barriers to Trade and Investment*. Brussels.

European Communities, Directorate-General for Research, Food Quality, and Safety. 2004. *Plants for the Future 2025: A European Vision for Plant Genomics and Biotechnology*. Luxembourg: Office for Official Publications of the European Communities. Available at http://europa.eu.int.

EU-US Biotechnology Consultative Forum. 2000. *Final Report*. December. Available at http://europa.eu.int.

Fara, G. M., G. Del Corvo, S. Bernuzzi, A. Bigatello, C. Di Pietro, S. Scaglioni, and G. Chiumello. 1979. Epidemic of Breast Enlargement in an Italian School. *The Lancet*, August 11, 295–97.

Fernandez-Cornejo, Jorge, and William McBride. 2000. *Genetically Engineered Crops for Pest Management in US Agriculture: Farm Level Effects*. ERS Economic Research Service, US Department of Agriculture, Agricultural Economic Report no. AER786. Washington: US Department of Agriculture. Available at www.ers.usda.gov.

Fernandez-Cornejo, Jorge, and William D. McBride. 2002. *Adoption of Bioengineered Crops*. ERS Economic Research Service, US Department of Agriculture, Agricultural Economic Report no. AER810. Washington: US Department of Agriculture. Available at www.ers.usda.gov.

First, Harry. 1995. Antitrust Enforcement in Japan. *Antitrust Law Journal* 64, no. 1 (Fall): 137–82.

Goldberg, Ray, and Hal Hogan. 2003. *Launching the European Food Safety Authority.* Harvard Business School Case Study N2-904-414. Boston: Harvard Business School.

Goldman, Patti, and J. Martin Wagner. 1996. *WTO Dispute Settlement Proceeding; European Communities—Measures Concerning Meat and Meat Products (Hormones).* Comments on behalf of Cancer Prevention Coalition, Public Citizen, Institute for Trade and Agricultural Policy, October 4. Sierra Club Legal Defense Fund.

Goreux, Louis, and John Macrae. 2003. *Reforming the Cotton Sector in Sub-Saharan Africa.* World Bank Africa Region Working Paper Series 47. Washington: World Bank.

Hightower, Jim. 1999. *If the Gods Had Meant Us to Vote They Would Have Given Us Candidates.* New York: HarperCollins.

Horlick, Gary N. 1995. WTO Dispute Settlement and the Dole Commission. *Journal of World Trade* 29 (December): 45–48.

Hudec, Robert. 1993. *Enforcing International Trade Law: The Evolution of the Modern GATT Legal System.* Salem, NH: Buttersworth Legal Publishers.

Hufbauer, Gary Clyde, and Ben Goodrich. 2003. *Next Move in Steel: Revocation or Retaliation?* Policy Brief 03-10. Washington: Institute for International Economics.

Hurd, Hilary. 1999. EU Says It Will Not Lift Ban on Hormone-Treated Beef (The EU Scientific Committee on Veterinary Matters Related to Public Health Decision). *Food Chemical News* 41, no. 12 (May 10).

ICAC (International Cotton Advisory Committee). 2002. Production and Trade Policies Affecting the Cotton Industry. Washington. Available at www.icac.org.

Iida, Keisuke. 2004. Is WTO Dispute Settlement Effective? *Global Governance* 10: 207–25.

Iklé, Fred Charles. 1964. *How Nations Negotiate.* New York: Harper and Row.

Ito, Takatoshi. 1992. *The Japanese Economy.* Cambridge, MA: MIT Press.

Jackson, John H. 1969. *World Trade and the Law of GATT.* Indianapolis, IN: Bobbs-Merrill.

Jackson, John H. 1997a. *The World Trading System: Law and Policy of International Economic Relations,* 2d ed. Cambridge, MA: MIT Press.

Jackson, John H. 1997b. The WTO Dispute Settlement Understanding—Misunderstandings on the Nature of Legal Obligations. *American Journal of International Law* 91, no. 2: 60–64.

Jackson, John H., William J. Davey, and Alan O. Sykes Jr. 1995. *Legal Problems of International Economic Relations: Cases, Materials and Text.* St. Paul, MN: West Publishing.

Josling, Timothy, Donna Roberts, and David Orden. 2004. *Food Regulation and Trade: Toward a Safe and Open Global Food System.* Washington: Institute for International Economics.

Kuchler, Fred, John McClelland, and Susan E. Offutt. 1989. Regulating Food Safety: The Case of Animal Growth Hormones. *National Food Review* 12, no. 3 (July–September): 25–30.

Lamming, G. E., G. Ballarini, E. E. Baulieu, P. Brookes, P. S. Elias, R. Ferrando, C. L. Galli, R. J. Heitzman, B. Hoffman, H. Karg, H. H. D. Meyer, G. Michel, E. Poulsen, A. Rico, F. X. R. van Leeuwen, and D. S. White. 1987. Scientific Report on Anabolic Agents in Animal Production. *Veterinary Record* 121 (October 24): 389–92.

Lawrence, Robert Z. 2004. *Crimes and Punishments? Retaliation Under the WTO.* Washington: Institute for International Economics.

Leamon, Ann K. 2003. *Robert Shapiro and Monsanto.* Harvard Business School Case Study N9-801-426, rev. ed. Boston: Harvard Business School.

Losey, J. E., L. S. Raynor, and M. E. Carter. 1999. Transgenic Pollen Harms Monarch Larvae. *Nature* 399: 214.

Marcus, Alan I. 1994. *Cancer from Beef: DES, Federal Food Regulation, and Consumer Confidence.* Baltimore, MD: Johns Hopkins University Press.

Moore, Christopher. 1996. *The Mediation Process.* 2nd ed. San Francisco, CA: Jossey-Bass.

Mulligan, Terence. 1999. *Chiquita Brands International (A).* Harvard Business School Case Study N9-797-015. Boston, MA: Harvard Business School.

Office of Technology Assessment, US Congress. 1991. *Biotechnology in a Global Economy.* OTA-BA-494. Washington: US Government Printing Office.

O'Halloran, Sharyn. 1997 Comments on David Vogel's Social Regulations as Trade Barriers. In *Comparative Disadvantages? Social Regulations and the Global Economy*, ed. Pietro S. Nivola. Washington: Brookings Institution Press.

Oxfam. 2004. *"White Gold" Turns to Dust*. Oxfam Briefing Paper No. 58. Available at www.oxfam.org.

Paarlberg, Robert. 2000. The Global Food Fight. *Foreign Affairs* 79, no. 3 (May/June): 24–38.

Patterson, Lee Ann. 2000. Biotechnology Policy: Regulating Risks and Risking Regulation. In *Policy-Making in the European Union*, ed. Helen Wallace and William Wallace. 4th ed. Oxford: Oxford University Press.

Patterson, Lee Ann, and Tim Josling. 2002. *Regulating Biotechnology: Comparing EU and US Approaches*. European Policy Paper Series. Pittsburgh: European Union Center, University of Pittsburgh.

Pew Initiative on Food and Biotechnology. 2003. *US vs. EU: An Examination of the Trade Issues Surrounding Genetically Modified Food*, rev. ed. Washington: Pew Initiative on Food and Biotechnology.

Pringle, Peter. 2003. *Food, Inc.: Mendel to Monsanto—The Promises and Perils of the Biotech Harvest*. New York: Simon and Schuster.

Putnam, Judith Jones. 1990. Food Consumption. *Food Review*, July 1: 1.

Robinson, Robert J. 1996a. *Errors in Social Judgment: Implications for Negotiation and Conflict Resolution*. Part 1, *Biased Assimilation of Information*. Harvard Business School Note 2897-103. Boston, MA: Harvard Business School.

Robinson, Robert J. 1996b. *Errors in Social Judgment: Implications for Negotiation and Conflict Resolution*. Part 2, *Partisan Perceptions*. Harvard Business School Note 2897-104. Boston, MA: Harvard Business School.

Robinson, R. J., D. Keltner, A. Ward, and L. Ross. 1995. Actual Versus Assumed Differences in Construal: "Naive Realism" in Inter-group Perception and Conflict. *Journal of Personality and Social Psychology* 68: 404–17.

Ross, L., and A. Ward. 1995. Psychological Barriers to Dispute Resolution. *Advances in Experimental Social Psychology* 27: 255–304.

Rubin, Jeffrey Z., Dean G. Pruitt, and Sung Hee Kim. 1994. *Social Conflict: Escalation, Stalemate, and Settlement*, 2d ed. New York: McGraw-Hill.

Sahel and West Africa Club Secretariat/OECD. 2005. *Economic and Social Importance of Cotton Production and Trade in West Africa*. Paris: OECD.

Scaglioni, Silvia, Carmelo DiPietro, Attilio Bigatello, and Giuseppe Chiumello. 1978. Breast Enlargement at an Italian School. *The Lancet*, March 11, 551–52.

Scherer, F. M. 1995. *Retail Distribution Channel Barriers to International Trade*. Cambridge, MA: John F. Kennedy School of Government, Harvard University.

Shaffer, Gregory C., and Mark A. Pollack. 2004. *Regulating Between National Fears and Global Disciplines: Agricultural Biotechnology in the EU*. Jean Monnet Working Paper 10/04, New York University School of Law, New York. Available at www.jeanmonnetprogram.org.

Sieg, Albert L., with Steven J. Bennett. 1994. *The Tokyo Chronicles: An American Gaijin Reveals the Hidden Truths of Japanese Life and Business*. Essex Junction, VT: Omneo.

Skelly, Carol, and Stephen MacDonald. 2003. Issues in the Global Cotton Market: A US Perspective. Paper presented at the 2003 China International Cotton Conference, Jiuzhaigou, China (October 27–31). Available at www.fao.org.

Specter, Michael. 2000. The Pharmageddon Riddle. *The New Yorker*, April 10, 58–71.

Sutherland, Peter, Jagdish Bhagwati, Kwesi Botchwey, Niall Fitzgerald, Koichi Hamada, John Jackson, Celso Lafer, and Thierry de Montbrial. 2004. *The Future of the WTO: Addressing Institutional Challenges in the New Millennium*. Geneva: World Trade Organization.

Taylor, Michael R. 2003. Rethinking US Leadership in Food Biotechnology. *Nature Biotechnology* 21, no. 8 (August): 852.

Torersen, Helge, Jürgen Hampel, Marie-Louise von Bermann-Winberg, Eleanor Bridgman, John Durant, Edna Einsiedel, Björn Fjæstad, George Gaskell, Petra Grabner, Petra Hieber, Erling Jelsøe, Jesper Lassen, Athena Marouda-Chatjoulis, Torben Hviid Nielsen,

Timo Rusanen, George Sakellaris, Franz Seifert, Carla Smink, Tomasz Twardowski, and Merci Wambui Kamara. 2002. Promise, Problems, and Proxies: Twenty-Five Years of Debate and Regulation in Europe. In *Biotechnology: The Making of a Global Controversy*, ed. Martin W. Bauer and George Gaskell. Cambridge: Cambridge University Press.

USDA (United States Department of Agriculture), Economic Research Service. 1998. *Agriculture in the WTO*. Washington.

Vogel, David. 2001. *Ships Passing in the Night: The Changing Politics of Risk Regulation in Europe and the United States*. EUI-RSCAS Working Paper 16, European University Institute, Robert Schuman Centre of Advanced Studies, Florence. Available at http://ideas.repec.org.

Vogel, David, and Diahanna Lynch. 2001. The Regulation of GMOs in Europe and the US: A Case-Study of Contemporary European Regulatory Politics. Council on Foreign Relations, Special Report, April 5. Available at www.cfr.org.

Watkins, Michael. 2000. *Diagnosing and Overcoming Barriers to Negotiated Agreement*. Harvard Business School Note 9-800-333. Boston, MA: Harvard Business School.

Watkins, Michael. 2002. *Breakthrough Business Negotiation: A Toolbox for Managers*. San Francisco, CA: Jossey-Bass.

Watkins, Michael, and Kim Winters. 1997. Intervenors with Interests and Power. *Negotiation Journal* 13, no. 2 (April): 119–42.

Weiler, J. H. H. 2001. The Rule of Lawyers and the Ethos of Diplomats: Reflections on WTO Dispute Settlement. In *Efficiency, Equity, and Legitimacy: The Multilateral Trading System at the Millennium*, ed. Roger B. Porter, Pierre Sauvé, Arvind Subramanian, and Americo Beviglia Zampetti. Washington: Brookings Institution Press.

Willkie Farr & Gallagher. 1995. *Rewriting History: Kodak's Revisionist Account of the Japanese Consumer*. Prepared for Fuji Photo Film USA. Washington: Willkie, Farr & Gallagher.

Wirth, David A. 1994. The Role of Science in the Uruguay Round and NAFTA Trade Disciplines. *Cornell International Law Journal* 817: 832–40.

WTO (World Trade Organization). 1999. *Trading into the Future*. 2nd ed. Geneva: WTO. Available at www.wetec.org.

WTO (World Trade Organization). 2005. *The GATT Years: From Havana to Marrakesh. Understanding the WTO*. Available at www.wto.org.

Zimbardo, Philip G., and Michael R. Leippe. 1991. *The Psychology of Attitude Change and Social Influence*. New York: McGraw-Hill.

Additional Readings

Introduction to the Current Dispute Settlement System

Hoekman, Bernard M., and Michel M. Kosetecki. 2001. Chapter 3 of *The Political Economy of the World Trading System: The WTO and Beyond*. Oxford: Oxford University Press.

Matsushita, Mitsuo, Thomas J. Schoenbaum, and Petros C. Mavroidis. 2004. Chapter 2 of *The World Trade Organization: Law, Practice, and Policy*. Oxford: Oxford University Press.

WTO Rules and Their Application in WTO Law

Horn, Henrik, and Petros C. Mavroidis, eds. 2003. *The WTO Case Law of 2001*. American Law Institute Reporter's Studies. Cambridge: Cambridge University Press.

WTO (World Trade Organization). 2003. *WTO Analytical Index: Guide to WTO Law and Practice*. Geneva: World Trade Organization and Bernan.

Analysis of the WTO Dispute Settlement System

Bagwell, Kyle, and Robert Staiger. 2002. *The Economics of the World Trading System*. Cambridge, MA: MIT Press.

Barfield, Claude E. 2001. *Free Trade, Sovereignty, and Democracy: The Future of the World Trade Organization*. Washington: American Enterprise Institute Press.

Bayard, Thomas, and Kimberly Ann Elliott. 1994. *Reciprocity and Retaliation in US Trade Policy*. Washington: Institute for International Economics.

Bown, Chad P. 2003. On the Economic Success of GATT/WTO Dispute Settlement. *Review of Economics and Statistics* 86, no. 3: 811–23.

Busch, Marc L., and Eric Reinhardt. 2002. Testing International Trade Law: Empirical Studies of GATT? WTO Dispute Settlement. In *The Political Economy of International Trade Law: Essays in Honor of Robert Hudec*, ed. David M. Kennedy and James D. Southwick. Cambridge: Cambridge University Press.

Horn, Henrik, Hakan Nordstrom, and Petros C. Mavroidis. 1999. *Is the Use of the WTO Dispute Settlement System Biased?* CEPR Discussion Paper 2340. London: Centre for Economic Policy Research.

Howse, Robert. 2000. Adjudicative Legitimacy and Treaty Interpretation in International Trade Law: The Early Years of WTO Jurisprudence. In *The EU, the WTO, and the NAFTA: Towards a Common Law of International Trade,* ed. J. H. H. Weiler. Oxford: Oxford University Press.

Petersmann, Ernst-Ulrich, and Mark A. Pollack, eds. 2003. *Transatlantic Economic Disputes: The EU, the US, and the WTO.* Oxford: Oxford University Press.

Conflict Resolution and Design of the Dispute Resolution System

Ury, William, Jeanne Bret, and Stephen Goldberg. 1988. *Getting Disputes Resolved: Designing Systems to Cut the Costs of Conflict.* San Francisco: Jossey-Bass.

Hormone-Treated Beef

Mavroidis, Petrus C. 2003. The Trade Disputes Concerning Health Policy Between the EC and the US. In *Transatlantic Economic Disputes: The EU, the US and the WTO,* ed. Ernst-Ulrich Petersmann and Mark A. Pollack. Oxford: Oxford University Press.

Pauwelyn, Joost. 1999. The WTO Agreement on Sanitary and Phytosanitary (SPS) Measures as Applied in the First Three SPS Disputes: EC–Hormones, Australia-Salmon, and Japan Varietals. *Journal of International Economic Law* 2, no. 4: 641–64.

Bananas

Cadot, Olivier, and Douglas Webber. 2002. Banana Splits: Policy Process, Particularistic Interests, Political Capture, and Money in Transatlantic Trade Politics. *Business and Politics* 4, no. 1: 5–39.

Weiss, Fred. 2003. Manifestly Illegal Import Restrictions and Non-Compliance with WTO Dispute Settlement Rulings: Lessons from the Banana Dispute. In *Transatlantic Economic Disputes: The EU, the US and the WTO,* ed. Ernst-Ulrich Petersmann and Mark A. Pollack. Oxford: Oxford University Press.

Kodak v. Fuji

Chua, Adrian. 1998. Reasonable Expectations and Non-Violation Complaints in GATT/WTO Jurisprudence. *Journal of World Trade* 32, no. 2: 27–50.

Dillon, Sara. 1999. Fuji-Kodak, the World Trade Organization and the Death of Domestic Political Constituencies. *Minnesota Journal of Global Trade* 8, no. 2: 197.

Komuro, Norio. 1998. Kodak-Fuji Film Dispute and the WTO Panel Ruling. *Journal of World Trade* 32, no. 5: 161–217.

Lawrence, Robert Z. 1993. Japan's Different Trade Regime: An Analysis with Particular Reference to Keiretsu. *Journal of Economic Perspectives* 7, no. 3 (Summer): 3–20.

Tarullo, Daniel K. 2000. Norms and Institutions in Global Competition Policy. *American Journal of International Law* 94: 478–504.

Steel

Hufbauer, Gary Clyde, and Ben Goodrich. 2003. *Steel Policy: The Good, the Bad, and the Ugly.* International Economics Policy Brief 03-01. Washington: Institute for International Economics.
Lawrence, Robert Z., and Nathaniel Stankard. 2004. America's Sorry Trade Performance. *International Economy* (Winter): 36–39.
Sykes, Alan. 2004. The Persistent Puzzles of Safeguards: Lessons from the Steel Dispute. *Journal of International Economic Law* 7, no. 3: 523–64.

Cotton

Newell, Matthew. 2005. Cotton, US Domestic Policy, and Trade Wars: The Future of WTO Agriculture Negotiations. *Minnesota Journal of World Trade* 14 (Summer): 301–44.
Steinberg, Richard, and Timothy Josling. 2003. When the Peace Ends: The Vulnerability of EC and US Agricultural Subsidies to WTO Challenge. *Journal of International Economic Law* 6, no. 2: 369–417.

Genetically Modified Organisms

Paarlberg, Robert. 2001. *The Politics of Precaution: Genetically Modified Crops in Developing Countries*. Baltimore, MD: Johns Hopkins University Press.
Vogel, David. 2001. *Ships Passing in the Night: The Changing Politics of Risk Regulation in Europe and the United States*. EUI Working Papers RSC No. 2001/16. Dan Domenico, Italy: European University Institute.

Index

Aaron, David, 203, 208, 211, 214
Abbott, Roderick, 130
acceptable daily intake (ADI) levels, 45n, 46
administrative guidance, under Japanese antitrust law, 153, 166
administrative surcharges, under Japanese antitrust law, 152
ADR mechanisms. *See* alternative dispute resolution (ADR) mechanisms
Africa, rejection of GMOs in, 318, 322, 339
African, Caribbean, and Pacific (ACP) former colonies, 99n
    preferential treatment for, 113, 139
        and banana dispute, 97, 99, 101–108, 102n, 118–19, 134, 137
        and cotton dispute, 250, 250n
        and GATT rules, 105
        as violation of trade rules, 120–22
agenda, narrowness of, as structural barrier, 12
Agfa-Gevaert, 168
aggregate measurement of support (AMS), 275
    and cotton dispute, 238, 238n, 239, 255
Agracetus, 288
Agreement on Import Licensing Procedures, 120
Agreement on Sanitary and Phytosanitary Measures (SPS), 8
    Annexes B and C, 344

and beef hormone dispute, 32, 56–59, 63, 80, 82, 91–96, 297
versus Biosafety Protocol, 310, 310n
and GMO dispute, 299–300, 307, 312–13, 324–28, 335, 335n, 338–39, 344
harmonization of standards under, 82, 92–93
negotiation of, 57–59
risk assessment under, 82, 93–95
Agreement on Subsidies and Countervailing Measures (SCM), 8, 232n, 243, 263, 263n, 264, 272–73, 272n
Agreement on Technical Barriers to Trade (TBT), 8
    Article 7, 46
    and GMO dispute, 328, 328n, 335
AgrEvo, 291
Agricultural Adjustment Act of 1933, 274
agricultural biotechnology. *See also* genetically modified crops
    business of, 290–93
    in developing countries, 319–20, 322, 333, 339
    EU regulation of, 284–85, 293–96, 333–34
    history of, 285–87
    US regulation of, 287–90, 293–96
agricultural chemicals, 285–86
agricultural exports, US, 283

355

agricultural lobbies
  in GM crops dispute, 320, 330
  importance of, 236–37, 262
agricultural policies
  EU, 19, 33–34
  US, 33–34
Agricultural Risk Protection Act (ARPA), 276
agricultural subsidies, 33–34, 58, 240–41, 255–56, 271–72
  compliance with WTO, 256, 258–61, 263–64, 265n, 267
  domestic, effect of international rules on, 262–63
  future of, 262
  reduction of, 236–38, 242, 256–57, 259–60
  trade-distorting, 238, 238n
agricultural trade
  pillars of, 236–37, 236n, 271
  as policy issue, 33–34, 57–58
  WTO reform of, 236–38, 251–52, 260–63
Agriculture Council (EU), and banana dispute, 122–23
AK Steel, 198
alcoholic beverages, US tariffs on, 56
Allied Mills, 36
alternative dispute resolution (ADR) mechanisms
  need for, 15
  spectrum of, 16–17, 16f
amber box subsidies, 238, 238n, 258, 272–73
Amehou, Samuel, 245
American Farm Bureau Federation, 76, 320
American Institute for International Steel, 221
American Iron and Steel Institute, 204
American Meat Institute, 76
American Soybean Association (ASA), 320, 330
AML. See Anti-Monopoly Law (AML)
Amorim, Celso, 257
AMS. See aggregate measurement of support (AMS)
Amstutz, Dan, 57
Anderson, Kym, 117
Anderson, Scott, 240, 243
Andriessen, Frans, 42, 47, 51, 66
antidumping laws, 195–96
  injury standards under, 208, 214, 232
  versus section 201 actions, 196, 201, 218
  use by steel industry, 197, 208, 211, 216, 231
  and WTO rules, 232–33

Anti-Monopoly Law (AML), 151–52, 159, 162
antitrust regulations, 150–54
  Japanese, 151–54
  US, 150–51, 172, 177
Appellate Body (WTO), 21, 68, 120, 228, 329
arbitration, 21, 21n, 22
  in banana dispute, 128
  binding, 17
  in cotton dispute, 260
Archer Daniels Midland Company, 303, 314
Argentina
  and Biosafety Protocol, 309
  and cotton dispute, 248
  and GMO dispute, 284, 321, 323–24
Arguedas, Irene, 107, 111–12, 116
ARPA. See Agricultural Risk Protection Act (ARPA)
Asanuma, Tokichi, 146–47, 147n
Asian financial crisis
  effect on agriculture, 240, 275, 276n, 279
  effect on steel industry, 200, 204–205
Askey, Thelma, 212, 218
Association of Biotechnology Companies, 288
Australia
  and Biosafety Protocol, 309
  and cotton dispute, 235, 248, 278
  GMO food labeling in, 303
Auto Basket of Framework Negotiations, 166
auto sales dispute (US-Japan), 158, 160, 166
Aventis CropScience, 313
Avery, Oswald, 286
Azevedo, Roberto, 254

baby food
  DES-contaminated, 38, 39n
  GMOs in, 303, 314
Baffes, John, 242, 252
Bair, James, 313
banana(s)
  Caribbean, 100
  EU domestic production of, 99, 102, 103n, 104
  EU market for, 99, 100t, 101, 101n, 102t
  US production of, 111n
  world prices of, 109, 109t
banana dispute (US-EU), 3, 97–141
  and beef hormone dispute, 65–66, 76–77, 126
  case analysis, 137–39

compromise in, 133–36
effect on EU, 137–38
effect on US, 137–38
and EU banana regime, 97, 101–108
framework agreement, 106–108
politics in, 110, 110*n*, 112, 114, 118, 125,
   125*n*, 127, 134–35, 135*n*, 137
and Regulation 404, 101–108, 140*f*–141*f*
resolution of, 79, 130–33
US retaliation in, 124–30, 137–39
winners and losers in, 137–38
WTO case, 97–98, 116–19
   compliance issues, 121–30, 137–39
   damage assessment, 127, 129, 129*n*
   EU appeal of, 120, 126
   panel ruling, 119–21
banana industry, composition of, 98–99,
   112, 113*t*
banana regime (EU)
   and banana dispute, 97, 101–108
   creation of, 101 (*See also* Regulation 404,
      EEC)
   EU members opposed to, 113
   international reactions to, 105–106
   as traditional border barrier, 137
Bananas Management Committee (EU), 123
banana trade
   exports, 99, 100*t*
   historic importance of, 98–101
   imports, 101, 102*t*
Barfield, Claude, 24–25, 80
Barringer, William, 197–98, 201*n*, 206,
   208–209
Barshefsky, Charlene
   and banana dispute, 123, 129
   and beef hormone dispute, 69–70,
      76–77, 77*n*
   and FSC dispute, 131
   and GMO dispute, 283
   and Kodak-Fuji dispute, 144, 163–69, 171
   and steel dispute, 203
   WTO cases under, 154, 154*n*
Basic Policy for Distribution
   Systematization, 165
Baucus, Max, 220, 320
Bayou Steel, 226*n*
Bebb, Adrian, 336
Becker, George, 200, 202, 204, 207, 212,
   212*n*, 213, 214*n*, 216
beef
   European supply of, 42–43
   labeling of, 68–69
   market protection for, 34
   slaughterhouse hygiene concerns, 56

UK-import, EU ban on, 70–71, 296
US consumption of, 54, 55*n*
US production of, without hormones,
   54–56
beef hormone(s)
   ban on, 37–44
      costs of, 72
      implementation of, 51–56
         date for, 47, 47*n*
   black market in, 48–49
   certification requirements for, and
      hormone-free proposal, 54
   Codex standards on, 46–47, 59–62,
      307–308
   history of, 34–35
   pharmaceutical firms manufacturing,
      35*n*
      lobbying by, 43
   safety of, 35, 51, 307–308
      EU risk assessment study, 68–69,
         80, 82
      international body to review, 44–47
      scientific review of, 40, 42, 46,
         60–61, 67, 69, 80
   US-EU task force on, 53–54
beef hormone dispute (US-EU), 2–3,
   31–96, 297–97
   and banana dispute, 65–66, 76–77, 126
   beginning of, 37–44
   case analysis, 81–85
   changing the rules during, 57–63, 84
   costs of, 72
   versus GM crops dispute, 317
   hormone-free proposal, 54–56
   and international institutions, 44–47, 57
   outcome of, 84–85
   politics in, 3, 32, 37–41, 66
   scientific versus social issues in, 52
   and SPS agreement, 32, 56–59, 63, 80,
      82, 91–96, 297
   standoff in, 52–53, 56, 72–80
   timeline of key events in, 86–88
   and trade rules, 82–83
   US industry pressure in, 76–77
   US retaliation over, 32, 50–56, 64, 70,
      72–79, 83, 85, 130, 304
      carousel, 76–79
      EU products included in, 73, 73*n*, 75
   WTO ruling on, 63–64, 66–70, 304,
      307–308
      and dispute resolution system, 32,
         89, 90*f*
      EU compliance with, 70, 80, 83–85,
         304

Belgium
    ban on sale of Coca-Cola products in,
        71
    dioxin-tainted foods in, 71, 301
    and GMO dispute, 311
Benin
    in cotton dispute, 235, 242, 245, 248–50
    cotton production in, 246–47, 247n
    WTO-World Bank conference in, 253
Bentsen, Lloyd, 49
Berg, Paul, 287
Bernal, Richard, 118
Bernauer, Thomas, 298
Bethlehem Steel, 198, 226
BEUC. *See* Bureau of European
        Consumer's Unions (BEUC)
Biais, Stephanie, 75
biases, effect on trade negotiations, 13–15,
        13n, 27
bilateral negotiations
    Japanese attitude toward, 160–61, 160n
    in Kodak-Fuji dispute, 169–70, 175–77
    versus multilateral challenges, 175–77
binding arbitration, 17
biological diversity, effect of GMOs on, 309
Biosafety Protocol, 309–11
    and GMO dispute, 309–11, 316, 322,
        328–30, 336, 338
    risk assessment under, 310
    versus SPS agreement, 310, 310n
Biotechnology Industry Organization, 288
Biotechnology Regulations Interservice
        Committee (BRIC), 293
Biotechnology Science Coordinating
        Committee, 290
Biotechnology Steering Committee (BSC),
        293
biotech pollution, 306
Birmingham Steel, 226, 226n
blue box subsidies, 258, 263, 272–73
Blunt, Roy, 320
Bolten, Joshua, 53, 53n
Bonino, Emma, 69
Boutry, Eric, 75
Bové, Jose, 74–75
bovine spongiform encephalopathy (BSE),
        70–71, 296
Bowles, Erskine, 125, 203
Bradley, James G., 221
Brainard, Lael, 203
Brazil
    Chamber of Foreign Trade, 256
    cotton case brought by (*See* cotton
        dispute)

cotton production in, 239, 239n, 278
cotton subsidies, 241–42, 281, 281t
Foreign Relations Ministry, 241, 245
GM crops in, 319
leadership at WTO, 236, 238, 256, 265
soybean production in, 239, 239n
steel imports from, 200, 202, 207, 218
Brazilian Rural Society (BRS), 237
Bretton Woods Conference (1944), 5
Brittan, Leon, 68, 70, 111–12
Brown, Nick, 74
Brown, Ron, 154n
BSE. *See* bovine spongiform
        encephalopathy (BSE)
Bt cotton (genetically modified), 247,
        247n, 278n, 283, 284t, 292
Bureau of European Consumer's Unions
        (BEUC), 38, 39n, 43
Burke, Derek, 298
Burkina Faso, and cotton dispute, 246–47,
        249–50
Bush, George H. W., administration
    beef hormone dispute during, 52, 55
    steel dispute during, 195, 201, 219
Bush, George W., presidential campaigns
        of
    and cotton dispute, 257
    and steel dispute, 212, 214–15
Bush, George W., administration
    banana dispute during, 133
    beef hormone dispute during, 79
    GMO dispute during, 320–21
    steel dispute during, 3–4, 193–94,
        216–18, 233
        and section 201 case, 218–21
    WTO cases under, 172, 233
business. *See also* industry influence
    competition with other political agents,
        8–9
Busquin, Philippe, 333
Byrd, Robert, 207, 210, 217, 217n
Byrne, David, 315–17, 322, 327, 330–32

CAFTA. *See* Central American Free Trade
        Agreement (CAFTA)
Callaway, C. Wayne, 292
Calumet Steel, 226n
Camargo Neto, Pedro de
    background of, 237–39
    on "box-shifting" by US, 258
    on farm bill, 254
    on G-20 coalition, 251
    at 2002 international conference, 242–43
    meetings with CAMEX, 245

Corbett, William, 213
corn, genetically modified, 283–84, 284t, 290–92, 297–99, 306, 313–15, 331, 340
Corzine, Leon, 336
Costa Rica
  and banana dispute, 105–107, 121–22
  section 301 case against, 111, 116
Côte d'Ivoire, and cotton dispute, 247, 249n
Cotonou Waiver, 139, 250n
cotton
  demand for, 278–79
  dumping of, 258
  genetically modified, 247, 247n, 278n, 283, 284t, 292
  global market for, 278–81
  supply of, 278
  US government support for, 276, 277t
  US share of market in, 244–45, 244f
  West African production of, 246
cotton dispute, 4, 235–81
  Brazil's case in, 240–46
  at Cancún ministerial meeting, 236, 249–53, 265
  case analysis, 262–66
  and Doha Round, 251–53, 256–58, 265
  lucky break in, 242–43
  milestones in, 250–51
  outcome of, 261, 264–66
  politics in, 236–37, 245, 249–51, 254, 257–60, 262
  retaliation in, 248, 258–60
  separate WTO initiative in, 248–50
  third-party signatories in, 248, 248n
  timeline of key events in, 268–70
  West African sectoral initiative, 245–53, 257, 261, 265
  WTO panel ruling, 253–54, 264, 265n, 267
    appeal of, 258–61
    compliance issues, 258–61, 264–65
    implications of, 254–58
cotton prices, 241, 244, 246, 246n, 247, 275–76, 278–79
  effect of US subsidies on, 243–44, 243n, 254, 265n, 267
  subsidies based on, 255–56, 267
cottonseed oil, genetically modified, 321
cotton subsidies, 241, 241n, 243–44, 243n
  elimination of, 236–38
  US, 276, 277t, 279, 281t
  worldwide, 279–81, 280t–281t
Council of Agriculture Ministers, beef hormone ban by, 42–43, 42n

Council of Economic Advisers (CEA)
  and banana dispute, 127
  and steel dispute, 203, 206, 209
countercyclical payments, agricultural, 240, 255, 257–58, 264, 267, 277
counterretaliation, in beef hormone dispute, 51–52
countervailing duties, 195–96, 216, 231–32, 237, 239
Crawford, Lester, 36, 36n, 40, 43, 307
  as chairman of CCRVDF, 45
  on Codex standards, 47, 60, 62
  on EU beef hormone risk assessment study, 68
  on hormone-free proposal, 54
  on scientific debate in beef hormone dispute, 52
  and SPS agreement, 58
  and USDA meat inspection program, 57
  on US-EU Hormone Task Force, 53
Creutzfeldt-Jakob disease, 70–71, 296
Crick, Francis, 286
"critical circumstances" policy, 202
Crowder, Richard, 336
cultural attitudes. See also public opinion
  to food safety, 81
  and Japanese antitrust policy, 153
Customs Service (US), countervailing duties imposed by, 196

Dagris. See Compagnie Française pour le Développement des Fibres Textiles (CFDT)
Dairy Coalition, 292
dairy products, unpasteurized, US ban on, 50
Daley, William, 200, 203, 207, 210
Dalian (China) mini-ministerial meeting, 260
Deaver, Mike, 159
de Clercq, Willy, 47, 50–51
Delaney Clause (Food Additives Amendment), 35, 36n
Delors, Jacques, 295
Denman, Roy, 50
Denmark
  biotechnology regulation in, 294–95
  and GMO dispute, 311
Department of Agriculture (US)
  and beef hormone dispute, 36
  biotechnology regulation by, 289, 303
  farm support programs, 240, 260
  and GMO dispute, 313
  and hormone-free proposal, 54

Department of Agriculture (US)—
    continued
    Meat Inspection Program, 36n
    The Sanitary and Phytosanitary Dispute
        Settlement Paper, 57
DES. See diethylstilbestrol (DES)
Devaney, Dennis, 218
developed countries. See also specific
    country
    cotton subsidies in, reform of, 250
developing countries. See also specific
    country
    agricultural biotechnology in, 319–320,
        322, 333, 339
    agricultural challenges brought by,
        236–38, 250, 262, 265–66 (See also
        cotton dispute)
    and Doha Development Agenda, 251,
        263
    exemption from steel tariffs, 222–23,
        222n
    and GMO dispute, 285, 318–320, 322,
        333, 339
    increasing demands from, 7, 265
    involvement in trade disputes, 10, 25
    special and differential treatment of, 7
Dewey Ballantine, 155, 158, 201
diethylstilbestrol (DES), debate over,
    35–37, 81
Diethylstilbestrol (DES) Proviso, 36
Dijon mustard, 75
dioxin-tainted foods, Belgian scare about,
    71, 301
Directive 90/219 (EC), 294, 294n
Directive 90/220 (EC), 294, 294n, 295, 299,
    299n, 315, 324, 326
Directive 2001/18 (EC), 315–16, 324, 330
dispute resolution systems. See also
    specific system
    alternative, need for, 15
    ambiguous rules under, 26
    caseload, 10–11, 11f
    compliance with, 18–20, 23, 25, 28–29
        and banana dispute, 121–30,
            137–39
        and beef hormone dispute, 70, 80,
            83–85, 304
        and cotton dispute, 258–61, 264–65,
            265n
    and deliberate rule-breaking, 28–29
    designing, 15–17, 16f
    difficulties with, 12
    effect of international alliances on, 27
    effect of issue linkage on, 27

gaming of, 25–27
issues covered by, 28
legalistic nature of, 19–20, 64, 335
and politics, 2, 26
reasons for bringing cases to, 29
roles of, 24
strategies for influencing, 26–27, 29–30
success of, 30
time factors in, 26
in the trade system, 17–25
Dispute Settlement Body (WTO), 11–12,
    21, 25
    and banana dispute, 127, 154
    and GMO dispute, 324
    and Kodak-Fuji dispute, 144, 170
Dispute Settlement Understanding
    (WTO), 15, 21, 21n–22n, 29
    and banana dispute, 139, 154, 176
    and cotton dispute, 239, 258, 272, 329,
        339
    and GMO dispute, 329, 339
DNA technology, recombinant, 286–87,
    290
Doha Development Agenda, 251, 263
Doha Round
    agricultural framework, 236–37, 240–42,
        245, 251–53, 253n, 257, 260–61
    and banana dispute, 139
    and cotton dispute, 251–53, 256–58, 265
    and GMO dispute, 334, 336
Dole, Robert
    and banana dispute, 110, 114, 114n
    and beef hormone dispute, 65
    and Kodak-Fuji dispute, 163n
Dole Food Co., Inc., 98
    cases against European Commission,
        133n
    and dollar bananas, 99, 99n, 100–101
    and GATT case, 106
    import category in EU banana regime,
        103–104, 108, 135
    participation in EU banana regime, 108,
        138
    political donations by, 135
    role in banana dispute, 124, 132, 135,
        138
    and section 301 filing, 108–10, 112, 112n,
        113–14
"dollar bananas," 98, 99n, 100–101
domestic policy agenda, effect on trade
    agreements, 9–10, 208, 262–63
Dominica, and banana dispute, 127
Domzalski, Yves, 39
Doneski, Ellen, 209–10, 215, 217, 219

DoPrado, Victor Luiz, 170
Downey, Tom, 159
Downey Chandler, 159
DSB. *See* Dispute Settlement Body (WTO)
DSU. *See* Dispute Settlement
    Understanding (WTO)
Dunkel, Arthur, 52
DuPont, 291, 302

Eastman, George, 147*n*
Eastman Kodak Co. *See also* Kodak-Fuji
    dispute
  attack on WTO by, 171, 171*n*
  competition with Fuji, 148–49
  effect of Fuji dispute on, 143
  history of, 145–46
  Japanese market share, 146–50, 149*t*, 155
  sale of technology to Japanese firms, 147
Ecuador, and banana dispute, 104, 107,
    115–17, 116*n*, 121–22, 126, 126*n*–127*n*,
    128, 130, 133, 135*n*, 138
Edelman, 159–60
EFSA. *See* European Food Safety
    Authority (EFSA)
Egypt
  cotton subsidies, 241–42, 281, 281*t*
  free trade agreement with US, 323
  in GMO dispute, 321, 323, 339
  elections, and steel dispute, 211–12, 213*n*,
    214–15
Emergency Steel Loan Guarantee Act, 210
enabling clause, 7
English, Philip, 207
environment, effect of GMOs on, 295,
    301–302, 306, 309, 313, 328
environmentalists
  in beef hormone dispute, 64
  competition with other political agents,
    8–9
  in GMO dispute, 284, 298, 313
Environmental Protection Agency (EPA),
    289, 303, 313
Esserman, Susan, 203–205, 214
estrogen, food contamination with, 38
ETI. *See* Extraterritorial Income Exclusion
    Act (ETI)
European Commission
  and banana dispute, 101, 122–23, 133,
    133*n*
  biotechnology regulation by, 293–96,
    294*n*, 298, 333
  directives (*See specific directive or
    regulation*)
  Environmental Directorate-General, 338

food safety regulatory system, 72
and GMO dispute, 301, 311–12, 315,
    321, 323, 335–337
  Scientific Group on Anabolic Agents in
    Animal Production (*See* Lamming
    Group)
European Committee of Enquiry into the
    Problem of Quality in the Meat
    Sector, 54
European Council of Ministers
  in beef hormone disputes, 39, 81, 83
  directives (*See specific directive or
    regulation*)
  and GMO dispute, 299, 315, 329
  Novel Foods and Novel Food
    Ingredients Regulation 258/97, 299,
    299*n*, 300, 324, 326
European Court of Justice, and banana
    dispute, 113
European Federation of Animal Health
    (FEDESA), 43, 48
European Food Safety Authority (EFSA),
    317–18, 322, 332
European Parliament
  in beef hormone dispute, 41, 54, 58,
    63, 83
  directives (*See specific directive or
    regulation*)
  and GMO dispute, 298–99, 315, 329
European Union (EU)
  agricultural biotechnology regulation
    in, 284–85, 293–96, 333–34
  agricultural policies, 33
  agricultural structure in, versus
    American agribusiness, 72
  agricultural subsidies, elimination of,
    256
  approaches to dispute settlement, 19–20
  bananas (*See also* banana dispute,
    US-EU)
    domestic production, 99, 102, 103*n*,
      104
    framework agreement with Latin
      America, 106–108
    market, 99, 100*t*, 101, 101*n*, 102*t*
    regime for (*See* banana regime, EU)
  beef hormones (*See also* beef hormone
    dispute, US-EU)
    approved for use, 37
    ban, 37–44
    risk assessment study, 68–69, 80, 82
  beef imports to
    UK, 70–71, 296
    US, 33

foot-and-mouth disease, 301
Foreign Correspondents' Club of Japan, 161
foreign sales corporation (FSC), US-EU dispute over, 78–79, 79*n*, 130–31, 139, 259*n*, 321
"fortress Europe," 137
France
 and banana dispute, 99, 101
 ban on Coca-Cola products in, 71
 and beef hormone dispute, 74–75
 DES-tainted veal in, 38, 39*n*
 and GMO dispute, 311
 wine from, 48*n*
Freedom to Farm Act, 264, 274–75
free trade
 and cotton dispute, 256
 and steel dispute, 203–204, 209, 215, 218–19, 223, 229–31
 and WTO rules, 232–33
free trade agreements. *See also specific agreement*
 exemption from steel tariffs, 222–23, 222*n*
Free Trade Area of the Americas, 219
Fresh Del Monte Produce, Inc., 98
Friends of the Earth, 298, 313, 336
Frito-Lay, 314
fruit production, by cotton farmers, prohibition on, 254–55, 265, 267, 267*n*
FSC. *See* foreign sales corporations (FSC)
Fuji Photo Film Company. *See also* Kodak-Fuji dispute
 competition with Kodak, 148–49
 history of, 146
 monopolistic practices of, 157–58
 network operated by, 156, 156*n*
 response to Kodak's section 301 case, 159–60
Fyffes Ltd., 98, 104, 104*n*, 137

Gall, Eric, 330
game dynamics in trade negotiations, 13, 29–30, 84
 and beef hormone dispute, 84
 and steel dispute, 230–31
gaming the system, 25–27
Gardner, Booth, 169
G-20 coalition, 251–52, 256, 260
Geest Ltd., 98, 104, 104*n*, 137
General Agreement on Tariffs and Trade (GATT), 1, 5–8
 agricultural issues under, 33, 262–63
 Article I, 6, 113
 Article II, 164, 181, 183–85

Article III, 6, 164, 170, 176, 182, 185–87, 331*n*
Article VI, 232*n*
Article IX, 187–88
Article X, 164, 170, 182, 188
Article XI, 335
Article XIII, 134, 134*n*, 189–91
Article XIX, 232*n*
Article XX, 46, 46*n*, 328, 328*n*
Article XXII, 18
Article XXIII, 18, 164, 170, 176–77, 181
Article XXX, 171
banana dispute, 105–106
beef hormone dispute, 46, 51–52, 57, 83
versus bilateral negotiations, 175–77
creation of, 6, 154
dispute resolution system, 1, 8, 17–20
 caseload, 10–11, 11*f*
 compliance with, 18–19
 dissatisfaction with, 20
 mediation within, 19
 retaliation under, 11, 20
 signatories to, 6
 success of, 6
 versus WTO system, 83, 24–25, 63, 114, 138
liberalization countermeasures, 164–65, 178*f*–180*f*
nonviolation provisions, 170, 172
plurilateral codes, 7–8
purpose of, 6
retaliation under, 232–33
trade rounds, 112 (*See also specific round*)
US attitude toward, 163
General Agreement on Trade in Services (GATS), 8
 and banana dispute, 114, 117, 120
 and Kodak-Fuji dispute, 165–66
 nonviolation provisions, 170
Generalized System of Preferences, 111
genetically modified crops. *See also specific crop*
 acreage in, 283–84, 284*n*, 284*t*, 292
 categories of, 290
 environmental effects of, 295, 301–302, 306, 309, 313, 328
 EU regulation of, 284–85
  versus US regulatory approach, 338–40
 food produced from
  EU moratorium on, 300–305
  labeling of, 299, 303, 305, 310, 316–17, 320, 322
  EU regulations for, 329–32
  traceability in, 316, 320, 322

genetically modified crops—*continued*
  history of, 283–87
  public opinion of, 284–85, 287–88,
    297–98, 300–303, 313–14, 317, 322,
    335, 338
  risk assessment of, 295, 305–306, 310,
    312, 317, 326–29, 339–40
  US regulation of, 303
    versus EU regulatory approach,
      338–40
genetically modified crops dispute
    (US-EU), 4–5, 71, 283–344
  versus beef hormone dispute, 317
  and Biosafety Protocol, 309–11, 322,
    328–30, 336, 338
  case analysis, 338
  new EU policy initiatives during, 333–34
  outcome of, 336–37, 339
  politics in, 284, 300, 317, 322
  and rejection of GM foods, 318–20
  and SPS agreement, 299–300, 307,
    312–13, 324–28, 335, 335n, 338–39, 344
  and StarLink corn, 313–15, 340
  timeline of key events in, 341–43
  WTO case, 285, 303–304, 311–13, 320–38
    arguments during, 324–29
    EU response to, 326–29
    preliminary decision, 334–37
    scientific basis issue, 326
    third-party signatories to, 321,
      321n, 323
    "undue delay" issue, 325–26
genetic engineering, 286–87, 290
Geneva Steel, 198, 217n
Georgetown Steel, 226
Gephardt, Richard, 65
Germany
  and banana dispute, 99, 99n, 100, 104
  biotechnology regulation in, 294–95
  GM food regulations, 316
Gingrich, Newt, 65, 68, 125
Glauber, Joe, 240, 252–55, 259, 276–77
Glavany, Jean, 31, 73, 75
Glenn, John, 65
Glickman, Dan, 63, 67, 69–70, 289
Global Trade Watch, 62
GMOs. *See* genetically modified crops
    dispute, US-EU
goal transformation, 14
Godfrain, Jacques, 74
Goldberg, Ray, 315
Goldman, Patti, 62
goods, banana dispute claims involving,
    117–18

Gore, Al, 206
  presidential campaign of, and steel
    dispute, 211–15
Goreux, Louis, 247n
Grassley, Charles, 220, 320, 323
Great Britain. *See* United Kingdom
Greece, and cotton dispute, 241, 278,
    281t
green box subsidies, 238, 254, 263, 265,
    271, 271n, 273
Greenpeace, 298, 301–302, 311, 313, 330
green revolution, 286, 286n
Griswold, Daniel, 195
Groser, Tim, 260
Gruber, Rick, 293
Guatemala, and banana dispute, 105–107,
    115–16, 121, 127
Guest, Gerald, 51
Guidelines for Rationalizing Terms of
    Trade for Photo Film, 165

Haeberli, Christian, 117, 324n
Hagin, Joseph, 65
Hanavan, Darrell, 314
Harbinson, Stuart, 117
Harbison, Earle, Jr., 288
Harkin, Tom, 320
harmonization of standards
  and beef hormone dispute, 42–43, 49,
    72, 81–82
  definition of, 95
  for food safety, 42–43, 49, 72, 81–82, 317,
    338
  and GM crops dispute, 317–18, 338
  under SPS agreement, 82, 92–93
Hashimoto, Ryutaro, 162, 162n
Hastert, Dennis, 209, 320
Havana Charter on the International
    Court of Justice, 18n
Hawaii, banana industry in, 111n
Hawaii Banana Industry Association, 97,
    110
Hayes, Rita, 73
Heck, Ron, 330
Heinz, 314
herbicides, 285
herbicide-tolerant crops, 290, 292
Hightower, Jim, 54–55
Hills, Carla, 52, 56
Honduras, and banana dispute, 107,
    115–16, 121, 127
Hong Kong ministerial meeting, 257–58,
    260, 334
Hormone Directive of 1981 (EC), 41

litigation
  and dispute resolution system, 19–20,
    64
  negotiation through, 239, 243, 335 (*See
    also* cotton dispute)
living modified organisms (LMOs), 310
Livingston, Robert, 35, 35*n*, 44
lobbying
  by farm industry, 236–37, 262, 320, 330
  by pharmaceutical industry, 43, 66
Logan Act of 1800, 55
Lomé Convention, and banana dispute,
    99, 101, 111, 113, 119–21
Losey, John, 306
Lott, Trent, 68, 78, 125, 131
LTV Steel, 216, 226
Lynch, Diahanna, 294–95
Lyng, Richard, 49, 51, 57

Maarbjerg, Peder, 219
Mable, Alison, 113
MacArthur, Douglas, 151
MacSharry, Raymond, 56
Macy, Adrian, 170
mad cow disease, 70–71, 296, 338
Maher, Ahmed, 323
Malan, Pedro, 245
Maldonado, Teodoro, 116
Mali, and cotton dispute, 242, 246–47,
    249–50
managed trade
  versus rules-based approach, 167,
    174–75
  and US-Japan trade disputes, 144
Mansito, Fernando, 53
market access, 271
  and Kodak-Fuji dispute, 143
  nonagricultural (NAMA), 261
marketing loan payments, agricultural,
    254, 275
marketing loss assistance program,
    agricultural, 240, 254
Market-Oriented Sector-Specific (MOSS)
    talks, 153
mass media
  and banana dispute, 65–66, 78
  and beef hormone dispute, 41, 50–52,
    65–66, 78
  and cotton dispute, 249–50
  and food scares, 301
Mastel, Greg, 199, 209, 213*n*
"material injury" standards, 232
Mauritius, and cotton dispute, 250, 250*n*
maximum residue levels (MRLs), 46

McClellan, Scott, 254, 256
McDonald's
  and beef hormone dispute, 31, 74–75
  and GMO crops, 314
mediation, 16, 16*n*
  under GATT, 19
Mehaignerie, Pierre, 38
Melchett, Peter, 302
melengestrol acetate (MGA), 45*n*
Mendel, Gregor, 286
Mesquita, Paulo, 260
Mexico
  and banana dispute, 107, 115–16, 127
  cotton subsidies, 241–42, 281*t*
  and Kodak-Fuji dispute, 168
MFN treatment. *See* most favored nation
    (MFN) treatment
Miami Group, 309
milk production, genetically modified
    hormone used in, 291–92, 308, 308*n*
Miller, Robert, 223
Mills, Richard, 80
Minder, Raphael, 334
Ministry of International Trade and
    Industry (MITI), 152*n*, 159
  in Kodak-Fuji dispute, 160–65, 168
Misuzu, 146
Mitsubishi, 151
Mitsui Group, 151, 156, 156*n*
Mondale, Walter, 158
Monsanto Company, 285, 288, 288*n*,
    314–15
  and Chinese rejection of GM crops, 319
  GM crop production by, 292, 297,
    314–15
  marketing of GMO foods in Europe by,
    302, 302*n*
  rbST production by, 291–92
moral issues, in banana dispute, 101
Morningstar, Richard, 304, 312, 315,
    317–18
MOSS (Market-Oriented Sector-Specific)
    talks, 153
most favored nation (MFN) treatment, 6
  for ACP former colonies, 139
  and banana regime, 113
MRLs. *See* maximum residue levels
    (MRLs)
Murdock, David, 135
Murphy, Jim, 311

NAFTA. *See* North American Free Trade
    Agreement (NAFTA)
Nagase & Co., 147–48

naive realism, 14, 14*n*
NAMA (nonagricultural market access), 261
National Academy of Sciences, 289
National Beef Cattlemen's Association, 34, 56, 68, 76
National Corn Growers Association, 320, 336
National Economic Council
  and Kodak-Fuji dispute, 167, 175
  and steel dispute, 203, 213, 219
National Grain and Feed Association, 320
National Institutes of Health (NIH), 72, 287
National Security Council, 219
national security interests, steel industry protection on basis of, 212*n*, 230
National Steel, 226, 226*n*
national treatment (GATT Article III), 6, 164, 170, 176, 182, 185–87, 331*n*
Negoro, Yasuchika, 162
Nestlé S.A., 298
"newcomer" category, in EU banana regime, 103, 134, 135*n*
New Zealand, GMO food labeling in, 303
Nicaragua, and banana dispute, 105–107, 122
Nixon administration, and steel dispute, 195, 219
Noboa Group, 98, 116, 132, 138
  import category in EU banana regime, 103, 134
nondiscrimination principle, and banana dispute, 137
nongovernmental organizations (NGOs).
  See also specific organization
  in cotton dispute, 248–50
  in GMO dispute, 284, 305, 335–36
nonviolation provisions, of GATT and GATS, 170, 172
North American Free Trade Agreement (NAFTA), 215
North American Millers Association, 313
Novartis, 291, 297–98, 303
Novel Foods and Novel Food Ingredients Regulation 258/97 (EC), 299, 299*n*, 300, 324, 326
Nucor Steel, 198, 200, 218

O'Driscoll, Gerald, 223
OECD. *See* Organization for Economic Cooperation and Development (OECD)
oestradiol-17b, 34, 39–40, 69, 80

Office Internationale des Epizooties (OIE)/World Organization for Animal Health, 44, 44*n*
Office of the US Trade Representative (USTR). *See also specific representative*
  and antitrust cases, 150–51
  and banana dispute, 3, 97, 105–106, 138
    framework agreement, 108
    resolution issues, 130–33
    section 301 filing, 106, 108–12, 138
    WTO case, 114–21, 123–24
  and beef hormone dispute, 43
  and cotton dispute, 254, 258
  and FSC dispute, 131
  and GMO dispute, 320–21, 330, 339
  influence of industry on, 66, 110–12, 127, 144, 163–64, 176
  and Kodak-Fuji dispute, 3, 144, 163–69, 175
    bilateral negotiations with Japan, 168–69, 175–77
    section 301 case, 158–59
  and steel dispute, 202–203, 208, 224
  WTO cases brought by, 154, 154*n*
Office of Trade and Investment (Japan), 162
Ohmiya, 146
Ohnishi, Minoru, 146, 159, 170
Okinawa, US soldiers on trial in, 161
Omnibus Trade and Competitiveness Act of 1988, 49*n*
  Super 301, 20
O'Neill, Paul, 218, 220–21, 224
Organization for Economic Cooperation and Development (OECD)
  and biotechnology regulation, 294
  and steel dispute, 225, 225*n*
Oxfam, 242, 245, 248–49, 253

Paarlberg, Robert, 288, 290, 293, 296, 316, 318, 323, 335–36
Pacific banana trade. *See* African, Caribbean, and Pacific (ACP) former colonies
Pakistan, cotton production in, 278
Panama, and banana dispute, 121–22, 127, 127*n*
Parlin, Christopher, 121
partisan perceptions, 14–15
patent protection, for agricultural biotechnology, 290
peace clause, and cotton dispute, 239, 243, 254, 263–64, 267, 272–73
Pension Benefit Guaranty Corporation, 226
perception biases, 13–15, 13*n*, 27

pharmaceutical firms, manufacturing beef
hormones, 35n
lobbying by, 43, 66
photographic film
dispute over (See Kodak-Fuji dispute)
Japanese prices for, 156–57, 157f
phytosanitary measures
agreement on (See Agreement on
Sanitary and Phytosanitary Measures
[SPS])
appropriate level of protection, 93–94, 96
definition of, 95
Pimenta Report, 54
Pioneer Hi-Bred, 291
plant-breeding techniques, 286–87, 290,
333. See also genetically modified
crops
Plant Pest Act, 290n
Plants for the Future: A 2025 Vision for
European Plant Biotechnology, 333
plurilateral codes, GATT, 7–8
Podesta, John, 203, 206, 212–13, 216
Polaroid, 166
political agents, competition between, 8–9
political barriers, to negotiated
agreements, 13
political donations, by industry, 110, 110n,
112, 118, 134–35, 135n
politics
and banana dispute, 110, 110n, 112, 114,
114n, 118, 125, 125n, 127, 134–35,
135n, 137
and beef hormone dispute, 3, 32, 37–41,
66
and cotton dispute, 236–37, 245, 249–51,
254, 257–60, 262
and dispute settlement, 2, 26
and free trade/protectionism debate,
230–31
and GMO dispute, 284, 300, 317, 322
and increasing complexity of trade
rules, 8–10, 136
and Kodak-Fuji dispute, 144, 163–64,
164n, 176
and steel dispute, 203–204, 207–209,
213n, 214–15, 223, 223n, 231, 233
pork products, in beef hormone dispute
retaliation, 73, 74n
Posilac, 291–92
power, distribution of, and politics of
trade agreements, 9
precautionary principle
and beef hormone dispute, 32, 64, 67,
81, 296

and GMO dispute, 303, 310, 312–13,
318, 329, 338–39
in risk assessment, 312, 329
preferential treatment, for former
colonies. See African, Caribbean, and
Pacific (ACP) former colonies
press. See mass media
price-based farm support, and cotton
dispute, 255–56, 258, 267
price floor, and cotton dispute, 255–56
primary importers, in EU banana regime,
104, 134
private barriers, and US-Japan trade
disputes, 144, 174
private behavior, WTO regulation of, 174
private interests. See also industry
influence
abuse of WTO dispute resolution
system by, 128
process and production method (PPM),
beef hormone use as, 46
procymidon, 48n
Prodi, Romano, 78, 304
production flexibility contract payments,
267
progesterone, 34, 39–40
protectionism
in European Union, 137
and GMO dispute, 285, 317, 319
and steel dispute, 203–204, 213, 218–19,
221, 223, 229–31
and WTO rules, 232–33
protests
of biotech foods, 291–92
at Cancún ministerial meeting, 252
Proxmire, William, 36
psychological barriers, to negotiated
agreements, 13–15, 13n
public opinion. See also cultural attitudes
of beef hormone dispute, 43, 55, 81, 297
of biotech foods, 291–92
of cotton dispute, 251, 266
on food safety, 291–92, 297, 300
of genetically modified crops, 284,
287–88, 297–98, 300–303, 313–14, 317,
322, 335, 338
Public Voice for Food and Health Policy,
59n, 60

Quinn, Jack, 207–208, 217
quota rents, in EU banana regime, 105, 117

Randall, Alan, 323
rational breach, 26, 231

steel industry (US)—*continued*
  subsidies, curbing of, 225
  trade figures, 219
  trade remedies sought by, history of,
    194–97
  use of antidumping laws by, 197, 211,
    216
steel mills, types of, 197
steel prices, 212, 217, 226
Steel Recovery Act, 208
Steel Revitalization Act of 2001, 217
Steinberg, James, 203
Step 2 program, 243, 243*n*, 254, 259–60,
    265*n*, 267
stilbenes, ban on, 39
structural barriers, 12–13
  in beef hormone dispute, 84
  in Kodak-Fuji dispute, 174
Structural Impediments Initiative (SII),
    153, 175
"substantial injury" standards, 232
sugar subsidies, EU, 235, 250*n*, 256–57,
    265
Sumitomo, 151
Summers, Law, 215–16
Sumner, Dan, 240, 243, 243*n*
Sundlof, Steve, 62, 72
Supachai Panitchpakdi, 79, 251, 257, 260,
    324*n*
Super 301 (Omnibus Trade Act of 1988),
    20
Supreme Commander for the Allied
    Powers (SCAP), 151
Syngenta, 319, 331

tariff(s)
  on photographic products, 146, 148
  reduction of, formulas for, 260
  on steel products, 222–24, 228
tariff-rate quota (TRQ)
  and agriculture trade rules, 263, 281
  in EU banana regime, 103, 132
    and GATT rules, 105, 117
    as violation of trade rules, 120–22,
      122*n*
taxation, of foreign sales corporations,
    WTO case over, 78–79, 79*n*, 130–31,
    139, 259*n*, 321
TBA. *See* trenbolone acetate (TBA)
technical barriers to trade, 7
terrorist attacks, 251
testosterone, 34, 39–40
Thailand, cotton case brought by, 235
Thatcher, Mary Kay, 320

"third country" sector, in EU banana
    regime, 102–108, 102*n*
third-party signatories
  to cotton case, 248, 248*n*
  to GMO case, 321, 321*n*, 323
Thomas, Bill, 227
Thompson, Bob, 240, 242, 252
time factors, in dispute resolution, 26
tobacco, genetically engineered, 288, 288*n*
Togo, in cotton dispute, 249*n*
tokuyakuten, 146–47, 156, 160
Tokyo Round (GATT), 7–8
  dispute settlement system, 8, 20, 20*n*
  and US politics, 9
tomato puree, genetically modified, 297,
    297*n*, 302
Toxic Substances Control Act, 290*n*
traceability, of GMOs in foods, 316, 320,
    322
Trade Act of 1974
  amendments to (*See* Trade and
    Development Act of 2000)
  Section 201 (*See* Section 201, Trade Act
    of 1974)
  Section 301 (*See* Section 301, Trade Act
    of 1974)
Trade and Competitiveness Act of 1988, 49
Trade and Development Act of 2000,
    section 407, 77
Trade Association Act of 1948, 151–52
trade barriers, 11–15
  institutional, in beef hormone dispute,
    84
  political, 13
  private, and US-Japan trade disputes,
    144, 174
  psychological, 13–15, 13*n*
  structural, 12–13
    in beef hormone dispute, 84
    in Kodak-Fuji dispute, 174
  traditional border
    European banana regime as, 137
    WTO focus on, 174
trade disputes
  case studies, 2–5 (*See also specific
    dispute*)
  and deliberate rule-breaking, 28–29
  developing countries involved in, 10, 25
  issues in, 10–11, 27–30
  number of, 10–11, 11*f*
  settlement of (*See* dispute resolution
    systems)
  trade-distorting subsidies, and cotton
    dispute, 238, 238*n*, 255–57, 262–63

trade negotiations
  elements of, 12
  game dynamics in, 13, 29–30, 84, 230–31
trade promotion authority (TPA). *See* fast-
    track negotiating authority
Trade-Related Aspects of Intellectual
    Property Rights (TRIPS) agreement,
    8, 260
Trade-Related Investment Measures
    (TRIMs) agreement, 8
trade rules
  deliberate violations of, 28–29
  effect on domestic farm support, 262–63
  increasing complexity of, 5–11, 136
Tramantano, Karen, 203, 206, 212
Treasury Department (US), antidumping
    investigations, 195*n*
Treaty of Westphalia (1648), 144
treble-damage remedy, 150
trenbolone acetate (TBA), 34, 39–40, 42*n*, 60
Trico Steel, 226
trigger price mechanism, 195
TRIMs. *See* Trade-Related Investment
    Measures (TRIMs)
TRIPS. *See* Trade-Related Aspects of
    Intellectual Property Rights (TRIPS)
True Food campaign, 301
Turkey, and cotton dispute, 241–42, 278,
    281*t*
Tyson, Laura, 167

Ukraine, steel imports from, 218
Unilever, 298
Union of French Consumers, 38, 39*n*
United Brands, 108. *See also* Chiquita
    Brands International
United Fruit Company Limited, 108. *See
    also* Chiquita Brands International
United Kingdom
  and banana dispute, 99, 101, 123
  beef imports from, 70–71, 74, 296
  foot-and-mouth disease in, 301
United Nations (UN)
  Convention on Biological Diversity, 309
  in dispute resolution system, 18
  Food and Agriculture Organization
    (FAO), 44–45, 307 (*See also* Joint
    FAO/WHO Expert Committee on
    Food Additives [JECFA])
  in GMO dispute, 309
  Resolution 39/248, 45*n*
United States (US)
  agribusiness in, versus European-style
    agriculture, 72

agricultural biotechnology regulation
    in, 287–90, 293–96
agricultural exports, 283
  effect of GMO dispute on, 284,
    299–300
agricultural subsidies, 33, 238*n*, 240–42,
    241*n*, 255–56, 274–77 (*See also* cotton
    dispute)
  compliance with WTO, 256,
    258–61, 263–64, 265*n*, 267
  price suppression caused by,
    243–44, 243*n*
  reduction of, 257, 259
antidumping regulations, 232
antitrust regulations, 150–51, 172
auto sales dispute with Japan, 158, 160,
    166
bananas (*See also* banana dispute,
    US-EU)
  domestic production, 111*n*
  effects of EU banana regime on,
    104–105, 110, 112, 113*t*
beef (*See also* beef hormone dispute,
    US-EU)
  consumption, 54, 55*n*
  imports to EU, 33
  UK, ban on, 70–71, 296
Biosafety Protocol support, 309–310
Codex standards adopted by, 45*n*
cotton (*See also* cotton dispute)
  exports, 244–45, 244*f*
dispute settlement approach, 19–20
domestic law prevalence over
    international law in, 208
Egyptian free trade agreement with,
    323
farm policy, 274–77
food industry, European targeting of,
    74–75
foreign sales corporation dispute
    involving, 78–79, 79*n*, 130–31, 139,
    259*n*, 321
genetically modified crops (*See also*
    genetically modified crops dispute,
    US-EU)
  acreage, 283–84, 284*t*, 292
  regulation of, 303, 338–40
government agencies (*See specific
    agency*)
and Japanese antitrust policy, 151, 153
Japanese trade disputes with, history
    of, 144
photographic film industry dispute (*See*
    Kodak-Fuji dispute)

World Meat Congress, 63
World Trade Organization (WTO)
  Agreement on Subsidies and
    Countervailing Measures (SCM), 8,
    232n, 243
  agricultural reform in, 236–38, 251–52
  Appellate Body, 21, 68, 120, 228, 329
  Article 5, 263
  banana case in, 97–98, 112–19
    compliance issues, 121–30, 137–39
    damage assessment, 127, 129, 129n
    EU appeal, 120, 126
    panel ruling, 119–21
  beef hormone ruling, 63–64, 66–68, 83,
    304, 307–308
    appeal of, 67–68
    compliance with, 70, 80, 83–85
    implementation of, 68–69
  border barriers focus of, 173
  and competition policy enforcement,
    172, 177
  cotton case, 235–81
    compliance issues, 258–61, 264–65
    outcome of, 261, 264–66
    panel ruling, 253–54, 264, 265n, 267
      appeal of, 258–61
      implications of, 254–58
    timeline of key events in, 268–70
  creation of, 112, 154
  dispute resolution system, 1, 15, 17,
    21–25, 117
    abuse of, by private interests, 128
    ambiguous rules under, 26
    and antitrust cases, 150–51, 172
    arbitration under, 21, 21n, 22
    Article 21.5, 125, 125n, 129, 139
    Article 22, 124, 125n, 129, 139
    and beef hormone dispute, 32, 80,
      89, 90f
    case load, 10–11, 11f
    compensation under, 22–23, 85
    compliance with, 23–25, 28–29,
      83–85, 125
      and banana dispute, 121–30,
        137–39
      and beef hormone ruling, 70, 80,
        83–85
    cost-benefit analysis of, 137
    enforceability of, 137
    evolution of, 5
    gaming of, 25–27, 231
    versus GATT system, 24–25, 63, 83,
      114, 138

    issues covered by, 25, 28
    remedies under, 23–24
    retaliation under, 11, 21–25, 29,
      137–39, 232–33, 272
    role of Codex standards in, 59
  Dispute Settlement Body (*See* Dispute
    Settlement Body [WTO])
  Dispute Settlement Understanding (*See*
    Dispute Settlement Understanding,
    WTO)
  FSC case at, 78–79, 79n, 130–31, 139,
    259n, 321
  GMO dispute in, 285, 303–304, 311–13,
    320–38
    arguments during, 324–29
    EU response to, 326–29
    preliminary decision, 334–37
    scientific basis issue, 326
    third-party signatories to, 321,
      321n, 323
    "undue delay" issue, 325–26
  Kodak-Fuji case in, 167, 169–73, 176
  ministerial meetings (*See specific*
    meeting)
  private behavior regulated by, 174
  protectionist rules under, 232–33
  Safeguards Agreement, 224, 232
  and sovereignty issues, 144–45
  SPS agreement (*See* Agreement on
    Sanitary and Phytosanitary Measures
    [SPS])
  steel case in, 224, 227–29, 232–33
  strengths and weaknesses of, 22, 138
  success of, 30

Yasuda, 151
Yellen, Janet, 203, 206
Yerxa, Rufus, 167
Yeutter, Clayton, 50–52, 54–56

zaibatsu, 151–52, 156n
Zambia, rejection of GM food aid from
  US, 218, 339
Zeneca Group, 291, 297, 297n
Zenren, 156, 156n
zeranol, 34, 39–40, 42, 42n
zero-sum game, negotiations as, 12, 84,
  138, 167
Zoellick, Robert
  and cotton dispute, 254
  and GMO dispute, 320–22
  and Kodak-Fuji dispute, 133–34, 172
  and steel dispute, 218–22, 225, 228

Other Publications from the Institute for International Economics

79 Trade Relations Between Colombia
    and the United States
    Jeffrey J. Schott, editor
    August 2006   ISBN 978-0-88132-389-4

BOOKS

IMF Conditionality* John Williamson, editor
1983   ISBN 0-88132-006-4
Trade Policy in the 1980s* William R. Cline, ed.
1983   ISBN 0-88132-031-5
Subsidies in International Trade*
Gary Clyde Hufbauer and Joanna Shelton Erb
1984 ISBN 0-88132-004-8
**International Debt: Systemic Risk and Policy
Response***   William R. Cline
1984   ISBN 0-88132-015-3
**Trade Protection in the United States: 31 Case
Studies*** Gary Clyde Hufbauer, Diane E. Berliner,
and Kimberly Ann Elliott
1986   ISBN 0-88132-040-4
**Toward Renewed Economic Growth in Latin
America*** Bela Balassa, Gerardo M. Bueno, Pedro-
Pablo Kuczynski, and Mario Henrique Simonsen
1986   ISBN 0-88132-045-5
Capital Flight and Third World Debt*
Donald R. Lessard and John Williamson, editors
1987   ISBN 0-88132-053-6
**The Canada-United States Free Trade Agreement:
The Global Impact***
Jeffrey J. Schott and Murray G. Smith, editors
1988   ISBN 0-88132-073-0
World Agricultural Trade: Building a Consensus*
William M. Miner and Dale E. Hathaway, editors
1988   ISBN 0-88132-071-3
Japan in the World Economy*
Bela Balassa and Marcus Noland
1988   ISBN 0-88132-041-2
**America in the World Economy: A Strategy for
the 1990s***   C. Fred Bergsten
1988   ISBN 0-88132-089-7
**Managing the Dollar: From the Plaza to the
Louvre***   Yoichi Funabashi
1988, 2d. ed. 1989   ISBN 0-88132-097-8
**United States External Adjustment
and the World Economy***
William R. Cline
May 1989   ISBN 0-88132-048-X
Free Trade Areas and U.S. Trade Policy*
Jeffrey J. Schott, editor
May *1989*   ISBN 0-88132-094-3
**Dollar Politics: Exchange Rate Policymaking
in the United States***
I. M. Destler and C. Randall Henning
September 1989   ISBN 0-88132-079-X

**Latin American Adjustment: How Much Has
Happened?*** John Williamson, editor
April 1990   ISBN 0-88132-125-7
**The Future of World Trade in Textiles and
Apparel***   William R. Cline
1987, 2d ed. June *1999*   ISBN 0-88132-110-9
**Completing the Uruguay Round: A Results-
Oriented Approach to the GATT Trade
Negotiations***   Jeffrey J. Schott, editor
September 1990   ISBN 0-88132-130-3
**Economic Sanctions Reconsidered (2 volumes)
Economic Sanctions Reconsidered:
Supplemental Case Histories**
Gary Clyde Hufbauer, Jeffrey J. Schott, and
Kimberly Ann Elliott
1985, 2d ed. Dec. 1990   ISBN cloth 0-88132-115-X
                    ISBN paper 0-88132-105-2
**Economic Sanctions Reconsidered: History and
Current Policy**   Gary Clyde Hufbauer,
Jeffrey J. Schott, and Kimberly Ann Elliott
December 1990   ISBN cloth 0-88132-140-0
                    ISBN paper 0-88132-136-2
**Pacific Basin Developing Countries: Prospects for
Economic Sanctions Reconsidered: History
and Current Policy**   Gary Clyde Hufbauer,
Jeffrey J. Schott, and Kimberly Ann Elliott
December 1990   ISBN cloth 0-88132-140-0
                    ISBN paper 0-88132-136-2
**Pacific Basin Developing Countries: Prospects
for the Future***   Marcus Noland
January 1991   ISBN cloth 0-88132-141-9
                    ISBN paper 0-88132-081-1
Currency Convertibility in Eastern Europe*
John Williamson, editor
October 1991   ISBN 0-88132-128-1
**International Adjustment and Financing: The
Lessons of 1985-1991*** C. Fred Bergsten, editor
January 1992   ISBN 0-88132-112-5
**North American Free Trade: Issues and
Recommendations***
Gary Clyde Hufbauer and Jeffrey J. Schott
April 1992   ISBN 0-88132-120-6
Narrowing the U.S. Current Account Deficit*
Alan J. Lenz/*June 1992*   ISBN 0-88132-103-6
The Economics of Global Warming
William R. Cline/*June 1992*   ISBN 0-88132-132-X
**US Taxation of International Income: Blueprint
for Reform***   Gary Clyde Hufbauer,
assisted by Joanna M. van Rooij
October 1992   ISBN 0-88132-134-6
**Who's Bashing Whom? Trade Conflict
in High-Technology Industries**
Laura D'Andrea Tyson
November 1992   ISBN 0-88132-106-0
Korea in the World Economy*
Il SaKong
January 1993   ISBN 0-88132-183-4

WORKS IN PROGRESS

Sustaining Reform with a US-Pakistan Free Trade Agreement Gary Clyde Hufbauer and Shahid Javed Burki

Reform in a Rich Country: Germany Adam S. Posen

Global Forces, American Faces: US Economic Globalization at the Grass Roots J. David Richardson

The Future of Chinese Exchange Rates Morris Goldstein and Nicholas R. Lardy

The Arab Economies in a Changing World Howard Pack and Marcus Noland

Economic Regionalism in East Asia C. Fred Bergsten

The Strategic Implications of China-Taiwan Economic Relations Nicholas R. Lardy

Financial Crises and the Future of Emerging Markets William R. Cline

US Taxation of International Income, 2d ed. Gary Clyde Hufbauer and Ariel Assa

Prospects for a Middle East Free Trade Agreement Robert Z. Lawrence

Prospects for a Sri Lanka Free Trade Agreement Dean DeRosa

Workers at Risk: Job Loss from Apparel, Textiles, Footwear, and Furniture Lori G. Kletzer

Economic Sanctions Reconsidered, 3d. ed. Kimberly Ann Elliott, Gary C. Hufbauer, and Jeffrey J. Schott

The Impact of Global Services Outsourcing on American Firms and Workers J. Bradford Jensen, Lori G. Kletzer, and Catherine L. Mann

Rethinking US Social Security: Drawing on World Best Practices Martin N. Baily and Jacob Kirkegaard

Policy Reform in Mature Industrial Economies John Williamson, ed.

The Impact of Financial Globalization William R. Cline

Banking System Fragility in Emerging Economies Morris Goldstein and Philip Turner

Second among Equals: The Middle-Class Kingdoms of India and China Surjit Bhalla

DISTRIBUTORS OUTSIDE THE UNITED STATES

**Australia, New Zealand,
and Papua New Guinea**
D. A. Information Services
648 Whitehorse Road
Mitcham, Victoria 3132, Australia
Tel: 61-3-9210-7777
Fax: 61-3-9210-7788
Email: service@dadirect.com.au
www.dadirect.com.au

India, Bangladesh, Nepal, and Sri Lanka
Viva Books Private Limited
Mr. Vinod Vasishtha
4737/23 Ansari Road
Daryaganj, New Delhi 110002
India
Tel: 91-11-4224-2200
Fax: 91-11-4224-2240
Email: viva@vivagroupindia.net
www.vivagroupindia.com

**Mexico, Central America, South America,
and Puerto Rico**
US PubRep, Inc.
311 Dean Drive
Rockville, MD 20851
Tel: 301-838-9276
Fax: 301-838-9278
Email: c.falk@ieee.org
www.uspubrep.com

Southeast Asia *(Brunei, Burma, Cambodia,
Indonesia, Malaysia, the Philippines,
Singapore, Taiwan, Thailand, and Vietnam)*
APAC Publishers Services PTE Ltd.
70 Bendemeer Road #05-03
Hiap Huat House
Singapore 333940
Tel: 65-6844-7333
Fax: 65-6747-8916
Email: service@apacmedia.com.sg

Canada
Renouf Bookstore
5369 Canotek Road, Unit 1
Ottawa, Ontario KlJ 9J3, Canada
Tel: 613-745-2665
Fax: 613-745-7660
www.renoufbooks.com

Japan
United Publishers Services Ltd.
1-32-5, Higashi-shinagawa
Shinagawa-ku, Tokyo 140-0002
Japan
Tel: 81-3-5479-7251
Fax: 81-3-5479-7307
Email: purchasing@ups.co.jp
*For trade accounts only. Individuals will find
IIE books in leading Tokyo bookstores.*

Middle East
MERIC
2 Bahgat Ali Street, El Masry Towers
Tower D, Apt. 24
Zamalek, Cairo
Egypt
Tel. 20-2-7633824
Fax: 20-2-7369355
Email: mahmoud_fouda@mericonline.com
www.mericonline.com

United Kingdom, Europe
(including Russia and Turkey), **Africa,
and Israel**
The Eurospan Group
c/o Turpin Distribution
Pegasus Drive
Stratton Business Park
Biggleswade, Bedfordshire
SG18 8TQ
United Kingdom
Tel: 44 (0) 1767-604972
Fax: 44 (0) 1767-601640
Email: eurospan@turpin-distribution.com
www.eurospangroup.com/bookstore

**Visit our Web site at:
www.iie.com
E-mail orders to:
IIE mail@PressWarehouse.com**